GLOBAL STU

D1033488

INDIA AND SOUTH ASIA

EIGHTH EDITION

Dr. James H. K. Norton

OTHER BOOKS IN THE GLOBAL STUDIES SERIES
- Africa
- China
- Europe
- Islam and the Muslim World
- Japan and the Pacific Rim
- Latin America
- The Middle East
- Russia, the Baltic and Eurasian Republics, and Central/Eastern Europe

Contemporary Learning Series

2460 Kerper Blvd., Dubuque, IA 52001

Visit us on the Internet
http://www.mhcls.com

Staff

Larry Loeppke	*Managing Editor*
Jill Peter	*Senior Developmental Editor*
Lori Church	*Permissions Coordinator*
Maggie Lytle	*Cover*
Tara McDermott	*Design Specialist*
Jean Smith	*Project Manager*
Sandy Wille	*Project Manager*
Jane Mohr	*Project Manager*

Sources for Statistical Reports

U.S. State Department *Background Notes* (2003).
C.I.A. *World Factbook* (2004).
World Bank *World Development Reports* (2002/2003).
UN *Population and Vital Statistics Reports* (2002/2003).
World Statistics in Brief (2002).
The Statesman's Yearbook (2003).
Population Reference Bureau *World Population Data Sheet* (2002).
The World Almanac (2003).
The Economist Intelligence Unit (2003).

Copyright

Cataloging in Publication Data
Main entry under title: Global Studies: India and South Asia.
     1. India—History—20th–21st centuries. 2. India—Politics and government—1947–.
     3. Asia, Southeastern—20th–21st centuries. 4. Asia—History—20th–21st centuries.
I. Title: India and South Asia. II. Norton, James H. K., *comp.*
ISBN 0-07-337971-9   954   91-71258   ISSN 1080-4153

Eighth Edition

Printed in the United States of America   1234567890QPDQPD987   Printed on Recycled Paper

India and South Asia

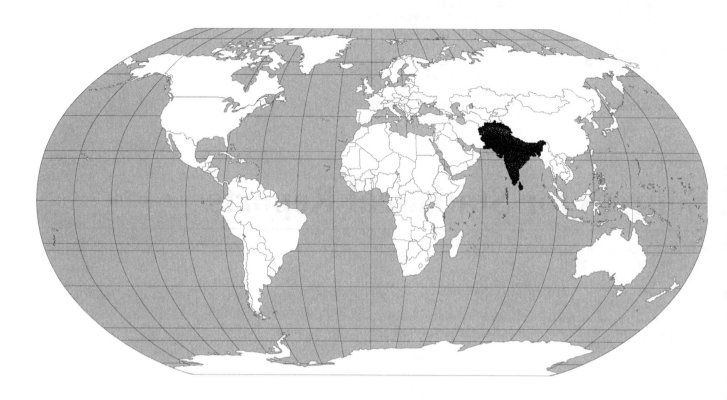

AUTHOR/EDITOR

Dr. James H. K. Norton

The author/editor of *Global Studies: India and South Asia, Eighth Edition*, received a B.S. degree from Yale University, B.A. and M.A. degrees in Sanskrit from Oxford University, and a Ph.D. in Indian philosophy from the University of Madras in India. He taught for 10 years at the College of Wooster, where he was associate professor of religion and chairman of the Department of Indian Studies. While at Wooster, Dr. Norton initiated a junior-year study program for college students in Madurai University, India, now part of the University of Wisconsin College Year in India program. He has also taught at Madurai University, Boston University, and Oberlin College. He is currently farming in Massachusetts, conducting continuing-education courses, and has served for many years on school boards and school advisory councils on Martha's Vineyard. Dr. Norton has spent five years in India, first as a Ford Foundation scholar while doing graduate work at the University of Madras. He has returned as a teacher and as a senior research fellow of the American Institute of Indian Studies. He is a member of the Association for Asian Studies. His articles on Indian philosophy, on comparisons of Eastern and Western thought, and on Martha's Vineyard local history appear in a number of books and journals.

Contents

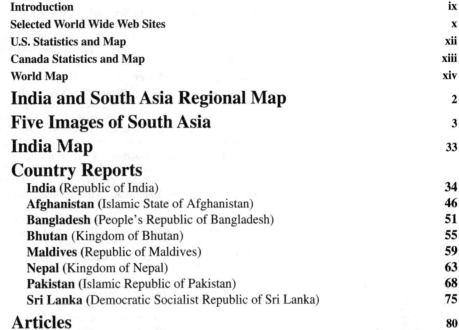

Sri Lanka

Using Global Studies: India and South Asia

THE GLOBAL STUDIES SERIES

The Global Studies series was created to help readers acquire a basic knowledge and understanding of the regions and countries in the world. Each regional volume provides a foundation of information—geographic, cultural, economic, political, historical, artistic, and religious—that will allow readers to better assess the current and future problems within these countries and regions and to comprehend how events there might affect their own well-being. In short, these volumes present background information necessary to respond to the realities of our global age.

Each of the volumes in the Global Studies series is crafted under the careful direction of an author/editor—an expert in the area under study. The author/editors teach and conduct research and have traveled extensively through the regions about which they are writing.

In this *India and South Asia* edition, the author/editor has written introductory essays on the South Asia region and country reports for each of the countries included.

MAJOR FEATURES OF THE GLOBAL STUDIES SERIES

The Global Studies volumes are organized to provide concise information on the regions and countries within those areas under study. The major sections and features of the books are described here.

Regional Essays

For *Global Studies: India and South Asia*, the author/editor has written an essay, "Images of South Asia," focusing on the religious, cultural, sociopolitical, and economic differences and similarities of the countries and peoples in the region. A detailed map accompanies the essay.

Country Reports

Concise reports are written for each of the countries within the region under study. These reports are the heart of each Global Studies volume. *Global Studies: India and South Asia, Eighth Edition*, contains eight country reports, including India.

The country reports are composed of five standard elements. Each report contains a detailed map visually positioning the country among its neighboring states; a summary of statistical information; a current essay providing important historical, geographical, political, cultural, and economic information; a historical timeline, offering a convenient visual survey of a few key historical events; and four "graphic indicators," with summary statements about the country in terms of development, freedom, health/welfare, and achievements.

A Note on the Statistical Reports

The statistical information provided for each country has been drawn from a wide range of sources. (The most frequently referenced are listed on pages x–xi.) Every effort has been made to provide the most current and accurate information available. However, occasionally the information cited by these sources differs to some extent; and, all too often, the most current information available for some countries is dated. Aside from these difficulties, the statistical summary of each country is generally quite complete and up to date. Care should be taken, however, in using these statistics (or, for that matter, any published statistics) in making hard comparisons among countries. We have also provided comparable statistics for the United States and Canada, which can be found on pages xii and xiii.

World Press Articles

Within each Global Studies volume is reprinted a number of articles carefully selected by our editorial staff and the author/editor from a broad range of international periodicals and newspapers. The articles have been chosen for currency, interest, and their differing perspectives. There are 38 articles in *Global Studies: India and South Asia, Eighth Edition*.

The articles section is preceded by an annotated table of contents. This resource offers a brief summary of each article.

Web Sites

An extensive annotated list of selected World Wide Web sites can be found on the facing page in this edition of *Global Studies: India and South Asia*. In addition, the URL addresses for country-specific Web sites are provided on the statistics page of most countries. All of the Web site addresses were correct and operational at press time. Instructors and students alike are urged to refer to those sites often to enhance their understanding of the region and to keep up with current events.

Glossary, Bibliography, Index

At the back of each Global Studies volume, readers will find a glossary of terms and abbreviations, which provides a quick reference to the specialized vocabulary of the area under study and to the standard abbreviations used throughout the volume. Following the glossary is a bibliography, which lists general works, national histories, and current-events publications and periodicals that provide regular coverage on India and South Asia. The index at the end of the volume provides reference to the contents of the volume. Readers seeking specific information and citations should consult this standard index.

Currency and Usefulness

Global Studies: India and South Asia, like the other Global Studies volumes, is intended to provide the most current and useful information available necessary to understand the events that are shaping the cultures of the region today.

This volume is revised on a regular basis. The statistics are updated, regional essays and country reports revised, and world press articles replaced. In order to accomplish this task, we turn to our author/editor, our advisory boards, and—hopefully—to you, the users of this volume. Your comments are more than welcome. If you have an idea that you think will make the next edition more useful, an article or bit of information that will make it more current, or a general comment on its organization, content, or features that you would like to share with us, please send it in for serious consideration.

Selected World Wide Web Sites for India and South Asia

(Some Web sites continually change their structure and content, so the information listed here may not always be available. Check our Web site at: http://www.mhcls.com/online/—Ed.)

GENERAL SITES

CNN Online Page
http://www.cnn.com
This is a U.S. 24-hour video news channel. News, updated every few hours, includes text, pictures, and film. Good external links.

C-SPAN ONLINE
http://www.c-span.org
See especially C-SPAN International on the Web for International Programming Highlights and archived C-Span programs.

International Network Information Center at University of Texas
http://inic.utexas.edu
This is a gateway that has pointers to international sites, including South Asia.

Penn Library: Resources by Subject
http://www.library.upenn.edu/resources/subject/subject.html
Rich in links to information about Asian studies, this vast site includes population and demography data.

Political Science RESOURCES
http://www.psr.keele.ac.uk
On this Web site, find a dynamic gateway to sources available via European addresses. A list of country names is available.

ReliefWeb
http://www.reliefweb.int
UN's Department of Humanitarian Affairs clearinghouse for international humanitarian emergencies.

Social Science Information Gateway (SOSIG)
http://sosig.esrc.bris.ac.uk
The project of the Economic and Social Research Council (ESRC) is located here. It catalogs 22 subjects and lists developing countries' URL addresses.

Special Issues
http://specialissues.com
This unusual site is the repository of transcripts of every kind, compiled by Gary Price, from radio and television, of speeches by world government leaders, and the proceedings of groups like the United Nations, NATO, and the World Bank.

United Nations System
http://www.unsystem.org
The UN's system of organizations presents this official Web site. An alphabetical list is available that offers: UNICC—Food and Agriculture Organization.

UN Development Programme (UNDP)
http://www.undp.org
Publications and current information on world poverty, Mission Statement, UN Development Fund for Women, and more can be found here. Be sure to see Poverty Clock.

U.S. Agency for International Development (USAID)
http://www.usaid.gov
The U.S. policy toward assistance to Asian countries is available at this site.

U.S. Central Intelligence Agency Home Page
http://www.cia.gov
This site includes publications of the CIA, such as the World Factbook, Factbook on Intelligence, Handbook of International Economic Statistics, and CIA Maps.

U.S. Department of State Home Page
http://www.state.gov/index.html
Organized alphabetically, this Web site presents: Country Reports, Human Rights, International Organizations, etc.

World Bank Group
http://www.worldbank.org
News (i.e., press releases, summary of new projects, speeches), publications, topics in development, countries and regions are available here. Links to other financial organizations are possible.

World Health Organization (WHO)
http://www.who.ch
Maintained by WHO's headquarters in Geneva, Switzerland, this comprehensive site includes a search engine.

World Trade Organization (WTO)
http://www.wto.org
Topics include a foundation of world trade systems, data on textiles, intellectual property rights, legal frameworks, trade and environmental policies, recent agreements, and others data.

The Economist
http://www.economist.com/asia
The Economist is a weekly international news and business publication offering clear reporting, commentary and analysis on world politics, business, finance, science and technology.

Foreign Affairs
http://www.foreignaffairs.org/asia
Founded in 1921, the Council on Foreign Relations is a non-profit and nonpartisan membership organization dedicated to improving the understanding of U.S. foreign policy and international affairs through the free exchange of ideas.

Human Rights Watch
http://www.hrw.org/asia
Human Rights Watch is dedicated to protecting the human rights of people around the world.

Terrorism Research Center
http://www.terrorism.com
Founded in 1996, the Terrorism Research Center, Inc. (TRC) is an independent institute dedicated to the research of terrorism, information warfare and security, critical infrastructure protection, homeland security, and other issues of low-intensity political violence and gray-area phenomena.

South Asia Terrorism Portal
http://www.satp.org
South Asia Intelligence Review (SAIR) brings regular assessments, data and news briefs on terrorism, insurgencies and sub-conventional warfare, counter-terrorism responses and policies, as well as on related economic, political, and social issues, in the South Asian region.

Wikipedia
http://www.wikipedia.org /(Country)
Wikipedia is a multilingual, web-based, free content encyclopedia project. Wikipedia is written collaboratively by volunteers from all around the world.

World Newspapers
http://www.world-newspapers/(Country)
A collection of world newspapers, magazines, and news sites sorted by country and region.

GENERAL INDIA AND SOUTH ASIA SITES

Asia Web Watch
http://www.ciolek.com/Asia-Web-Watch/main-page.html
Here is a register of statistical data that can be accessed alphabetically. Data includes Asian Online Materials Statistics and Appendices about Asian cyberspace.

Asian Arts
http://asianart.com
This online journal for the study and exhibition of the arts of Asia includes exhibitions, articles, and galleries.

Asian Studies WWW Virtual Library
http://coombs.anu.edu.au/WWWVL-AsianStudies.html
Australia National University maintains these sites, which link to many other Web sources, available at each country's location.

Asia-Yahoo
http://www.yahoo.com/Regional/Regions/Asia/
Access a specialized Yahoo search site that permits key-word searches on Asian events, countries, and topics from here.

History of the Indian Sub-Continent
http://www.stockton.edu/~gilmorew/consorti/1aindia.htm
As part of Stockton's World Wide Web Global History Research Institute, the history of the Indian subcontinent has been arranged chronologically at this site. This excellent resource contains maps, pictures, short writings, and scholarly writings.

South Asia Resources
http://www.lib.berkeley.edu/SSEAL/SouthAsia/
From this University of Berkeley Library site there is quick access to online resources in Asian studies as well as to South Asian specialists and other special features.

See individual country report pages for additional Web sites.

The United States (United States of America)

GEOGRAPHY

Area in Square Miles (Kilometers): 8,711 sq. mi. (9,631,420 sq. km.) (about 1/2 the size of Russia)

Capital (Population): Washington, DC (570,898, 2003 est.)

Environmental Concerns: air and water pollution; limited freshwater resources, desertification; loss of habitat; waste disposal; acid rain

Geographical Features: vast central plain, mountains in the west, hills and low mountains in the east; rugged mountains and broad river valleys in Alaska; volcanic topography in Hawaii

Climate: mostly temperate, but ranging from tropical to arctic

PEOPLE

Population

Total: 298,444,215 (July, 2006 est.)

Annual Growth Rate: 0.91% (2006 est.)

Rural/Urban Population Ratio: 19.2/80.8 (UN 2005)

Major Languages: 82.1% English; 10.7% Spanish; 7.1% other (2000 census)

Ethnic Makeup: 81.7% white; 12.9% black; 4.2% Asian; 1% Amerindian (2003 est.)

Religions: 52% Protestant; 24% Roman Catholic; 10% none or unaffiliated; 14% others (2002 est.)

Health

Life Expectancy at Birth: 75.02 years (male); 80.82 years (female) (2006 est.)

Infant Mortality: 6.43/1000 live births (2006 est.)

Physicians Available: 1/365 people

Per Capita total expenditure on Health: $5,771 (WHO)

HIV/AIDS Rate in Adults: 0.6% (WHO 2005 est.)

Education

Adult Literacy Rate: 99% (2003 est.)

Compulsory (Ages): 7–16; free

COMMUNICATION

Telephones: 268,000,000 (2003)

Cell Phones: 194,479,364 (2004)

Daily Newspaper Circulation: 238/1,000 people

Televisions: 776/1,000 people

Internet Users: 203,825,428 (2005)

TRANSPORTATION

Highways in Miles (Kilometers): (6,407,637 km) (2004)

Railroads in Miles (Kilometers): (226,105 km) (2004)

Usable Airfields: 14,858 (2006)

Motor Vehicles in Use: 206,000,000

GOVERNMENT

Type: federal republic

Independence Date: July 4, 1776

Head of State/Government: President George W. Bush is both head of state and head of government

Political Parties: Democratic Party; Republican Party; others of relatively minor political significance

Suffrage: universal at 18

MILITARY

Military Expenditures (% of GDP): $518.1 billion (FY 2004 est.); 4.06% (FY 2003 est.)

Current Disputes: various boundary and territorial disputes; "war on terrorism"

ECONOMY

Per Capita Income/GDP: $41,800 / $12.49 trillion (2005 est.)

GDP Growth Rate: 3.5% (2005 est.)

Inflation Rate: 3.2% (2005 est.)

Unemployment Rate: 5.1% (2005 est.)

Population Below Poverty Line: 12% (2004 est.)

Natural Resources: many minerals and metals; petroleum; natural gas; timber; arable land

Agriculture: food grains; feed crops; fruits and vegetables; oil-bearing crops; livestock; dairy products

Industry: diversified in both capital and consumer-goods industries

Exports: $723 billion (primary partners Canada, Mexico, Japan)

Imports: $1.727 trillion (primary partners Canada, China, Mexico, Japan)

Human Development Index (ranking): 10 (UNDP 2005)

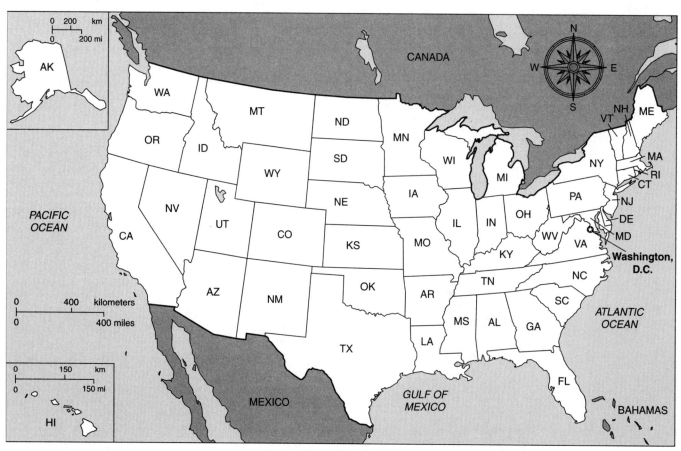

Canada

GEOGRAPHY

Area in Square Miles (Kilometers): 3,855,102
sq. mi. (9,994,670 sq. km.)
Capital (Population): Ottawa (1,142,700
(2004 est.))
Environmental Concerns: air and water
pollution; acid rain; industrial damage to
agriculture and forest productivity
Geographical Features: permafrost in the north;
mountains in the west; central plains; lowlands
in the southeast
Climate: varies from temperate to arctic

PEOPLE

Population
Total: 33,098,932 (July, 2006 est.)
Annual Growth Rate: 0.88% (2006 est.)
Rural/Urban Population Ratio: 18.9/81.1
(UN 2005 est,)
Major Languages: English (Official) 59.3%;
French (Official) 23.2%; Other 17.5%
Ethnic Makeup: 28% British Isles origin; 23%
French origin; 15% other European; 6%
others; 2% indigenous; 26% mixed
Religions: 42.6% Roman Catholic; 23.3%
Protestant; 4.4% Others Christian; 1.9%
Muslim; 11.8% Other; 16% none (2001
Census)

Health
Life Expectancy at Birth: 76.86 years (male);
83.74 (female) (2006 est.)

Infant Mortality: 4.69/1000 live births
Physicians Available: 1/534 people
Per Capita expenditure on Health: $2,989
(WHO 2003)
HIV/AIDS Rate in Adults: 0.3% (WHO 2005 est.)

Education
Adult Literacy Rate: 99%
Compulsory (Ages): primary school

Communication
Telephones: 18,276,400 main lines (2005)
Cell Phones: 14,984,400 (2004)
Daily Newspaper Circulation: 215/1,000 people
Televisions: 647/1,000 people
Internet Users: 20.9 million

TRANSPORTATION
Highways in Miles (Kilometers): (1,042,300 km)
Railroads in Miles (Kilometers): (48,467 km)
Usable Airfields: 1,337 (2006)
Motor Vehicles in Use: 16,800,000

GOVERNMENT
Type: constitutional monarchy that is also a
parliamentary democracy and a federation
Independence Date: July 1, 1867
Head of State/Government: Queen Elizabeth II /
Prime Minister Stephen Harper
Political Parties: Conservative Party of Canada,
Liberal Party, Green Party, New Democratic
Party, Bloc Quebecois
Suffrage: universal at 18

MILITARY

Military Expenditures (% of GDP): $9,801.7
million (2003); (1.1%) (2003)
Current Disputes: maritime boundary disputes
with the United States

ECONOMY

Currency (U.S. equivalent): 1.2118 Canadian
dollars to $1 US (2005)
Per Capita Income/GDP: $34,000 (2005
est.)/$11,035 trillion (2005 est.)
GDP Growth Rate: 2.9%
Inflation Rate: 2.2%
Unemployment Rate: 6.8%
Population Below Poverty Line: 15.9% (2003)
Labor Force by Occupation: 75% Services;
14% Manufacturing; 5% Construction, 2%
Agriculture, 3% other (2004)
Natural Resources: petroleum; natural gas; fish;
minerals; cement; forestry products; wildlife;
hydropower
Agriculture: grains; livestock; dairy products;
potatoes; hogs; poultry and eggs; tobacco;
fruits and vegetables
Industry: oil production and refining; natural-gas
development; fish products; wood and paper
products; chemicals; transportation equipment
Exports: $364.8 billion f.o.b. (2005 est.) (primary
partners United States, Japan, United Kingdom)
Imports: $317.7 billion f.o.b. (2005 est.) (primary
partners United States, China, Mexico)
Human Development Index (ranking): 5
(UNDP 2005)

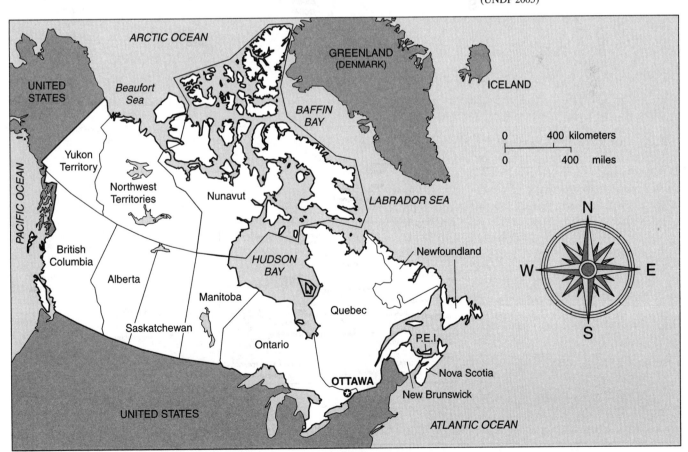

GLOBAL ● STUDIES

This map is provided to give you a graphic picture of where the countries of the world are located, the relationship they have with their region and neighbors, and their positions relative to major trade and power blocs. We have focused on certain areas to illustrate these crowded regions more clearly. The India and South Asia region is shaded for emphasis.

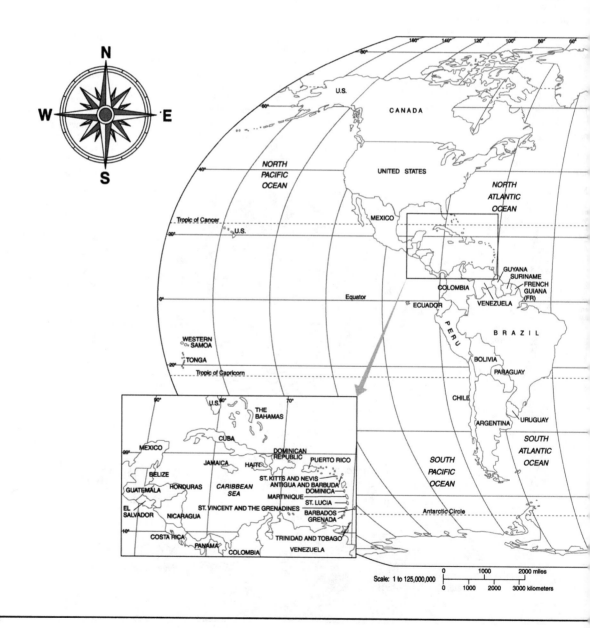

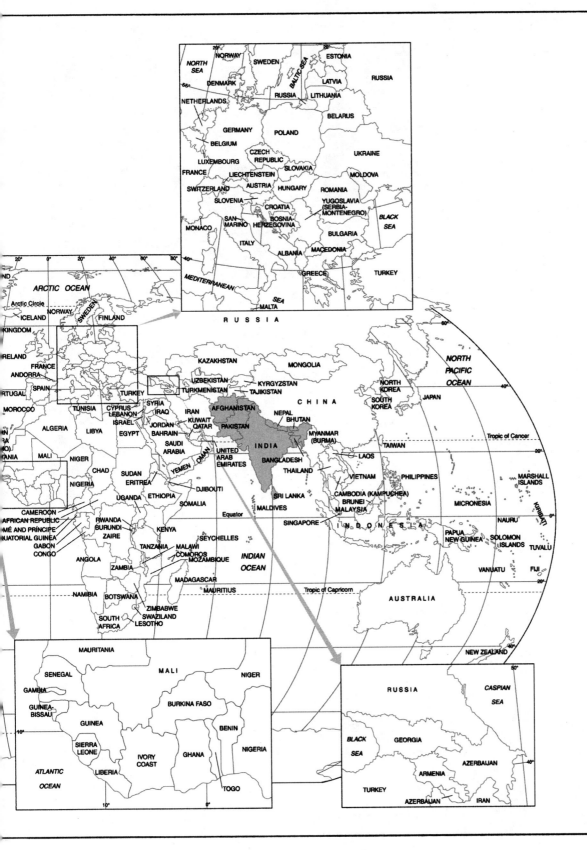

India and South Asia

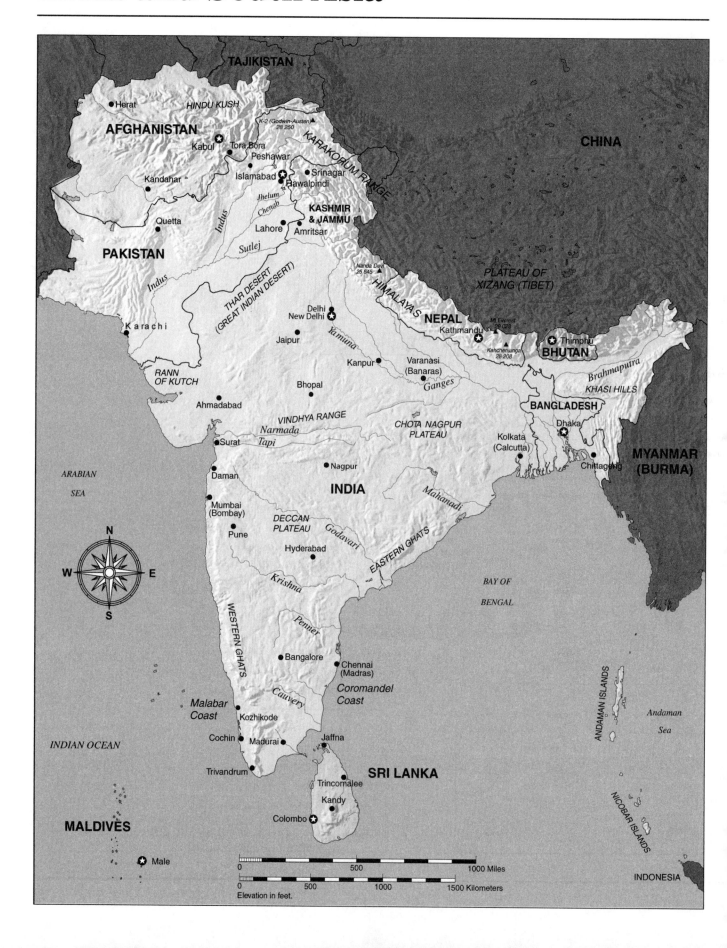

TAJIKISTAN

Herat

HINDU KUSH

AFGHANISTAN

K-2 (Godwin-Austen) 28,250

CHINA

KARAKORUM RANGE

Kabul Tora Bora
Peshawar
Kandahar
Islamabad Srinagar
Rawalpindi

Quetta

KASHMIR & JAMMU

Jhelum
Chenab

Lahore Amritsar

PAKISTAN

Indus

Sutlej

Nanda Devi 25,645

HIMALAYAS

PLATEAU OF XIZANG (TIBET)

Indus

THAR DESERT (GREAT INDIAN DESERT)

Delhi
New Delhi

NEPAL

Mt. Everest 29,028

Kathmandu

Thimphu
BHUTAN

Karachi

Jaipur

Yamuna

Kanpur

Kahchenjunga 28,208

Varanasi (Banaras)

Brahmaputra

KHASI HILLS

RANN OF KUTCH

Bhopal

Ganges

CHOTA NAGPUR PLATEAU

Kolkata (Calcutta)

BANGLADESH

Dhaka

Ahmadabad

VINDHYA RANGE

Narmada

Tapi

Chittagong

MYANMAR (BURMA)

ARABIAN SEA

Surat
Daman

Nagpur

INDIA

Mahanadi

N
W   E
S

Mumbai (Bombay)

Pune

DECCAN PLATEAU

Hyderabad

Godavari

EASTERN GHATS

BAY OF BENGAL

Krishna

Penner

WESTERN GHATS

Bangalore

Cauvery

Chennai (Madras)

Coromandel Coast

ANDAMAN ISLANDS

Andaman Sea

Malabar Coast

Kozhikode

Cochin Madurai

Jaffna

INDIAN OCEAN

Trivandrum

Trincomalee

SRI LANKA

Kandy

NICOBAR ISLANDS

MALDIVES

Colombo

Male

0   500   1000 Miles

0   500   1000   1500 Kilometers

Elevation in feet.

INDONESIA

Five Images of South Asia

OUT OF MANY VIEWS, A PORTRAIT

We begin with five images to portray the uniqueness of South Asia. They are not definitive. Every assertion about the suncontinent, it is said, is a contradiction. Rather, they intend to create illuminating foci toward a picture of this immensely varied, fascinating and increasingly important part of our world.

IMAGE 1: SOUTH ASIA, A DISTINCT LAND AND AN ANCIENT CIVILIZATION

A. K. Ramanujan used to tell the story of a Mongolian conqueror who had a certain species of nightingale brought to him from Kashmir because he had heard that this bird sang the most beautiful song in the world. But when the bird arrived, it did not sing. It was explained to the enraged conqueror that it sang only when perched on the branch of a chinar tree, and that the chinar tree grows only on the hillsides of Kashmir. Ramanujan concluded this story of what the conqueror needed to do to get his captured nightingale to sing with these words of St.-John Perse:

We know the story of that Mongolian conqueror, taker of a bird in its nest, and of the nest in its tree, who brought back with the bird and nest and song the whole natal tree itself, torn from its place with its multitude of roots, its ball of earth and its border of soil, a remnant of home territory evoking a field, a province, a country, and an empire.

—St.-John Perse, *Birds*
(cited in A. K. Ramanujan, *Poems of Love and War*)

A DISTINCT LAND

The land on which the people of South Asia live is clearly set apart from the rest of Asia. Geologically speaking, it is a recent addition to the continent. About 100 million years ago, it broke away from the east coast of Africa and drifted slowly on a separate geological plate east and north, until it collided, about 28 million years ago, into the southern edge of the Asian continent. The immense power of this impact pushed the Tibetan plateau more than 3 miles into the air and created a high ridge of snow-clad peaks. The Himalayan mountain range, the highest in the world, is still rising at a rate of about 10 inches per century as a result of that massive collision.

This same India plate is sliding under and pushing down the Burma plate. The sudden release of the western edge of that plate from the India plate's push caused the devastating earthquake and tsunami that brought such wide-spread death and havoc along the South Asian coastlands on December 26, 2004.

The Himalayan Mountains on the north set the subcontinent apart from the rest of Asia, and the waters of the Arabian Sea, the Bay of Bengal and the Indian Ocean enclose its coastal shores to the south. The high mountain peaks and the vast ocean waters also produce the annual monsoons, seasonal torrents of rain upon which the livelihood of the people of South Asia depends.

Within these natural borders is a wide range of topography and climate that divides into four distinct regions.

Farthest to the north are the frigid heights of the south face of the Himalayas. All of Bhutan, most of Afghanistan and Nepal, and small portions of India and Pakistan fall within this region.

The second region stretches across the north-central portion of the subcontinent in three wide, alluvial river valleys. Three river systems—the Indus, the Jumna-Ganges, and the Brahmaputra—begin within 100 miles in the Himalayas, and flow in three directions through the mountains. The Indus flows to the west through Pakistan to the Arabian Sea. The Jumna-Ganges Rivers flow to the south out of the Himalayan region and then join to flow east across the great northern plain of India, to where they merge in Bangladesh with the Brahmaputra River. The Brahmaputra flows to the east from its Himalayan source, then south into Bangladesh. Both river systems flow together through many tributaries into the Bay of Bengal.

These river systems provide the north-central plains region with a steady, though uneven, flow of melting snow. Because of this flow through the temperate northern plains, this region is the most widely irrigated and has the most productive agricultural lands of the subcontinent.

To the south of the northern plains region are the highlands of peninsular India, which projects out into the Indian Ocean. The highlands rise to a wide plateau, called the Deccan, bordered to the east and west by mountains smaller, but older, than the Himalayas. The central portion of Sri Lanka also rises to highlands, which, together with the Deccan, form the third geographical region of the subcontinent. Because these highlands are not high enough to be snow-covered, farmers in this region are entirely dependent upon the seasonal monsoons for sufficient water to cultivate the land.

From these highlands the land slopes down into the fourth region, the coastal plains and tropical beaches of India, Pakistan, Bangladesh, Sri Lanka, and Maldives. Most of South Asia's largest cities, which developed as trading posts during the seventeenth century and are now great centers of commerce, are in this coastal region.

These four distinct regions, which also include desert and rain forest, contain as wide a range of topography and climate as exists anywhere in the world.

AN ANCIENT CIVILIZATION

Maritime Commerce

The earliest evidence of a distinctive South Asian culture is found in the archeological sites of the world's earliest known urban civilization. This Harappan city culture flourished in the Indus River valley, in the northwestern portion of the subcontinent, from 3000 to 1500 B.C.

3

What He Said

As a little white snake
with lovely stripes on its young body
troubles the jungle elephant

this slip of a girl
her teeth like sprouts of new rice
her wrists stacked with bangles
troubles me.

Catti Natanar, *Kur* 119
(Translated by A. K. Ramanujan)

(Courtesy of James Norton/Norton 01)

This small statue of a dancing girl was caste in bronze over 4000 years ago in Mohenjo Daro, the ancient city of the Harappan Civilization in the Indus River Valley. Lost in the sands that buried that city so long ago, her image was captured 2000 years ago by a South Indian poet at the other end of the subcontinent, some 2000 miles away, in this love poem found in the classical Tamil Sangam anthology called the Kuruntokai. Now recovered in the twentieth century from the excavations of the ancient city and in the translations of the classical Sangam poetry, we, too, are tantalized by this tiny, yet enduring image of India.

Excavations of these ancient sites reveal that the Harappans produced enough surplus, primarily in cotton and grains, to carry on trade well beyond their own region. Their commercial activity extended into the developing civilizations in the Fertile Crescent, Africa and Europe to the west, and Southeast Asia and China to the east. This trade brought peacocks from the subcontinent to embellish the throne of King Solomon in ancient Israel. It also brought the number zero to Europe during the Renaissance to change the mathematics of the West, and Buddhism to become a major religious faith in East Asia and the rest of the world.

Maritime commerce from the shores of South Asia, begun in the days of Harappan mercantile enterprise, continued through the era of silk trade, to the fiercely competitive activity of European trading companies in the seventeenth and eighteenth centuries and into the present day.

Because of the extent and intensity of this trade, it is difficult to trace the origin of many of the concepts and practices that came the other way—brought from other parts of the world to become part of South Asian daily life. We do not know, for example, the origin of the Harappan city builders, whose layout of streets and water use reveal a clear understanding of urban planning. We have no earlier instances of city dwelling to learn how or where these skills were developed. The practice of spiritual discipline called yoga is also of unknown origin, as is the Dravidian culture of south India. Both are old enough to have developed within the Harappan city culture. Attempts have been made to establish links between them. But they could have come from other sources that have been lost, and of which they are the only trace.

Also difficult to unravel is the persistence of so many indigenous cultural threads that have continued to evolve into a wide variety of patterns. So much has been added, and nothing ever appears to be thrown away.

The earliest agrarians on the subcontinent used a large slab and rolling stone, called a saddle-quern, over 6,000 years ago to grind grain into the flour. This implement was made obsolete long ago by grinding mills. But it is still used in village kitchens to pulverize condiments to season food and to crush peanuts into peanut butter.

Old practices, many times intermingled with newer things, are still recognizable as significant elements in the heritage of the peoples of South Asia. In the western world of planned obsolescence, such tenacity is hard to imagine. Geeta Mehta, in *Snakes and Ladders*, describes this contrast in a slightly different way: Whereas westerners struggle to recover their past, the problem for the people of India is to discover their present.

The Aryan Migration

In contrast to the more elusive impact of maritime commerce on South Asia, migrations of peoples from other parts of the world are a clearer source of new life and perspective in South Asia. They have come for the most part overland, across the Central Asian trade routes between China and the Middle East, down into the northwestern approach to the north-central plains region of the subcontinent.

The Aryan people are the earliest recorded migration of major impact. Around 1500 B.C., this tribal, martial and pastoral people from Central Asia drove their horse-drawn chariots and herds of cows into the subcontinent, destroying what remained of the Harappan cities and irrigation channels in their path.

They brought with them an Indo-European language, which later evolved into Sanskrit, the classical language of ancient India, and the many contemporary languages spoken throughout the northern portion of the subcontinent and on the islands of Sri Lanka and Maldives. They also brought collections of religious songs, which formed the basis of a tenth century B.C. anthology of 1,028 poems called the Rg-Veda, the oldest surviving religious literature in the world. The Veda is still considered *sruti*—that is, inspired; literally, "heard by ancient seers"—the most sacred of all Hindu religious texts. And the Aryans either brought or soon developed a mythic understanding of the world as a sacred reality. This perspective blossomed as Vedic culture during the time of their expansion and settlement across the northern plains of the subcontinent.

During the era of the Aryan settlement, Brahmin priests developed, celebrated, and interpreted an elaborate scheme of sacrifices as expressive of the total sanctity of the world in which they lived. They instituted daily rituals to assure long life, progeny and prosperity, ceremonies to celebrate the consecration of their leaders and assure them of victory in battle, and disciplines to enhance their sacred powers. They also asserted a dominant role in restructuring Aryan society around their religious activity. One of the later Vedic hymns celebrates the creation of the universe through a cosmic sacrificial offering of primordial Man. It sets forward the earliest description of the *varna*, or classical, model of the hierarchical caste system, which divided mankind into four groups. And it placed the priesthood at the top:

> When they divided the Man [in the cosmic sacrifice], into how many parts did they apportion him? What do they call his mouth, his two arms and thighs and feet? His mouth became the Brahmin; his arms were made into the Warrior, his thighs the People, and from his feet the Servants were born.
>
> Rg-Veda 10.90,11-1 (O'Flaherty translation)

Next in order of preference on the scale are the Kshatriya, the warriors, or rulers by might. Then came the Vaisya, citizens, with landholding or commercial status. And at the bottom were the Sudra, laborers and craftspeople.

People were grouped on this scale according to the inherited occupation of their extended family, community, or tribe. The ranking was based on a combination of the ritually purifying-polluting status in a sacrifice of a group's traditional occupation, as determined by the priesthood, and the ability of that social group to maintain social order. Maintaining social order was everyone's responsibility, but it held a specific and elevating prerogative for the priests because they had unique recourse to sacred power, *brahman*, which emanated from their performance of sacrificial rites. This scale clearly envisioned a Brahmin-dominated society.

Subsequent periods in South Asian history and literature do not show general acceptance of this dominant role for the priesthood. In the period between 500 B.C. to A.D. 200, the Sanskrit epics, the Mahabharata and the Ramayana, and early Buddhist literature, give more prominence to the warrior, or princely community, to which the heroes of the epics and the Buddha belonged. Social and world order was not based on the rite of sacrifice, nor was it maintained by the Brahmin priests. It was based, rather, upon princes' strict adherence to their chivalrous obligations, called Dharma.

Rama, the hero of the Ramayana, is portrayed as a prince who is severely righteous in order to assure the peace and well-being of the people over whom he is called to govern. In that same tradition, Siddharta Gautama, the prince who became the Buddha, the "Enlightened One," taught to his religious com-

(Courtesy of James Norton/Norton 02)

The east ornamental gateway (gopuram) of the temple of Meenakshi at the center of the city of Madurai in south India. Meenakshi is an ancient, primordial mother goddess, benefactor and protector of the city, who became incorporated into the Shaivite tradition by being married to Shiva. Their wedding is performed by Lord Vishnu, in the annual Chitirai Festival.

munity an eight-fold path of righteousness, which he called *dhamma*, the "Way." Heinrich Zimmer, in *Philosophies of India*, describes this path as a "spiritual physician's program of psycho-dietetics" to lead them to realize their Buddha nature and, ultimately, attain the transcendence of *nirvana*.

The high point of Buddhist expansion came upon the conversion of the Mauryan emperor Asoka to the Buddha's Way in the third century B.C. In the eighth year of his reign, Asoka was so deeply moved by the devastation caused by warfare in his defeat of a neighboring kingdom, he decided to reject the use of military force to add to his kingdom. He would rule his realm rather by moral force. His new policy, which he proclaimed on a series of pillars erected throughout his kingdom, was to shun aggression and to seek "safety, control, justice and happiness for all beings." He thus gave a wide legitimacy across the span of his empire in the northern plains region to the Buddhist *dhamma*, upon which his policy was based.

Also during his reign, Asoka sent his son, Mahinda, to bring the teachings of the Buddha to Sri Lanka. Mahinda's arrival in 246 B.C. marks the beginning of the Theravada Buddhist tradition on that island.

Brahmin religious authority continued to spread through the northern plains and peninsular regions of South Asia. But its full cultural impact was not realized until the Gupta imperial dynasty in the fourth century A.D. Sanskrit, the sacred language of the priesthood, had by then become accepted as appropriate for the royal court and all of the intellectual and artistic endeavors that the court supported. The influence of other religious communities, especially Jains and Buddhists, led the Brahmins to become vegetarian in their diet. And a great surge of popular religious lore, long practiced but unrecognized in courtly circles, infused courtly life with new perspectives, enthusiasm, and theistic fervor. The austere righteousness and the intricate, sacrificial purity of the earlier eras were augmented by a sense of divine playfulness spun out in recitations of exemplary cosmic exploits of unnumbered gods and goddesses, of heroes and heroines from a mythic past.

The Gupta Era, from A.D. 300 to 650, was a time of great creative activity, drawing upon and affirming enhanced Sanskritized models devised by the Brahmin priesthood. The poetic works of Kalidasa, the philosophical writings of Shankara, and the artistic creations found at Ajanta, Ellora, and Elephanta all portray the imaginative insight, excitement, and refinement achieved in that eclectic, yet highly disciplined and politically stable, era.

In the centuries following the Gupta era, the Brahmin community gained economic dominance in addition to their intellectual and religious authority. In reward for the Brahmins' courtly and religious services, they received land grants—even entire villages—as gifts from Hindu monarchs. Their increasing prominence in all of these aspects of courtly life established a pattern for social change in those regions of the subcontinent where Hindus predominated. Today, to achieve higher status in the hierarchical caste structure, other communities emulate the patterns of behavior practiced by high-caste Brahmins, a process called Sanskritization.

This label indicates how the pastoral religious traditions of the ancient Aryan cow herders in the central portion of the subcontinent have developed and gained stature and authority during the many centuries since the early Vedic Age.

The Moghul Migration

The second migration to have a major impact on the peoples of South Asia came 3,500 years later, and reveals a different pattern of acceptance. This migration was of militant Turks from Persia, called the Moghuls, who were forced to move into South Asia by the Mongols' triumphant marches across Central Asia.

Babur was the first, when he established a tenuous foothold in 1504 with the capture of the city of Kabul, in what is now Afghanistan. Competition for control of the north-central plains was fierce; and not until the reign of his grandson, Akbar (1556–1605), did Moghul rule begin to establish firm imperial control in that commanding region of the subcontinent.

During his reign, Akbar established an extremely effective administrative network to maintain authority over the realms he conquered. He also maintained a luxurious court, which supported an extensive creativity in art, music, architecture, and literature. Akbar's rule was a magnificent time, driven by his own desire to absorb the best of the wealth of traditions—Persian, Indian, and even European—that he welcomed into his domain.

The fruits of Akbar's attempts to achieve cultural synthesis remain in the arts. The greatest triumph is architectural: the Taj Mahal. Shah Jahan, Akbar's grandson, built this exquisitely beautiful mausoleum in Agra, in memory of his beloved wife, Mumtaz Mahal, who died in 1631. Miniature painting and Hindustani music continue to reveal the integration of art forms introduced under Akbar's imperial patronage. And remnants of his administrative structure adopted by the British colonial government are also evident in village life today.

The Moghuls were not the first Muslims to enter South Asia. Arab traders plying the coastal ports had introduced the new Islamic faith as early as the eighth century. They were followed by itinerant Sufi teachers, who settled in villages throughout the subcontinent. Their commitment to a religious life drew respect and veneration from a number of indigenous peoples receptive to spiritual insight and leadership. The more mystical quality of the faith of these masters converted large numbers to Islam, mostly in the northwest corner of the region, the Punjab, and the northeast, Bengal—areas where Buddhists had previously been the most numerous.

Further conversions took place during the militant rule of the Sultans, who dominated portions of the Gangetic plain for three centuries prior to the arrival of the Moghuls. The mosque, the daily calls to prayer, Muslim festivals, and Islamic law became an authentic part of the social fabric of South Asian life. They were accepted, even though these Muslims were a small religious minority in the central regions of the subcontinent.

The imperial stature, administrative acumen, and grandeur of Moghul rule gave immense institutional status to Islam as a distinct religious faith and political legitimacy to an extensive Muslim community. Even today, Pakistan's aspiration to identify the nation as a modern Islamic Republic builds upon this heritage of that Moghul imperial presence.

But Moghul domination in the political realm did not lead to mass conversions among the much larger Hindu population who resided in the central and southern portions of their empire. Akbar tried to synthesize his refined, imperial Islamic faith within a common South Asian culture. His hope was that all his subjects might share in a single, universalist religion, which he called "Divine Faith," Din-i-Ilahi. Inspired Hindu leaders like Kabir also sought a more inclusive religious perspective among their followers.

Because of the structural integrity and diversity of the many religious communities that fell under the inclusive umbrella of Hinduism, their attempts to unify Islam and Hinduism were not successful. Under British colonial rule during the nineteenth century, the separate religious identities of Hindus and Muslims were affirmed. Their difference as religions became the basis for the division of Bengal in 1905, and the creation of Pakistan separate from India with the departure of the British Raj in 1947.

Religious identity has been at the heart of antagonism and warfare between Pakistan and India since their independence. It is the source of terrorism and communal riots throughout the subcontinent to this day.

The Aryan and Moghul migrations reveal two very different experiences of incorporating foreign peoples into the social fabric of the subcontinent during the long course of its history. But they also identify a single pattern of cultural integration. The early Aryan culture, through continuing interaction and adaptation over a long period of time, came to dominate the social

(Royalty-Free/CORBIS/DAL_DAS0100)
The greatest period of Muslim influence in South Asia began in the sixteenth century, when the Moghuls dominated the north-central plains. This period was a time of grandeur and elegance. The Taj Mahal is one of the most famous monuments in the world.

realm—not by political force but by intellectual and religious authority, which set the norms that define the culture. One of those norms is to maintain the integrity of differing linguistic, religious, and ethnic groups who live in the subcontinent by isolating them as discrete cultural units within an abstract, hierarchical framework called the caste system.

The Moghul migration reveals that even extensive political domination, both military and administrative, is not sufficient to create or coerce cultural assimilation in a social environment that accepts cultural pluralism as normal.

Both of these migrations contributed significantly to the development of South Asian civilization. They also demonstrate that the social diversity of language, religion, ethnic community, and social status is deeply rooted in South Asia. As celebrated in the creation hymn (10.90) in the Rg-Veda, social distinctions are a part of cosmic order, and not easily homogenized.

The British Raj

The British colonial empire brought another significant impact on evolution of the distinct culture of South Asia. It was not a migration; and, unlike the Moghul experience, it had little impact on the creative arts on the subcontinent. The British Raj was primarily political, imposing colonial rule over the subcontinent from the mid-nineteenth century until the 1940s. Its impact lies largely in the introduction of democracy, industrial development, and technology.

British presence on the subcontinent began in the early 1600s, when the East India Company, with head offices in London, England, established trading centers, first in Indonesia, and then along the Indian coast. In these activities, the British entrepreneurs were following a pattern of maritime commerce in this region that goes back to the Harappan cities in the millennium B.C., during the earliest days of South Asian civilization.

This British commercial interest became dominant in South Asia during the eighteenth century, had no intention of establishing any political authority in the subcontinent. The British were there primarily for economic advantage, spending much of their time and effort with local authorities trying to curry favor and exclusive licenses for trade. But as they became more entangled with these authorities, especially as they struggled to diminish competing European interests in the region, they began to bring the peoples of the subcontinent increasingly under their own political control.

In the early 1800s, their greater political involvement stimulated a concern to bring social reform to the subcontinent as well. The character of their reform was most strikingly expressed in a famous "Minute on Education," written by an East India Company Supreme Council member, Thomas Macauly, in 1835.

Macauly urged that the British administrators create a special class of South Asian people who would be "Indian in blood and color, but English in taste, in opinions, in morals, and in intellect." These clerks of the company would be groomed to bring the new ideas of individualism, technology, democracy, and nationalism, which were then evolving in Europe and America, to usher South Asia into the modern world.

This energizing—but ethnocentric—reform movement received a resounding jolt in British India in 1857, when an isolated British Indian Army unit rebelled. Eighty-five soldiers were jailed for refusing to use ammunition greased with animal fat. Initially it was a minor incident. But among other things, it revealed a British insensitivity to Hindu religious attitudes toward the use of beef fat (for Hindus, the cow is sacred) and Muslim religious attitudes toward pork (that it is polluting). This minor rebellion became the stimulus for a popular uprising across the entire north-central region of the subcontinent. People took it as an opportunity to express a shared and growing sense of dissatisfaction with the British domination of their land. It grew into the "Great Mutiny" of 1857.

The spontaneity of this revolt contributed to its lack of organization and direction. It was soon subdued by British military might. But its widespread appeal revealed that, for all of the enthusiasm and goodwill the British rulers felt toward their South Asian subjects, their intentions—which appeared appropriate in their Western context—were not going to be readily accepted. The cultural context of South Asia was too substantial, too complex, and too different to be easily reformed.

The reform movement of the early nineteenth century gave way to a more blatant colonial domination of the subcontinent during the second half-century. In 1858, the British Crown assumed direct control of British India. Queen Victoria became the first to bear the title "Empress of India."

(World Bank 427-IN-12)

The crush of peoples and cultures poses significant challenges to democracy in South Asia. Here, afternoon traffic builds near the India Exchange in Calcutta, India.

The impact of the British Raj is still evident in the setting of the dividing lines that established the boundaries between the nations in Bhutan and Nepal with Tibet by a line drawn along the peaks of the Himalayan Mountains—the McMahon Line. British authorities also secured the other borders of these two countries, which were determined before British rule by Gurkha and Tibetan conquests. The Raj used the existing natural and political realities to assert its own governing authority within them.

By contrast, the setting of the borders of Afghanistan did not appear to have recognized any indigenous factors. They were established by treaty between Czarist Russia and Great Britain in 1907, in response to British colonial interests to contain any Russian aspirations to gain access to the Arabian Sea. As a consequence, the Pashto-speaking people in the northwest corner of the subcontinent were divided. In 1979, at the time of the Soviet invasion of Afghanistan, about 6 million—more than a third of the total population of that country—lived on the Afghan side. Another 16 million lived on the other side of the border, constituting the dominant population in the Northwest Frontier Province of Pakistan. Their separation as dominant minorities between two nationalities remains a significant factor in South Asian politics to this day.

The border determination of greatest impact was the decision by the Raj in 1947 not only to grant independence to a large portion of British India as a new republic, but also to establish a separate Islamic country, called Pakistan ("Land of the Pure"). At that time, those administrative districts under direct British control with a majority Muslim population were assigned to Pakistan, and those with a Hindu majority to India. The accession of the princely states that were not under direct British control—about 40 percent of the subcontinent—into

either India or Pakistan, was to be based on the preference of the ruling maharajas of these states.

There were two large exceptions to this process of accession. The princely state of Hyderabad, in the Deccan, had a Muslim leader and a Hindu majority population. It was absorbed into India when Indian troops rushed into the state to quell riots that came in the wake of the partition of India and Pakistan in 1947. The princely state of Kashmir, on the other hand, had a majority Muslim population and a Hindu maharaja. It was nominally acceded to India by Maharajah Hari Singh in October 1947, as Pakistani forces had begun to enter Kashmir and were fast approaching the city of Srinagar.

The result of this process of border determination was a Pakistan divided into two sections, East and West, on the shoulders of the subcontinent, separated by 1,000 miles of India; and a Kashmir still divided between the unresolved claims of both India and Pakistan and a United Nations (UN) resolution to encourage the people of Kashmir to have a choice.

Even with the setback experienced in the Mutiny of 1857, Western political ideas of democracy, social reform, and freedom of expression continued to spread through South Asia. The Indian National Congress was formed in 1887 to seek opportunities for South Asians to shape and to participate in a growing body politic. In 1919, Mohandas Gandhi emerged as the leader of this movement. Through the power of his example and his great organizational skills, he was able to build grassroots support for the Congress throughout British India. Enlivened by a spirit of democracy and of political freedom, this movement first paralleled and then superseded British colonial rule.

The British imperial presence also brought to South Asia the concept of a modern nation. An independent, democratically elected government was the goal—certainly for those who were under foreign colonial domination; but also for those who had been under traditional, autocratic rule of hereditary maharajas, tribal leaders, and vestigial imperial domains. Upon achieving independence, South Asian peoples awoke from a long era of unrepresentative leadership. Forceful ideas began to take on relevance: liberty achieved through democracy, prosperity through economic growth, and individual human rights sustained by law. These have become the standards by which the success of a nation's quest for modernization is measured. The British colonial government set them as its expectation of the countries to which it granted independence in the middle of the twentieth century—to India and Pakistan in 1947, and Sri Lanka in 1948. The other smaller nations—Afghanistan, Bhutan, Maldives, and Nepal—which trace the origin of their governments to more autocratic traditions of long standing in the subcontinent, are challenged to hold these same standards to their performance for recognition as modern states. They are all seeking new opportunities for expression, for economic growth, and for taking control of their destiny as politically free peoples among the nations of the world.

The British colonial interaction with South Asia is now over. Yet it continues, like the Aryan and Moghul experiences, to have a discernible impact in the subcontinent. Significant changes are occurring in the political and economic life because of the British Raj, just as the artistic and Islamic influences of the Moghul era are also evident in contemporary South Asia. The religious and intellectual heritage shaped by the evolution of Aryan culture continues to be profoundly present.

All of these threads—Aryan, Moghul, and British Raj—contribute to a unique and distinctive culture. They are intricately interwoven among themselves and with the many other influences both indigenous and brought by centuries of maritime commerce to form the tapestry of the long, rich, and varied heritage of the peoples who belong to South Asia.

IMAGE 2: A DIVERSE SOCIAL ENVIRONMENT

It is the endurance of this civilization, despite its encounter with a host of other cultures and other political influences, that has led many observers to conclude that the Hindu style is absorptive, synthesizing, or tolerant. What they see is something quite different, namely, Indian civilization's ability to encapsulate other cultures and make it possible for many levels of civilization to live side by side. But encapsulation is neither toleration, absorption, nor synthesis.
—Ainslie T. Embree

The 1.487 billion people who live in South Asia represent more than a fifth of the total population of the world, and they are growing in numbers at an alarming pace. The World Bank projects that at the current rate of growth, the population of the subcontinent will exceed 1.8 billion by the year 2025.

The countries of South Asia have tried to curb this rate, with varying success. The most effective effort has been in Sri Lanka. Analysts relate this achievement to the high level of literacy that the country has attained. Education, especially of women, appears to be the key to limiting population growth.

South Asia is not only crowded, but it is also a land of immense human contrasts. There are many different social groups across the subcontinent, each displaying distinctive beliefs and customs, language, and culture. Sikhs and Buddhists and Jains; fishermen and pit weavers along the tropical shores of the coast lands; elegant urban aristocrats and naked religious mendicants; tribal peoples and computer engineers; beggars, film stars, and Kathakali dancers; and many more are all interwoven into the multi-stranded fabric of South Asian life. It is a rich panoply of activities and conditions of humanity.

Endogamous extended family groupings called jatis are the most extensive and dominant social structures in the subcontinent. They provide by birth the most cohesive and enduring sense of where everyone fits into the society as a whole. Belonging to one's jati provides a greater sense of identity than that asserted for everyone in isolation by individualism in the United States. American students are often troubled that their Indian hosts do not feel secure in their presence until they can label them as another one of the students at the university. The students are doing their own thing by taking up studies in India, and want to be accepted as individuals. Their hosts feel more comfortable when they can identify them as belonging to a recognized group.

Jatis are traditionally identified by a family's occupation, from which each derives its name, such as dhobi (washerman community), gujar (herder community), or jat (farmer community). There are hundreds of thousands of such kinship groups throughout the country. In a normal village setting, individuals will interact on a daily basis with others from about 20 different jatis. The locally accepted position of their jati in a social hierarchy, generally called the caste system, will determine the expected social norms of their daily interactions. One's position in the immediate family is also highly proscribed by traditional expectations, maintained in most instances by the patriarchal structure of the family.

To the unfamiliar eye, individuals in these jati communities may look the same. Their distinguishing characteristics must be delineated by very fine strokes to convey their diversity. Regional differences among South Asians are the most obvious. They can be more readily identified in broader sweeps. Religion and language are also valuable descriptors. Because religious communities and majority language areas tend to concentrate in specific regions of the subcontinent, many can be identified by region. But because so many languages are spoken in each region, and the religions extend so widely, the people of South Asia can be more specifically defined by the religious faith to which they belong and the mother tongue that they speak. As traditional sources of identity firmly rooted in their heritage, religion and language remain persistent and vital indicators of who the people of South Asia are.

MANY RELIGIONS

Hinduism and Islam—one indigenous, the other imported—are by far the largest of the world's religions on the subcontinent. Approximately 62 percent of the population is Hindu and about 31 percent Muslim. Hinduism is the dominant religion in India (80.3 percent of the population) and Nepal (80.6 percent). Islam is dominant in Pakistan (97 percent), Bangladesh (83 percent), Afghanistan (99 percent), and Maldives (100 percent). Buddhism, though started in India, is practiced by only 1.8 percent of the total population of the subcontinent. But it is the predominant religion in Sri Lanka (70 percent) and Bhutan (75 percent). Jains are an even smaller religious community that originated in the subcontinent. They trace their faith to Vardhamana Mahavira,

(Courtesy of James Norton/Norton 03)

As with rituals, festivals, innumerable temples, and shrines, daily worship called puja, this man responds to transcendence at a convenient place along the road.

a religious leader who lived in northern India at the same time as the Buddha, in the sixth century B.C. There are also Sikhs, whose religion was founded by Guru Nanak during the sixteenth century A.D., in the northwestern part of South Asia known as the Punjab.

Other religious communities, originating outside of the subcontinent, include Christians, Jews, and the Parsis, whose Zoroastrian faith had its origin in ancient Persia at the time of the Vedas, more than 3,500 years ago.

All of these religious communities, even when influencing each other, continually reaffirm the structural integrity of their own faith as separate from the faiths of others. Recognition of the integrity of other religious became the basis for the wide and rapid spread of the influence of Islamic mystics, called Sufis, during the early years of Islamic influence in the subcontinent. Where Sufi teaching and practice were consistent with the values and experience of the religious communities already there, they were readily venerated and even co-opted. People of many different faiths participated in worship at shrines honoring Sufi saints. The Islamic faith of the Sultans and the Moghuls who followed the Sufis into South Asia was also recognized, but not so readily accepted.

This persistence of the structural integrity of different communities' sacred identity also accounts for the immense variety of Hinduism. Hinduism is actually a composite term that includes a multitude of diverse religious groups. Hindus do share some common teachings and perspectives. They all, for example, affirm the transmigration of the soul after death to some other form of life. This belief they share with Buddhists and Jains, which is why many Hindus consider Buddhists and Jains to be within the inclusive umbrella of Hinduism. But the many different communities within Hinduism follow separate religious traditions in an immense variety of ways, each the result of an evolution over a distinct path during many centuries.

The earliest record of the Hindu religious tradition is the Rg-Veda, an anthology of 1,028 poems drawn together from the collections of several families of Vedic priests into its current form around the tenth century B.C. Many of the poems were composed earlier, and presuppose an even earlier history of religious belief and practice. Traditionally the sacred preserve of

the Brahmin priesthood, the Veda is not widely known or understood among Hindus today. And the Vedic sacrifices around which the collection of sacred poems was initially created—and upon which the religious authority of the Brahmin priesthood was initially established—are rarely performed.

More characteristic of Hindu life today are the rituals, traditions, and festivals celebrated at the innumerable temples and shrines that dot the countryside, daily worship called puja, and the sanctity of an epic fragment called Bhagavad Gita ("The Song of the Lord"). All of these have been added to the religious practices of the Hindus after the Vedic period (1500 to 500 B.C.).

These later additions reveal that Hinduism has changed significantly since Vedic times. But it has not evolved as a single religious tradition. By incorporating and encompassing many diverse strands at different times in separate ways, it has become a vast array of schools and sects and disciplines, all encompassed within the Hindu fold today.

Among these sects are the Vaishnavites, who worship God as first revealed in the Rg-Veda as Vishnu. They recognize His manifestation in a number of avatars (incarnations) drawn from other and later traditions. These incarnations include Krishna, the Buddha, and Kalki (the "One who is to come"). Shaivites belong to a separate sect that traces the origin of its faith even farther back, to representations of Shiva as Pasupati (the "Lord of animals"), found in the artifacts of the Harappan Civilization, and as Nataraj (the "Lord of the Cosmic Dance"). The gods of other regional religious traditions have been incorporated into the Shaivite fold as children of Shiva and his consort Parvati. Ganapati, the elephant-headed god, remover of obstacles, becomes one such deity, who remains the primary focus of worship in the Indian state of Maharastra.

In addition, Hinduism includes worshipers of Krishna and Ram and of the Goddess in a variety of manifestations: in the Great Tradition as Kali, Durga, or Devi, but also among innumerable regional and local deities who benefit specific villages or protect against certain diseases. Their virtues and powers are enthusiastically celebrated throughout the country in an annual cycle of religious festivals unique to every village. And there is yoga, a spiritual discipline that does not affirm the existence of

(Courtesy of James Norton/Norton 04)
The central back panel on a tenth century Chola Shaivite temple in Tamil Nadu, which portrays Shiva at the center of the verticle image of the lingam, the creative energy of the universe. It expresses the extent of Shiva's transcendence in the images of Brahmá, the god of creation, as an eagle at the top, and Vishnu, the sustainer of the universe, portrayed in his incarnation (*avatar*) as a boar, when he rescued the earth from the depths of the cosmic flood. Neither can reach to the awesome heights nor the hidden depths of the ultimate power of God.

any deity. Any description of Hinduism must attempt to contain all this array of forms and practices, each with its own history, tradition, and authority, for a vast number of religious communities who consider themselves Hindu.

Buddhism also originated in South Asia and has evolved as a separate religion since the sixth century B.C. Siddhartha Gautama, the founder of the faith, was born a prince in a remote north Indian kingdom not under the sway of a Brahmin priesthood. He renounced his royal inheritance to seek an ultimate meaning for his life. After many years of diligent search, he received the enlightenment of the "Four-fold Truth." His teaching to his disciples about the pervasive presence of misery (*dukha*), of its cause and its removal, was the basis on which this religion developed and expanded throughout the subcontinent.

Buddhism was originally the faith of a monastic community, the sangha. It was composed of those who, attracted by the Buddha's example and teaching, abandoned their worldly activities to commit themselves to following his path, or *dhamma*, in communal and meditative isolation. The conversion of the Mauryan emperor Asoka to the Buddha's teaching in the third century B.C. brought about a significant change in the Buddhist

tradition. His political authority gave greater currency to the Buddha's *dhamma* throughout the society. He also endowed the community with royal patronage, which encouraged not only its growth but also spawned a creative outburst of Buddhist art, literature, and philosophy. Tributes to this heritage have survived in the exuberant carvings and frescoes in the caves at Ajanta, and in the majestic tranquility of the sculpture of the Buddha teaching at Sarnath. It was this highly expressive and energetic Buddhism that, during the centuries following Asoka, burst forth into the far reaches of Asia—to Sri Lanka, Southeast Asia, and to China, Japan, Mongolia, and Tibet.

As in the case of Islam under Moghul Rule, Buddhism, though indigenous, remained among a dominant Hindu society an encapsulated religious community, even when favored by imperial patronage for several centuries after Asoka. During that time it did manage to introduce vegetarianism as a social virtue to be observed by Brahmins among the Hindus. Unlike Hinduism, it declined dramatically in the north-central region of the subcontinent toward the end of the first millennium, as many were drawn to the teachings of Sufi mystics. Beginning in the eleventh century A.D., that region was subjected to the military attacks and religious zeal of Islamic potentates from Central Asia.

Buddhism survives today in enclaves along the borders of South Asia: in Ladakh, the section of Kashmir closest to China; in Bhutan, also along the Himalayan border, next to Tibet; and in Sri Lanka, off the southeastern coast of peninsular India. It has recently been revived in India by the Mahar community in Maharashtra under the leadership of Dr. Bhim Rao Ambedkar. He converted to Buddhism in 1956 in protest against the Hindu attitude of abhorrence and discrimination toward them and other communities designated by Hindus as "untouchable."

Islam was brought initially to the subcontinent by Arab traders plying the coastal shores of peninsular India soon after the hegira, or flight of Mohammed from Mecca in A.D. 622. Itinerant Sufi mystics then spread their faith across the subcontinent. Sultans who began to rule portions of the northern plains during the eleventh century finally established Muslims as a distinct religious community. The predominance of their numbers on the western and eastern ends of the north-central plains region led to the creation of the separate western and eastern arms of the original nation of Pakistan in 1947. Although several million Muslims migrated from India to Pakistan at the time of independence in 1947, 150 million still reside in India today, forming a significant religious minority (14 percent). The population of all Muslims in the subcontinent—close to 467 million—is more than three times the number of Muslims in the Arab world. Only Indonesia, with 215 million, has more Muslims in a single nation.

Most of the Muslims in South Asia belong to the Sunni tradition. In Maldives, one has to be Sunni as a requirement of citizenship. Significant minorities of shi'ite Muslims live in Afghanistan, Bangladesh and Pakistan, in which the Islamic faith is the predominant religion, and are subject to some discrimination. In Pakistan and Bangladesh, Sunnis also challenge the legitimacy of members of the Ahmadhiya sect of Islam.

According to legend, the Apostle Thomas first introduced Christianity to the subcontinent during the first century A.D. It was certainly known to silk traders from Egypt passing through Afghanistan to China during the second century. A small community of Syrian Christians migrated to the southwest coast of the subcontinent in the fourth century.

(Courtesy of the Archeological Survey of India/Norton05)
This sculpture dating from the fifth century A.D. is a majestic portrayal of the heaven body (*sambhogakaya*) of the Buddha teaching at the deer park in Sarnath, soon after he had attained enlightenment. His earth body is portrayed on the base by the wheel of dharma among his disciples, the content of his teaching as what remains on earth after his entering nirvana.

The Portuguese first brought Roman Catholicism to the western coast of India during the 1400s. Under the restraining eye of the English East India Company, Protestant missions were not permitted to work in the subcontinent until the early 1800s.

Today, these Christian communities add up to less than 3 percent of the total population of South Asia. They have become a significant force in the political life of the subcontinent only in the state of Kerala, at the southwestern edge of the Indian peninsula, where they form nearly one third of the population. Because religious minorities tend to concentrate in specific regions of the subcontinent, Sikhs, who represent only 1.9 percent of the population of India, are a majority of 62 percent in the State of Punjab. Persecution against religious minorities does occur in a variety of forms throughout the subcontinent. Recent studies show that Muslims in India are significantly disadvantaged. Persecution against religious minorities does occur in a variety of forms throughout the subcontinent. Recent studies show that Muslims in India are significantly disadvantaged.

Persecution against religious minorities does occur in a variety of forms throughout the subcontinent. Recent studies show that Muslims in India are significantly disadvantaged. Ahmadiyas are discriminated against in Pakistan, Hindus in Sri Lanka and Bhutan. Of recent concern, Christians in northern India, where the conservative wing of the ruling Bharatiya Janata Party (BJP) asserted its Hindu nationalist zeal, have come under attack. More normally these religious communities are generally accepted where their presence has not become a political issue.

MANY LANGUAGES

Foreign visitors to the growing commercial city of Kolkata (Calcutta) during the late eighteenth century were struck by the immense diversity of languages encountered there. The language of the city marketplace was Portuguese, a vestige of the early domination of East Indian trade by Portugal. The language of government was Persian, also a vestige of the Moghul imperial past. By contrast, the languages of the courts were Sanskrit and Arabic (depending upon which tradition of law those pursuing legal redress belonged). Though each had a specific context in which it was considered appropriate, none of these languages originated there; and none was the common tongue, or vernacular language, of the people who lived in Calcutta.

Had the visitors wandered into the streets or into homes, they would have discovered another variety of languages. Different tongues spoken by the common people reflected the places of origin of those who moved to Calcutta to take part in the growing activity and prosperity there. Because most of these people came from the immediate surrounding area, the most prevalent vernacular was Bengali.

Today, the English language has replaced the many foreign languages used in the more formal aspects of contemporary urban life, and Bengali remains the language of most of the people. But many other languages are spoken in the streets and homes of the city.

Hundreds of vernaculars are spoken throughout South Asia today. In India alone, thirty-five different languages are spoken by more than a million people. These languages belong to four distinct language families broadly distributed across specific regions of the subcontinent. The major dialects in the northernmost, Himalayan region are Tibeto-Burmese, related to the languages across the northern and eastern borders of the subcontinent. Their presence reveals that those living in the remote valleys of that region had more extensive cultural interaction through the rugged and forbidding mountains and jungles along those borders than with the more settled plains to the south.

(UN Photo 153,017/Oddbjom Monsen)

These young women of Pushkar, India, are part of the vast cultural mosaic of peoples in South Asia.

The prevalent languages of the northern plains region, Sri Lanka, and Maldives belong to the Indo-European family of languages, distant cousins of Latin, Greek, and the Germanic tongues of the West. They were introduced in their earliest form by Aryans, migrating cattle herders from Central Asia who wandered into the subcontinent almost 3,500 years ago.

A totally separate family of languages is spoken among the tribal peoples who still inhabit the remote hill regions of peninsular India. These are generally called Munda languages, and are related to those spoken by the Aboriginal peoples of Australia to the southeast. The Indo-European and tribal families of languages reveal far-reaching interconnections that existed thousands of years ago among peoples who are now widely separated.

Dravidian is yet another language family. Its roots can be traced only to the South Asian subcontinent itself. Today the Dravidian languages are spoken mostly in the south of India and the northern part of Sri Lanka, but they are not confined to the subcontinent. They have been carried to East Africa, Singapore, the Fiji Islands, and the West Indies by immigrants who continue to affirm their South Asian heritage in these many other parts of the world.

Each of the numerous languages that belong to these four families has a specific area in the subcontinent in which it is spoken by the vast majority of the people. It is easy to see where these languages predominate in India and Pakistan, because state borders within these countries have been drawn to enclose specific dominant-language groups. Afghanistan and Sri Lanka are also divided into language-area sections.

The integrity of these languages is retained even beyond the region where they are predominant as minority linguistic pockets in other language areas. Thus, a variety of languages may be found anywhere, especially in cities, where migrants from many parts of the country tend to settle in sections of the city with others who share their native language.

Some of these many languages have developed literary and classical forms of expression, but all are most widely familiar as colloquial dialects, which, like accents, reflect common usage among specific groups of people in particular places. Colloquial dialects would seem to be the form of language most subject to assimilation with other languages that are spoken around it. Because of the diverse social context in which they are spoken, these languages do interact and influence each other. But this interaction has not led to their becoming assimilated into a common tongue. That each continues distinct in its integrity as a separate language is a primary example of encapsulation as a way of describing the social dynamic of the people of South Asia.

The language one learns first in childhood is one's "mother tongue." This way of describing one's native language reveals that, for the people of South Asia, one is born into a language community that is intrinsic to one's identity as a person, even when residing in countries far away from the subcontinent. The same is true for an individual's caste community and religion. One is born into them, and they remain inherently descriptive of who one is. A map that delineates the predominant language areas throughout the entire subcontinent, like a map of the religious communities described earlier, looks like an intricate patchwork quilt. The pattern of the language quilt, however, is not the same as for religions.

Generally speaking, people belonging to different religions in the same place speak the same language, but those belonging to the same religion speak many languages. Only in the smaller countries of the subcontinent—Bhutan, Maldives, and Sri Lanka—do religious identities and language identities tend to correspond. Only in Maldives, the smallest of the countries of the subcontinent, do these categories coincide with its national boundaries; only there does being a citizen of the country generally mean that one speaks the same language and worships in a common faith.

RELIGIOUS NATIONALISM

Differences in religious and language identities continue to play an important role in South Asian life. Because of their importance in defining distinct social groups, they are easily invoked in conflicts, which result from so many densely populated groups striving for limited resources. Social unrest, communal disputes, and outright rioting occur frequently. Even when disputes originate between individuals, they rapidly become characterized by the religious or linguistic identity of the participants.

The Sikh nationalist movement in the Punjab during the 1980s—even though it was pursued by an unrepresentative splinter group led by the headmaster of a rural Sikh school, a young religious zealot named Bhindranwale—was a war that engaged large segments of the Sikh community. Newspapers reported almost daily on what appeared as random, indiscriminate strafing of buses along the highways and shootings into wedding parties by snipers on passing motor scooters. These acts of violence were sanctioned by the Damdami Taksal militants and the All India Sikh Students Federation because they had Hindus—as well as Sikhs unsympathetic to their cause—as targets.

Bhindranwale's death in 1984 at the hand of Indian Army in the Golden Temple, the sacred center of Sikhism in Amritsar, led to the assassination of Indira Gandhi, then prime minister of India, by Sikh members of her bodyguard. Her death was followed by massive riots in the streets of Delhi, India's capital, and the murder of many Sikhs throughout the country. It was a "holy war."

In neighboring Kashmir, the quest for independence is also expressed in religious terms. It is a battle for the freedom of a predominantly Muslim population from what is experienced as an oppressive Hindu India. Armed bands of militants ambush, burn, and kidnap throughout the mountain valleys and in the once placid Vale, all in the name of their religion. Thousands of Hindu families have fled their homes in fear of this violence.

The issue of whether India is, in fact, a Hindu or a secular nation was put to the test in two recent events. In 1992 in the northern city of Ayodhya, an old, abandoned mosque was destroyed by an unruly mob. Built at the time of the first Moghul emperor, Babur, in the sixteenth century A.D., it had been identified by the BJP, a Hindu nationalist political party, as the site of an earlier Hindu temple claimed to be the birthplace of Lord Rama. Destruction of the Babari Masjid mosque by a band of Hindu pilgrims, unrestrained by local police reinforced with military units on December 6, 1992, led to widespread communal rioting across India and retaliatory destruction of Hindu temples in Pakistan, Bangladesh, and even in Britain.

Again, in 2002, communal violence broke out in the town of Godhra in Gujarat in response to the death of 58 Hindus, mostly women and children, in the burning of a railway car, while returning from a pilgrimage to Ayodhya. In reprisal, more than 1,000 Muslims in slum dwellings were killed, and many more left homeless. The state government, accused of not acting sufficiently to control the violence, used the event to gain support among the Hindu population for its reelection in December that year.

Both of these events made clear that the religious identity of the people of India is a powerful political force. Religious nationalism, especially in India, with its large Hindu majority, severely challenges the quest for a unifying political identity to include all its people who belong to many different religions. Yet the defeat of the BJP in the most recent national elections in April 2004 suggests that, although Hindu nationalist sentiment is a formidable political force, it does not command a majority. The ideal of a secular national identity, inclusive of all its religious minorities, has been reaffirmed as a viable objective. By contrast, Bhutan and Pakistan are deliberately seeking to affirm modern religious national identities—Bhutan as a Buddhist nation and Pakistan as an Islamic republic.

Sri Lanka represents a different configuration. There, linguistic identity reinforces the separation between the regions of the country where different religions are predominant. The majority of Sri Lankans are Buddhists who speak the Sinhalese language. In the northeast region of the country, however, most of the people are Hindu, with significant Muslim enclaves, and are Tamil-speakers. The regional basis of this separation has allowed these communities to coexist for centuries. But the quest to achieve a single national identity since the independence of the country in 1948 has resulted in intense warfare between nationalist groups. Because of the importance of their language differences, these militant groups see the conflict more as cultural—as tigers against lions—rather than as religious.

LINGUISTIC NATIONALISM

Even though the Muslim population of Pakistan is divided between Sunnis and Shi'ites (71 percent to 20 percent of the total population), political identity based on language has played a much more important role than religion. During their early years of independence, the common Muslim faith of the peoples of East and West Pakistan did not override the ethnic and linguistic differences between the Bengali speaking peoples of the east and the Punjabi dominated western wing of the country. That opposition led to the break away and independence of Bangladesh as a separate country in 1971.

Even today, language identity is a vital factor in the distinction between the muhajirs—families who migrated from India at the time of Pakistan's independence in 1947—and the indigenous peoples of the country. The muhajirs retain and cultivate the use of Urdu, the mother tongue they brought with them. They are also primarily an urban community, living mostly in the city of Karachi.

To maintain their identity as a distinct community in the Islamic Republic of Pakistan, about 20 million muhajirs formed a political party, now called the Muttahida Quami Movement (MQM), to represent their interests in the affairs of state. Members in this party have been subjected to severe harassment in Karachi, a city that recorded 1,800 people killed on its streets, most believed to be politically motivated, in 1995. The imposition of federal rule and the creation of military courts in the city in November 1998 was understood by the MQM as an effort to destroy the movement as a political force. The leader of the party, Altef Hussain, now resides in self-imposed exile in London.

Afghanistan, which, like Pakistan, is predominantly Sunni Islamic, also has many language groups throughout the regions of the country. The distinct ethnic identity of these language groups did not prevent their leaders from joining together to resist the Soviet invasion of their country in 1979.

They were unable, however, to get together to forge a single government after the Soviet withdrawal in 1989, and even after the downfall of the surviving Communist government in Kabul in 1992. A fundamentalist religious revival called Taliban then arose amongst the Pastho-speaking peoples of southern Afghanistan. Their reforming zeal swept across the country during the last half of the 1990s, and by 1999, forces allegiant to it controlled most of the country. Only a small force of mostly Dari-speaking Tajiks from the northern corner of Afghanistan held out. Following the terrorist attacks in the United States on September 11, 2001, and the refusal of the Taliban leadership to extradite or exile Osama bin Laden, United States and coalition forces backed the Tajik-led Northern Alliance to recapture Kabul.

In June 2002, a grand council, called a loya jirga, held in Kabul, elected Hamid Karzai, a Pashtun, as interim president with the hope that a new government might be formed by him to attract the support and allegiance of all of the many ethnic and linguistic groups that live in different regions of the country. In the early stages, its authority extended little beyond the city of Kabul itself, where it is protected by international peace keeping forces.

Hazid Karmai was elected president in national elections held in October 2004 by 54 percent of the vote. This support came substantially only from Kabul and the Pashto-speaking areas to the south of the city. Even though selecting a Tajik to be his vice presidential candidate, he gained little support from the other language areas of the country.

The difference between the more cosmopolitan environment of Kabul and the conservative countryside has contributed to political instability in Afghanistan for some time. It divided the People's Democratic (Communist) Party from its beginning in the early 1960s. This rift gave occasion for Soviet forces to invade the country in 1979. And the Taliban movement, which emerged out of the provincial city of Kandahar in 1996 and enveloped most of the country, had a devastating disdain for those urbanites in Kabul who did not share its reactionary religious agenda. The dominating power of indigenous local leaders, called warlords, has been even more divisive for a much longer time. Their continuing power, based on regional ethnic and language identity, will remain a significant factor in efforts to achieve a unifying national identity for the people of Afghanistan.

AN ENCAPSULATED SOCIETY

The distinction between urban and rural life in South Asia as defining the identity of its people is important because the subcontinent has a much greater rural population than urban. The total urban population is only 24 percent, as compared with 74 percent in the United States. India will soon have the second-largest urban population in the world, but urban dwellers still constitute less than a quarter of the total population of the country. Rural ways and the rural voice still have a significant role, and, as the 2004 elections in India reveal, a significant voice in determining the priorities and direction of South Asian political life.

There is also a vast disparity between the wealthiest and the poorest of the poor. Recognition of these inequalities has led to the development of SEWA (Self-Employed Women's Associa-

tion) in India and the Grameen Bank in Bangladesh, institutions that have created effective methods for providing capitalization of assets among the poor. Cooperatives modeled on these programs have been set up throughout the subcontinent, primarily to help women develop self-supporting careers.

Religion, language, urban/rural difference, and wealth/ poverty all reveal the immense diversity and variety in the social fabric of South Asia. The violence that often results from their interaction reveals the depth and the extent of these differences as establishing the unique identity of each of the many social groupings into which the nations of South Asia are divided. Religions and languages in particular affirm in their integrity divisions that have existed sometimes in harmony, sometimes in conflict for many centuries.

Social pressure toward bonding and conformity within these groups is so strong that they are not expected to assimilate or fit in with the distinguishing characteristics of others. This process functions among the smallest of social groupings, on the level of the jati caste communities.

Extended kinship groups, tribes, migrant peoples, religious communities, and even highly mobile urban classes are accepted as they are, as distinct communities within a stratified social hierarchy. They thus remain an encapsulated yet integral part within the whole fabric of South Asian society.

Although there have been periods of great confrontation, discrimination, and violence, the wide diversity among the many different peoples of South Asia is generally accepted as both inevitable and normal. Like the fourfold layering of humanity set forth in the Vedic hymn celebrating the sacrificial offering of primordial man in the creation of the universe, social diversity is a cosmic reality.

IMAGE 3: THE WORLD AS SYMBOL

The first function [of a symbol] is the representative function. The symbol represents something which is not itself, for which it stands and in the power and meaning of which it participates.... And now we come to something which is perhaps the main function of the symbol—namely, the opening up of levels of reality which otherwise are hidden and cannot be grasped in any other way.

Every symbol opens up a level of reality for which non-symbolic speaking is inadequate. The more we try to enter into the meaning of symbols, the more we become aware that it is the function of art to open up levels of reality; in poetry, in visual art, and in music, levels of reality are opened up which can be opened up in no other way.

But in order to do this, something else must be opened up—namely, levels of the soul, levels of our interior reality. And they must correspond to the levels in exterior reality which are opened up by a symbol. So every symbol is two-edged. It opens up reality and it opens up the soul. There are, of course, those people who are not opened up by music or who are not opened up by poetry, or more of them who are not opened up at all by visual arts. The "opening up" is a two sided function—namely reality in deeper levels and the human soul in special levels.

—Paul Tillich, *Theology of Culture*

A Vedic householder, himself a priest, or accompanied by a priest, starts his day before sunrise with a series of rituals. The basic rite, which may be accompanied by acts of purification, is to remove the coals from the household hearth, called the lord of the home hearth, upon which the meals of the house are cooked each day. These coals are moved to another hearth, outside of the house to the east, called the hearth of offering. There, in anticipation of the rising of the sun, the fire is rekindled using special sacrificial grass collected for this ceremony. This act is accompanied by reciting a hymn from the Rg-Veda, which celebrates the sacred power revealed in the beauty of the dawn as a moment filled with heightened anticipation. This time of the day is portrayed by a symbol, as a young maiden rising to stir all living creatures into life:

> Daughter of Heaven, she has appeared before us,
> A maiden shining in resplendent raiment,
> Thou sovereign lady of all earthly treasure,
> Auspicious Dawn, shine here today upon us.
>
> Arise! the breath of life again has reached us:
> Darkness has gone away and light is coming.
> She leaves a pathway for the sun to travel.
> We have arrived where men prolong existence.
> from Rg-Veda 1.113, A. A. Macdonell translation

Having invoked this charmed natural presence around the fire of offering in the eastern hearth, the householder awaits the appearance of the sun above the horizon.

This daily ritual, still practiced by some orthodox Brahmins in India today, is a symbolic act that portrays the natural sun, with all of its awesome energy, as representing something beyond itself as a physical reality. It points to a level of transcendent, auspicious power that cannot be grasped in any other way. For the sun is the primary symbol in the householder's life of the cosmic energy that creates order out of chaos and generates prosperity for all mankind. He thus invokes into his household through the fire of offering the blessing of that sacred power of the sun as it rises to fill the world with the bounty of its light.

To reaffirm this sacred level of meaning that lies within, but beyond the natural reality of the visible sun, he recites as it appears the words of the Gayatri mantra, one of the most sacred verses of the Veda.

> O face of the True Sun, now hidden by a disc of gold,
> May we know thy Reality, and see thee face to face.

Peoples from ancient times around the world have endowed the sun with symbolic meaning. Because of its awesome height in the sky above the earth, its brightness as a source of light for the entire world, and its consistency of motion as manifesting cosmic order, the sun has stirred man's creative imagination. He sees in it much more than a natural object to be observed in the common understanding as, in the English visionary William Blake's pejorative image, "a round disc of fire somewhat like a Guinea." The consistency and beauty of its moment of arrival, and of the light and blessing it brings, is simply too awesome, too intense to be experienced objectively. Like his response to the resplendence of the dawn, the Vedic householder enters into that moment passionately and creatively. He celebrates it each morning as a sacred time.

The transcendence revealed in this moment "now hidden by a disc of gold" in the words of the Gayatri mantra, is an ultimate level of reality pointed to by the sun. In Vedic mythology, special recognition was given to a goddess called Aditi. Retaining vestiges of ancient, pre-Aryan mother goddess worship, she is celebrated in the Rg-Veda as the Mother of the solar gods called Adityas, who are revealed in the phases of the sun during the course of a day. The god Varuna, the protector of moral order in the universe, appears at the apex of the day, and Martanda, "the death egg," her eighth child, appears at sunset. Her sacred power is also affirmed in her name, which means literally "without limit," "infinite," she who is beyond human understanding. Aditi gives birth out of chaos to cosmic order as manifest in the daily course of the sun. This, for the Vedic priests, was a sacred mystery.

This celebration of the dimension of transcendence at sunrise in the Vedic householder's daily ritual goes back to the religious musings of that robust, cow-herding people called Aryans, who drove their horse-drawn war chariots into the subcontinent from Central Asia more than three thousand years ago. From these early times, Vedic priests saw the world as an experience of sacred celebration rather than as an objective natural reality. Their ritual activity and intellectual pursuits to affirm the world as sacrifice sought to identify that deeper level of reality that gives the experiences and objects of this world the quality of being sacred.

They expressed this level of reality in symbols, as what experiences and objects represent, rather than just the fact of their objective reality. They saw the world as an arena for the refinement of human experience—to realize not just what is, but also what is beyond—to deeper levels of their being.

The pervasive authority of scientific thinking in Western culture encourages the perception of objects as things. They are acknowledged to be as they are observed, and our understanding of the world is built around relationships revealed and confirmed by perceptual data. These relationships are called models, whether they be of things observed directly, such as gravity, or, of abstract patterns, like atomic structure or galaxies. All of these descriptions are based on, and authenticated by, what we perceive as an objective natural world.

We also understand in perceiving an object or experience something more than the facts of its existence. It represents something more as a symbol by pointing to a special meaning or interpretation that it is not itself. If we recognize the pattern of a flag, for example, as belonging to a specific group of people, like a tribe or a country, it is more than a natural object. It stands as a symbol for what defines the identity, allegiance, and destiny of the people for whom it is their flag. So also, certain events are significant to a people not just because they happened.

The Fourth of July is celebrated to this day and uniquely by the American people with stories of the Revolutionary War and other quests for freedom, with fireworks and parades. Also important for the American people is the Exodus experience, an event that happened many centuries ago for the ancient people of Israel when they were freed from slavery in Egypt and found new life in a promised land.

The ancient Vedic priests' celebration of a dimension of transcendence in human experience appears in the poems of an anthology called the Rg-Veda, collected some 3,000 years ago, after their settlement in the subcontinent. As in the poem to Dawn, we can see in them "myth in the making."

They also developed an elaborate system of rituals to reenact, express, and celebrate the cosmos as a sacrificial event. In reciting these poems in this context, they took upon themselves the exclusive task of developing and giving authenticity to this symbolic perception of the world. This role also became the basis for asserting their social priority, as in the Vedic passage that described them as the mouth of primordial man, whose offering of himself brought about the creation of the universe.

As time went on these scholar-priests began to hold extensive discussions during their sacrifices to explore the meaning of the transcendent reality their ritual activity, as symbols, represented. Out of this discourse came a collection of narrative works called Upanishads.

In the centuries that followed, the priests further coalesced, elaborated, appended, and refined this appreciation of the sacredness of our world into classical forms. These forms provided the structure for immense intellectual and artistic creativity, which produced many outstanding works of thought and art on different aspects of human experience. Their analytical works, called sastras, were based on careful observation of the natural world around them. But they were not so much descriptions as they were reflections on what this world might be as expressive of a deeper level or order of being.

One of these sastras, called the Laws of Manu, is a remarkable treatise on social structure. It presents an elaborate set of rules of appropriate behavior for a society as though it were divided and ranked into the four *varna,* or classical caste, grouping as set forward in the Rg-Veda: Brahmin (priests), Kshatriya (rulers), Vaisya (citizens), and Sudra (laborers). It also divides one's life into four stages, called ashramas, each one occupying one-quarter of a lifetime: that of being a student, householder, mendicant, and ascetic. The Laws, rather than assuming that a single behavioral norm can apply to all of life, prescribe a distinct set of rules appropriate for each stage. A clear structure was thus imposed upon people's lives that placed upon them specific expectations of how they ought to act in a wide variety of conditions of class and of age. It was a comprehensive and authoritative model for social behavior, not because it described what actually happens, but because it expressed a vision of cosmic social order. It was something to live up to.

Other sastras focus on such topics as statecraft, poetics, philosophy, music, ritual and the visual arts. These works are [still] remarkable for the depth and precision of analysis that their author's undertook. They reveal that the classical scholar-priests who composed them did not find order or ultimate meaning immediately in the natural world about them. They had too great a sense of the flux and uncertainty in their normal human experience. They sought consistency, rather, in more abstract intellectual patterns, in the refinement rather than the description of what was about them. In art, for example, they suggested that aesthetic value was not in the experience of raw emotion (bhava), but in the refinement of that emotion into an aesthetic essence (rasa) that generates a sense of awe and beauty. Their attention was thus on what their experience pointed to as symbol rather than what it was as fact.

It was out of this refining analysis that the concept of the number zero emerged—it was in the classical South Asian way of looking at objects that the idea arose that there is something in our number system that is to be counted, even if it is not here.

Of all of the works of analysis during the classical tradition, none is greater than the earliest: the description of the structure of language by Panini, the classical grammarian of the Sanskrit language. Every language is a symbol system where particular sounds articulated in a distinct way represent a specific meaning to those who share in understanding that language. Its symbolic character also reveals levels of experience beyond the physical world. Words, sentences, stories, even myths not only express, they also create the significance of what happens to make real for us other dimensions of our experience. Through language, we become part of and celebrate whole new worlds.

Panini probably lived during the fourth century B.C. He analyzed how sounds, as the basic structural units of a language (morphemes), fit together to form words and sentences. Only specific combinations of sounds form words, and specific combinations of words form sentences. When we use them to communicate, words and sentences reveal patterns that are used to relate their meanings. Panini's insight was that these patterns are not established by the meanings of words and sentences, but rather by the structure of language itself.

To analyze the patterns of language, Panini did not focus on the way words and sentences are used in ordinary, colloquial language. He looked at the highly refined, classical form of the Sanskrit language of the priesthood. (The word *sanskrit* means "refined," or "perfected," and identifies the level of abstraction to which the formal use of that language had progressed among the intensively trained scholar-priests during the late Vedic period.) In this quest to discover the structure of this highly refined language, Panini identified its abstract form as a profound source of order in human life. Its greatest potential as language was not to describe what is, but, rather, as in Vedic poetry, to point to and affirm what is ultimately real in human experience: to the reality of the sun, for example, hidden in its appearance.

Panini reduced his study of Sanskrit to eight concise chapters of grammatical rules, wherein each successive rule was an exception to all the rules that preceded it. This impressive intellectual achievement appears even more remarkable in that he achieved this structure without the use of writing; he did it all in his head.

Panini's achievement was matched by other important intellectual quests during the classical period. Elaborations of the concept of cosmic time, time that is not linear, but ceaselessly revolving, are mind-boggling because of the vast span of the cycles proposed. These cycles were described in the Puranic literature, dating from the early years A.D., as extending through four eras, called yugas, of from 432,000 years to 1,728,000 years long. One thousand of these four-era periods add up to a Kalpa, or a day of Brahma. At the end of a 4,320,000,000-year day of Brahma, the created universe comes to an end, or is dormant during Brahma's night, of equal duration, before the cycle begins again.

Brahma is now in the first kalpa of his fifty-first year. Six Manus of that kalpa have passed away. We are living in the Kaliyuga of the twenty-eighth four-age period (*chaturyuga*) of the seventh *manvantara* of Brahma's fifty-first year. The Kaliyuga began on February 18, 3102 B.C. This would seem to indicate that we have a little less than 426,933 years to go until the Kaliyuga with its twilight comes to an end, and we have to face dissolution!

—W. Norman Brown, *Man in the Universe*

This concept of time also generated many imaginative images in Sanskrit literature. One is the account of an apsara, a celestial being who lived in the realm of heaven within a different time frame. One heaven day, while at play with her friends in a garden, she fell off of a swing and fainted. While unconscious, she went to earth to be born as a child. She lived to reach adulthood, married and give birth to children, attended her eldest son's wedding, and saw her grandchildren before she died. She then returned to her apsara friends in the heaven garden. They had anxiously gathered around upon her fall from the swing, and were fanning her. Upon reviving, she told her friends of her earthly experience. They were astounded that so much could have happened to her in so short a span of their time.

Imaginative and creative intellectual effort was also devoted to find an understanding of self—an answer to the question "Who am I?" And again, the analysis pursued not the question "What am I?" but "Of what is my being a symbol?"

The Upanishads distinguished early on between the self who acts, the agent—"I am the one who does, thinks, feels things"—and the self who observes this agency the witness. The active self was called *jiva* (the living thing), the aspect of self to which the acts of karma (acts having moral consequences), become attached. Yajnavalkya in the Brhadaranyaka Upanishad was the first to assert that this karma determines into what form of life the *jiva* transmigrates when reincarnated.

Other early scholar-priests devoted to the study of self affirmed another dimension of self standing apart from oneself as acting, thinking, feeling, hidden behind the visible self. Because this witness self is detached, observing rather than doing, it transcends the activity in which the *jiva* is involved. This aspect of self is called atma. The atma, because it transcends the natural self, is affirmed as more real, as the ultimate self, of which the natural, active self is a symbol.

> "Bring me a fig," Uddalaka said to his son Shvetaketu.
> He then asked him to break open and extract a tiny seed out of the fig.
>> "Break it open.... What do you see there?"
>> "Nothing at all, sir."
>> "Truly, my son, that subtle essence which you do not see, from that does the great fig tree grow. Believe me, the whole world has that essence for its Self. That is the Real. That is who you really are (*tat tvam asi*).
>>> from Chandogya Upanishad, 6.12.1–3

The Vedanta philosopher Shankara, who lived during the eighth century A.D., ranks with Panini as an intellectual giant among the classical scholars of South Asia. Shankara identified the experience of consciousness in our being as the primary designation of the true self, the atma. It is in witnessing ourselves as being conscious as a symbol that we gain some insight into who we really are, of our ultimately real self.

This way of thinking is not available to those who are literalists, who think that what they see is all that there is to human experience. The classical thinkers of South Asia envisioned and opened up impressive avenues of awareness and expression realized in creative works of art, music, dance, sculpture, and literature. They also discovered and affirmed a transcendent unity in human experience in the world, which can be realized through a multitude of symbols. This unity can even be discovered in

(Courtesy of James Norton/Norton 06)

A vast sculpture on a huge rock at Mahabalipuram along the Coromandel Coast in South India in the seventh century. It is an illustration of an episode in a Sanskirt poem by Bharavi about Arjuna's penance to acquire the sacred bow of Shiva for use in the culminating battle of the Indian epic, the Mahabharata. Notice the cat in lower right corner also doing penance to lure the mice at its feet. In classical art much in artistic form is crafted from literary images.

experiencing the transcendence of our own, isolated, individual selves, should we discover the "ultimate beyond" within.

Such a theme in modern times is expressed by Rabindranath Tagore, artist, educator, in this verse from the Gitanjali, for which he received the Nobel Prize in Literature in 1913:

> The same stream of life that runs through my veins night and day runs through the world and dances in rhythmic measures.
>
> It is the same life that shoots in joy through the dust of the earth in numberless blades of grass and breaks into tumultuous waves of leaves and flowers.
>
> It is the same life that is rocked in the ocean-cradle of birth and death, in ebb and flow.
>
> I feel my limbs are made glorious by the touch of this world of life. And my pride is from the life-throb of ages dancing in my blood this moment.

This heritage helps to explain why encapsulation as a social process is such an integral part of the culture of South Asia. The classical scholars understood that languages and religions are cultural constructs. No language or religion is natural in the sense that each has to be what it is, nor that what each language or religion is can be fully explained in natural terms. Different peoples express their experiences of identical things, even the same event, in very different ways. They even experience them differently.

Thus, attempts to construct a universal language, religion, or nationality have failed because the cultural contexts in which the necessary claims to absolutism are expressed, be it truth or allegiance, are not shared by all peoples. We see things, experience them, and talk about them in different ways, based upon the cultural context in which we are raised.

This understanding of the cultural relativity of language and religion is clearly evident in the pluralistic social context in which the peoples of South Asia live. It does not negate the absolute claims to meaning and truth of the many separate languages and religions around them. Each is recognized to have a functional integrity that distinguishes it from all other languages and religions.

A specific religion evolves as a structural abstraction among a group of people to reflect the uniqueness of their experience of transcendence as a group. Thus the group's religious practices become symbols that point to their identity and integrity of those who acknowledge and worship what is ultimately real for them, together as a community.

Among the Brahmin community, it is not the colloquial or even ritual use of Sanskrit that makes that language sacred. It is, rather, the structure of that highly refined language that makes it symbolically expressive of the ultimate meaning of the universe.

A Brahmin teaching states that when God came to create the universe, He did not create objects and then allow Adam, a human being, to invent language by naming what he saw. Instead, He went to the ultimate meaning of what is universally expressed symbolically in the language of the Rg-Veda to find out what He was to create. That level of reality is for the classical tradition more real than the reality of the natural world. Nothing can be literally true in the Veda unless it be ultimately true.

Recognition of structural integrity as characteristic of differing languages and religions is the basis for understanding them as symbols. They are not absolutes in themselves but rather point to a transcendent level of reality that is. One can accept the ultimate claim to universality of others for their religious faith to the degree that one understands the ultimacy of that universal reality to which one's own faith is a symbol. It is not a matter of accepting, or even tolerating, another's religion. It is, rather, the challenge of discovering that transcendent level of reality within one's own faith. To people of great faith, the ultimate reality affirmed by all religions is one.

Encapsulation as a social process in South Asia is based on an appreciation for the symbolic way each language and each religion is expressive of what is ultimately true for each social group. It affirms a vital sense of community among those who speak the same mother tongue and join in common religious practices. That is why language and religion play such an important role in the unfolding of democracy as a way of affirming a political identity for the peoples of South Asia.

Sharing a language and a religious faith clearly separates one from all those who do not. Problems arise when one takes this difference as affirming what is exclusive and absolute. Such literalism leads to isolation, antipathy, and violence. It is particularly dangerous in seeking viable national identities among people within geographical boundaries on the basis of religious and language identity.

The classical tradition teaches that the structural integrity of languages and religions is symbolic, and not exclusive nor absolute. When this perspective is understood as opening up oneself to other, deeper levels of reality, the pluralistic social environment of South Asia has not been assimilating nor conforming, but both resilient and accepting of difference.

IMAGE 4: DEMOCRACY IN SOUTH ASIA

"The spirit of democracy is not a mechanical thing to be adjusted by the abolition of forms. It requires a change of the heart."

—Mohandas K. Gandhi

The nations of South Asia have faced many obstacles in their quest for modern democratic governments.

First of all, the ideology of nationalism based on the will of the people established by adult franchise came from the west through British colonial rule. The formation of such nations evolved over several centuries in western Europe and America among dominant groups of culturally homogeneous people. Those of different cultural backgrounds, those who spoke different languages, and even women, were simply ignored in this process. Because this assumption of a dominant male ethnicity was unchallenged, it was taken for granted that the male citizens shared sense of identity as a nation would take precedence over any cultural differences among residual minority groups within the nation. All participants in the political process would blend into the culture of the politically dominant.

The assumption that dominant ethnicity determines the distinctive character of a nation could not be easily transposed into the diverse cultural environment of the peoples of South Asia. They are so accustomed to living in what Shashi Tharoor calls "a singular land of the plural," in which no ethnic nor linguistic group is in a majority. They do not understand common citizenship to be something that would demand greater allegiance than the community identities that separate them from all other linguistic, religious, and social groups among whom they live. They were not prepared to think of themselves as having a shared political identity as a nation.

The idea of modern democracy introduced by colonial rule also did not enter a political vacuum. Traditional sources of honor, allegiance, and identity based on patriarchal structures within the family, in the villages and among petty kingdoms continued to dominate public life. The Great Mutiny of 1857 in British India demonstrated widespread resistance to British colonial attempts to enlighten its South Asian subjects. The British recognized this indigenous authority when they invited the maharajas who fled during the Mutiny to return to administer their former kingdoms. It is also recognized by those who seek to work with the "warlords" in Afghanistan today.

Efforts in the twentieth century to encourage public participation in the political process, to realize a government of the people, reveal the adaptability of village level, caste community, and language area institutions. Established patterns of grassroots governance continue to be significant factors in

(UN Photo 87,040/WTARA)

Pluralism in South Asia complicates the establishment of a workable political base as minorities strive to find a legitimate place and voice in national life. The religious influence is exemplified by their Sikh teacher addressing some of his followers at the Golden Temple in Amritsar, India. What he tells people is likely to be more relevant to social and political change than what any politician may say.

implementing and shaping the transition from traditional power structures into democratic forms.

India and Bangladesh have both adopted policies that reserve public offices for women. Even there, those women elected to responsible positions still meet strong resistance to their authority from entrenched patriarchal power elites.

Sirimavo Bandaranaike and Chandrika Kumaratunga, who served as prime ministers and presidents in Sri Lanka, Prime Ministers Indira Gandhi in India, Khaleda Zia and Hasima Wajed in Bangladesh, and Benazir Bhutto in Pakistan are all remarkable women who have served their countries with distinction. Yet, each of them has gained prominence in national political life because of the dominant roles of their fathers or husbands. Traditional power structures do not relinquish their authority easily, if at all.

Religion and National Identity

Because language, religion, and nationality all establish self-authenticating corporate identities, leaders of the freedom movements during the twentieth century drew upon established language and religious communities to create national allegiances and encourage participation in the public domain. The traditional affiliations of dominant religious groups were especially convenient for this purpose.

The most obvious example of this exploitation of religious identity to create political involvement and unity was the division of British India under its direct control into India and Pakistan in 1947. The colonial government assigned those districts in which the majority of the population was Muslim to Pakistan, and Hindu-majority districts to India.

Muhammad Ali Jinnah, in his appeal for the founding of Pakistan, claimed the uniqueness of their identity to be based on cultural rather than religious difference. More recently, the Bharatiya Janata Party, the ruling party in India from 1999 to 2004, similarly framed its quest for a policy of Hindu nationalism as cultural, as Hindutva (Hindu-ness). They both wanted to avoid the appearance of religious discrimination.

The use of a religious community's bonding dynamic for political ends changes the nature of the relationship it affirms among the people. It reduces religious identity from a symbolic expression of ultimate truth, a *mythos*, to an ideology that is historically concrete, literally true, and both socially and geographically exclusive. At its worst, the political use of religious symbols has led to absolutizing the nation-state itself.

The reduction of religious identity to national identity is pervasive throughout our world today. The intensity and fervor created by appealing to people's religious allegiances to pro-

(United Nations/BP)

With the partitioning of India and Pakistan, masses of people migrated because of their religious affiliations. More than 14 million people fled, including these refugees, making it the largest migration in history.

mote a political cause or ideology has led to communal rioting, terrorism, and terrible bloodshed. It has left a trial of human misery in the Middle East, Africa, Northern Ireland, the former Yugoslavia, and in South Asia.

The Partition of British India in 1947

The ethnic, linguistic, religious groupings used in Western Europe to build the political identity of nations became especially divisive in South Asia's pluralistic social environment. The creation of the new nations of India and Pakistan out of the British Indian Empire isolated vast numbers of people not included in the dominant religious identity around which the national borders were drawn. Millions of Hindus and Sikhs living in areas of the subcontinent that became Pakistan, and Muslims finding themselves in an independent India, felt threatened as minorities in these newly established nations. Communal violence erupted across the subcontinent.

Children of many faiths and backgrounds who had grown up together, had learned and played together in the same classes in school for years, suddenly, on the day of the independence of their country, became enemies. They thought that they were going to be free. What they experienced, inexplicably, was severe division and hatred. Dazed and mystified, those of minority faiths were whisked away during the night to seek asylum across the border. Many did not make it.

Fourteen million people fled, the largest refugee migration ever experienced in the world. Homeless and threatened in their own lands, they were forced to flee in haste, destitute of any possessions, to cross the new national borders in a quest for survival. As Hindus and Sikhs moved toward India and Muslims toward Pakistan in opposite directions across the border drawn between the two countries, many hundreds of thousands were senselessly killed.

Kushwant Singh writes of the devastating impact of that violent confrontation on a Sikh village near the border, in his novel *Train to Pakistan*:

Early in September the time schedule in Mano Majra started going wrong….

Goods trains had stopped running altogether, so there was no lullaby to lull them to sleep…. All trains (now crowded with refugees) coming from Delhi stopped and changed their drivers and guards before moving on to Pakistan.

One morning, a train from Pakistan halted at Mano Majra railway station. At first glance it had the look of trains in the days of peace. No one sat on the roof. No one clung between the bogies. No one was balanced on the foot-boards. But somehow it was different. There was something uneasy about it. It had a ghostly quality.

(That evening) the northern horizon, which had turned a bluish gray, showed orange again. The orange turned into copper and then into luminous russet. Red tongues of flame leaped into the black sky. A soft breeze began to blow towards the village. It brought the smell of burning kerosene, then of wood. And then—a faint acrid smell of searing flesh.

The village was stilled in deathly silence. No one asked anyone else what the odour was. They all knew. They had known it all the time. The answer was implicit in the fact that the train had come from Pakistan.

That evening, for the first time in the memory of Mano Majra, Imam Baksh's sonorous cry did not rise to the heavens to proclaim the glory of God.

Those who survived this massive migration found themselves bewildered refugees. They did not experience the exhilaration of political freedom. They were homeless in the lands of their birth, unwelcome in the lands to which they fled. The

Partition of British India led to a human catastrophe that has left an abiding scar on the subcontinent.

The dividing of British India based on religious identity continues to unsettle the region. Particularly damaging has been the unresolved claim of both Pakistan and India to the princely state of Jammu and Kashmir. This dispute led to outright warfare between the two countries, in 1948 and 1965, which divided that state along a Line of Control. On either side of this line, both India and Pakistan describe the other's portion as foreign occupied. More recently, in 1999, Pakistan military units advanced into the Kargil region of Kashmir. And both countries built up their forces in confrontation along the entire Line of Control following the terrorist attempt to blow up India's Parliament Building in New Delhi on December 13, 2001. This lengthy dispute, and particularly the terrorist violence it has produced, continues to poison not only the relationship between the two countries, but also among the other South Asian nations and the international community.

Terrorism

Terrorist threats against innocent people to obtain ideological objectives have been felt in both the West and South Asia for many years. The IRA held the British in threat of terrorist acts from 1972 to 1997. Civil War in Sri Lanka, which began in 1983, introduced suicide bombing as a modern terrorist tactic. Muslim militants drove a bomb into an American barracks in Beirut, Lebanon, in 1983, killing 241 marines. An American airliner blew up over Lockerbie, Scotland, in 1988, killing all 259 passengers and flight crew aboard, and 11 more below them on the ground.

In 1993, terrorists attempted to blow up the World Trade Center in New York City. That same year, twelve bombs exploded simultaneously, one near the Stock Exchange, in Bombay killed 287 and wounded 713. The Oklahoma City bombing took 168 lives on April 19, 1995.

The landscape of terrorism changed with the destruction of the twin towers of the World Trade Center on September 11, 2001, and with the "war on terror" in response. The 9/11 attack confirmed to Islamic fundamentalist militants the symbolic power of terrorism, even against overwhelming economic and military odds, as they had overcome in resisting the Soviet military occupation in Afghanistan in the 1980s. And they saw the "war on terror" in response as an attack on Islam, which legitimized the violence of their jihad to protect their faith.

The Terrorism Research Center (TRC) recorded 19 major terrorist attacks in the world in 2001. That number rose to 43 in 2002, to 175 in 2003, and 655 in 2004. In 2005, the total number of incidents in the world rose to 11,111. Of these, 4,230 happened in the Middle East, and 3,974 in South Asia.

In India, there were 1,404 terrorist incidents in 2005. The military occupation and the insurgency in Kashmir accounted for nearly half of them. Close to 45,000 people have been killed there since 1989.

The Kashmir Crisis

When India and Pakistan became independent in 1947, 40 percent of British India was under the direct control of independent Maharajas. In recognition of their sovereignty, it was determined that they should decide to which country they should accede, to either India or Pakistan. In most cases, as they were not given any other choice, that was an easy decision. The state of Jammu and Kashmir was unusual in that it had a Muslim majority under the rule of a wavering Hindu Maharaja, Hari Singh. He was already facing an indigenous independence movement closely tied to the Indian National Congress, led by Sheikh Abdullah, the "Lion of Kashmir."

For Pakistan, it was an issue of their religious identity as an Islamic state. Because the majority of the population of the state was Muslim, under the rules set by the British Raj for partition, it should be part of Pakistan. India illegally invaded Kashmir in 1947, and has been forcefully occupying ever since all that portion of the former princely state that was not liberated by Pakistan in 1948. Because Pakistan became a separate country to protect the freedom and the cultural integrity of the Islamic peoples in the subcontinent, its support for the freedom of the Kashmiri people from Hindu India's oppression is integral to its identity as an Islamic state. Since then Pakistan has been eager to engage international support to implement 1948 UN resolutions for a plebiscite to let the people of Kashmir decide to which country they want to belong.

For India, it is an issue of the sovereignty of a secular state. It asserts that Kashmir became an integral part of the country when the Maharajah of Jammu and Kashmir, even under duress, acceded it to India in 1947, according to those terms of the partition of India and Pakistan. Only in the Vale of Kashmir do the Muslims outnumber the Hindus, who predominate in the Jammu section of the state, as do the Buddhists in Ladakh. Because of this diversity of religious groups, India's response is framed in its constitutional commitment to secularism. In Kashmir, as in the nation, the religious identity of any segment of the population should not determine the political status of the whole.

Its claim to sovereignty has been validated, India contends, by elections held for public office in their portion of the state since 1952, although sporadically after 1980. These elections obviate the need for a UN plebiscite. Such elections, it also points out, have never been held in Pakistan occupied Kashmir, which is ruled by a governor appointed by the central government in Islamabad.

The people of Kashmir are caught between India's national secular identity and Pakistan's religious nationalism. Both ideologies are worth fighting for, and their opposition has led to a deadly conflict on their soil. Kashmiris' hope to preserve their own independent, more accepting, traditional life was jolted first by heavy-handed Indian administration in the name of their being part of India. Then they were devastated by the rise of an extreme Islamist resistance movement inspired by the success of the Mujahedeen in Afghanistan, with United States, Saudi, and Pakistani support, to repel Soviet occupation there. Its intense jihadist zeal to free their land from Indian military occupation both inflicted and invited horrific atrocities against military and civilians alike.

The level of violence drove some 300,000 Hindu pandits from their ancient homes in the Vale of Kashmir, many as refugees into Jammu. Life in the Vale became for them a living hell.

Salmon Rushdie describes a pandit's loss of harmony and the peaceful beauty of the sonorous mountains of Kashmir in his novel *Shalimar the Clown*.

[Pandit Pyarelal Kaul] closed his eyes and pictured his Kashmir. He conjured up its crystal lakes, Shishnag, Walur,

Nagin, Dal; its trees, the walnut, the poplar, the chinar, the apple, the peach; its mighty peaks, Nanga, Parbat, Raka-poshi, Harmukh. *The pandits Sankritized the Himalayas.* He saw the boats like little fingers tracing lines in the sur-face of the waters and the flowers too numerous to name, ablaze with bright perfume. He saw the beauty of the gold-en children, the beauty of the green- and blue-eyed women, the beauty of the green- and blue-eyed men. He stood atop Mount Shankaracharya which the Muslims called Takht-e-Sulaiman and spoke aloud the famous old verse concerning the earthly paradise. *It is this, it is this, it is this.* Spread out below him like a feast he saw gentleness and time and love. He considered getting out his bicycle and setting forth into the valley, bicycling until he fell, on and on into the beauty. *O! Those days of peace when we all were in love and the rain was in our hands wherever we went.* No, he would not ride out into Kashmir, did not want to see her scarred face, the lines of burning oil drums across the roads, the wrecked vehicles, the smoke of explosions, the broken houses, the broken people, the tanks, the anger and fear in every eye. *Everyone carries his address in his pocket so that at least his body will reach home.*

India has identified large numbers of Islamic militants trained in camps in Pakistan to conduct terrorist acts in the name of jihad (holy war) in Kashmir, increasingly since the withdrawal of the Soviet Union from Afghanistan in 1989. Lashkar-e-Taiba, Jaish-e-Mohammad, and Hizbul Mujahideen are Pakistani based terrorist organizations with purported contacts with Pa-kistan Military Intelligence (ISI), were among the groups that provided such camps for jihadists to infiltrate into Kashmir to fight with local insurgents and to organize terrorist cells there.

The terrorist attack on the World Trade Center and the Pen-tagon on 9/11/2001 brought the United States with the military force of its "war on terror" into South Asia to rout al Qaeda and the Taliban out of Afghanistan. Pakistan became a critical ally in this effort. President General Musharraf of Pakistan sought to use his prominence as an ally to bring his country's claim for Kashmir to the international community for resolution.

India saw the situation differently. Both countries accepted the Talibans accountability for terrorism for harboring al Qaeda terror-ists in Afghanistan. But India thought that the United States should hold President Musharraf to the same standard for his government's support for those committing terrorist acts in India. After numer-ous diplomatic encounters to improve relations between the United States and India, the American government applied strong diplo-matic pressure on President Musharraf to rein in recognized ter-rorist groups in Pakistan, and to limit infiltrators and support from them to the insurgency. This he agreed to do in January 2002.

In return, the United States asked India to enter into dialogue with Pakistan toward a resolution of the Kashmir dispute. India, skeptical about Musharrafs declaration, did not see these initia-tives as comparable. It set as a condition for any dialogue that the infiltration of insurgents from Pakistan be stopped.

The number of terrorist incidents dropped significantly in 2006. According to an Indian government report, terrorist at-tacks have been reduced by 19 percent and deaths by 29 percent in Kashmir between November 2005 and October 2006. But a significant number of deadly terrorist attacks occurred in other parts of India.

An explosion in the Sarojini Nagar Bazaar in New Delhi on October 29, 2005, killed 62 people, and injured 155 more. A sniper killed an Indian Institute of Technology professor in Ban-galore on December 27, 2005. Bombs were set off in a railway station and a Hindu temple in Varanasi on March 7, 2006, kill-ing 21 and wounding 62. Bombs set in seven commuter trains leaving Mumbai on July 11, 2006, exploded within a span of 11 minutes, killing 187, and injuring over 700. And on Septem-ber 8, terrorists set off three bombs in Malegaon, in northern Maharashtra, killing 31 people, and injuring over 200 others.

Indian authorities have determined all of these to be initiated by militant cells based in Kashmir with ties to terrorist groups in Pakistan. Police and covert services report interrupting an aver-age of three such Pakistani-supported terrorist cells per month.

These cells are not the only source of terrorist activity in India. Naxalite Maoists are conducting a terrorist insurgency in the mineral-rich forests of eastern India, causing havoc, mostly among the tribal peoples there. And nationalist insurgencies in the northeastern states sporadically carried out deadly attacks. They all present an imminent threat to innocent people in many different parts of the country.

With so much terrorist activity going on in India, Prime Minis-ter Manmohan Singh proclaimed at a police academy graduation ceremony on October 27, 2006: "Terrorism is the most danger-ous threat today and it has become a hydra-headed monster."

Secret negotiations to find a solution to the Kashmir dispute have intensified among private parties and public officials. At the meeting of the Non-Aligned Nations in Havana in Sep-tember 2006, Prime Minister Manmohan Singh and President Musharraf initiated a framework toward resolving their differ-ences over terrorism and other issues of the Kashmir conflict.

Public announcements confirm Pakistan's desire to find a common resolution for all Kashmiris, and specifically to reject any proposal to make the Line of Control permanent. In this demand it is following the lead of the All Parties Hurriyat Con-ference seeking a united Kashmiri voice in deliberations about their future.

The two governments are now looking for a mutually agree-able way to decentralize their control of their respective por-tions of the state, for which there are already some provisions in Article 370 of India's Constitution. Mutual withdrawal from the disputed Siachen glacier, 20,000 feet high in the Himalayas along the Line of Control, and Sir Creek in the Thar Desert are two places where the process could begin reducing the military confrontation. And the opening up of bus routes across the Line of Control is bringing families long separated together.

But the essential issue of the national identities of India and Pakistan, which is at the base of all of the devastating military and terrorist activity, remains. Any agreement that grants more local autonomy might help to reduce other major sources of terrorism, as in Balochistan in Pakistan and among the north-eastern states in India.

The Independence of Bangladesh in 1971

A second unsettling consequence of the 1947 partition was the separation in 1971 of East Pakistan to form the independent country of Bangladesh. The religious identity of the original Pakistan was not able to hold the country together. The eth-nic and linguistic identity of the Bengali Muslims, which they share with the people of West Bengal in India, proved stronger than their religious identity as Muslims in a Pakistan dominated by the ethnically and linguistically different, and financially advantaged, Muslim population of West Pakistan.

The result of this failure of religious nationalism was no less severe than the reign of terror that befell upon the people of Kashmir. The Bengali freedom fighters movement survived an intense military assault from West Pakistan in a desparate attempt to hold the country together. The Pakistan government, then under the martial rule of General Yahya Khan, sought to preserve its union by military repression. According to a *New York Times* report at that time (June 7, 1971):

> People have killed each other because of race, politics, and religion; no community is entirely free of guilt. But the principal agent of death and hatred has been the Pakistani Army. And its killing has been selective. According to reliable reports from inside East Pakistan, the Army's particular targets have been intellectuals and leaders of opinion—doctors, professors, students, writers.

That reign of terror caused over 200,000 deaths. And eight million people fled across the East Pakistan border into the squalor of refugee camps in the neighboring states of India. That number included over 1,500 physicians and 10,000 teachers. The International Rescue Committee reported in 1971:

> With the closure of the borders by the Pakistani military, large numbers are continuing to infiltrate through the 1,300-mile border with India through forest and swamps. These groups, with numbers sometimes up to 50,000 in a 24-hour period, have for the most part settled along major routes in India. They are found wherever there is a combination of available ground and minimal water supply.… The refugee camps may vary in size from small groups to upwards of 50,000. There has been an extraordinary effort on the part of the West Bengal and Indian governments to organize these camps and supply them with at least minimal amounts of food and water.
>
> The refugee diet…consists of rice boiled in open clay pots, some powdered milk which is occasionally available, and dall, which is a lentil type of bean used for a thin soup.… At this point the diet would be classified as barely adequate.

Political turmoil along with annual heavy flooding of its many rivers has sustained the flow of refugees out of the country. It is estimated that anywhere from 7 million to 12 million Bangladeshis are living in India today. Lack of documentation and of will has hampered sporadic attempts to repatriate these rufugees to their homeland.

A military coup killed the leader of the freedom movement, Prime Minister Mujibur Rahman, just four years after independence. And a second coup killed his successor, General Ziaur Rahman in 1981. Their deaths initiated an intense rivalry between Mujibur Rahman's daughter, head of his Awami League, and Begum Zia, the widow of General Zia, head of his Bangladesh National Party. As leaders of the country's two largest political parties, their opposition has denied the country political stability for almost twenty years.

Islamist militancy and terrorism have grown during this time of political turmoil, particularly on a wave of fundamentalist Islamist fervor throughout the Muslim world following the 9/11 terrorist attacks in the United States. Begum Zia's Bangladesh National Party (BNP) defeated Sheikh Hasina Wajed's Awami League government in October 2001, with the support of the Jamaat-e-Islami. That radical Islamist party had sided with the Pakistani army during the quest for Bangladesh independence in 1971, and has continued to push its agenda for a fundamentalist religious identity for both Bangladesh and Pakistan.

Terrorist incidents rose from 60 in 2004 to 90 in 2005, in which 396 people died. Notable among these incidents were grenade attacks at Awami League political rallies, in Dhaka on August 21, 2004, which killed 22 party members, and in Habiganj on January 27, 2005. The deaths of five Awami League activists there included Shah A.M.S. Kibria, former Finance Minister, Foreign Secretary, and Executive Secretary of the United Nations Economic and Social Commission for Asia and the Pacific.

A dramatic sequel of terrorism happened seven months later. As described by Haroon Habib in *The Hindu,* August 23:

> August 17, 2005, will go down in the annals of Bangladesh history. In an unprecedented act of terror, nearly 500 bombs went off simultaneously in 63 of Bangladesh's 64 districts killing 2 people and injuring at least 200. The targets were government and semi-government establishments, especially the offices of local bodies and court buildings.

The Zia government did little to investigate the attacks on its political opposition, nor to check the rise of further terrorist acts. Public opinion attributes this reluctance to its tenuous control of power needing the support of the Islamic fundamentalist parties.

The government did make a claim to "successfully combat terrorism in the name of Islam" by two high-profile arrests in March 2006. Shaikh Abdur Rahman is leader of a terrorist organization called the Jamaat'ul Mujahideen Bangladesh (JMB), which claimed responsibility for the August 17 bombings. The second person arrested was "Bangla Bhai," leader of the Jagrata Muslim Janata Bangladesh (JMJB). Like Shaikh, he fought as a jihadi in Afghanistan in the 1980s. Both of these organizations have close links with, and the protection of, the Jamaat-e-Islami party, a fundamentalist coalition member in Begum Zia's government.

The capture of these two leaders in anticipation of national elections in 2007 suggests that the ruling Bangladesh National Party is concerned that, when the will of the majority has opportunity to express itself, popular support for religious extremism declines. Because it has depended on the support of Islamic fundamentalists to stay in power, the outcome of the election will determine how much latitude a successor government will grant to militant Islamist organizations to continue their violent jihadist activities.

The large number of refugees and continuing incidents of terrorism in Bangladesh since 1971 reveal the heavy toll in human displacement and suffering caused by religious nationalism in seeking political identity among the culturally diverse peoples of the subcontinent.

This pattern is not unique to the partition of British India into districts of Hindu and Muslim majorities. Large numbers of people have become refugees in both Sri Lanka and Bhutan, where the overwhelming majority of their populations are Buddhist. That those belonging to religious minorities also speak a different language adds to their separation from the dominant religious majorities in both of these countries.

The Sri Lankan Experience

Free and general elections for political office in Sri Lanka were first held under British colonial rule in 1931. The country also has the highest levels of per capita income, education and literacy, and the lowest birthrate and population growth rate in the subcontinent.

Despite all of these achievements, the country has been entangled since 1983 in devastating communal warfare between the government and a militant faction of Tamil-speaking Hindus called the Liberation Tigers for Tamil Eelam (Nation), the LTTE. This dispute has caused over 65,000 deaths and displaced more than a million people, 400,000 of whom fled the country as refugees.

Tamil speakers make up about 18 percent of the total population of the country. They live mostly in the north and eastern part of the island, which has been a Tamil homeland for more than 2,000 years. There they constitute a plurality if not an outright majority in the political districts of that region. The example of the creation of India and Pakistan would have suggested the division of the island into two countries, based on the majority populations in each of the districts of the British Crown colony, then called Ceylon. But in 1948, it was hoped that the political identity of a unified island nation would take precedence over the religious and linguistic identities of its constituent regions. It was also hoped that such a unifying political identity would prevail over any cultural and linguistic affinity of the Tamil population in northern Sri Lanka with the larger neighboring state of Tamil Nadu, across the Palk Strait in south India.

At the time of independence, there were an additional 800,000 Indian Tamils in Ceylon. They were distinct from the indigenous Tamil community of the north, imported by the British from Tamil-speaking south India during the nineteenth century to work on the coffee, rubber, and tea plantations in the southern hills of the colony. The new Ceylonese government declared these Tamils stateless and pushed for their repatriation of India. In 1964, and again in 1974, the government of India agreed to receive 600,000 "plantation Tamils" back into India. The Ceylonese Tamils saw these deportations as ominous.

Tensions between the Sinhalese majority and Tamil minority increased during a period of uneasy accommodation. In 1956, which marked the 2,500th anniversary of the Buddha's attaining *nirvana*, the newly elected Sri Lanka Freedom Party passed the "Sinhala Only" act to make the language of the Buddhist majority the one official language of the country. In response to Tamil protests, originally nonviolent, communal riots broke out, leading up to 1983, when anti-Tamil riots throughout the country killed over a thousand people. The LTTE, a small, militant separatist group, then rose with a vengeance to defend the linguistic identity and political freedom of the Tamil people. Guerrilla warfare broke out in the predominantly Tamil-speaking areas of the north and east.

The devastation caused by this violent insurgency and the Sinhalese Army response to to put it down forced many Tamils to flee the country. By May 1991, some 210,000 refugees were reported to have made it to south India. Another 200,000 sought asylum in Europe. But most have continued to suffer the ravages of civil conflict in Sri Lanka, dependent upon relief efforts set up within the country itself. They became refugees in their own land.

In 1987, the Sri Lankan government invited India to send a "Peace Keeping Force" to attempt to suppress the LTTE. But

(Courtesy of Tamil Week)
Internal displaced Tamils, who surivived the tsunami in December 2004, are rescued from crossfire between Sri Lanka army and Tamil Tiger force in Pettalai along the east coast of Sri Lanka. In this incident, one child died and six are missing.

the deployment of the Indian army was not able to bring the two sides together, and the invitation was withdrawn in 1990.

Between 1983 and 2002, in spite of two brief cease-fires and talks between the LTTE and the Sri Lanka government, warfare increased in intensity and devastation.

With encouragement from the Norwegian government, both sides of the conflict agreed to a cease-fire in 2002, and entered into negotiations toward a political settlement of their dispute. Refugees from the northeast region of the country began to return to their homes.

There has been little progress in negotiations during a period of military restraint. The LTTE strengthened its forces, abducting children into its military according to UNICEF reports. It also established de-facto administrative control in the north and east region. Because of bickering over control of relief and rehabilitation efforts even the shared catastrophic impact of the Indian Ocean tsunami did not bring the opposing forces any closer together. Military encounters have recently increased in intensity, around the vital eastern port city, Trincomalee, and along Highway 9 to Jaffna.

Deadly acts of terrorism in this coflict included a LTTE cell assassination of Prime Minister Rajiv Gandhi in India with a suicide bomb in 1991. More recently Sri Lanka's Foreign Minister, Lakshman Kadirgamar was assassinated in Columbo on August 12, 2005, and a year later, acting Peace Coordinator, Kethesh Loganathan. Both were outstanding Tamils who rejected the LTTE's claim to represent the Tamil community in Sri Lanka.

Despair over the restoration in the lives of the Tamil people and a compassionate resolution of their civil conflict is summarized in the plain words of Tamil, Jagan:

"We carry a double burden now. We have to fight the Sinhalese racism and the tyranny of the Tigers, both together."
Nirupama Subramanian, *Sri Lanka Voices from a War Zone*

Bhutan: A Nagging Refugee Problem

Even the small country of Bhutan, tucked away in the high Himalayan mountains on the northeast side of the subcontinent, has not been immune from a refugee crisis. The shape of the issue appears discouragingly familiar: Can the identity of the nation include all those living within its borders who belong to distinct ethnic, religious, and linguistic minorities?

The gradual move toward modernization in this mountain kingdom has led to the migration of laborers, some from India, but in greater numbers from Nepal. The Nepali immigrants have settled almost entirely in the more productive southern part of the country, where they live as a distinct minority called Lhotshampas. In 1988 they were estimated to constitute as much as 42 percent of the population of Bhutan.

This trend toward modernization challenged the traditional way of life of the Bhutanese people. To meet this challenge, made more intense by the awareness that other Buddhist kingdoms in that region—Tibet, Sikkim, and Ladakh—have not survived, the government of Bhutan took a number of actions to create a national identity based upon its Buddhist heritage. These actions included the adoption of Dzongkha as the national language and the mandating of a national dress for formal occasions. These actions were not specifically aimed at the Nepali population. However, they were taken with the clear recollection that it was the agitation of Nepalis living in the neighboring kingdom of Sikkim that led to its absorption into India in 1974.

In 1985, the government passed a Citizenship Act, which allowed citizenship only to those Nepalis who could claim residency before 1958. In 1988, this act was enforced by a census in southern Bhutan, to identify those immigrants who could not claim legal residency. The rigor of this census became a direct assault on the Nepalis. The deportations, social unrest, and terrorist acts that followed led to the flight of many Nepalis from the country. By July 1993, 85,000 had made their way into refugee camps set up by the United Nations High commission for Refugees in eastern Nepal.

The governments of Nepal and Bhutan have met 16 times to seek a solution to the plight of these refugees. In 2001, the Bhutan government offered a process selecting those eligible for repatriation. But its terms were so restrictive that little was accomplished. There is hope that international pressure can encourage an early and just solution. The United States has recently offered to accept 60,000 of these refugees over a period of six years in hopes of getting things moving.

These refugees destined to live in deteriorating conditions in the UNHCR camps in Nepal pose a very specific question: can a way be found to include them within the national identity of the people of Bhutan? The same question also applies to all those who are minorities as non-Buddhist, Dzonkha speakers living in Bhutan itself. Can they be accepted and protected as full citizens in the Kingdom of Bhutan if its identity is defined exclusively by religion and language?

Terrorism in Nepal

Nepal, by contrast, experienced a dramatic change in terrorist activity. Seventy-seven terrorist incidents occurred in the first three months of 2006. Then they suddenly dropped to almost none.

Maoist militants have ravaged the country since 1996, an insurgency against the "feudal autocracy" of the king that has claimed more than 12,500 lives. But in May, the Maoists joined in a cease-fire with a Seven Party Alliance, which the previous month broke by public protest the absolute rule of King Gyanendra, which he had decreed on October 4, 2002.

Prachanda, the leader of the Maoist insurgency, declared in February that his party plenum agreed to abandon armed struggle to remove the oppression of the feudal monarchy in Nepal. To participate in competition with the parliamentary political parties has become for them a more promising way to achieve their revolutionary goals, in a democratic republic free of royal interference.

Many remain skeptical, but the leaders of the Maoists and the Seven Party Alliance agreed on November 21, 2006, to a UN-supervised disarmament of both Maoist and Royal Nepali Army forces and the creation of an interim parliament, in which the Maoist will hold 73 of 330 seats. The government will be run by a Council of Ministers, and the king will be deprived of all power during the interim period. They further agreed to establish a nationally elected Constituent Assembly in June 2007, and for it to vote at its first meeting on the removal of the monarchy.

The immense significance of this Comprehensive Peace Agreement was proclaimed by Girija Prasad Koirala, the leader of the Seven Party Alliance, at the time of signing: "This has given a message to the international community and terrorists all over the world that no conflict can be resolved by guns. It can be done by dialogue."

Political Crisis in Afghanistan

Afghanistan continues to experience severe consequences of warfare and terrorism since 1979, when the Soviet Union sent 85,000 troops into Afghanistan to suppress those opposed to the Afghan People's Democratic (Communist) Party rule. The arrival of these forces led some 400,000 Afghan Pashtuns to flee into Pakistan, to live in refugee camps among the 16 million Pashtuns who live on the other side of the Durrand line that separates them into the two countries.

During the period of Soviet occupation (1979–1989), in order to resist Soviet expansion into the region, the U.S. government contributed not only advanced military weapons, but also medical assistance, terrorist training and encouragement to those who fled the devastation of Soviet attacks on their lands. The Pakistan government also aided its strategic neighbor by providing arms and logistical support to the resistance, finding support for its own military government by assisting the United States. Iran and Saudi Arabia also made significant contributions to the Afghan cause. As a result, the refugee camps became not just places of refuge for those displaced from Afghanistan, but also staging and rehabilitation areas for those returning to fight against Soviet forces in their country.

Most came across in groups of fifty or one hundred, villages or nomad clans led by maliks, the local tribal chieftains. They brought more than 2 million animals with them—goats, sheep, buffaloes and camels. It was a timeless sight. The men in turbans or woolen or embroidered caps, baggy pants and vests or robes like academic gowns, bandoliers of cartridges across their chests, old rifles or new machine guns on one shoulder. Their sons were dressed the same way, miniatures of their fathers. The animals and the women walked behind. When they stopped, they sometimes took the tents offered by the United Nations or, sometimes, just recreated their katchi villages on the other side of the mountains. Then the men, many of them, went back to kill Russians.

> —Richard Reeves, *Passage to Peshawar*

The Soviet's devastating scorched earth policy over the next decade forced many more across the borders into refugee camps in Pakistan and Iran. By 1989, the number of refugees rose to six million, more than one-third of the country's total population.

The withdrawal of the Soviet army in 1989, and consequently of U.S. support to Afghanistan, was followed by intense internal fighting among rival warlords, called the mujahideen, who were united only to oppose Communist rule in their country. Their warfare for control of Kabul caused immense destruction to the city. Hundreds of thousands fled, reducing by half its prewar population of close to 1 million. Countless others abandoned their blown-out villages.

In 1994, the Taliban, a militant Islamic revolutionary movement, arose amidst the country's political chaos, violence and corruption with an urgent call for reform. With Pakistani and al Qaeda support, it was able to capture Kabul in 1996, and, by 1999, to dominate some 90 percent of the country. It imposed upon the lands it controlled a welcome sense of peace, together with an extremely oppressive fundamentalist religious order.

Refuge camps, when they had strong international support, provided some opportunities for education, social reform, health care, and employment not available under Taliban domination in their homelands, especially to women. Any semblance of civic order and public services had simply disappeared during these years of internal conflict. Hazardous also were land mines planted through wide, unmapped areas of the country. Reports in the fall of 2002 recorded over 300 land mine injuries a month throughout the country. And then came the intensive bombing of U.S. forces to destroy al Qaeda and Taliban in response to the terrorist attacks in the United States on 9/11/2001. All of these offered small inducement for the refugees to return to their former homes.

By the end of 2001, 12 years after the Soviet withdrawal, 2.2 million refugees were still in Pakistan, 2.4 million in Iran, and around 1 million in refugee camps in Afghanistan itself. Two million refugees returned in 2002, overwhelming the meager resources available in Afghanistan. In January 2003, the UN Commission on Refugees recommended that no more return because of the lack of security, facilities, and humanitarian aid to support them. Since the fall of the communist government in 1992, in the solemn words of Barnett R. Rubin, "Afghanistan has been ruled, in whole or in part, at times badly and at times atrociously, but it has not been governed."

The UN-sponsored Bonn Agreement in December 2001, provided for a provisional government, with Hamid Karzai elected as its leader. Steps toward a permanent government began with preparations for a national election for president in October 2004. These included more than 1,600 polling stations set up by the International Organization for Migration in Pakistan for 738,000 refugees still in that country who registered to vote. Eighty percent of them voted. About half of the 500,000 refugees who registered in seven offices in Iran also voted. The IOM achieved the largest refugee participation ever in a national election. Overall, Karzai won 55 percent of the vote, and became president for a five-year term.

Elections for Parliament and 34 provincial assemblies were held in September 2005. The results of these elections reaffirmed the religiously conservative bases of power in the countryside. It is revealed even more in the resurgence of the Taliban among Pashtuns on both sides of the Durand Line since the elections, supported by the illicit wealth of opium production. Increasing acts of terrorism, and the devastating military battles between the Taliban and the NATO forces assigned to suppress them are creating havoc and destruction among the civilian population. These circumstances present a huge challenge to the world where efforts for the rehabilitation of the Afghan people are successively diminishing in impact. The country has too long been punished by superpower competition, and divided by opposing regional and ethnic forces within the country.

The Afghan people, even though voting, are still far from realizing a common political identity, let alone the exercise of any instruments of a stable democratic government.

Other Refuges

Not all of the many refugees in the subcontinent are South Asian. The Chinese takeover of Tibet in 1951 led to the flight of the Dalai Lama, the religious and temporal leader of the Tibetan people, into India in 1959. Hundreds of thousands of his followers also fled into India and into neighboring Nepal and Bhutan, seeking refuge from the repression of Chinese domination in their homeland. In their adopted home, these Tibetan refugees continue to search for ways to maintain their identity as a Buddhist people in exile.

And the military repression that followed upon the thwarting of elections in Myanmar (Burma) in May 1990 has caused many to flee across its border into Bangladesh and the eastern states of India. Some 280,000 refugees were recently reported to be in camps along the border of eastern Bangladesh. They remain hopeful that the courageous Nobel Laureate, Aung San Suu Kyi, and her National League for Democracy will succeed in their quest to achieve a stable, democratically elected government, accountable to all the people of that country and protective of their human rights.

The extensive presence of refugees and the continuing threat of terrorist acts by political insurgents throughout the subcontinent bear witness to the challenge in every country in South Asia to achieve a basis for its political identity as a nation that includes the unique, multicultural diversity within each of its borders.

Still, the nations of South Asia are making strides toward democracy. All of them, with the exception of Bhutan, and notwithstanding the military coup in Pakistan in 1999, have held more than one national election since 1993, with high levels of voter participation. With the exception of Maldives, which limits the activity of opposition political parties, most of the recent elections have resulted in the civil transfer of power from one political party to another. This result in the national elections in

India in the spring of 2004 was dramatic evidence that democracy is taking hold in South Asia today.

The nations of South Asia still face many other challenges. As the diversity among the nations might suggest, none of them has responded to these challenges in the same way. How each of these countries is progressing on its separate path toward democracy is discussed in each of the country reports that follow.

A common thread among these varied responses has been the attempt to achieve a political solution to adversarial relations among peoples that are based on more traditional and profound expressions of human identity than that of the nation-state. A political solution to human strife was the assumption and the promise in the formation of nations in Western Europe during the eighteenth and nineteenth centuries. But the experience of two world wars in the twentieth century and the continuing presence of refugees throughout the world suggest the inadequacy of nationalism based on self-determination as a way to achieve lasting unity and peace.

The independence of nations and freedom of the individual are worthy political goals. But the South Asia experience reveals to us that they are not ends in themselves. Nor can they be imposed.

Alexis de Tocqueville observed in the early years of the nineteenth century that the long-term success of democracy in the United States depends not upon the structure and institutions of the government, but upon the habits of the heart of the American people. Mahatma Gandhi, on the threshold of political independence for the people of India, also realized that democracy was not just a matter of form. It is a matter of the heart and soul of a people.

IMAGE 5: MAHATMA GANDHI

Generations to come, it may be, will scarce believe that such a one as this ever in flesh and blood walked upon this earth.

—Albert Einstein

The name of Mahatma Gandhi comes up in a number of contexts in looking at the uniqueness of South Asia. His role in shaping the freedom movement on the subcontinent was immense. He identified himself with the common people, adopted their dress and simplicity of life, and traveled from village to village to spread his message of reform. He encouraged everyone to use the spinning wheel and to wear clothes made of the hand-spun cloth called khadi. He called for national boycotts. And he fasted. In these many ways, he managed to get everyone involved in the political process of becoming a new nation.

In this way he was able to restructure the Indian National Congress as the instrument for India's freedom. The power base of this movement had resided in an intellectual elite, who had shaped its policies for achieving independence since 1887. Gandhi, building on a large number of grassroots initiatives, brought the power base to the village level. Under his leadership, removing the oppression of colonial rule was something that was happening to everyone, in every corner of the land.

Of greater international significance is the method of nonviolent protest against social injustice that Gandhi developed during his years in South Africa. He applied this method with confounding consistency in leading the peoples of British India

to freedom in 1947. Its effectiveness was partly the result of his ability to discipline people in the deployment of his method. He was also able to command accountability from those who were the oppressors. In this way he established a viable alternative to power politics to achieve historic goals. Gandhi called this method satyagraha, or Soul Force. And he encouraged its use to empower all who are oppressed and powerless to gain the courage, the discipline, and the vision to become free.

In the time since his death in 1948, a number of important events have changed the course of history. The rise of the Solidarity movement in Poland initiated the crumbling of the Soviet Union and its grasp on Central/Eastern Europe. The civil rights movement in the United States, under the leadership of Dr. Martin Luther King, Jr., initiated a national policy on race relations to correct historic injustices to minority students and workers.

The election of Nelson Mandela and his African National Congress to political leadership in 1994 brought the end of Apartheid in South Africa. These events released new energy and a vision of hope for positive change in the world. All traced their inspiration for how to disarm oppressive political power with nonviolent public protest to Mohandas Karamchand Gandhi, the man who came to be called the Mahatma.

Early Years

Gandhi was born in Porbandar, a small seaport town on the western coast of the Kathiawar peninsula in western India, on October 2, 1869. His father was a diwan, or prime minister, in the employ of maharajas in that region. Although Mohandas was the youngest, the fourth child of his father's fourth wife, it was expected that he would continue his father's and grandfather's political careers. He was groomed from an early age for leadership.

Yet Gandhi proved to be an indifferent student. He found mathematics particularly difficult. When he was 13, his parents arranged for his marriage to Kasturbai, a young woman his age. In spite of her gentle and accepting nature, he accounted himself an immature, jealous, and domineering husband. He was later to credit her example as a patient and devoted wife in leading him to see the virtues of a life committed to nonviolence.

Gandhi's mother also had a deep influence on his life. A devout Hindu, she revealed to him by her life of devotion the power of religious faith and fasting. When, at 18, Gandhi went to England to study law, he vowed to her that he would abstain from meat and wine while away. His determination to honor this vow set a pattern of discipline in keeping commitments for the rest of his life.

Gandhi stayed in England for just three years. He proved himself an able enough student to pass the London Matriculation examinations in Latin, French, and chemistry, and, a year later, his law examinations. He was admitted to the Bar on June 10, 1891, enrolled in the High Court on June 11, and sailed for India on June 12.

Shy and sensitive, Gandhi was not able to establish a law practice in Bombay, nor with his brother back in Porbandar. So he leapt at an opportunity with a local firm of Muslim merchants to work on a case in South Africa. The original assignment was for one year. In the course of that year he became so involved in the plight of Indians living in that country that he stayed for more than 20 years—and changed the course of history on two continents.

(Margaret Bourke-White, used by permission GSPEMG1946505013)

Mahatma Gandhi spent time every day spinning as an act of self discipline and meditation. He encouraged his followers to do the same and to wear home spun khadi garments as symbolic acts of self reliance expressive of the freedom he sought for his people from British rule. "Be the change you wish to see in the world."

In South Africa

Gandhi's first encounter with discrimination against Indians in South Africa came in 1893, when he was thrown out of a first-class compartment of the train he was taking to Johannesburg. His enraged reaction to this affront convinced him that an appropriate response would be to encourage the diffuse group of Indians living there to work together to protest the many abuses they all experienced as nonwhites in that country. He became engrossed in organizing campaigns and demonstrations for Indian rights. Finding this work demanding and effective, he decided to stay on in Africa. He established a law practice in Johannesburg to support his reform efforts and his family, whom he called from India. He also set up a weekly newspaper, *Indian Opinion*, and purchased a farm on which to set up a commune to maintain the paper's publication.

As the South African government imposed more and more restraints on the Indian people living in the country, Gandhi orchestrated a series of nonviolent protest demonstrations that engaged increasing numbers of Indians. His last protest march recruited more than 2,000 men, women, and children, and was joined in sympathy by 50,000 miners and indentured laborers. Such wide participation led the government to reconsider its policy and enact a law in 1914 to prohibit offensive discriminatory practices against all Indians living in South Africa. This movement was so ordered and disciplined by his commitment to nonviolent resistance that Gandhi emerged from this experience a leader of immense stature. He was someone to be reckoned with in South Africa—an achievement that was noticed in England and in India.

The direction of Gandhi's growth in South Africa was, in a significant way, thrust upon him. He could have been treated there with polite respect, done his job, and returned to India unnoticed. Being thrown out of a railway car because of his color and national origin was something Gandhi neither anticipated nor felt he deserved. In responding to this immediate experience of social injustice, he gained a sense of something much greater than just what was happening to him. He discovered a personal mission that he felt compelled to fulfill: to bring together an oppressed people in a quest for social justice.

Being by temperament introspective, deliberate, even fastidious, Gandhi searched within himself for resources to meet this challenge. This quest brought him to affirm intuitively, for he had no formal training in its conceptual intricacies, two precepts drawn from the classical heritage of South Asia. First, and more consciously, Gandhi identified his mission with the ancient concept of dharma, of cosmic moral order. This concept was set forward in the early Sanskrit epics, the Mahabharata and the Ramayana, as the proper behavior for ruling princes—not only as the moral foundation of their authority to rule, but also as the source of the well-being of their subjects.

Gandhi pursued the private aspect of dharma (the moral foundation for leadership) with determination. His autobiography, *The Story of My Experiments with Truth*, written mostly in 1926, is replete with descriptions of his attempts to discipline his personal life around issues of celibacy, vegetarianism, purification, and self-control. He continued this pattern of moral exploration and testing throughout his life, always seeking to be better prepared (by which he meant morally adequate) to undertake the public tasks he felt compelled to perform. Even toward the end of the long struggle for national independence, the primary issue was not whether the British would grant freedom to the people of the subcontinent. His greatest concern was whether he, personally, was morally pure enough to lead the people of India to this goal.

Equally important to Gandhi was the public aspect of dharma that it was to be realized for everyone's benefit. The cosmic dimension of dharma is realized not in the abstract, nor just in one's personal life, but in the public affairs of humanity. This awareness made his personal experience of discrimination in South Africa a public offense, which would be righted only when discrimination would not be practiced against any Indian residing there. Gandhi's awareness of the epic precept of dharma made him sensitive not only to the stringent moral demands of his mission, but also to the magnitude of its objective. He ultimately sought to liberate a people not just from the injustice of colonial rule, but from all oppression, to allow them to become truly free.

The second precept of the classical heritage Gandhi affirmed by his experience in South Africa was an awareness of a truer, deeper reality of "self" than he normally experienced in the everyday world. He experienced glimpses of a more ultimate reality of being, what in the classical heritage of South Asia was called atma. In his quest for this higher being of self, Gandhi intuited that a vital quality that distinguishes it from the ordinary experience of self is that it is by nature nonviolent: "Non-violence is not a garment to be put on and off at will. Its seat is in the heart, and it must be an inseparable part of our very being." It was this deeper, more refined self that was to define the distinctive character of the mission to which he had been called—that only the means could justify the end. Above all else, the means must be nonviolent.

Gandhi's concern for reducing the level of violence in our everyday lives and in the world around us reinforced his moral image of dharma. Joined with an intimation of the atma, nonviolence requires a discipline that identifies and refines our awareness of our true self.

> The acquisition of the spirit of non-violence is a matter of long training in self-denial and appreciation of the hidden forces within ourselves. It changes one's outlook on life.… It is the greatest force because it is the highest expression of the soul.

Gandhi's living out of these important concepts of dharma and atma identified him on a profound level with the people from India then living in South Africa. He spoke to them out of a context to which they were uniquely prepared to respond as a distinct group of people. It is also significant that his initial steps to leadership took place far from India. Author V.S. Naipaul, recalling his own upbringing as an Indian in Trinidad, describes an important social dimension to Indian life that Gandhi would have only experienced outside of India.

> These overseas Indian groups were mixed. They were miniature Indias, with Hindus and Muslims, and people of different castes. They were disadvantaged, without representation, and without a political tradition. They were isolated by language and culture from the people they found themselves among; they were isolated from India itself. In these special circumstances they developed something they never would have known in India: a sense of belonging to an Indian community. This feeling of community could override religion and caste.

Naipaul added that it was essential for Gandhi to have begun his freedom movement for the Indian peoples in South Africa. "It is during his.…years in South Africa that intimations came to Gandhi of an all-India religious-political mission." Had he begun in India, he would not have known for whom he was seeking independence. In South Africa, Gandhi discovered a destiny for a people to become a free nation. As in the case of his own sense of mission, Gandhi returned to India with the conviction that this free nation could not be born until the people of India had discovered their soul.

Return to India

Gandhi returned to India in 1915, at the age of 45. By then he was recognized as a national hero to a people without a nation. Soon, he was widely acclaimed as the Mahatma, the "Great Souled One."

Gandhi worked toward the removal of British colonial domination in India much as he had worked to overcome discrimination in South Africa: by addressing particular instances of oppression. Initially these did not involve the government. Gandhi first addressed the inequities between English plantation owners and peasants in the eastern province of Bihar, and Indian mill owners and mill workers in the western city, Ahmedabad. Feeling that Indian independence from British colonial rule should not replace one oppression with another, he attacked the subservient role imposed upon women in Indian society. He also took up the plight of "untouchable" communities—what he called "the ulcer of untouchability" in Indian life. Between 1915 and 1948, Gandhi initiated hundreds of nonviolent protest actions against a wide range of social injustices and abuses throughout the country.

One of Gandhi's most important achievements in the independence movement of India was his ability to lead the diverse people of the subcontinent to a shared vision of what it meant to be free. Drawing upon the importance of symbolic thought as developed in the classical heritage of his people, he insisted that people of all stations and walks of life take on the daily discipline of spinning thread for their clothing on a spinning wheel. This action not only freed them from the economic tyranny of dependence upon cloth manufactured in England; more important, spinning encouraged them to be self-reliant even while living under the burden of British colonial rule.

Gandhi's most dramatic act of satyagraha was in 1930, when he led his followers from Ahmedabad on a 200-mile walk to collect salt from the sea, in protest against the salt tax imposed by the British government. What began as a march of 78 men and boys, specially trained to undertake the journey, gathered more and more people as it made its way through the Gujarati countryside. When the column reached Dandi on the shore, the company had grown to thousands. The Oscar-winning film *Gandhi* gives a vivid picture not only of the energetic figure of Gandhi himself leading the march, but also of the dramatic swelling of the crowds who joined behind him to make the salt march a powerful expression of public support. Gandhi compared the march to the Boston Tea Party, which anticipated the war for independence in America. It was the culminating act of a series of nonviolent protests against British rule that led to the beginning of home rule in 1937 and the total withdrawal of British colonial government in 1947.

These examples reveal Gandhi's immense power to draw people into the modern political process by creating powerful symbolic actions. In performing them, people in all reaches of British India began to assert and discover the qualities of freedom among some of the simplest, most immediate elements of their lives: their clothing and food. These simple acts were symbolic in the classical sense in pointing beyond themselves to express what it is to be truly free.

Fasting became another aspect of Gandhi's leadership role during his years in India. He conducted 17 fasts "to the death." The first happened soon after his return from South Africa, as a part of his efforts to resolve the dispute over wages between the mill workers and the mill owners in Ahmedabad in 1918. Like his earlier actions, it was not premeditated, but grew out of the circumstances in which he found himself. The strike that he was urging the workers to sustain was exhausting their resources and their resolve. To encourage them to continue, he decided to subject himself to the same threat of starvation the prolonged strike was imposing upon them. He could not demand of the striking workers more than he would demand of himself. So he began a fast that would continue until the workers received the wage they were demanding from the mill owners.

Unlike later fasts, this gesture prompted neither wide public awareness nor concern. And Gandhi himself was not entirely comfortable about the coercive elements of his action. But the mill owners were moved by this dramatic placing of himself on the line. After the third day of his fast, they agreed to a compromise in which all parties could feel some gain. Of more lasting significance, Gandhi's action and resolution did not allow the workers to abandon their commitment to improve their lot. He taught them by example to become empowered by their own inner strength.

In 1932, Gandhi began a series of fasts based on his concern for the plight of the "untouchable" communities in India. His initial protest was against the attempt on the part of the British government to set up separate untouchable electorates in a provisional government in British India, a policy that was supported by Dr. Ambedkar and other leaders of the untouchable communities. Gandhi's objection was that giving the untouchable communities separate political status removed from the Indian community as a whole the need to reform itself by eliminating the scourge of discrimination and oppression based on caste. Dr. Ambedkar saw Gandhi's objection as an attempt to keep untouchables under Hindu oppression. But Gandhi was adamant, and on September 20, he began a fast to raise Hindu consciousness about the evils of caste discrimination and to alter the British proposal. Resolutions against discrimination and intense discussions with the untouchable leaders immediately ensued. Five days later, a compromise pact was achieved and sent to London, where it was accepted by the prime minister. By this fast, Gandhi made a significant impact, for the first time, on a specific British government policy in India. And, as fate would have it, all of this happened while he was imprisoned by the colonial government in Yeravda Prison under a century-old regulation, which allowed the government to hold him for suspected sedition without sentence or trial.

During the spring of 1933, Gandhi fasted again on behalf of the untouchable communities as an act of purification. He described it as "an uninterrupted twenty-one days' prayer."

Gandhi fasted twice during the final year of his life, in Calcutta from September 1 to 5, 1947; and in New Delhi, beginning on January 13, 1948. In both instances he was responding to the communal rioting between Hindus and Muslims following the partition of British India and the independence of India and Pakistan on August 15, 1947. By this time, as Gandhi entered his 78th year, people throughout the subcontinent were caught up in daily reports on the state of his health during the fasts. And they were stirred to meet his expectations of amity between the two new countries and among the religious communities that resided in both. In January, Gandhi specifically demanded as a condition of ending his fast the reparation to Pakistan of its share of British India's assets retained by the Indian government. When that was done, the Pakistan foreign minister before the United Nations Security Council directly attributed to Gandhi's fast a "new and tremendous wave of feeling and desire for friendship between the two Dominions."

By his many and creative acts for freedom and by his fasting, Gandhi was able to command enormous authority among the people—all without the benefit of holding any political office. During his many years of leadership in the independence movement, he held only one elective position. He was elected president of the Indian National Congress in 1925, but held the office for only one year. He stepped down to give a place to Sarojini Naidu, the first woman to be elected to that office.

Being out of political office seemed to increase the impact of his singular, moral basis for authority. It was even more commanding when he took moral positions in direct confrontation with the authority structures of his time. For his opposition to the colonial rule of the British Raj, he spent 2,049 of his politically most active days (more than five years) in jail. His self-affirming authority as a political figure and his commitment to nonviolence as the guiding principle for political action won for Gandhi universal recognition as the conscience of an empire and the "Father of the Republic of India."

Any sense of achievement that Gandhi might have felt because of India's independence in 1947 was negated by the scourge of communal rioting and bloodshed that swept across the subcontinent as the specter of partition of British India into two separate nations loomed. As the time of independence approached, Gandhi did not go to the capital to see the reins of power passed. Instead, he walked from village to village in the Noakhali district of East Bengal, seeking to quench the flames of violence that scorched that land. Gandhi was deeply shaken, doubting his effectiveness to bring the message of nonviolence to the people. But Lord Montbatten, who was in New Delhi as the governor-general of newly independent India, described Gandhi's effectiveness in a very different way: "In the Punjab we have 55,000 soldiers and large scale rioting is on our hands. In Bengal our forces consist of one man, and there is no rioting."

The Light Endures

Gandhi remained convinced that Muslims and Hindus could live at peace together in a single, secular nation. For Gandhi, truth was not the exclusive possession of any religious community but, rather, what revealed the transcendent unity of all people. This conviction was to cost him his life.

A young Hindu, passionately afraid that Gandhi was threatening Hinduism by being too accommodating to Muslims, assassinated him at his evening prayer meeting on January 30, 1948. That evening, Gandhi's longtime friend and protege, the prime minister of the newly formed government of India, Jawaharlal Nehru, announced his death over the radio:

Our beloved leader, Bapu, as we call him, the father of our nation is no more.... The light has gone out, I said, and yet I was wrong. For the light that shone in this country was no ordinary light. The light that has illumined this country for these many years will illumine this country for many more years....and the world will see it and it will give solace to innumerable hearts.

In leading the vastly diverse peoples of India to their independence through the first half of the twentieth century, Mahatma Gandhi learned that political power is normally based on oppression and the use of force. That coercive power leads only to bondage, violence, and suffering. He became convinced that political freedom cannot be achieved by force. It can be realized only in discovering within ourselves a more profound and demanding quality of human identity and relationship, a quality that is characterized by nonviolence. Only when we become genuinely nonviolent in ourselves and in our relationships with others can we become truly ourselves. Nations also must become genuinely nonviolent. Then they, too, will discover an identity as a people that is inclusive of all who live within their borders. Only then can we begin to think about achieving peace among nations.

Eric Ericson, in his perceptive biography, *Gandhi's Truth*, describes this insight as a profound source of hope for the survival of the human race:

To have faced mankind with nonviolence as the alternative to [such policing activities as the British massacre in Amritsar] marks the Mahatma's deed in 1919. In a period when proud statesmen could speak of a "war to end war"; when the superpolicemen of Versailles could bathe in the glory of a peace that would make "the world safe for democracy"; when the revolutionaries in Russia could entertain the belief that terror could initiate an eventual "withering away of the State"—during that same period, one man in India confronted the world with the strong suggestion that a new political instrument, endowed with a new kind of religious fervor, may yet provide mankind with a choice.

India (Republic of India)

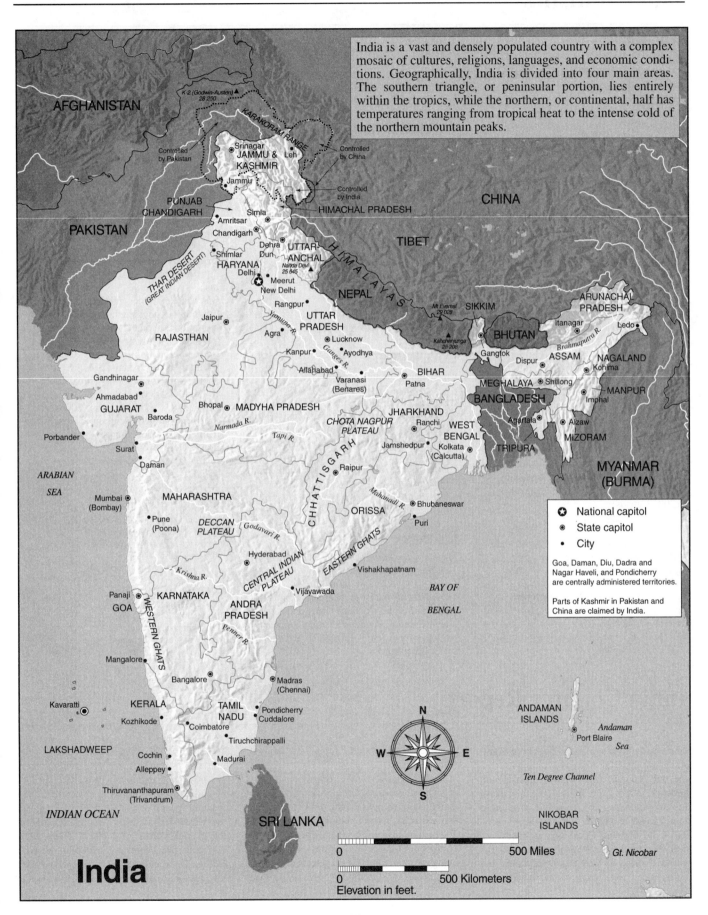

India is a vast and densely populated country with a complex mosaic of cultures, religions, languages, and economic conditions. Geographically, India is divided into four main areas. The southern triangle, or peninsular portion, lies entirely within the tropics, while the northern, or continental, half has temperatures ranging from tropical heat to the intense cold of the northern mountain peaks.

AFGHANISTAN

K-2 (Godwin-Austen) 28,250

KARAKORAM RANGE

Controlled by Pakistan

Srinagar
JAMMU & KASHMIR
Leh
Controlled by China

Jammu
Controlled by India

CHINA

PUNJAB
CHANDIGARH
Simla
HIMACHAL PRADESH

PAKISTAN

Amritsar
Chandigarh

TIBET

Shimlar
Dehra Dun
UTTAR ANCHAL
Nanda Devi 25,645

HARYANA
Delhi
Meerut
New Delhi

THAR DESERT
(GREAT INDIAN DESERT)

Rangpur

HIMALAYAS

NEPAL

Mt Everest 29,028

SIKKIM

ARUNACHAL PRADESH

Jaipur

UTTAR PRADESH

Yamuna R.

Itanagar
Ledo

RAJASTHAN

Agra

Lucknow
Ayodhya

Kahchenjunga 28,208

BHUTAN

Gangtok

Brahmaputra R.

ASSAM

NAGALAND
Kohima

Kanpur
Ganges R.

Dispur

Allahabad
Varanasi (Benares)

BIHAR
Patna

MEGHALAYA
Shillong

MANPUR
Imphal

Gandhinagar

Ahmadabad
GUJARAT
Baroda

Bhopal
MADYHA PRADESH

Narmada R.

JHARKHAND
Ranchi

BANGLADESH

Agartala
TRIPURA

MIZORAM
Aizaw

CHOTA NAGPUR PLATEAU

WEST BENGAL

Porbander

Surat
Daman

Tapi R.

CHHATTISGARH

Jamshedpur
Kolkata (Calcutta)

MYANMAR (BURMA)

ARABIAN SEA

Mumbai (Bombay)

MAHARASHTRA

Raipur

Pune (Poona)

DECCAN PLATEAU
Godavari R.

ORISSA

Mahanadi R.
Bhubaneswar
Puri

BAY OF BENGAL

Hyderabad

CENTRAL INDIAN PLATEAU

EASTERN GHATS

Vishakhapatnam

Krishna R.

Panaji
GOA

KARNATAKA

Vijayawada

ANDRA PRADESH

WESTERN GHATS

Penner R.

National capitol
State capitol
City

Goa, Daman, Diu, Dadra and Nagar Haveli, and Pondicherry are centrally administered territories.

Parts of Kashmir in Pakistan and China are claimed by India.

Mangalore

Bangalore

Madras (Chennai)

Kavaratti

KERALA
Kozhikode

TAMIL NADU
Pondicherry
Cuddalore

ANDAMAN ISLANDS

Andaman Sea

Port Blaire

Coimbatore

Tiruchchirappalli

LAKSHADWEEP

Cochin
Alleppey

Madurai

Ten Degree Channel

N
W   E
S

Thiruvananthapuram (Trivandrum)

INDIAN OCEAN

SRI LANKA

NIKOBAR ISLANDS

Gt. Nicobar

India

0   500 Miles

0   500 Kilometers

Elevation in feet.

33

India Statistics

GEOGRAPHY

Area in Square Miles (Kilometers):
1,269,010 (3,287,590) (about 1/3 the size of the United States)
Capital (Population): New Delhi (15,334,000 metro area; 9,817, 439 city proper)
Environmental Concerns: soil erosion; deforestation; overgrazing; desertification; air and water pollution; lack of potable water; overpopulation
Geographical Features: upland plain (Deccan Plateau) in south; flat to rolling plain along the Ganges; deserts in the west; Himalaya Mountains in the north
Climate: varies from tropical monsoon to the south, to temperate in the north, to arctic in the Himalayas

PEOPLE

Population

Total: 1,095,351,995 (July, 2006 est.)
Annual Growth Rate: 1.38% (2006 est.)
Rural/Urban Population Ratio: 71.3/28.7 (UN 2005 est.)
Major Languages: Hindi; English; Bengali; Telugu; Marathi; Tamil; Urdu; others; 24 languages each spoken by 1 million or more persons; numerous other languages and dialects
Ethnic Makeup: 72% Indo-Aryan groups; 25% Dravidian: 3% Mongoloid and others
Religions: 80.5% Hindu; 13.4% Muslim; 2.3% Christian; 1.9% Sikh; 2.8% other (2001 Census)

Health

Life Expectancy at Birth: 63.9 years (male); 65.57 years (female) (2006 est.)
Infant Mortality: 54.63/1000 live births (2006 est.)
Physicians Available: 1/2,173 people
Per Capita total expenditure on Health: $82 (WHO 2003 est.)
HIV/AIDS Rate in Adults: 0.9% (5.7 million) (WHO 2005 est.)

Education

Adult Literacy Rate: 59.5% (48.3% female) (2003 est.)
Compulsory: theoretically compulsory in 23 states to age 14

COMMUNICATION

Telephones: 49.75 million main lines (2005)
Cell Phones: 69,193,321 (2006)
Daily Newspaper Circulation: 21/1,000 people
Televisions: 68/1,000 people
Internet Users: 50.6 million (2005)

TRANSPORTATION

Highways in Miles (Kilometers): 1,991,786 (3,851,440 km.)
Railroads in Miles (Kilometers): (63,230 km.)
Usable Airfields: 341 (2006)
Motor Vehicles in Use: 6,700,000

GOVERNMENT

Type: federal republic
Independence Date: August 15, 1947 (from the United Kingdom)
Head of State/Government: President Abdul Kalam; Prime Minister Manmohan Singh
Political Parties: Congress Party; Bharatiya Janata Party; Bahujan Samaj Party; Communist Party of India/Marxist; Janata Dal Party; Samajwadi Party; All-India Forward Bloc; United Front; many regional parties
Suffrage: universal at 18

MILITARY

Military Expenditures (% of GDP): $19.04 billion (2.5%) (2005 est.)
Current Disputes: communal unrest; militant nationalist movements; claims to Kashmir with Pakistan; border disputes with China, Bangladesh, Nepal, Pakistan; refugee repatriation, territorial, and water-sharing disputes

ECONOMY

Currency ($ U.S. Equivalent): 44,101 rupees = $1 U.S. (2005)
Income Per Capita GDP: purchasing power parity $3,300/$3,611 trillion (2005 est.)
GDP Growth Rate: 7.6% (2005)
Inflation Rate: 4.2% (2005 est.)
Unemployment Rate: 8.9%
Labor Force by Occupation: 60% agriculture; 23% services; 17% industry
Population Below Poverty Line: 25% (2002 est.)
Natural Resources: coal; iron ore; manganese; mica; bauxite; titanium ore; chromite; natural gas; diamonds; petroleum; limestone
Agriculture: rice; wheat; oilseed; cotton; jute; tea; sugarcane; potatoes; livestock; fish
Industry: electronics; textiles; chemicals; food processing; steel; machinery; transportation equipment; cement; mining; petroleum; software
Exports: $76.23 billion f.o.b. (2005 est.) (primary partners United States, Hong Kong, United Kingdom, China, UAE, United Kingdom, Hong Kong.)
Imports: $113.1 billion f.o.b. (2005 est.) (primary partners Belgium, United States, United Kingdom, China, Singapore, Australia, Germany)
Human Development Index (ranking): 127 (UNDP est.)

SUGGESTED WEBSITES

http://www.wcoc.org.uk/igcmc/main.htmlHAPP
http://www.economictimes.com
http://www.indiaserver.com/thehindu/thehindu.html
http://www.newaindia-times.com
http://www.gorp.com/gorp/location/asia/india/npintro.htm
http://www.indnet.org
http://www.123india.com
http://southasia.net/India/
http://www.hinduonnet.com
http://www.whatisindia.com

India Country Report

India is the largest of the countries of South Asia, and the land of greatest contrasts. It is the only country to extend through all the subcontinent's geographical regions, from the snowy peaks of the Himalayas, more than 25,000 feet high, to the tropical beaches of the Malabar Coast on the Laccadive Sea. And its population is phenomenally diverse, divided by languages, religions, and cultures, by cities and villages, by extremes of poverty and wealth. India is a land of many contrasts.

India is crowded and getting more so every day. On May 11, 2000, the government of India officially recognized the birth of the child that extended its population to one billion. Today more than 1,095,000,000 people, about 16 percent of the entire world population, are living on approximately 2.3 percent of its total landmass. Almost four times more people than are living in the United States occupy one-third the amount of space. And their numbers are growing at an annual rate of 1.38 percent.

India reaches farthest to the north among the high peaks of the Karakuram Range in the western Himalayan Mountains, beyond the glacial plateau of Ladakh. There, west of Tibet, India shares a disputed border with China. This boundary extends east through the high ridges of the Himalayas, skirting the mountainous kingdoms of Nepal and Bhutan to the hill country of the northeast frontier. There it encounters another portion of its 2,000-mile contested border with China. It then swings south along the western edge of Myanmar (Burma) and back around Bangladesh to the Bay of Bengal.

Because of the unrelenting arctic cold of the barren glaciers coursing the steep, southern slopes of the Himalayas, much of the northern border area of India is uninhabitable. The average population density of this mountainous region is a sparse 70 people per square mile. They are interspersed in protected gorges and fertile valleys that sustain isolated settlements. Most of the Himalayan peoples tend flocks of sheep, yak, and goats, or work the tea plantations and orchards on the lower foothills. In warmer seasons they form small bands of traders and bearers making arduous, heavy-laden treks through snow-clad passes over the divide into Tibet. The extreme height, isolation, and breathtaking beauty of this region have found expression in distinctive folk traditions of colorful art, music, and dance. Numerous Buddhist monasteries and an occasional Hindu shrine dot the rugged mountain landscape.

DEVELOPMENT

 With the freeing of the economy of government controls in 1991, India has become the leader in Intelligence Technology and Business Process Outsourcing. It has a large, young labor force, a GDP approaching 10% annual growth, but is lagging in employment growth and infrastructure. Two thirds of the work force is in agriculture, which produces less than 1/4th of GDP. Almost 30 percent of the population lives in poverty.

This remote Himalayan region is the source of a great river system, the Jumna-Ganges. These rivers provide an uneven but unbroken flow of life-sustaining water down the mountain valleys and into the great northern plains, the bread basket of northern India. The cultivation of grains and rice is the main economic activity on these plains, by people who live closer and closer together as these rivers, joined at Allahabad, extend to the east toward the Bay of Bengal. The density of the rural population rises to over 2,000 people per square mile in the delta of the Ganges River.

The great central plain of northern India has the most arable and irrigated land. It is also the most populated, and historically the dominant region. The great empires of India—the Mauryan (320–125 B.C.), Gupta (300–650 A.D.), and Moghul (1508–1857 A.D.) Dynasties—rose to prominence in this region. New Delhi, the capitol of India, lies at the upper end of the central plains region, on the

Jumna River. Although it became the capitol of British India only in 1911, it is from this site that the Islamic Sultans of the thirteenth century and the Moghul kings in the sixteenth century controlled the plains to the east and the Deccan plateau to the south.

Farther east along the Ganges River are the even more ancient cities of Varanasi and Patna, known before the time of the Buddha in the sixth century B.C. as Kasi and Pataliputra, renowned for their commerce and learning. Much of India's wondrous classical tradition in art, literature, music, and philosophy evolved in this region during the times of imperial dominance and patronage. Even today, the Gangetic plain retains its traditional importance in the political and cultural life of India.

Rising to the south of the Gangetic plain, in peninsular India, is a wide plateau flanked by two mountain ranges. These ranges, though smaller and warmer than the Himalayas, are also sparsely populated. They have long provided refuge for renegade princes, slopes for coffee and tea plantations, shelter for wild game, and homes for most of India's tribal population.

As in the central plain, most of the people in the Deccan live in small villages and depend upon agriculture for their subsistence. Because the only sources of water for farming are the unpredictable seasonal rains brought by the southwest monsoon, this region has not had the economic base for the political domination experienced in the Gangetic plain. Only when the great empires of the north have swept south has this region shared in a common history with the rest of the country. Otherwise, separated by geography and language, the Deccan has supported many local kingdoms and developed its own traditions and cultures.

Three of India's larger industrial cities—Hyderabad, Ahmedabad, and Bangalore—are in the Deccan region. Ahmedabad, long known for its textile mills, is today the capitol of India's fastest-growing industrial state. Bangalore has become the center of the nation's high-technology industries—telephones, jet engines, and computers. Hyderabad is also rapidly developing its own high-tech industries and the base for Microsoft operations in India.

The fourth region of India is the coastal plain, a narrow strip of low-lying, tropical land around the edge of the Indian peninsula. During the monsoon seasons, this plain is filled with luxuriant growth, especially along the southwest Malabar Coast. Its rich harvests of rice and fruits support the highest rural population density in the country—more than 4,000 people per square mile. This region also experienced the devastating impact of recent natural disasters. The official death toll of the Indian Ocean tsunami on December 26, 2004, on the Andaman and Nicobar

Islands just north of Sumatra, Indonesia, and the coastlands of Tamil Nadu approached 11,000. That is comparable with the tolls caused by the earthquake in Gujarat in 2001, and by the cyclone in Orissa in 1999.

India's two largest urban centers, the port cities of Mumbai (Bombay) and Kolkata (Calcutta), and its fourth-largest city, Chennai (Madras), are in this coastal region. These cities were built during the expansion of European commerce in the sixteenth and seventeenth centuries and became thriving hubs of commerce under British colonial rule. Today, they are the most important centers for banking, investment capital, and international trade for all of India.

The growth of the population in all of the cities of India is immense. In the metropolitan region of Mumbai (Bombay), India's largest city, the population rose from 9.9 million in 1991 to 16.4 million in 2001, and to 18.1 million in 2004. By 2015, India is projected to have the largest urban population in the world, and Mumbai to be the world's second largest city.

This increase is due as much to immigration from the villages with the lure of urban opportunity as to the birth rate and increasing life expectancy of the urban population itself. With this dramatic increase, the pressure on urban lands and services is staggering, the ability to cope near—many people would say past—its limit.

This limit was certainly passed by an outburst of urban rioting, with widespread destruction and bloodshed that erupted in Mumbai for 10 days in January 1993. It began in a climate of communal tension between Hindus and Muslims throughout India following the destruction of a Muslim mosque in Ayodhya in the north-central region of the country on December 6, 1992. Mobs swept through the slums of the city, burning, stabbing, and looting. According to Human Rights Watch, more than 1,000 people were killed and thousands more wounded. Many more fled, homeless, to other parts of the country in the wake of this devastation. Although based on tensions of national scope, the Mumbai riots also revealed the latent social unrest and uncontrollable violence that lurk amid the increasing poverty and oppression of a fast-growing urban population.

Even with this staggering urban growth over the next decade, India's cities will still hold less than 35 percent of its total population. Today, about 71 percent of the population lives in small agricultural villages, tied to the traditional patterns of a rural countryside. India will be for the foreseeable future a nation of villages.

The pattern of population growth in India presents a picture of uneven, but significant change. Nine of the states and Union

(Courtesy of James Norton/Norton 07)

Women in Tamil Nadu transplanting young rice plants in paddy supplied by water brought by pipes through the mountains from Periyar Lake in Kerala.

territories, mostly in the south of India, who govern about 12 percent of the total population, have made remarkable progress in reducing their annual rate of growth in recent years to less than 1.2 percent. Two states, Maharashtra and Punjab, according to the 2006 National Family Health Survey, have achieved what is called a "replacement level" of population, producing an average of no more than two children per family. These states have shown that family-planning policies can control the rate of growth However, 12 states with 55 percent of the population still have growth rates close to 2 percent. It is their lack of progress toward limiting growth that places the national growth rate at 1.38 percent.

In February 2000, in response to this imbalance, the national government adopted for the first time a 10-year "population policy" encouraging all of the states to work toward replacement levels of growth. It also proposed not to change the number of representatives from each state in the national legislature for the next 25 years, so that no state would be penalized politically for reducing its proportion of the nation's population.

THE SOCIETY

The differences between the geographic regions of India and between urban and rural life within these regions are not the only sources of contrast in this diverse country. They contribute to, but do not account for, the complex mingling of culture and societies that are found in such wide array throughout the country. Even within a single region, people are divided in many other ways—by language, religion, and complex social groupings called castes.

Language

The original linguistic survey of British India in 1898 identified 188 languages and 544 dialects. A more recent comprehensive ethnographic study, "Peoples of India," identified 324 distinct languages in the country. Hindi is the most prevalent among the major languages in the northern plains region. Others that belong to the Indo-European family of languages include Bengali, Punjabi, Bihari, and Urdu. Oriya, Marathi, and Gujarati extend beyond the northern plain region into the northern parts of the Deccan and the coastal plains. Tamil, Telugu, Kanarese, and Malayalam, the major languages in the southern part of peninsular India, belong to a totally different family of languages, called Dravidian.

The Constitution of the Republic of India recognizes 17 Indo-European and Dravidian languages. This list does not include English, which is still the link language, the language of higher education, the professions, and national business and government in most parts of the country. Nor does it include the many tongues spoken by the mountain and tribal peoples who live in the remote parts of the north, east, and peninsular India. These languages belong to very different families of languages that are spoken by Tibetans, Burmese (people of Myanmar), and even by the Aboriginal peoples of Australia.

The people of India have long been separated into language groups; or, in their terms, they share a unique identity with those who speak the same mother tongue. These language groups are predominant in particular parts of the country, a native place toward which those language-speakers venerate a sense of social roots, even when they have traveled far afield.

The government of India recognized the importance of this language identity in 1956,

soon after the country's independence, when it established new state boundaries. One was drawn to divide the old British province of Bombay between those who spoke the Marathi language and those for whom Gujarati is the mother tongue. This division created the states of Maharashtra and Gujarat. The Presidency of Madras was divided into Tamil Nadu for Tamil speakers, and Andhra Pradesh for those who speak Telegu.

Identification with a particular language is through the family into which one is born, by one's mother, not by one's location. Adjusting the boundaries of the new states to coincide with the predominance of a language group did not change the linguistic identity of those who spoke other mother tongues in that state. Other-language-speakers live as minority groups, many times in enclaves, to preserve the distinctive ethos of their linguistic identities. These different linguistic groups stand out in the cities, where Bengalis and Tamils live in Mumbai (Bombay), for example, and Malayalis and Telugus in Chennai (Madras).

No single language is spoken or understood by more than 40 percent of the people. There have been attempts to establish Hindi, the most prevalent language among the states in the north-central region of India, as the national language. The states of the other regions of the country have resisted this status for any language, particularly one that is not their own. They cannot easily accept having their political identity defined, nor their primary education taught, in any other language than their own mother tongue.

Religion

India is also divided by religions, but in a different pattern. Whereas Hindi is nationally a minority language, Hindus are 80 percent of the total population and command a majority in almost every region of the country. Islam is the largest of the minority religions. There are close to 150 million Muslims in India, slightly less than the total population of Muslims in Pakistan, and more than in Bangladesh. India's Muslims are 13.4 percent of the total population of the country. All other religious minorities—Sikhs, Jains, Christians, Buddhists, and others—together make up only 6.6 percent.

The minority religions tend to concentrate in specific regions of the country in large enough numbers to become politically significant. Muslims are an overwhelming majority in Kashmir, and they are a sizable minority in the north-central state of Uttar Pradesh. Sikhs are close to 62 percent of the population of the state of Punjab. And Jains are in sufficient numbers in Gujarat, and Christians in Kerala, along the southwest Malabar Coast, to have an impact on the cultural, educational, and political aspects of life in those states.

With so many differences, one wonders how India holds together. From the day of its independence as a nation, it has been challenged to find its political identity as a multi-ethnic, multi-religious, multi-language country.

Economic Disparity

A four-year-old girl with her legs crippled by polio drags herself to the nearest open drain in Bombay's shantytown Dharavi. She cups the foul-smelling water and pours it on her body. That is her daily morning bath, a ritual repeated by children in thousands of slums across the country.

Some 15 miles south of Dharavi in the expensive neighborhood of Altamount Road, the six-year-old son of a wealthy businessman has a massive birthday bash on the manicured lawns of his father's palatial villa as similar rich children from the neighborhood ride around on camels and ponies supplied for the occasion.

What bonds these two children are the extremes of life that India's 350 million children face every day. By all accounts, the children in the condition that the Dharavi girl finds herself grossly outnumber those who can afford the lifestyle of the boy on Altamount Road.

—Neelish Misra, *India Abroad*, (November 1, 1996)

Another challenge in modern India is the extent and the visibility of poverty. Meager subsistence is the rule for the 193 million people in rural areas who live below the poverty line. Because village economy is based upon the production and distribution of food

in exchange for craft services or labor—the *jajmani* system—low income means barely above starvation. Sixty-seven million people live in urban slums, living on less than $1 a day. In Kolkata (Calcutta), beyond the slum-dwellers, some 700,000 people sleep on the streets each night.

The scope of India's urban poverty is hard to imagine. V. S. Naipaul gives this vivid description of his visit to a large slum in Mumbai (Bombay) called Dharavi:

> Back-to-back and side-to-side shacks and shelters, a general impression of blackness and grayness and mud, narrow ragged lanes curving out of view; then a side of the main road dug up; then black mud, with men and women and children defecating on the edge of a black lake, swamp and sewage, with hellish oily iridescence. . . . [It] was also an industrial area of sorts, with many unauthorized businesses, leather works and chemical works among them which wouldn't have been permitted in a better-regulated city area. . . . Petrol and kerosene fumes added to the stench. In this stench, many bare-armed people were at work: gathering or unpacking cloth waste and cardboard waste, working in gray-white dust that banked up on the ground like snow and stifled the sounds of hands and feet, working beside the road itself or in small shanties: large scale rag-picking.
>
> —*India, A Million Mutinies Now*

The Green Revolution in the late 1950s introduced new, hybrid strains of rice and wheat, and grain production has increased dramatically. Since 1970, India has imported grains only once, in 1987, when lack of monsoon rains diminished the yields enough to create a national shortage. Other times of famine have occurred in different regions when drought, earthquakes, storms, and political unrest have left large numbers of people in both cities and villages with barely enough to eat. Without further reduction in India's birth rate and an increase in urban development, it is hard to imagine how the nation's economic progress will be able to reduce the anguish of poverty and environmental decay for an increasing population. All of the gains now have to be distributed among too many needy people.

Remarkable in this context has been the emergence of a significant middle class, of households that are earning more than necessary for simple survival: food, clothing, and housing. A report to the Millennium Conference held in New Delhi in February 2000 estimated that 25 percent of the total population in India is affluent and upper middle class, with sufficient income to stimulate a market economy as consumers. This class

almost equals the population of the United States. Another 40 percent of the population is identified as lower middle class. They have risen for the most part out of the throes of subsistence and are increasing the level of household incomes at impressive rates. These new incomes are creating new markets and opportunities for a population long characterized as impoverished, austere and protected by restrictive economic planning and import controls. Today, with the rate of growth of the gross domestic product (GDP) edging toward 10 percent, it is well on the way to becoming a consumer-driven economy.

This rapidly developing middle-class market, combined with the collapse of the Soviet Union, led to a dramatic change in India's economic policy. Its earlier, restrictive import policies, which forced IBM and Coca-Cola to withdraw during the 1970s, established a good indigenous industrial base and encouraged aggressive entrepreneurial talent among its own. Dr. Manmohan Singh, then finance minister (now prime minister), initiated reforms to liberalize the economy by divesting some of the government's public-sector industries, reducing government red tape, and decreasing restrictions on foreign investment. All of these factors led to a spurt of an average annual real growth rate in the gross domestic product (GDP) of more than 6 percent. The industrial sector itself is growing in 2006 at an impressive 9 percent per year. Growth in the steel, textile, and automotive parts industries have been impressive. With a growing young labor force to employ in this sector as it expamds (a resource not so available to China), the economy is expected to improve for many years to come.

An even more stimulating part of India's economic development has been the rapid rise in its service sector of information technology (IT) and information technology enabled services (ITES), especially since the Y2K crisis. In a more globalized economy today, India has taken the lead in software creation, professional-service consulting, and setting up call centers to provide a myriad of financial and support services to companies across the world. Business process outsourcing (BPO) in the IT sector of India's economy grew at an annual rate of 29 percent in 2002, to command 80 percent of the world market, making it the fastest growing industry in India. Exports in the IT sector worth $36 billion in 2005—one quarter of India's total exports—are expected to grow to $60 billion in 2010.

This phenomenal growth is built upon a young, educated elite, now 1.3 million strong, which promises to grow to over 2 million by 2008. Although they represent but a small portion of India's labor pool of 464 million, their success and new incomes are producing a ripple effect on the entire economy. They are also producing a new class of "zippies," young adults looking for designer products in high-rise malls around the centers of IT activity in cities across the country.

Reforms leading to further growth will certainly continue under the leadership of Manmohan Singh as prime minister following the Congress Party victory in the elections of 2004. His Minimum Common Programme will, however, place greater emphasis on human resource development to address the issues of unemployment and poverty in the country.

FREEDOM

The world's largest democracy, India has maintained stable parliamentary and local government through free elections and rule of law since the adoption of its constitution in 1950. Jihadis in Kashmir, Naxalites in east central, and separatist groups in northeast India perpetrate terrorist acts against civilians.

Today, even Dharavi slum in Mumbai is the site of a major urban project of the Mumbai Slum Redevelopment hAuthority. It envisions five "townships," in which 72 seven-story apartment buildings are being built to house 56,000 households. The project, which will allow space for extensive industrial development, community services, and the Kumbharwada potters' colony, is expected to be finished by 2013.

India faces a number of challenges in its economic development. India does not have adequate infrastructure investment to provide necessary transportation and energy for its industrial expansion. Its labor laws, some of which go back to 1947, discourage increasing and seasonal adjustments in employment, and are overly restrictive and protected by political populism. And consumer demand, growing four times faster than the economy, is outstripping the production that generated it. This increase is creating an imbalance in imports and adding to inflation.

The agricultural sector employs two-thirds of the labor market, but produces less than a quarter of the GNP. And it is growing at only 3 percent. Problems of globalization and water supply are increasing stress and hindebtedness for farm communities, which are experiencing an increasing number of suicides. That means that 600 million people in 600,000 villages across the country are largely untouched by the benefits of the new prosperity. And then there are most of the 67 million who live in urban slums.

Promises for the economic future of India are tempered by the overwhelming demands of teeming population and extensive poverty in both cities and villages, environmental degradation, and strife.

"Excess," V. S. Naipaul calls them, recognizing that so much of the conflict and violence is the result of an awakening of a new political consciousness in the country. "A million mutinies supported by twenty kinds of group excess, sectarian excess, religious excess, regional excess." Yet he finds even in this awakening a vision of hope: "the beginnings of self-awareness . . . the beginning of a new way for the millions, part of India's growth, part of its restoration."

A Country of Change

Change is expected in India. It has to do with the dramatic annual anticipation of the monsoon, when flood-producing torrents of rain end an intolerably hot, dry season each spring; with the unpredictable terror of disease and sudden death; with the rise and fall of fortunes and of transient petty kingdoms and even mighty empires. The people have a conscious heritage of many thousands of years during which countless changes have taken place.

A word for "life" in India is *samsara,* which literally means "flowing," like a river. Sometimes, like a river in flood, change can be traumatic. Such was the partition of India and Pakistan at the time of their independence from British colonial rule in 1947. Fourteen million people were suddenly displaced from their homes, and close to a million lost their lives in senseless, random massacres. For the most part, however, life in India flows in a single direction, never at quite the same pace, but usually within its banks. Life's flow is never entirely predictable, but there are sufficient patterns to give a sense that in India, even in times of great change, everything is very much the same.

INDIA SINCE INDEPENDENCE

The substantial economic development and control of population growth in India have happened in the context of an even greater growth and restoration in the lives of the Indian people. With the achievement of independence in 1947, India became a democracy.

As a new nation, India had first to establish an independent, sovereign government, free of colonial domination. This task was achieved by the transition of the Indian National Congress, which since 1885 had led the movement for India's political freedom, to the majority political party in a Constituent Assembly set up by the British Raj in 1935. At the time of independence, the Congress Party formed an interim government, with its leader, Jawarhalal Nehru, serving as prime minister. With the adoption of its Constitution on January 26, 1950, the Republic of India became a democratic, secular nation.

The Constitution established a parliamentary national Legislature: the Lok Sabha (House of the People), with 545 members to

five year terms, and the Rajya Sabha (Council of States), with 12 members appointed by the president and 238 members elected proportionately by the legislative assemblies in each of the 28 states and seven Union Territories.

Five uninterrupted years in office was the rule during the early years of the Republic, when the government was firmly under the control of Prime Minister Jawarhalal Nehru. Nehru's charismatic leadership and commitment to democracy brought together many disparate interests into the Congress Party. Since his death in 1964, many of the country's social and regional factions have become more politically savvy in gaining representation for their own interests in the national legislature. The Lok Sabha has thus become more representative of the diversity of the country. But with regional, ethnic, and special interests more dominant, its institutional authority and its ability to achieve a national political agenda have diminished.

The Congress Party began to win less than a majority of seats in the legislature in the 1990s. The process of selecting a prime minister became more complex and tenuous.

By the elections in the spring of 1996, the Bharatiya Janata Party (BJP) became the first party to compete with the Congress Party on the national level. It won 186 seats, mostly from the north-central plains states. The Congress Party came in a distant second, with 136 seats. The president initially invited Atal Behari Vajpayee, leader of the BJP, to become prime minister. But he could not garner the support of a 273-seat majority needed to gain the confidence of the Lok Sabha. He resigned even before the newly elected legislature convened.

In the 1998 elections, the BJP again won the most legislative seats, but still fell short of commanding a majority. This time Vajpayee was able to bring together a coalition of 19 parties. The vote to install his government was 274 seats in favor. His victory was achieved only through the last-minute support of a regional party from the state of Andhra Pradesh.

Vajpayee managed to hold this coalition together to remain in office as prime minister for a little more than a year. Then Jayalalitha, leader of another coalition party from Tamil Nadu, withdrew her party's support because she was unsuccessful in getting the Vajpayee government to intervene on her behalf in lawsuits accusing her of mismanaging state funds. Without her support, Vajpayee lost his majority, and was forced to resign.

With no alternative leadership able to achieve a majority, new elections were held in the fall of 1999. The BJP won 183 seats and returned to power in a newly formed coalition of 24 parties, called the National Democratic Alliance. Vajpayee remained in power for almost five full years. Feeling confident of his party's success based

(UN Photo 42,950)

In 1950, India adopted its Constitution, thus formally establishing itself as a democratic, secular nation. The first prime minister of this new country was Jawarhalal Nehru (far left), the head of the Congress Party, standing next to Lady Mountbatten.

upon their Hindu nationalist platform and economic reforms, he called for elections in April 2004.

Much to everyone's surprise, the BJP was routed in the polls. The Congress Party eked out a plurality. With a coalition of 15 other parties to form the United Progressive Alliance, and the support of the communist parties, it was able to form a government. On the urging of Sonia Gandhi, leader of the Congress Party, Dr. Manmohan Singh, a Sikh and former finance minister, became prime minister. He immediately set forward a "Common Minimum Programme" to establish a political agenda acceptable to all members of the coalition and the communist parties needed to hold a majority of the Lok Sabha.

Other political parties that represent specific minority interests in the political spectrum are gaining strength. The Bahujan Samaj Party (BSP) and the Samajwadi Party (SP), represent Dalits (traditional untouchable communities, 16 percent of the nation's population) and Muslims (13 percent). Though aligned in opposition to each other, they won increasing numbers of legislative seats in recent national and state by-elections. Based on its victories in the 1996 state election, the BSP joined forces with the Bharatiya Janata Party in Uttar Pradesh. Its leader, Mayawati, became the first woman Dalit to hold the office of chief minister of an Indian state.

The Samajwadi Party won the second largest number of votes in the 1998 national elections in Uttar Pradesh, reducing the BJP's dominance in that state and preventing it from winning a majority in the national legislature. The election results suggest that, if the BSP and the SP had joined together, they might have routed the BJP in its greatest stronghold in India. In the 2002 state by-elections, the SP and the BSP won more seats than the ruling BJP, which fell from 158 seats in 1999 to 88. The BJP remained in power in Uttar Pradesh only by joining again with the BSP to form a majority of one in the state Legislative Assembly.

The success of these parties representing the "underclasses" reveals a growing awareness on the part of the disadvantaged communities of how democracy can work to their advantage. Such recognition can only strengthen the role of democratic government to address the needs of all of the people in the nation.

Parliamentary democracy founded in the Constitution of the Republic of India has worked well. Political parties and the ballot box have identified the public will and determined the direction of policy in the Lok Sabha, even for some of the most secessionist-minded groups in the country. The unexpected defeat of the Bharatiya Janata Party (BJP) in the elections of 2004, and the continuing rise of the Bahujan Samaj Party (BSP) and Samajwadi Party (SP) give dramatic witness to the power of the voice of the people.

The ballot box has also worked to determine the membership and agendas of the similarly structured, though less orderly, legislative assemblies on the state and municipal levels of government.

Elections have become an important part of Indian life. Among the many villages in the country, they are taking on the character of a festival, as reported under the headline "Joy and Order as India's Voting Starts":

> What seemed important was not so much which of the dozens of political parties was up or down, or which local candidate from among the 15,000 running across India was likely to win. What permeated the mood was something as old as independent India itself: the sheer pleasure of taking part in a basic democratic rite, the business of appointing and dismissing governments, that has survived all of the disappointments that Indians have endured in the past half-century. In a troubled land, democracy means there is hope.
>
> —*The New York Times*
> (April 18, 1996)

CHALLENGES TO DEMOCRACY

Many factors have contributed to the success of democracy in India. Some will point to the example and the many years of preparation promoted by British colonial rule. Others look to the inspiration of Mahatma Gandhi and his leadership of the Indian National Congress, which brought the independence movement to the people of the subcontinent. Also important has been the Constitution and the vital leadership and vision of Jawarhalal Nehru and the Congress Party in implementing its guarantees. Other factors include the remarkable restraint of the Indian army, the dedicated service of the Indian Administrative Service, and an enlightened press. Yet with all of their important contributions, democracy still faces many challenges in India today.

An unusual challenge came in 1975, unusual because it arose totally in the context of constitutional government itself. And it was quickly met by the power of the ballot box.

In 1975, Prime Minister Indira Gandhi, to protect herself from a legal challenge to her office, asked President Ahmad to declare a "National Emergency," under the "President's Rule" provision in the Constitution. That act suspended for two years the normal function of government and the civil liberties protected by the Constitution. National elections were postponed, opposition leaders were put in prison, and press censorship was imposed. But when national elections were reinstated in 1977, the people of India voted her and the Congress Party out of office. They were not going to have their political freedom eroded. And their's was the final say.

Indira Gandhi had gained prominence as the only child and home provider of Jawaharlal Nehru. She became a widow in 1960, upon the death of her husband Feroze Gandhi, a Parsi Journalist, and no relation to the Mahatma. That she became prime minister of India in 1966, and was reappointed in 1980, is itself remarkable because the Indian cultural environment assigns a more subservient role to women, and especially to widows. Her achievement underscores another, more far-reaching challenge to democratic government in India: that the institutions of government, not indigenous to India, function somewhat like a superstructure imposed upon traditional patterns and mores that are both substantial and persistent even as the Indian people become more modern.

HEALTH/WELFARE

India's commitment to village development and universal education has improved diet, hygiene, medical services, and literacy. Birth-control policies are implemented unevenly, and poverty is extensive, especially in urban slums.

Laws, for example, have been enacted to protect women against abuses sanctioned by traditional practices. Dowry has long been expected to be paid by a bride's family to her perspective in-laws as an inducement and condition of marriage. It was outlawed by the Dowry Prohibition Act, enacted in 1961 and strengthened by amendments in the 1980s. The government of India also in 1993 ratified the international Convention on the Elimination of All Forms of Discrimination Against Women. The practice of dowry nevertheless continues unabated, sanctioning instances of manslaughter or suicide, excused as "dowry death" or "bride-burning," when subsequent dowry demands by the groom's family are not met or issues of incompatibility surface. Dowry demands have increased and spread more widely across India as the society has become more consumer conscious. And the incidence of "accidental" death has increased to 7,000 per year among newlywed women.

With more recent policies to limit population growth and with advanced gender detection technology, India is recording a significant decline in the ratio of girls to boys in the population less than six years old. The national average of sex ratio in the 2001 census was 927 girls to 1000 boys, with many, states falling below 800. Government laws in 1994 to prohibit the use of technology for prenatal sex determination have had limited or no impact on the traditional preference for a male heir sustained by the patriarchal structure of the family. Discrimination against women has increased in these and many other ways, even as India adjusts to more modern economic conditions.

Equality for all citizens is another example of an issue affirmed by the Constitution of India, but not observed in practice. The framers of the Constitution even included affirmative action provisions to reserve places for those of traditionally untouchable and scheduled castes in education and government. Yet many belonging to lower castes who have benefited by affirmative action in education are not able to get jobs upon graduating from college because of continuing discrimination in the marketplace. This discrimination functions openly in the daily lives of villagers throughout India, and even among Indian nationals who have moved to other, more socially liberal parts of the world.

The Challenge of Caste

Because of its hierarchical structure, the caste system is by definition inequitable, and thus a contradiction to the equality presupposed by democracy. Particularly, those who find themselves of lower rank feel the tremendous weight of its oppression. Those with higher or improving rank are not so troubled by this inherent inequality. One's attitude toward the caste system may depend largely on one's place in the system.

To many the caste system is a rigid structure that divides people into distinct social groups that are ranked in a fixed hierarchy. For others, the system is seen not as separating basically similar people into isolated groups, but rather, as a structure that holds very diverse groups of people together. And its hierarchical structure, rather than fixing people into permanent levels, provides them with some opportunity for social mobility. As with so much about India, the caste system is more complex and more flexible than appears on the surface.

The caste system is based upon a social group for which Westerners do not have a counterpart. In the north of India, the caste community is generally called a jati (a word based on a verbal root meaning "to be born"). It is an extended kinship group whose perimeters extend beyond the natural family. The jati is also endogamous, which means that it provides the pool of acceptable marriage partners. Natural family members are excluded from this pool by generally accepted rules of incest. A jati thus extends the idea of a family to a larger social group made up of extensive cousins and potential in-laws.

Jati is important to an Indian's self-identity. Whereas Westerners tend to think of themselves in society primarily as individuals, in India, one is more apt to think of oneself primarily as belonging to one's jati. It provides a context for all of one's interactions with others, with respect to working, socializing, eating, and especially as regards marriage. In India, where marriages are mostly arranged by parents, the expectation to marry someone of one's own jati is generally the rule.

The jati is further defined by a traditional occupation, passed on from generation to generation, which gives each jati its name. There are many thousands of jati caste communities throughout India, most of them confined to a single linguistic region. There may be as few as two or three jatis in the remote mountain valleys of the Himalayas. Generally, in the more densely populated areas of India, a villager will interact with about 20 different such caste groups in his normal daily life.

The jati is the social unit that is placed in the hierarchical ranking of the caste system. Here is where the possibility of flexibility, or mobility, arises. That one belongs to a certain jati is fixed by birth. Where that jati is ranked in the hierarchical caste order is not. Its rank is based on some general rules that are accepted by almost everyone. For example, Brahmin jaits of traditional priest are placed at the top of the caste hierarchy. That they are expected to abjure wealth, practice asceticism, and revere learning is a significant feature of this system. It does not hold as high esteem for those who hold political power, are famous, or pursue money and become conspicuous spenders.

The hierarchical ranking of this system demeans in rank jatis that perform menial tasks such as cleaning latrines, sweeping streets, and removing the carcasses of dead animals. People belonging to these jatis are called "untouchables," a designation that reveals the ancient priestly caste's understanding of its own supremacy in rank. Brahmins as a community had to remain ritually pure in order to retain the efficacy and respect for their priestly functions. Those who performed "polluting" functions in the society—those dealing with human waste and animals—had to be avoided for fear of their diminishing the priests' sacred power. They were thus placed lowest on the hierarchical scale and declared "outcastes."

Mahatma Gandhi, in his crusade to remove the scourge of the demeaning term "untouchable," called them Harijans, "children of God," and encouraged members of his religious community to perform the "polluting" functions for themselves. In many parts of India today people in these jatis prefer to be called Dalits (the "oppressed"), and are seeking recognition as equal members of Indian society. Their quest, however, still meets a great deal of resistance throughout the country.

For those jatis that fall between the high-ranked Brahmins and the low-ranked Dalits, though every jati has its own rank, the basis of ranking is not so clear or consistent. Some occupations, such as land cultivators or carpenters, are generally accepted as higher than potters, herders, and washermen. Land or industrial ownership, and thus control over production in a village, called dominance, is an important determinant in caste rank. Social practices, such as ritual observance, dress, vegetarian diet, and with whom one eats, may also determine rank. Different rules apply in different situations. As norms and conditions change, so is the rank of one's jati open to change.

Many examples illustrate this fluidity of ranking. The jati names of several ancient emperors betray an absence of royal blood, or, at least, of earlier royal rank for their caste. Such did not prevent them from becoming kings. A striking, more contemporary example is the Nadar community in south India. It was considered an untouchable community in the nineteenth century, but is now accepted as a merchant caste. K. Kamaraj, a Congress Party member in the Lok Sabha, led the syndicate that first proposed Indira Gandhi to be Congress Party's candidate for prime minister in 1966, following the death of her father. He was a Nadar.

Even Mahatma Gandhi's family was not fixed in jati rank. The family name (*gandhi* means "grocer") identifies a bania, merchant, background. Both Gandhi's grandfather and father served as chief ministers for maharajas of small Indian states, a role traditionally reserved for Brahmins. Gandhi was himself thrown out of his jati by the elders of his community when he went to England to study law. He stepped out of the caste system altogether when he was accepted as a person committed to a religious life, when he became the Mahatma.

The position of any specific jati in the social hierarchy is based primarily on the acceptance of its claim to rank by members of the other jatis with which it interacts. Because mobility is open only to the entire jati, and not to individuals within it, and members of other jatis need to agree, change in rank does not happen quickly. Nevertheless a social dynamic extends through the system that asserts a claim to higher rank and encourages others to accept that claim.

The Caste System and Political Change

The cohesion and flexibility in the caste structure provides the dynamic within the traditional social context for democracy to work. The right of all adults to vote to determine who will represent them is new to India. In a system in which rules of ascendancy are continually being worked out, the role of the vote to grant political power emerged as an acceptable way to affirm rank status that already existed within the village hierarchy. The system does not have to change; it simply has to adapt itself to an additional way to assert ascendancy.

Winning of elections by commanding votes has found a place in the traditional caste structure in two important ways. First, because jatis extend through many villages within a linguistic region, they provide cohesive units for regional associations formed to promote political causes important to their jati members, as voting blocks in elections. They also function as lobbies in the halls of government between elections. Such blocks have led to the rise of political parties to assert the rights of the Dalits in northern India.

Within a single village, the traditional caste structure adapts to democratic elections by creating voting blocks out of the local authority structures, called factions, already in place in the villages. The power of higher castes in a village faction is based on the control of production and distribution of food that is harvested from village lands. Those who dominate these village resources are quick to convert into votes for their chosen candidates the allegiances created by the dependency of those of lower jati rank in the village who serve and get food from them. Thus democracy is co-opted to support traditional patterns of social life rather than to reform them.

The slow pace of land reform in India, in contrast to the rapid acceptance of new methods of agriculture that produced abundant supplies of grain in the Green Revolution, is evidence of this adaptation of democracy to traditional sources of power. New laws have broken up large land estates and reduced absentee landlordism. But politically active regional landholder jati associations have been able to block legislative action on some of the most difficult village problems: landlessness and under employment, the inequities of wealth and privilege, and landowner-laborer relations. Disputes between landowners and their laborers are still mostly resolved by force, with little interference by the police or protection from the courts.

This amazing, and sometimes horrifying, capacity for persistence and adaptation of India's traditional social institutions is a basis for concern. But these institutions have also provided a stabilizing and receptive context in which democracy has been able to develop. Democracy as a form of government does not happen in a social vacuum.

ACHIEVEMENTS

 Through its Green Revolution, India has been self-sufficient in grains since 1970. Technology and a growing middle class have attracted increasing direct investment in the economy. The impact of India-Americans and popular artists like musician Ravi Shankar reveal the vitality of India's heritage of creativity in language, art, and human relations.

The continuing burden of poverty has been another real threat to democracy in India. While Americans have tended to view economic improvement and prosperity as direct consequences of political democracy, the developing world in general, and India in particular, have shown that the two are not necessarily connected. Prosperity is the result of many factors other than just political structure. Population density and population growth, for example, have had greater impact on economic growth than form of governance in India. Cultural factors, geo-commercial considerations, international economic forces, and specific economic policies of the government of India have also contributed to its continuing struggle to provide economic well-being for all of its people. In India, democracy has not yet lived up to its economic promise not contributed to radical social change.

But the large participation of the rural poor in the national elections in 2004 contributed significantly to the victory of the Congress Party. Their vote became the mandate for Prime Minister Manmohan Singh "to carry forward the process of social and economic change which benefits the poorer sections of our community, particularly farmers and workers."

The Challenge of Religious Nationalism

Another persistent challenge to democracy has been the quest for an inclusive national identity for the wide diversity of peoples in the country. Nothing in their heritage affirms for them this kind of unity.

The writer V. S. Naipaul realized this contrast from his childhood experience in Trinidad. Immigrants of many different languages and religions from India, shared an identity as Indians. This was not true for the same diversity of people who lived in India itself:

> When I got there I found [the idea of being an Indian] had no meaning in India. In the torrent of India, with its hundreds of millions, that continental idea was no comfort at all. People needed to hold on to smaller ideas of who and what they were; they found stability in the smaller groupings of region, clan, caste, family.
> —*India: A Million Mutinies Now*

None of these smaller ideas of identity are based on political associations. They are, rather, linguistic, religious, and social, such as caste, into which the people of India are grouped not by events, but by birth.

Because 82 percent of the people of India are Hindu, their religious identity is readily available to create a political majority to establish the national agenda. Their overwhelming number is still a source of great concern to those who are in a religious minority: Muslims, Sikhs, Parsis, Buddhist, Jains, Christians, and Jews. The call for the separate nation of Pakistan was due in large part to this anxiety among the Muslim community in British India. How could a predominantly Hindu society, determined to meet its own objectives in a democracy, not discriminate against, if not actually oppress, people of other religions?

The Indian National Congress, which for 60 years worked constructively and diligently for the independence of India from British rule, was committed to realizing a free India as a secular state. Mahatma Gandhi's vision of a universal religious identity and the democratic idealism of India's leaders in its early years as a republic held to the goal that the government must recognize the presence and the integrity of its many different religious communities. In the words of India's Constitution, "all persons are equally entitled to freedom of conscience and the right freely to profess, practice, and propagate religion." This separation between the secular objectives of the nation-state and

(UN Photo 87,052)

In India, religious identity often takes precedence over the idea of belonging to a nation. Many religious sects demand political recognition. In 1984, the Indian Army stormed the Golden Temple in Amritsar (pictured above), the sacred shrine of the Sikh community. This action was in response to Sikhs' demand for the establishment of an independent state in Punjab. In retaliation, a group of Sikhs assassinated Prime Minister Indira Gandhi.

the religious identity of its peoples has not, however, always been clear. More recently, religious identity has taken precedence over the more abstract idea of "belonging" to a democratic nation.

Three specific movements have challenged the commitment to political secularism in India today. First is the outright demand by a militant wing of the Sikh community for an independent state, called Khalistan, to be established in the current state of Punjab, in northwest India.

To quell the violence of this nationalist demand in its frequent, random terrorist attacks and kidnappings, the Indian army went into the Golden Temple in Amritsar to rout out of the temple's protective walls a militant Sikh separatist leader who had sought sanctuary there. The outrage felt by the Sikh community over this assault on the sacred shrine of the entire Sikh community led to the assassination of Prime Minister Indira Gandhi later that year by two Sikh members of her bodyguard. Her death stirred reprisals against Sikhs, killing 3,000 in riots across the north of India.

Continuing violence caused the suspension of the 1991 elections in Punjab. After political order was restored, they were held in February 1992, and a moderate Sikh, Prakash Singh Badal, was elected chief minister of the state. His assassination in August 1995 revealed that tension still existed among Sikhs and with surrounding Hindu communities. Yet, the 1996 and all subsequent elections in Punjab have been conducted with a remarkable reduction of violence.

Indira Gandhi's response to Sikh militancy was secular in intent: to hold India, with all of its religious differences, together as one nation. But their religious rather than their political identities defined the participants in this confrontation. The drastic consequences were the result of Sikhs and Hindus having greater allegiance to their religion than to the nation.

The second recent challenge to political secularism in India has been the rise of religious nationalism as a political movement. The man who assassinated Mahatma Gandhi in 1948 did so in the name of Hindu nationalism. He felt that Gandhi's attempts to accommodate the Muslim communities into an independent India were compromising his Hindu faith too much. By this action, he affirmed the greatest fears of those advocating an independent Pakistan: that they would not receive equal status as a religious minority in the new nation of India. As a consequence of Mahatma Gandhi's example and his death, the quest to achieve a truly secular nation took on great urgency during the early years of India's independence.

As political awareness and participation increased among India's peoples, their religious identity has also been stimulated. One impetus was a television extravaganza. In 1987, a film producer, at the invitation of the national government, created a television series based on the Ramayana, a classical Indian epic.

The original Sanskrit account of the ideal Indian prince, Rama, recognized by Hindus as an incarnation of the Supreme God

Vishnu, was composed 2,000 years ago. The story is more popularly known and celebrated among the Hindi-speaking population in a translation of this epic done by a religious poet, Tulsidas, in the sixteenth century A.D. Doordarshan, the national television channel, broadcast the modern television serial, described as "a mixture of soap opera and national mythology," on Sunday mornings in 104 half-hour episodes.

During its broadcast, almost all of India came to a halt. More than 100 million viewers were glued to any television set (some 25 million of them) they could find. The serial was an immense success, both in telling the story and in spreading the virtues of television among millions of new viewers.

The intent of the government and the serial's producers had been to extol India's ancient, albeit Hindu, heritage as a way of encouraging a greater sense of national pride. The serial actually stirred up religious sentiments of both Hindus and the minorities who had reason to fear the arousal of such passion.

The television serial also coincided with the rise of a new political party committed to Hindu nationalism, the Bharatiya Janata Party (BJP). In a country where many have risen to political prominence through the film industry, it is not difficult to ascribe increasing popularity of this new party directly to the broadcast of the Ramayana. Even more did the BJP gain from a sequel television serial. India's other, older and longer epic, the Mahabharata, was presented in 93 hour-long episodes from October 1988 to July 1990. Like the Ramayana, this epic extols the virtues of an ancient Hindu past. And it includes the original recitation of the most revered text of contemporary Hinduism, Bhagavad Gita, "The Song of the Lord."

The Bharatiya Janata Party had won only two seats in Parliament in the elections of 1984. In 1989, its holdings jumped to 89. In the 1991 elections, they won 118 seats, then second only to the Congress Party, which won 225 seats, briefly diminishing that party's hopes for a majority in the Lok Sabha. The BJP won a slim majority that year in the legislative assembly of India's largest state, Uttar Pradesh, a long-time Congress Party stronghold.

In this rise to political prominence, the Bharatiya Janata Party tied its fortunes directly to another incident, which is also related to Rama, the hero of the Ramayana, and that also received extensive television-viewing attention, but this time as national news. The BJP leadership became actively involved in a campaign to build a temple to Rama on the site of his legendary birthplace in the city of Ayodhya, in eastern Uttar Pradesh. Through a number of public demonstrations, including a chariot procession across northern India, the party was able to rouse a large amount of public support for the building project and for its leadership as a political force. Such a mingling of religion and politics was effective, but potentially dangerous.

What made the building campaign particularly volatile was that the location for the temple to Rama was on the site of the Babri Masjid, a historic, but unused, Muslim house of prayer. This mosque was built in 1528 (purportedly on the site of a temple that had been destroyed) for Babur, the first of the Islamic Moghul Emperors in India. Because the Muslim community was equally eager to preserve the vestiges of its own glorious past in India, the project placed the BJP in direct conflict with the Indian Muslim minority. In hopes of working out a political compromise that would not stimulate further religious antagonism between Hindus and Muslims, Prime Minister Narasimha Rao placed the dispute over the ownership of this land in the hands of the Supreme Court of India.

The BJP, in control of the Uttar Pradesh government, became impatient with the maneuvering by the prime minister. It supported a rally on Dec. 6, 1992, at the Babri mosque/proposed Rama temple site in Ayodhya. The BJPs aim was to keep national attention on its objective to promote the interests of Hindus, and to urge approval to build the temple. A crowd of over 700,000 people from across the country gathered for the rally in that city of some 70,000 residents. Even though the national government had assigned 15,000 troops there to maintain order, the situation got out of control, and a small group of enthusiasts scaled the Babri mosque and pulled it apart.

The response throughout the country was immediate and devastating. Dormant feelings of anger, fear, frustration, and hatred erupted into communal riots across India. Hundreds of people were killed, and vast numbers of shops and homes destroyed, from Assam to Kashmir to Kerala. The violence quickly spread into neighboring Pakistan and Bangladesh, where Hindu temples and homes were destroyed in reprisal. A tinderbox of communal resentment based on religion had exploded.

Realizing its complicity in the far-reaching violence caused by the mosque's demolition, the BJP government of Uttar Pradesh resigned. Prime Minister Narasimha Rao imprisoned the national leaders of the BJP, and urged the president to invoke Presidents Rule to dismiss the governments in three other states where the BJP held power: Madhya Pradesh, Rajasthan and Himachal Pradesh. And recognizing the challenge to his own government that the destruction of the mosque created, Narasimha Rao called for the resignation of his entire cabinet.

The Babri Masjid episode severely challenged India's commitment as a secular democratic republic. The outbursts of communal rioting and the increasing strength of the BJP as a political party both suggested that the Hindu religious identity of the majority of the Indian people was defining their national character more powerfully than the political institutions, which were established by the Constitution in 1950. The dawn of Ram Raj, an idyllic age of government led by the power of God, was proclaimed, and the specter of Hindu religious fundamentalism was on the rise.

The BJP continued to increase in political strength. The party's greatest appeal was among an emerging rural middle class throughout north India. This more traditional support suggests that the real power of the BJP was not religious, but rather, the conservative forces of the privileged who dominate India's agrarian society. Even though this political base built on communal sentiment that identifies India as exclusively a Hindu nation, it never got wide support.

To gain a majority in the Lok Sabha, the BJP had to form coalitions with other parties, which caused it to temper some of its extremist Hindu positions. It continued to rewrite India's history in school textbooks and to permit attacks against Christian missionaries and converts. But its assertions of Hindutva (Hindu-ness) were presented as cultural, not religious. Its main concern was to be a national political party, not to establish a national religious identity.

The BJP, under the leadership of Prime Minister Vajpayee, in a 24-party coalition called the National Democratic Alliance, stayed in power from 1999 until the elections in 2004 on the national level, But during this time it lost control of legislatures in seven states, retaining

its power in only four others. An important exception was in Gujarat, where the BJP survived a challenge in by-elections held in December 2002, in response to communal violence that broke out on February 27, 2002.

That violence began when 58 passengers, mostly women and children, were killed in a train on which they were returning from a pilgrimage to Ayodhya to visit the Ram temple site. The train was allegedly set on fire by a band of Muslim slum dwellers from the town of Godhra, in eastern Gujarat. Attacks in reprisal against Muslim communities in the state led to the destruction of many homes and the death of more than 1,000 people.

Accusations were made that the BJP government in Gujarat did not act to contain the violence against the Muslim population. It was suspended by Presidents Rule and by-elections were set to be held after a cooling-off period. The party used this episode of communal violence, and a terrorist attack on a Hindu temple in September, to generate political support among the Hindu majority in the state. In the December by-election, the BJP won a commanding majority, 117 out of 182 seats in the state Assembly.

Nationally, however, the violence against Muslims in Gujarat stirred a reaction against Hindu nationalist sentiment. Prime Minister Vajpayee felt called upon to stress the need for a more balanced, secular approach to government. And in the elections in the spring of 2004, the BJP won only 138 of the 543 seats in the Lok Sabha.

Their defeat suggested that their religious agenda had played itself out in Indian national politics. Shashi Tharoor expressed a more respectful understanding of the religious integrity of Hinduism than its reduction to political policy when he wrote in response to the communal violence that followed the Ayodhya temple episode:

It pains me to read in the American newspapers of "Hindu fundamentalism," when Hinduism is a religion without compulsory fundamentals. That devotees of this essentially tolerant faith are desecrating a place of worship and assaulting Muslims in its name is a source of both sorrow and shame. India has survived the Aryans, the Mughuls, the British; it has taken from each—language, art, food, learning—and outlasted them all. The Hinduism that I know understands that faith is a matter of hearts and minds, not bricks and stone.

Indian Express
(January 20, 1993)

The third challenge to political secularism is in the state of Jammu and Kashmir, the one state in India where Muslims are an overall ma-

(Press Information Bureau, Government of India/NP16196)   (Press Information Bureau, Government of India/NP16195)
Women and men voting at separate voting stations in Guraz, Jammu and Kashmir on September 16, 2002.

jority. The government of India first attempted to suppress an independence movement in Kashmir by successively courting and jailing Sheikh Abdullah, whose quest for Kashmiri freedom was from Maharajah Hari Singh, before the independence of India in 1947.

After his death in 1982, Prime Minister Indira Gandhi, upset by initiatives by his son, Farooq, to obtain greater autonomy for Kashmir, appointed a dedicated civil servant, Jagmohan, as governor of the state. He dismissed the state legislature under the "Presidents Rule" provision in the Constitution, and instituted severely aggressive measures by India's military in Kashmir to enforce his control.

The Muslim separatist movement, energized by this repression, received additional religious fervor and support from militant Muslims, *jihadis,* mostly from Pakistan, who had been fighting in Afghanistan during the 1980s to free that country from Soviet military occupation. Using the weaponry and terrorist tactics learned to overcome the massive strength of the Soviet army, the insurgents attacked the Indian military and many civilians with deadly force. More than 45,000 people were to die in this conflict.

During this time of violence, India's military presence, mismanagement of elections and human rights abuses continued to erode public support. But the government of India still asserted its claim to sovereignty in the state by calling for legislative elections in the fall of 2002. It even attempted to encourage the All Parties Hurriyat Conference, a conglomerate of 23 separatist parties in Kashmir, to participate in the elections. The Hurriyat declined, stating that a dialogue between India and Pakistan about their rival claims for Kashmir should occur before any elections that presuppose India's sovereignty over them. A comprehensive opinion poll taken in the spring of 2002 recorded 65 percent in all regions of the state believing that elections were not possible because of the violence. But it also recorded that 61 percent still preferred to be citizens of India.

Even with increased security arrangements, the 2002 elections led to the killing of more than 600 candidates, political workers, security personnel and civilians attending political rallies and going to the polls. But 44 percent of the electorate participated, leading to the defeat of the incumbent party and the formation of a new government coalition of the Peoples Democratic Party (with 16 seats), the Congress Party (with 20 seats), and the Peoples Democratic Forum, a Communist party (with seven seats), for a slim majority in the 87-seat assembly. The new chief minister, Mufti Mohammad Sayeed, head of the PDP and a former member and home minister in the Congress Party, promised to "heal the wounds of militancy" in this terribly ravaged state.

American forces, which went to Afghanistan after 9/11, urged President Musharraf of Pakistan to stop Pakistani terrorist groups from supporting the insurgencies in both Afghanistan and Kashmir. The violence has diminiahed in Kashmir, but terrorist acts have continued, suggesting that Pakistan may remain convinced that the tension created by these tactics to destabilize both India and Afghanistan have been the best means to obtain their political objectives in the region.

President Musharraf and Prime Minister Manmohan Singh met at the Non Allignment Movement meetings in Havana, Cuba, in September 2006, and agreed on a framework to set up high-level dialogue between their governments. With all this attention, and with the opening up of transportation links across the Line of Control, there is renewed hope that the people of Kashmir can rebuild their lives, and live in peace.

But Kashmir is still caught between the conflicting national ideologies of India's need to affirm its commitment to an inclusive, secular state and Pakistans claim that it is the only legitimate government for Muslims in the northwestern portion of the subcontinent.

REGIONAL POLITICAL CONCERNS

As India becomes more economically productive, it enters into a global arena with both the United States and China to find more sources of energy. Its economy at the present rate of growth will demand double what it uses today in twenty years. India has significant coal reserves, but 90 percent of its oil is imported. That India looks to Iran as a major supplier places it in an adverse relationship with the United States politically as well.

India's quest to be recognized as a nuclear power makes nuclear proliferation another major issue in its relations on the world scene. The world was shocked when both India and Pakistan tested nuclear bombs in May 1998. The United States was especially outraged by these tests. Nuclear-armed India and Pakistan threaten the stability of South Asia and give precedent for developing nuclear arms in other volatile areas of the world. The U.S government responded by imposing sanctions on both India and Pakistan. They turned out to be small in terms of India's foreign-aid support, and largely ineffective. Their greatest impact was on American investors and farmers, who brought pressure to bear on the U.S. Congress. Eventually the sanctions were removed, as an act of goodwill in response to India's joining the United States in the war on terror in 2001.

Pakistan, because it recognizes India as a continuing threat to its existence, does not feel secure with India's overwhelming nuclear advantage. The rise to power of the Bharatiya Janata Party as a Hindu nationalist party added to Pakistan's apprehensions. It felt compelled to answer India's test with tests of its own two weeks later.

India did not react to Pakistan's tests. Nor did it respond to Pakistan's nuclear threats during the Kargil incursion in the summer of 1999, which it repulsed with conventional arms. And it did not assert its nuclear capability in its military build-up in 2002 to stop further terrorist acts following the attempt to blow up the Parliament Buildings in New Delhi on December 13, 2001.

Both countries recognize the potential power of the rhetoric of nuclear deterrence, particularly in getting America's attention, while avoiding any circumstance for the actual use of nuclear weapons. Both realize that nuclear warfare in South Asia would be a catastrophic end of both countries. India's need for nuclear deterrence, ever since 1971, has been to defend itself not from Pakistan, but from other atomic powers, especially China.

India is concerned that U.S. nuclear policy is not committed to a workable timetable to eliminate all nuclear weapons in compliance with the Nuclear Non-Proliferation Treaty, which the United States signed in 1968. India also does not have any confidence that the United States can restrain, specifically, China's ability to destabilize South Asia by providing nuclear materials to Pakistan. And it has clearly demonstrated that it did not pre-vent Pakistan from providing nuclear know-how to other countries. In the absence of such assurance, India, for its own security, requires that it retain its nuclear testing option. In spite of immense diplomatic pressure, India, like the United States, has not signed the Comprehensive (Nuclear) Test Ban Treaty.

India's one attempt to confront its large Asian neighbor, China, with conventional arms was to settle a border dispute in 1962. This confrontation led to a humiliating rout of India's border forces. Relations with China since have been formal, and inconsequential, due in large part to a lack of interest on China's part. India cannot help feeling that its nuclear capability has been an important protection, and is reluctant to participate in any regional nuclear agreement that excludes China. Its preference would be to have all the major powers, including the United States, join in an enforceable nuclear disarmament treaty.

Ironically, the American response to India's nuclear tests did not acknowledge that U.S. policy itself contributed to India's need to acquire what its strategic planners call "credible minimum nuclear deterrence." In the absence of binding international disarmament or control over nuclear weapons development, India's security depends upon its developing sufficient second-strike capability to have a credible response to a threat of nuclear attack. Deterrence and a unilateral commitment not to make a first-strike use of nuclear arms are the two pillars of India's nuclear policy. India has signed a no-first-strike agreement with China.

The most recent step in India and the United States' dance on nuclear capability came with an agreement for the United States to provide India with nuclear fuel and technology, with certain restrictions on its use. It was initiated at a joint meeting of Prime Minister Manmohan Singh and President George W. Bush at the White House on July 18, 2005 and ratified by the U.S. Congress on December 8, 2006. It passed partly because the United States does not see India's nuclear arms capability as a threat because of its history of stable, civilian government. Also significant was the influence of the India lobby in the United States, reflecting an increasing population, now some 2 million, of professional class Indians who have migrated from India to form the wealthiest ethnic minority in the United States. But the strongest incentive was the hope that a democratic and economically expanding India would become a strategic security partner in future engagement with China.

Because of its size, and now with its increasing economic clout, India remains dominant in South Asia. Bhutan's economy is, for example, totally dependent upon Indian investment, and its foreign relations are, by longstanding treaty, handled by the government of India. Though the issue of terrorism in India is most seriously emanating from jihadis trained in Pakistan and infiltrating through Kashmir, Bangladesh and Nepal, Bhutan acted quickly at India's request to eliminate hideouts and training camps for militant insurgent groups active in Assam and Nagaland in northeastern India.

Because of the terrorism issue, relations with Pakistan and Bangladesh have been more contentious. They are both aware that India, by attacking Pakistan in 1971, determined that they are two nations instead of one. Also important, the rivers that represent the major source of water for irrigation in both of these countries originate in and are controlled by their powerful neighbor.

India remains supportive of the Sri Lankan government in its protracted war against the Tamil separatist LTTE, but is wary of giving any military support to this effort. India was the first to send naval ships for relief work in Sri Lanka, and to the Maldives and Sumatra, following the tsunami disaster in December 2004.

India continues to pursue avenues of wider economic and diplomatic cooperation. It maintains an active role in the 113-nation Non-Aligned Movement, which met in Havana, Cuba, in September 2006. It also became a full dialogue partner in the Association of Southeast Asian Nations (ASEAN) in January 1997. This status in ASEAN is shared with the United States, the European Union, Australia, Japan, and South Korea. India's admission overcame the concerns of Southeast Asian leaders that they not be drawn into such South Asian issues as the Kashmir dispute.

With its promising eeconomic growth and political stability, India is seeking recognition in the world. It is now a nuclear power. It aspires to become a permanent member of an expanded United Nations Security Council.

Afghanistan (Islamic State of Afghanistan)

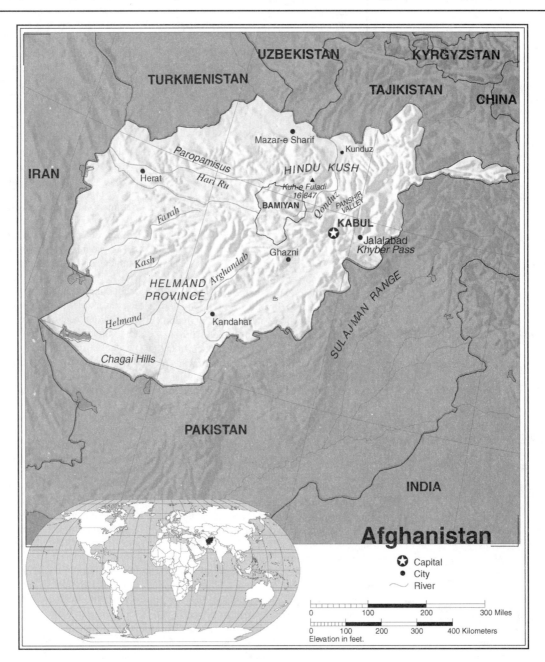

Afghanistan Statistics

GEOGRAPHY

Captial (Population): Kabul (2,206,300) (2003 est.)

PEOPLE

Population

Total: 31,056,997 (July, 2006 est.)
Annual Growth Rate: 2.67% (2006 est.)

Rural/Urban Population Ratio: 75.7/24.3 (UN 2005 est.)
Major Languages: 50% Afghan Persian or Dari (official), 35% Pashtu (official), 11% Turkic languages (primarily Uzbek and Turkman), 4% minor languages (primarily Beloch and Pashai), much bilingualism
Ethnic Makeup: 42% Pushtun (Pashtun, or Pathan); 27% Tajik; 9% Hazara; 9% Uz-

bek; 4% Aimak; 3% Turkman; 2% Baloch; 4% other
Religions: 80% Sunni Muslim; 19% Shi'a Muslim; 1% other

Health

Life Expectancy at Birth: 43.16 years (male); 43.53 years (female) (2006 est.)
Infant Mortality: 160.23/1000 live births

46

Physicians Available: 1/6,690 people
Per Capita total expenditure on Health: $26 (WHO 2003 est.)
HIV/AIDS Rate in Adults: 0.01% (2001 est.) (N/A WHO 2005 est.)

Education

Adult Literacy Rate: 36% (21% for females) (1999 est.)
Compulsory (Ages): 7–14

COMMUNICATION

Telephones: 50,000 main lines (2004)
Cell Phones: 600,000 (2004)
Daily Newspaper Circulation: 11/1,000 people
Televisions: 10 per 1,000 people
Internet Users: 25,000 (2005)

TRANSPORTATION

Highways in Miles (Kilometers): (34,789 km.) (21,000)
Railroads in Miles (Kilometers): 15.4 (24.6)
Usable Airfields: 46
Motor Vehicles in Use: 67,000

GOVERNMENT

Type: Islamic Republic
Independence Date: August 19, 1919 (from United Kingdom control over Afghan foreign affairs)
Head of State/Government: President Hamid Karzai is Chief of State, Head of Government
Political Parties: 43 parties approved by Ministry of Justice.
Suffrage: 18 years of age; universal

MILITARY

Military Expenditures (% of GDP): $122.4 million (1.7%) (2005 est.)
Current Disputes: severe internal conflicts; border disputes with Pakistan

ECONOMY

Currency ($ U.S. Equivalent): 541 afghanis = $1 U.S.
Per Capita Income/GDP: $800/$21.5 billion (2004 est.)
GDP Growth Rate: 8% (2005 est.)
Inflation Rate: 16.3% (2005 est.)
Unemployment Rate: 40% (2005 est.)

Population Below Poverty Line: 53% (2003)
Labor force by Occupation: 80% agriculture; 10% industry; 10% services
Natural Resources: natural gas; petroleum; coal; copper; talc; barite; sulphur; lead; zinc; iron ore; salt; precious and semiprecious stones
Agriculture: opium; wheat; fruits; nuts; sheepskins; lambskins; wool; mutton
Industry: small-scale production of textiles, soap, furniture, shoes, fertilizer, and cement; handwoven carpets; natural gas; coal; copper
Exports: $471 million (not including illicit exports) (primary partners United States, Pakistan, India)
Imports: $1.007 billion (primary partners Pakistan, United States, India, Germany, Turkmenistan, Russia, Kenya, Turkey) (2005)
Human Development Index (ranking): N/A (UNDP 2005)

SUGGESTED WEBSITES

http://www.afghan-web.com
http://cia.gov/cia/publications/factbook/geos/af.html
http://www.afghanistans.com

Afghanistan Country Report

Afghanistan is a rugged and mountainous country, nearly the size of Texas, divided through its center by the western extension of the high Himalayan mountain range known as the Hindu Kush. The land slopes away from this range in three different directions into jagged foothills and stark river valleys.

DEVELOPMENT

Twenty-nine years of warfare and religious repression have devastated the economy and welfare of the people. Continuing Taliban insurgency, terrorism, and corruption have hindered reconstruction. Poppy cultivation for heroin is the primary source of wealth.

Only 12 percent of this rugged land is arable; and it receives an average rainfall of less than 12 inches a year. Severe drought conditions throughout the country since 1996 have drastically reduced even that rainfall for agricultural production and decimated the livestock of the Kuchi people, Afghanistan's nomadic herders. Toward the south, the land is normally inhospitable desert, racked by seasonal sandstorms that have been known to bury entire villages. The mountainous terrain in the north has mineral resources, primarily iron ore and natural gas, which are unexploited but hard to obtain. This part of the country

experienced a severe earthquake in February 1998, which destroyed more than 20 villages, killing several thousand people. The country, once celebrated for lush oases and luxuriant gardens of fruit, nowhere today can be characterized as naturally comfortable or abundant, except in the growing of poppies.

The three-way slope of the landscape from the high ridge of the Hindu Kush divides Afghanistan into three distinct ethnic and linguistic regions. Northern Afghans are predominately Uzbeks and Turkmen, who share a strong sense of identity as well as the Turkic language with the peoples who live across their northern border in Turkmenistan, and Uzbekistan—former republics of the Soviet Union.

The Tajik and Hazara peoples, who are 25 and 19 percent of the population, live in the central section on the western slope of the Hindu Kush toward Iran. The Tajik, of ancient Persian origin, are primarily Sunni Muslim. The Hazara are Shi'a Muslims who trace their descent from the invaders of Genghis Khan from Mongolia in the thirteenth century A.D. They share a common language, Dari, which is a dialect of Farsi, the language of Iran (where Shi'a Muslims are predominant).

The Pashtuns (also called Pathans or Pushtuns) are the largest ethnic group, 12 million strong, about 42 percent of the total population. They live on the southeastern

slope of the country, and are themselves divided into tribal groups, such as the Durrani and the Ghilzai. The Durrani Pashtuns have been politically the most dominant during the past 300 years.

FREEDOM

National elections were held in 1955, but public life is still controlled by local and regional clan leaders and war lords. Millions remain as refugees in Pakistan and Iran, and NATO forces are assigned to restore order and security.

The Pashtuns are mostly Sunni Muslims, but they speak a different language, Pashto. They share this language and ethnic identity with some 16 million Pashtuns, who live across the Durand Line, established as the boundary between them by the British in 1907. The Pakistani Pushtuns provided shelter to more than three million Afghan Pashtun refugees during the Soviet occupation of Afghanistan from 1979 to 1989, and to unnumbered Taliban insurgents since their defeat in 2001. Their common identity also sustains a latent aspiration for a single Pashtun nation. It is a source of genuine threat to the unity of Pakistan that has given it urgency to be involved in Afghan affairs.

Emperors briefly united Afghan lands in the twelfth and eighteenth centuries, but neither empire lasted more than a generation. Fiercely independent local chieftains and clan leaders, sometimes called warlords, long the bearers of their clan's sense of identity, allegiance, and honor, have been the most powerful political force in the country.

Afghanistan's traditional wealth was based on its position along the silk route between China and Europe. The petty chiefs extracted from travelers significant bounty of customs fees, commissions for protection, or loot. The prominent role of drug trafficking and arms dealing in Afghan life draws on this heritage. According to United Nations reports, Afghanistan produces 92 percent of the world's supply of heroin, worth bilions of dollars annually in poppy cultivation.

MODERN HISTORY

British forces marched into Afghan territory in 1878, but soon withdrew. They left Abdur Rahman Khan as the Emir of Kabul. During his reign, from 1880 to 1901, he committed himself to "breaking down the feudal and tribal system and substituting one grand community under one law and one rule." But the many local chieftains and clan leaders, some claiming independent authority for generations, resisted. They did participate in a succession of national councils, called loya jirga, to legitimize royal claims for ceremonial leadership.

In 1953, Sadar (Prince) Mohammed Daoud Khan, then commander of the Afghan army, seized the authority of prime minister to the Emir of Kabul, Zahir Shah. He instituted many economic and social reforms, leading up to the adoption of a constitutional monarchy with a nationally elected legislative assembly in 1964. His reforming zeal allowed women to remove the chadri (the traditional heavy veil worn in public), and to participate for the first time in that election. Also participating was a newly formed, but already fractious, Communist Party.

Elections were held again in 1969, but this time the religiously and socially conservative clan leaders better understood the electoral process. They gained control of the Assembly in order to preserve their traditional authority, and effectively limited further reform.

Impatient with this resistance, Sadar Daoud overthrew the government in 1973. He sent Zahir Shah into exile and set himself up as military dictator. With both American and Soviet aid, he improved agriculture by irrigation and health services, and encouraged an industrial sector to increase the country's wealth. In 1977, he promulgated a new Constitution that outlawed all political parties except his own, including the largely urban and intellectual communist party. A new as-sembly then elected Daoud President of the Republic of Afghanistan.

The Soviet Occupation

Resistance to Daoud's nationalist reform program came from both sides of the political spectrum. From the more conservative elements in the countryside, a zealous group of militant clan leaders, armed and trained by Pakistan, arose to harass his government. Strengthened by a rising Islamic-fundamentalist zeal, they called themselves mujahideen—fighters for the faith. But Daoud was more concerned about the growing influence, encouraged by the Soviets, of the leftist, modernizing groups in Kabul. He began to purge suspected communist from the military and the bureaucracy. Within a year, army officers, threatened by this purge, assassinated him. Nur Mohammed Taraki, leader of the Peoples Democratic (communist) party, took over the reins of government.

President Taraki was assassinated in 1979, to be followed by an archrival, Hafizullah Amin.

Both leaders had adopted vigorous campaigns to break up the landholdings of the local chieftains and to increase literacy among the people. Mujahideen resistance intensified to a point where President Amin sought Soviet aid to protect his government. The Soviet government, fearing that continuing civil strife would diminish their influence and investment and threaten the security of the adjoining Soviet states to the north, sent troops in December 1979. They came, but they deposed Amin and his radical faction of the communist party, and installed Babrak Karmal to undertake a more moderate approach to socialist reform.

HEALTH/WELFARE

Because of warfare and insurgency, public services are very limited. The traditional repression of women also contributes to the lack of human resource development in health and education.

Forces of resistance in the countryside intensified in their opposition to foreign intervention in addition to the reforms seeking centralization, industrialization, and modernization. In the face of Soviet military repression, more than 3 million Pashtuns crossed the border into Baluchistan and the Northwest Frontier Province of Pakistan. The affluent established residences in Peshawar and Quetta. The vast majority moved into hastily constructed refugee camps. Another 2 million fled across the western border into Iran. Having gathered their families into the safety of camps across the border, supplied by Pakistani, Iranian, Arabic, and U.S. military and logistical support, they began to fight back as holy adversaries (mujahideen).

This incursion of Soviet military forces in 1979 also intensified the Cold War competition between the United States and the Soviet Union, which transformed Afghanistan into a proxy international battlefield. During their years of occupation, the Soviets increased their military strength to 120,000 troops. Increasing forces on both sides, armed with advanced weaponry, ravaged the countryside. Twelve thousand of 22,000 villages and more than 2,000 schools were destroyed, and 1 million Afghans and 13,000 Soviet soldiers were killed.

The Soviet Withdrawal

In 1986, President Babrak Karmal resigned and was replaced by Dr. Muhammed Najibullah. In 1988, the leaders of seven mujahideen groups joined in Pakistan to form an interim government in exile. Faced with this resistance, the Soviet Union became unwilling to sustain the losses of an intensifying military stalemate. In 1989, it withdrew its forces, and in 1991, agreed with the United States for both to stop arming the warring factions in Afghanistan.

Lack of cohesion—religious, ethnic, and military—among the mujahideen hampered their attempts to overthrow the Kabul government for three years after the Soviet troops departed. President Najibullah offered to form a joint government with them, but they could only agree that they did not want to share any part of a new government with the Communists.

In March 1992, Najibullah's army overthrew him, and mujahideen forces, under the command of Ahmad Shah Masood, a Tajik from Panshir, overtook the city of Kabul. Their victory was followed by a loya jirga, "national council," to elect Burhanuddin Rabbani, a Tajik, as interim president and draw up a new Constitution for nationwide elections to be held in 1994. But the rivalry among the majuhideen leaders, particularly between Rabbani and Gulbuddin Hekmatyar, a Ghilzai Pashtun, led to intense fighting in Kabul and a further collapse of civil order throughout the country. The periodic assaults and bombings among rival mujahideen parties seeking control of the city reduced much of it to rubble.

In 1993, a group of Pashtun religious students called the Taliban ("seekers of religious knowledge") from the southern city of Kandahar rose up in indignation against the militancy and corruption of the mujahideen. Their reforming fervor spread rapidly among a people weary of uncontrolled violence, fear, and destruction.

(UNHCR/16046/A. Hollmann)

Millions of refugees who fled to Pakistan and Iran during the Soviet occupation of Afghanistan were reluctant to return to Afghanistan. This was due, in no small part, to the constant fighting among the mujahideen and then to problems with the Taliban. Women and children are particularly vulnerable groups of refugees.

ACHIEVEMENTS

National elections for president were held in 2004, and for national and regional legislators in 2005. Given the continuing devastation and lack of security, the greatest achievement may simply be their survival.

The Taliban became a formidable force, supplied by arms and logistics from Pakistan, manpower from local clan militias, war orphans from Islamic parochial schools called madrasas, religious volunteers (jihadis) from many countries, and financial support and training from al Qaeda. By the fall of 1996, they controlled the southern two-thirds of the country. Then they drove the mujahideen out of Kabul. They established a reign of reactionary religious terror in a city that has aspired for so long to become modern.

Their reforming zeal countenanced many human rights abuses. Most oppressed were women, particularly widows, who were deprived of jobs, humanitarian aid, and education. By 1999, Taliban forces controlled 95 percent of the country. Only a small vestige of the anti-Soviet resistance called the Northern Alliance held out in the northeastern corner of the country.

The Soviet incursion, the deadly fighting among the mujahideen and the rise of Taliban subjected the Afghan people to the ravages and repression of more than twenty years of war. Many who became refugees during the Soviet occupation, because of the destruction of their homes, the depletion and mining of their fields, and, after October 7, 2001, fear of American bombing, remained in squalid refugee camps. Women especially hesitated to return, because of fear of repression in their homelands by the Islamic fundamentalist fervor of both the mujahideen and Taliban leaders. By the end of 2001, there were still 2.2 million refugees in Pakistan, 2.4 million in Iran and around 1 million in refugee camps in Afghanistan itself.

Restoration

Following the terrorist attacks in the United States on September 11, 2001, an international coalition led by the United States joined forces with the Northern Alliance to oust the Taliban from Kabul. Pakistan withdrew its support to the Taliban. And al Qaeda training camps were dismantled. The coalition victory created a new beginning toward political stability and reconstruction in the country. The Tajik leaders of the Northern Alliance were initially the strongest: former president Burhanuddin Rabbani, and Muhammad Fahim and Yunus Qanuni, both successors to Ahmad Shah Masood, military commander of the Northern Alliance before his assassination on September 10, 2001.

An impressive list of regional leaders emerged to share in this effort. Some had joined the mujahideen in opposition to Sardar Daoud's reforms in the 1970s. All had a part in the violent in-fighting following the Soviet withdrawal, based on their identification with the many diverse ethnic and tribal groups in the country. The most powerful of them retained their own private militias, and many were sustained by foreign aid and a flourishing trade in heroin production.

The United Nations initiated the rebuilding of Afghanistan by gathering representative leadership from across the country in Bonn, Germany, in December 2001. The intent of the Bonn meeting was to establish institutions of government with authority separate from that of the indigenous leaders. Despite the good intentions, according to Barnett Rubin, "the result was an Afghan government created at Bonn that rested on a power base of warlords."

An international peacekeeping force (ISAF) was set up first to establish security in Kabul. It began with 8,000 soldiers from over 30 countries, but had limited reach outside the city. Then in June 2002, a loya jirga, a council of 1,500 selected leaders, convened in Kabul on terms set under United Nations auspices in Bonn. This council created a transitional government, and elected as interim president, Hamid Karzai, a Pashtun with strong American support. Because he did not have an indigenous political base, he seemed most suited to hold the office above the taint and fray of traditional local clan power struggles and to attract international contributions for rehabilitation.

In October 2004, Hamid Karzai was elected president, with 55.4 percent of the vote. But his largest support came mostly from Kabul, where the evidence of foreign investment was most visible, particularly in the person of the U.S. ambassador, Zalmay Khalilzad, (known in Kabul as "the Viceroy"). Karzai also had support from Pashtun regions to the south, where local leaders and the Taliban have retained control. The other candidates also lined up with their ethnic bases. Yunus Qanuni, a Tajik, briefly interior minister and head of intelligence in the interim government, won 16.3 percent of the vote, mostly from the Northern Alliance strongholds in the north-central region of the country. He was subsequently elected Speaker of the Afghan Parliament. Mohammad Mohaqiq, the Hazara leader, received 11 percent from Hazara dominant districts, and 10 percent voted for Rashid Dostum, an Uzbek from the northern region. President Karzai did not appoint any of them to his cabinet.

Parliamentary elections for the Wolesi Jirga, or lower house, and Provincial elections were finally held on September 18, 2005. With the Taliban calling for a boycott, 53 percent of 12 million registered voters cast their ballot.

The results, included 68 seats, or 27 percent, for women. But overall they reaffirmed the traditional bases of power in the country. One of the first acts of the Parliament was toward reconciliation: to provide amnesty to Afghans suspected of "war crimes" during the past twenty-five years of warfare in the country.

A survey conducted a year after the elections by the Post-Conflict Reconstruction Project of the Center for Strategic and International Studies found the people less hopeful in four categories of their public life: security, justice, social well-being, and economic opportunity. Their survey concludes:

Gains have been made in education, communication, government processes, institutional capacity, roads and the private sector. Yet, the big issues from the beginning of the intervention remain: how to manage warlords and continued impunity, how to decrease poppy and drug trafficking, how to stop support for the Taliban, how to deliver electricity and revitalize the judiciary, and how to provide economic development in areas with limited access and infrastructure and serious security constrains.

Because of the horrible destruction that the terrorist attacks and the ISAF air strikes were inflicting on their homes and shops and their lives, the elders in the district of Musa Qala in Helmond Province. Negotiated in 2006 a ceasefire and withdrawal from their district of both the Taliban and the British forces sent to destroy them. This initiative became for them a sign of hope. "For four months we had fighting in Musa Qala and now we have peace. What is wrong with it, if we have peace?"

Timeline: PAST

A.D. 1747–1973
Loose tribal federation

1907
The British and Russians establish the boundaries of modern Afghanistan

1973–1978
Military dictatorship

1978–1992
Communist Party rule

1979–1989
Soviet military occupation

1980s
A mujahideen resistance is formed in Pakistan; A constitution was shaped, but the Bonn Agreement and subsequent constitution are what are in place now.

1990s
Taliban forces capture Kabul and control nearly all of the country

PRESENT

2000s
Deeming them "un-Islamic," the Taliban destroys ancient Buddhist statues

Afghanistan is invaded by forces from the international coalition against terrorism

The Taliban is forced from power; an interim government is formed

2002
Provisional government set up under terms of UN initiated 2001 Bonn Agreement. Hamid Karzai elected interim president.

2004–2005
Presidential and National Assembly elections were held. Taliban resurges. Intense conflicts with NATO forces sent to secure country.

2006–2007
Poppy cultivation grows as percentage of GDP and world heroin market, supports local clan leaders and insurgency.

Their success suggests that a people desparate for peace have the resources within themselves to seek it on their own.

Afghanistan has for too long been torn asunder by too many levels of conflict: those who hold adamantly to their traditional lifestyles in the countryside are still violently opposed to the cosmopolitan urban society in Kabul. Superimposed on this conflict have been the competing claims for democratic and socialist ideals and between fundamentalist and reform movements in Islam. These competing claims have played out within a context of long-standing animosities between ethnic and linguistic groups and rivalries and disputes among tribes, clans, and factions within parties and religious sects.

The country has also been torn between the conflicting interests of neighboring countries, especially Iran and Pakistan. And the global agendas of the United States and the Soviet Union during the final years of the Cold War introduced a whole new scale of mass destruction, arms trading, international drug dealing, and terrorist training.

War-ravaged and impoverished for years, the people of Afghanistan still seek for security and governance to lead them to social welfare and democracy.

Bangladesh (People's Republic of Bangladesh)

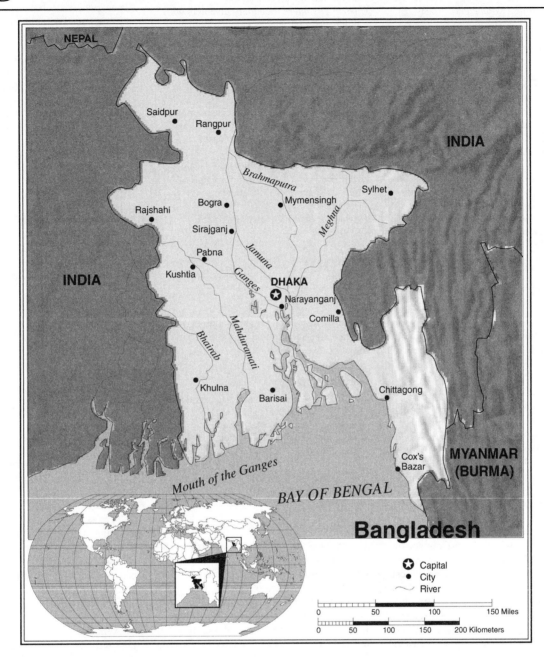

Bangladesh Statistics

GEOGRAPHY

Captial (Population): Dhaka (5,378,023)

PEOPLE

Population

Total: 147,365,352 (July, 2006 est.)
Annual Growth Rate: 2.09% (2006 est.)
Rural/Urban Population Ratio: 75/25 (UN 2005 est.)
Ethnic Makeup: 98% Bengali, 2% tribal groups and non Bengali Muslims. (1998)

Religions: 83% Muslim, 16% Hindu, 1% other (1998)

Health

Life Expectancy at Birth: 62.47 years (male), 62.45 years (female)
Infant Mortality: 60.83/1000 live births (2006 est.)
Physicians Available 1/4,759 people
Per Capita total expenditure on Health: $68 (WHO 2003 est.)
HIV/AIDS Rate in Adults: less than 0.1% (11,000) (WHO 2005 est.)

Education

Adult Literacy Rate: 43.1%; (31.8% female) (2003)
Compulsory (Ages): 6–11; free

COMMUNICATION

Telephones: 1.07 million main lines (2005)
Cell Phones: 2,781,600 (2004)
Daily Newspaper Circulation: 0.4/1,000 people
Internet Users: 300,000 (2005)

TRANSPORTATION

Highways in Miles (Kilometers): 128,926
  (239,226 km)
Railroads in Miles (Kilometers): 1,681
  (2,768 km)
Usable Airfields: 15
Motor Vehicles in Use: 227,000

GOVERNMENT

Type: parliament democracy
Independence Date: December 16, 1971
  (from West Pakistan)
Head of State/Government: President
  Iajuddin Ahmed; Prime Minister
  Zhaleda Zia
Political Parties: Bangladesh Nationalist
  Party, Awami League, Islami Oikya Jote;
  Jamaat-e-Islami, Jatiya Party (Ershad),
  Jatiya Party (Manzur).
Suffrage: universal at 18

MILITARY

Military Expenditures (% of GDP): $1.01
  billion (2005 est.) (1.8%)
Current Disputers: boundary disputers with
  India, terrorists attacks among political
  parties

ECONOMY

Currency ($ U.S. equivalent): 64.328 taka =
  $1 U.S.
Per Capita Income/GDP: purchasing power
  parity $2,100 (2005 est.)/$304.3 billion
GDP Growth Rate: 5.7% (2005 est.)
Inflation Rate: 7% (2005 et.)
Unemployment Rate: 2.5% (2005 est.)
Labor Force by Occupation: 63% agricul-
  ture, 26% services, 11% industry
  (FY 95/96)
Population Below Poverty Line: 45%
  (2004 est.)

Natural Resources: natural gas; arable land;
  timber
Agriculture: rice; jute; tea; wheat; sugar-
  cane; potatoes; tobacco; pulses; oilseeds;
  spices; fruit; beef; milk; poultry
Industry: jute; garments; textiles; food
  processing; newsprint; cement; light engi-
  neering; fertilizer; sugar
Export: $9,372 billion (2005 est.) (primary
  partners United States, Germany, United
  Kingdom, France)
Imports: $12.97 billion (2005 est.) (primary
  partners India, China, Kuwait, Singapore,
  Japan, Hong Kong)
Human Development Index (ranking): 139
  (UNDP 2005)

SUGGESTED WEBSITES

http://www.virtualbangladesh.com
http://southasia.net/Bangladesh
http://www.bangladesh.gov.bd

Bangladesh Country Report

Bangladesh, the youngest nation of South Asia, won its independence from Pakistan in 1971. It is a delta country fed by three major rivers, the Brahmaputra, the Ganges and the Maghma. They expand into 700 rivers to flow in intricate and shifting channels into the Sundarbans—tide country—leading into the Bay of Bengal. The Sundarbans is a land of sandbars and great reefs, many of which are submerged at high tide, with only treetops standing above the water. Its marshy thickets are also the home of crocodiles and the Royal Bengal tiger.

In the monsoon season, flooding waters frequently overflow the embankments surrounding settlements along these many rivers. The worst flood of the last century, in 1988, paralyzed the central part of the country, killing 800 people and leaving almost 30 million homeless. A single cyclone in May 1991 killed 130,000 people. Devastating flooding also occurred in 1998 and again in 2004, when 39 of the country's 64 districts where overrun with water. Natural disasters remain a constant threat to all aspects of life in Bangladesh.

More than 147 million people, nearly half the population of the United States, live in an area smaller than the state of Wisconsin, at an average rural density 2,600 per square mile.

It remains one of the poorest countries in the world; 61 percent of the urban population is below the poverty line, according to a recent Asian Development Bank survey, and over half of the total population lives on less than $1 a day. Among the poor are almost 300,000 tribal peoples isolated among the hills and jungles in the eastern regions of the country. The Lushai, Murung, and Kuki subsist as they have for thousands of years, practicing slash-and-burn agriculture and the rite of bride capture.

DEVELOPMENT

Primarily an agricultural country subject to natural disasters, political instability, and unemployment, Bangladesh has made remarkable progress in human resource development by its many NGOs. Natural gas and textiles have become the greatest producers of wealth.

Independence

The origin of Bangladesh as an independent nation began in 1905, when Lord Curzon, the British viceroy in India, attempted to divide the Colonial Province of Bengal into a predominantly Muslim East Bengal (which then included Assam) and a Hindu West Bengal. In the 1947 partition, when Pakistan became independent, a truncated yet predominantly Muslim province of East Bengal became the eastern wing of Pakistan.

East Pakistan had the larger population, but economic and political power resided in the western wing. Attempts to impose the Urdu language as the national language of Pakistan, and favoritism toward the western wing in economic development, led to student demonstrations in East Pakistan in 1952.

In 1970, in Pakistan's first popular national elections, the Awami League Party in East Pakistan, led by Sheikh Mujibur Rahman, won a majority of seats in the national legislature. But the political leaders in West Pakistan refused to accept Mujibur Rahman as prime minister. In response to this state-

mate, President Yahya Khan suspended the Assembly. The people of East Bengal rioted in protest. President Yahya Khan tried to suppress this public outcry by military force.

During eight months of military repression, the Pakistan army killed many hundreds of thousands, and eight million people fled as refugees into India.

In December 1971, India attacked Pakistan in support of the Bengali resistance movement to free the people of East Bengal from Pakistan military rule. Mujibur Rahman then became prime minister of the new nation of Bangladesh.

Almost all citizens of Bangladesh shared a common Bengali ethnic and language identity, and most are Sunni Muslims. With so much upon which to build a democratic nation—language, religion, culture, and a successful fight for its independence—the country still struggles to achieve political stability.

Although he was a popular leader, Mujibur Rahman did not prove an effective administrator in the face of severe overpopulation, poverty, famine, and natural disasters. His increasingly authoritarian rule as an executive president led to a military coup in 1975, in which he and most of his family were killed.

FREEDOM

Elections are held on a regular basis and 30 percent of local government offices are reserved for women. Rivalry between the two major parties, corruption, and license for terrorism have led to instability on the national level.

General Ziaur Rahman, army chief of staff, took over as martial-law administrator with the intent to lead the country back to democracy. He created his own political party, the Bangladesh Nationalist Party (BNP), and encouraged others to participate in national elections to elect 300 members to the national Legislature. (Thirty women members were subsequently to be elected by vote of the Legislature under a constitutional provision that expired in 2001.) He also developed an economic policy to increase agricultural production, education and health care.

Zia retained the independent executive presidency established by Mujibur Rahman, and won the presidential election held in 1978. In the legislative elections in 1979, his BNP won two-thirds of the seats in the national Legislature.

In 1981, dissident military officers assassinated General Zia. The political chaos following his death again led to martial law in 1982, under General Hussain Muhammed Ershad, chief of staff of the army.

Ershad continued General Zia's policies of economic development and social reform. But he instituted a National Security Advisory Council to increase military participation in government. This move caused political unrest among the people that led to his downfall. Although he won the presidential election in 1986, his party won only a very slim and widely questioned majority in the legislative elections that followed.

Two new leaders, each related to Ershad's more charismatic predecessors, came onto the national scene in protest against the 1986 election. Begum Khaleda Zia, the widow of General Zia, became head of the Bangladesh National Party (BNP) after her husband's death. Sheikh Hasina Wajed, the sole surviving daughter of Mujibur Rahman, led the Awami League (AWL). The rivalry and mistrust between these two has unsettled any political agenda for the country ever since.

President Ershad first attempted to suppress their protest. Then, in December 1987, he dissolved the Legislature and called for new elections. The BNP and the Awami League together boycotted these elections. Voter turnout was very small as public opinion began to turn against Ershad. In 1990, in response to public outcry, he resigned. Justice Shahabuddin Ahmed of the Supreme Court was appointed acting president.

National elections to restore the government were held in February 1991. Begum Zia was elected president, and her BNP, polling 31 percent of the votes, won 140 seats in the 300-member legislature. The Awami League, although gaining almost the same percentage of the popular vote, came in a distant second, with 84 seats.

A national referendum in September 1991, supported by both the BNP and the Awami League, placed executive power in the hands of the prime minister of the national legislature. Begum Zia then stepped down as president. Because her party did not command a majority of legislature seats, she needed the support of the Jamaat-e-Islami, a conservative Islamic party, to win the prime minister's office. Though a small minority, it persuaded Begum Zia's government to condemn a young doctor-turned-author, Dr. Taslima Nasreen, for alleged "blasphemy" in her popular novel, Lajja. The government arrested Nasreen for "outrage[ing] the religious feelings" of the people of Bangladesh. Having posted bail, Dr. Nasreen escaped to live in exile in Sweden, Germany, and the United States. This episode raised international concern, not only for the right of freedom of expression, but also as an indicator of the political strength of religious fundamentalism in Bangladesh.

HEALTH/WELFARE

Through the activity of many NGOs, Bangladesh has made significant gains in literacy, health care, and reduction in birth rate from 3.3% to 2% since 1971.

The close split of the popular vote between the two leading parties in the 1991 elections led Sheikh Hasina's Awami League to protest the outcome, and call for new elections. In 1994, the party boycotted the Legislature, and legislative activity was stymied. New elections were held in June 1996. The BNP's standing was reduced from 140 to 116 seats, and the Jamaat-e-Islami to three seats. With the support of what remained of General Ershad's party, Sheikh Hasina garnered the votes to become prime minister. This time it became the BNP's turn to boycott the Legislature.

The new Legislature still enacted an important initiative for women in government. This law reserves for them three of the 10 directly elected seats in the 4,298 local councils that form the lowest tier of government in Bangladesh. Elections for these councils started in December 1997, and 14,500 women were elected to council seats. This was an important step toward increasing the place of women in a country where traditional religious teachings and social custom have accepted their repression.

Sheikh Hasina's Awami League government was able to complete a full five-year term in control of the national legislature. But her liberalizing initiatives to establish modern secular rule in Bangladesh and build its relationship with India came to a sudden and surprising end in the elections of October 2001. Begum Zia's BNP campaigned on a pro-Islamic and isolationist platform, in alliance with three other conservative parties in order not to split their votes. Their alliance came to power in a landslide victory with 191 seats for the BNP, with 46 percent of the popular vote, and 18 for the Jamaat-e-Islami. The Awami League, with 42 percent of the vote, won only 62 seats. There were many indigenous causes for the rout of the Awami League. But the terrorist attacks in the United States the month before stirred Islamic fundamentalist fervor in Bangladesh, as they did in many places in the Islamic world.

ACHIEVEMENTS

Professor Yunus received the Nobel Peace Prize in 2006 for creating microcredit opportunities for the poor.

Islamist militancy increased in the country. Sixteen major terrorist incidents led up to grenade attacks on Awami League political rallies in Dhaka on August 21, 2004, and in Habiganj on January 27, 2005. On August 17, 2005, five hundred bombs exploded simultaneously across the country. Rioting broke out in the streets, followed by strikes in protest called by the Awami League. The BNP denied any involvement in any of these incidents. It did arrest two high-profile terrorists in March 2006. But it does not appear committed to reining in the forces of religious and sectarian violence as it seeks continuing Islamic fundamentalist support in the next national elections.

The elections were set for January 21, 2007, and a caretaker government installed 90 days prior, in October, in a process to assure free and fair voting. The Awami League, now part of a 14 party alliance, immediately protested the composition of the interim government as being pro-BNP and contested some 14 million false names that appear on the voter rolls. The alliance carried out a series of crippling transportation strikes throughout the country. The election, when it happens, will be a referendum on the role of Islamist terrorism in the country.

Outside of government channels, the picture is more positive. The people by themselves have shown outstanding initiative in human development to meet the challenges of population growth and rural poverty through grassroots, voluntary organizations. Such non-government organizations (NGOs) as the Bangladesh Rural Advancement Committee and Proshika, which encourages organic sustainable farming, have built schools, improved farming practices, and reduced the average number of births per Bangladeshi woman from more than seven in 1975 to 3.15 today. Human resource development indicators are improving.

The Grameen Bank is another important initiative to improve the plight of the poor from the ground up. Founded in the 1970s by economics professor Mohammed Yunus, it provides small loans to poor people without collateral. It has been successful in creating credit for more than 6 million borrowers, 96 percent of whom are women, and recovers more than $5 billion a year. The bank also trains its borrowers in nutrition, management skills, public health and family planning. Its effectiveness among the impoverished in Bangladesh has established it as a model for economic empowerment of the poor in many other countries. Professor Yunus received the Nobel Peace Prize in 2006 for his work to alleviate poverty with the Grameen Bank microcredit initiative.

CHALLENGES

Because of its large and growing population, its limited resources, unemployment, corruption and a succession of natural disasters, Bangladesh has struggled since its independence to achieve prosperity for its people. Cyclones and floods severely reduce agricultural production, which is barely sufficient to feed Bangladesh's population even in good times. The floods in the summer of 2004 left 35 million with severe losses estimated at $7 billion.

Timeline: PAST

A.D. 1757–1947
British control over Bengal

1947–1971
East Pakistan

1971
The birth of Bangladesh

1972–1975
Mujibur Rahman's presidential rule

1974
Severe flooding causes 400,000 deaths

1975–1989
Martial law

1990s
In 1991, a cyclone causes 130,000 deaths; flooding in 1998 kills 800 and leaves 30 million homeless; Bangladesh returns to parliamentary government

PRESENT

2000s
Women seek more reserved seats in the national Legislature

Bangladeshis continue to seek grassroot solutions to their country's severe economic and social problems

2004
Almost 2/3 of country flooded by monsoon, causing $7 billion in damage

2005
Professor Mahammad Yunus wins Nobel Peace Price for providing microcredit to the poor.

2006
Elections for National Assembly held.

Natural gas is the country's greatest potential resource, with reserves sufficient to provide for its energy needs. But without other natural resources to broaden its industrial base and create new employment, and with a decline in the world market for their jute and textiles, the country's largest exports, a sustained GDP growth of 5.3 percent is difficult to maintain. In earlier times, many skilled workers found jobs in the Persian Gulf region. In 1998–9, they sent back to Bangladesh $1.71 billion in remittances. But recent unrest there has led to their return to flood the country's already overcrowded job market.

With continued grants of humanitarian and economic aid, and with hopes for a stable, democratically elected leadership, a resilient and responsive people remain committed to providing education, health care, meaningful employment, and prosperity for all in their nation.

Bhutan (Kingdom of Bhutan)

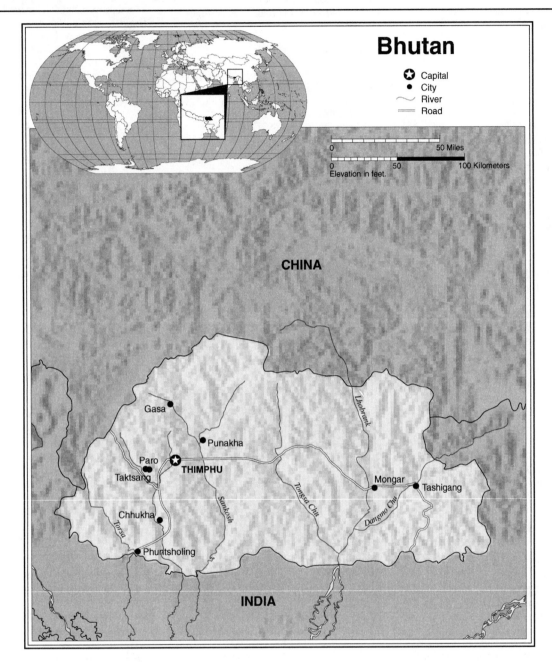

Bhutan Statistics

GEOGRAPHY

Captial (Population): Thimphu (60,200)

PEOPLE

Population

Total: 2,279,723 (July, 2006 est.); some
  estimates as low as 810, 000
Annual Growth Rate: 2.1% (2006 est.)
Rural/Urban Population Ratio: 90.9/9.1
  (UN 2005 est.)

Health

Life Expectancy at Birth: 55.02 years
  (male); 54.53 years (female) (2006 est.)
Infant Mortality: 98.41/1000 live births
  (2006 est.)
Per capita total expenditure on Health: $59
  (WHO 2003 est.)
Physicians Available: 1/8,000 people
HIV/AIDS Rate in Adults: less than 0.1%
  (WHO 2005 est.)

Education

Adult Literacy Rate: 47%
Compulsory (Ages): none

COMMUNICATION

Telephones: 30,300 main lines (2005)
Cell Phones: 22,000 (2005)
Televisions: 182/1,000 people
Internet Users: 20,000 (2003)

TRANSPORTATION

Highways in Miles (Kilometers): 2,292
(8,050 km)
Railroads in Miles (Kilometers): none
Usable Airfields: 2

GOVERNMENT

Type: monarchy; special treaty relationship
with India
Independence Date: August 8, 1949 (from
India)
Head of State/Government: King Jigme
Singye Wangchuk; Chairman of Council
of Ministers Sangay Ngedup
Political Parties: none legal
Suffrage: each family has one vote in
village-level elections

MILITARY

Military Expenditures (% of GDP): $8.29
million (2005 est.)/(1%)
Current Disputes: internal unrest; refugee
issues

ECONOMY

Currency ($ U.S. equivalent): 44.101 ngul-
trum = $1 U.S. (2005)
Per Capita Income/GDP: $1,400 (2003
est.)/$2.9 billion
GDP Growth Rate: 5.3% (2003 est.)
Inflation Rate 3% (2002 est.)
Labor Force by Occupation: 93% agricul
hture, 5% services, 2% industry
Natural Resources timber: hydropower;
gypsum; calcium carbide

Agriculture: rice; corn; root crops; citrus
fruit; food grains; dairy products; eggs
Industry: cement; wood products; distilling;
food processing; calcium carbide; tourism
Exports: $154 million (primary partners
Japan, Germany, France, South Korea,
United States, Thailand, Italy) (2005)
Imports: $196 million (primary partners
Hong Kong, Mexico, France) (2005)
Human Development Index (ranking): 134
(UNDP 2005)

SUGGESTED WEBSITES

http://www.cia.gov/cia/publications/factbook/
geos.bt.html
http://southasia.net/Bhutan
http://www.bhutannewsonline.com
http://www.hrw.org/nepal-bhutan

Bhutan Country Report

Bhutan is a small Himalayan country, about the size of Vermont and New Hampshire combined. Its highest point reaches 24,783 feet along the border with Tibet. The land falls through a series of cascading river valleys down the southern slopes toward Bangladesh, on the eastern side of the subcontinent. Its southern border—barely 100 miles away, yet more than 24,000 feet below—touches the edge of the Brahmaputra River plain, through narrow, humid, gorgelike valleys of bamboo jungle.

Most of the people in the country (population estimates vary widely, from 810,000 to more than 2.28 million) live in the broader, fertile, pine-filled valleys of the central region, from 5,000 to 9,000 feet above sea level. Isolated by its terrain and eager to preserve its Mahayana Buddhist heritage, the country has moved very cautiously into the modern world.

DEVELOPMENT

Ninety-three percent of Bhutan's labor force is in self-sufficient agriculture. Concerned to preserve its Buddhist heritage, it is cautiously developing a tourist industry and, with India's help, expanding its vast hydroelectric potential.

Culturally, religiously and linguistically, 65 percent of the people of Bhutan are closely related to Tibet. Dzongkha, the most common language spoken in the northern and western regions, is the official language of the country. Other Tibetan dialects are spoken in the eastern regions, where the people are more closely related by custom to Assam. The remaining 35 percent are Nepali and Hindi-speaking peoples, most of whom have

(Courtesy of Richard Ishida/www.w3.org/
People/Ishida01)
The Tiger's Lair (Taktsang) Hermitage.

recently migrated into the country as laborers, and have settled in the southern region closest to India. Several thousand Tibetans fled into Bhutan following the Chinese takeover of their country and subsequent repressions during the 1950's.

The Mahayana Buddhist religion in Bhutan—as distinct from the Theravada Buddhism of Sri Lanka and Southeast Asia—also traces its origin to the earliest tradition of Buddhism in Tibet: the Nyingmapa school of the Red Hat sect. Important monasteries,

as at Taktsang, celebrate the learned Indian monk Padma Sambhava, who introduced Buddhism into Tibet in the eighth century. He is described as the heroic Guru Rimpoche ("Precious Teacher") coming on a flying tiger to drive the forces of evil out of Druk Yul, "Land of the Thunder Dragon."

A Tibetan lama, Shabdrung Ngawang Namgyal, brought the isolated valley peoples under a single authority in the 1600s. He also established a tradition of religious leadership sustained by identifying the embodiment of his mind reincarnation (Dharma Raja) through successive generations. The religious authority of his Dharma Raja was finally subsumed during the 1930s under the temporal authority of a dynastic monarchy that was established in 1907 under British colonial rule.

THE MONARCHY

British military forces advanced into Bhutan in 1864 to repel Tibetan and Chinese claims of control over the Himalayan Mountains. In gratitude for his help in their successful attack of Tibet in 1903, the British rewarded Ugyen Wangchuk, then feudal lord (Penlop) of the north-central district of Tongsa, by assisting him to become Druk Gyalpo, the hereditary "Dragon King" of Bhutan, in 1907.

The British continued to oversee the external affairs of the country, but allowed the new king to rule independently in domestic matters. In 1949, with the end of the British Raj, Bhutan extended this agreement "to be guided in regard to its foreign relations" to the government of India. India has allowed Bhutan latitude in establishing international agreements, including support of Bhutan's admission to the United Nations in 1971.

(Courtesy of BhutanNewsOnline.com/Bhutanonline01)
His Majesty, the King Jigme Singye Wangchuck, and his four wives, Her Majesty Ashi Tshering Yangdon Wangchuck, Her Majesty Ashi Tshering Pem Wangchuck, Her Majesty Ashi Dorji Wangmo Wangchuck, and Her Majesty Ashi Sangay Choden Wangchuck, all sisters.

(Courtesy of Kaptan/Kaptan01)
His Royal Highness Dasho Jigme Khesar Namgyal Wangchuck, Crown Prince of Bhutan. He studied at Magdelen College, Oxford University, from which he was awarded M Phil in politics.

Jigme Dorji Wangchuk, grandson of Ugyen Wangchuk, instituted a number of reforms to bring his country cautiously into the modern era. To encourage more participation in government, in 1952, he established a National Assembly, the Tshoghdu. The Assembly had 151 members, 31 of whom were appointed by the king. The rest were elected by hereditary village headmen in the districts. They also served as local judges in a judicial system in which the king was the chief justice. As king, he also remained the religious head and chief executive of the country.

In 1968, the king granted the Assembly powers to limit his absolute authority. He could no longer veto legislation passed by majority vote of the Assembly. Also, by a two-thirds vote, the Assembly could force the king to abdicate. But in that case, only the next claimant in his hereditary line could succeed him. This provision reproduces on the national level the traditional family expectation that a landholder will pass on his lands to his eldest son as soon as the heir comes of age.

Jigme Dorji Wangchuk's reforms also included the elimination of serfdom by granting public lands to landless servants. But in order not to disrupt traditional social patterns and create unemployment, he did not break up large private landholdings.

Jigme Singye Wangchuk, then 17 years old, succeeded Jigme Dorji Wangchuk upon his death in 1972. He continued his father's policies of gradual reform. During the summer of 1998, he expanded the powers of the National Assembly by replacing his royal Council of Ministers with a cabinet elected by the Assembly. It was to be "vested with full executive powers to provide efficient and effective governance of our country." The Assembly, with some reluctance, carried out his wishes by electing a cabinet from a list of candidates that he provided.

In 2002, the government began a process to elect its village headmen by popular vote rather than hereditary appointment. In 2005, in his National Day Address, King Jigme Singye Wangchuk announced "that the first national election to elect a government under a system of parliamentary democracy will take place in 2008." At the same time, he announced that he will delegate his kingship to his eldest son, Jigme Khesar Namgyel Wangshuk, who is now 25, before 2008.

A draft constitution is being prepared for a referendum in 2007, in anticipation of the national elections. Its provisions now require a graduate degree for all candidates for seats in the new parliament. The King is leading the country toward the beginnings of democracy, while at the same time is concerned to maintain stability of the government.

ECONOMIC DEVELOPMENT

India has been the largest investor in the development of Bhutan's economy. In the face of Chinese threats of invasion over border disputes during the 1950s, the Indian government built a road from Bhutan's southern border to the capital, Thimphu. It took 112 miles of winding roadway to cover a straight-line distance of 45 miles. In 1996, India began a project to extend this roadway into eastern Bhutan.

With India's help, Bhutan has also increased the country's energy potential. The largest of six hydroelectric generators, the 336-megawatt Chuka Hydroelectric Project, financed by the Indian government, was completed in 1987, to export electricity to India. It now produces over 35 percent of Bhutan's annual revenue. The 1,020-megawatt Tala Hydroelectric Project, started in 1997, began production in 2006. India is providing 60 percent of the cost and technical assistance for this project. Another 1,000-megawatt project is in the works.

The importance of this relationship with India was affirmed by Bhutan's response to India's request in 2004 to remove camps set up within its borders by insurgents from Assam and Nagaland. The Royal Bhutan Army destroyed 30 camps in a swift military operation.

THE CHALLENGE OF MODERNIZATION

Bhutan has extensive forestry reserves that remain virtually unexploited. Twenty percent of the country has been set aside for preservation. The Royal Manas National Park, a 165-square-mile sanctuary established along its southern border, is designed to protect the natural wildlife of South Asia. Many of the species there are endangered. Tourism in this incredibly beautiful natural environment is being developed on a "low-volume and high-value" policy to develop its economic potential so as not to undermine the traditional Buddhist life of its people, and to maintain its natural preserve.

The development of the human resources of the country has also taken a measured pace. Canadian Jesuit Father William Mackey has led the development of the nation's educational system to provide 180 schools and a national college. Still, only a small percentage of school-age children attend, and the adult literacy rate is estimated at 47 percent, the lowest in Asia.

Health services are also meager; the expectation is that the family unit will remain the primary source of social welfare. The annual birth rate is a significant 2 percent, but the level of infant mortality is also high. The average life expectancy among the Bhutanese people is estimated to be 55 years.

Immigration has presented another challenge of modernization to the values of its rich natural and religious heritage. Most of the work force of Bhutan is employed in subsistence farming on the 16 percent of the land that is available for cultivation and pasture. Because this sector is self-sufficient, the country has had to import workers from neighboring Nepal and India to provide the labor needed to develop its industry. Their migration has challenged the country's efforts to preserve a national identity out of the exclusive culture of the dominant Buddhist community. To protect this identity, the government passed a law in 1985 to deny citizenship to all who could not claim legal residency before 1958.

A census taken in 1987 to enforce this exclusive nationalistic policy stirred political unrest among the Nepalis living in the southern part of the country, which led to terrorist attacks on schools and other public buildings. Government deportations in response moved eighty-five thousand people out of Bhutan into refugee camps set up by the United Nations High Commission on Refugees in the eastern part of Nepal.

After thirteen futile attempts to resolve the issue, in 2001, the governments of Bhutan and Nepal agreed to conduct a pilot screening of 12,000 refugees residing in one of the camps in Nepal. The Bhutan representatives divided these refugees into four categories. Only 2.5 percent of them were determined to be bona fide citizens eligible for repatriation to Bhutan. Those assigned to Category II (70 percent) were described as "voluntarily" migrated from Bhutan more than a decade ago. In order to return, they would be required to apply for citizenship. The requirements for readmission include a two-year probationary delay and proof of fluency in the Dzonkha language of northern Bhutan.

Screening began in a second refugee camp. But bilateral talks in 2003 failed to resolve issues of screening and of rights and security of those readmitted. The plight of the discouraged and restive 105,000 refugees remaining in seven camps in Nepal continues to challenge Bhutan's traditional values in the modern world.

Within Bhutan, increasing interaction with western lifestyles introduced by satellite television and the Internet is also changing attitudes and expectations among the youth. As a traditional and cautious Bhutan seeks to become more democratic and developed, an enlightened role of the king holds the greatest promise for resolving the cultural and political tensions created by the modernization of his country.

ACHIEVEMENTS

Twenty percent of the country has been set aside for the preservation of its vast forest and wildlife reserves. In keeping with its Buddhist heritage, it seeks to achieve as a nation increase in Gross Domestic Happiness, rather than GDProductivity.

Timeline: PAST

A.D. 1616–1950
Dharma Raja of Tibetan lamas

1907
Tongsa Penlop becomes hereditary king

1910–1947
British control over Bhutan's external affairs

1949
Indian control over Bhutan's external affairs begins

1953
A constitutional monarchy is established; the national Assembly has power to limit authority of king

1972
Jigme Singe Wangohuk becomes king

1980s
The Citizenship Act was enacted to limit citizenship to Nepali migrants. Unrest led to flight and deportation of 85,000 refugees to camps in eastern Nepal.

Building of hydroelectric power and limited tourism begin to contribute to country's economic growth.

1990s
Many Nepali immigrants are denied citizenship; demonstrators protest government policies toward Nepalis

PRESENT

2000s
Gradual government reforms leading to a parliamentary democracy begin.

Attempts to repatriate Nepali refugees from camps in eastern Nepal stall.

Maldives   (Republic of Maldives)

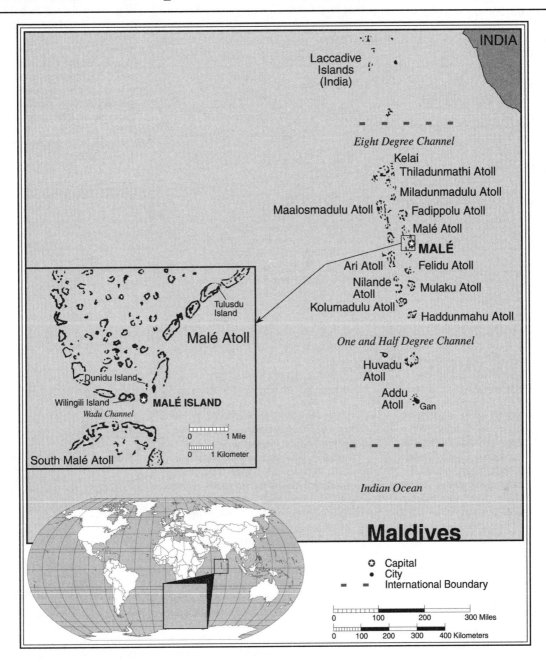

Maldives Statistics

GEOGRAPHY

Area in Square Miles (Kilometers): 186 (300) (about 1 1/2 times the size of Washington, D.C.)
Capital (Population): Male (81,600)
Environmental Concerns: depletion of freshwater aquifers; global warming and sea-level rise; coral-reef bleaching
Geographical Features: flat, with white sandy beaches
Climate: tropical; hot; humid; monsoon

PEOPLE

Population

Total: 359,008 (July, 2006 est.)
Annual Growth Rate: 2.78% (2006 est.)
Rural/Urban Population Ratio: 70.3/29.7 (UN 2005 est.)
Major Languages: Maldivian Dhivehi; English is spoken by most government officials
Ethnic Makeup: South Indians; Sinhalese; Arab
Religion: 100% Sunni Muslim

Health

Life Expectancy at Birth: 64.41 years; (63.08 years male; 65.8 years female)
Infant Mortality: 54.89/1000 live births
Per capita total expenditure on Health: $364 (WHO 2003 est.)
Physicians Available: 1/2,587 people
HIV/AIDS Rate in Adults: N/A (WHO 2005 est.)

Education

Adult Literacy Rates: 97.2.%

COMMUNICATION

Telephones: 31,500 main lines (2004)
Cell Phones: 113,200 (2004)
Daily Newspaper Circulation: 32/1,000 people
Television: 19/1,000 people
Internet Users: 19,000 (2005)

TRANSPORTATION

Highways in Miles (Kilometers): (88 km.; 66 km in Malé)
Railroads in Miles (Kilometers): none
Usable Airfields: 5

GOVERNMENT

Type: republic
Independence Date: July 26, 1965 (from the United Kingdom)
Head of State/Government: President Maumoon Abdul Gayoom is both head of state and head of government
Political Parties: registered in June, 2005: Adhaalath (Justice) Party AP, Dhivehi Rayyithunge Party DRP, Islamic Democracy Party IDP, Maldivian Democratic Party MPD
Suffrage: universal at 21

MILITARY

Military Expenditures (% of GDP): (5.5%) (2005 est.)
Current Disputes: none

ECONOMY

Currency ($ U.S. Equivalent): 12.8 rufiyaa = $1 U.S.
Per Capita Income/GDP: $3,900 / $1.25 billion (2002 est.)
GDP Growth Rate: −5.5% (2005 est.) (7.6% 1995–2004 average)
Inflation Rate: 5.6% (2005 est.)
Unemployment Rate: negligible
Labor Force by Occupation: 62% services, 20% agriculture, 18% industry (2000 est.)
Natural Resource: fish

Agriculture: fish; corn; coconuts; sweet potatoes
Industry: tourism; fish processing; shipping; boat building; coconut processing; garments; woven mats; rope; handicrafts; coral and sand mining
Exports: $123 million f.o.b. (2004 est.) (primary partners Thailand, United Kingdom, Sri Lanka, Japan, Algeria) (2005)
Imports: $567 million f.o.b. (2004 est.) (primary partners Singapore, UAE, Sri Lanka, India, Malaysia, Thailand, Bahrain) (2005)
Human Development Index (ranking): 96 (UNDP 2005)

SUGGESTED WEBSITES

http://www.maldive.com/hist/mhisto.html
http://www.cia.gov/cia/publications/factbook/geos/mv.html
http://www.undp.org/missions/maldives
http://southasia.net/Maldives/
http://www.hinduonnet.com
http://www.mv.undp.org

Maldives Country Report

Maldives is a string of 1,190 tiny tropical islands grouped into 26 atolls in the Indian Ocean about 400 miles southwest of India. The island chain stretches 510 miles north to south across the equator. Most of the islands are small, the largest being less than five square miles in area. The highest elevation is only 80 feet above sea level, but many rise barely six feet above the ocean waters. They were easily submerged under the Indian Ocean Tsunami on December 24, 2004, and more frequently by storm swells. They are fragile, remote, but enticingly beautiful.

DEVELOPMENT

Fishing and Tourism are the major industries of this nation of islands. Both were severely damaged by the 2004 tsunami. Tourism is recovering rapidly, while fishing boats and housing remain restoration issues.

Most of the islands are covered with lush scrub growth, some have coconut-palm groves, and all are surrounded with coral reefs and clear waters abundant with fish. The mean daily temperature remains at 80°F year-round. The climate is humid, especially during the monsoon season from June to August. Because of a shortage of fresh water and arable land on most of the islands, only 200 of them are inhabited. More than one fifth of the total population of 359,008 lives in the capitol city on the island of Malé, which is just 7/10 of a square mile.

The earliest inhabitants of Maldives came from south India and Sri Lanka. Remains of shrines indicate the migration of Buddhists around the second century B.C. Divehi, the prevailing language of the islands, is further evidence of early Buddhist settlement. It is derived from Pali, the classical language of Buddhism in India, from which the Sinhalese language of Sri Lanka also comes.

Because the Maldive islands lie across the maritime trade route between Africa and East Asia, Arab traders often stopped there. The arrival of an Islamic Sufi saint in 1153 A.D. led to the conversion of the people to Islam. Since then Divehi is written in Arabic script, with the addition of many Arabic and Urdu words. The Moroccan explorer Ibn Battuta visited Male in the fourteenth century, during his extensive travels through North Africa and Asia. Because of his Islamic scholarship, he was invited to stay on Malé as a judge. His accounts give a colorful description of island life at that time. Today, citizenship is restricted to Sunni Muslims, and the country's legal system is based on Shari'a, Islamic law.

Two immense global currents challenge the Maldives today: the revolution of self-determination through democracy and the rise of ocean waters by global warming.

FREEDOM

Rights of citizenship are restricted to Sunni Muslims. Although declared a democratic republic in 1968, it has slowly moved toward legislative reforms and an independent judiciary. Political parties became legal in 2005.

THE BEGINNINGS OF REPRESENTATIVE GOVERNMENT

Strongly united under the authority of a sultan (an Islamic monarch), the Maldivians remained fiercely independent through the centuries. A local leader, Bodu Muhammad Takurufanu, repulsed a brief Portuguese colonial intrusion in 1573. Maldives became a protectorate under the British crown in 1887. Even then, the Maldivian leaders did not permit British interference in local governance.

The British established a military base on the southern island of Gan during World War II and an air base in 1956. But strong anti-foreign sentiment forced the closing of the base in 1976, 14 years before the end of a 30-year lease with the British. The following year, Maldives rejected a Soviet offer to lease the base for $1 million per year.

In 1953, the sultan, Muhammad Amin Didi, declared Maldives a democratic republic, with himself as president. But the power of governance remained with an appointed "Regency Committee." In 1968, Amin Ibrahim Nasir, who had served since 1957 as prime minister in the committee, instituted a new Constitution with an elected legislature (Majlis). This body selected him as its nominee to become president of the country. The Constitution prohibited political parties to form any opposition.

During his tenure as president, Ibrahim Nasir abolished the post of prime minister and increased his presidency to quasi-sultan status. He won a second five-year term in 1973. He did not seek reelection in 1978, and was succeeded by Maumoon Abdul Gayoom.

President Gayoom was elected for six terms as the single candidate in the national referendum to approve his nomination by a majority vote of the 42-member Citizen's Majlis. Each time he received more than 90 percent of the popular vote.

HEALTH/WELFARE

The government developed an emergency rescue service able to reach 97% of the population widely dispersed among the habitable islands of the country. Its literacy (97.2%) is the highest in South Asia.

ECONOMIC DEVELOPMENT

President Gayoom's enlightened economic policies encouraged significant growth in the fishing and tourism industries. Almost half of the country's workforce is employed in fishing, mostly using traditional craft called dhonis. In the 1980s, government funds helped to construct canning and cold-storage facilities, as well as more than 200 modern fishing boats, to expand the catch—and the markets—for this valuable resource.

ACHIEVEMENTS

With substantial international help, the country has made substantive recovery from the tsunami damage. To preserve its fragile environment and its peace-loving character, it is a strong advocate for reducing global warming and making the Indian Ocean a nuclear-free zone.

In 1981, an international airport was constructed on an island near Malé to serve an increasing number of tourists. It, together with airports on the islands of Hulule and Gan, the number of tourist visitors rose to 615,000 to vacation in 87 tourist zones on isolated atolls in 2004. With continuing foreign aid, the country sustained an impressive growth rate, around 7 percent from 1995 to 2004, and the second highest per capita income in South Asia.

These industries, together with a reviving coconut crop and a modest shipping fleet, did not balance the import needs of the country, especially for food. The country received more than 20 percent of its revenue as foreign aid, and it continued to accumulate debt.

Then came the devastating tsunami. Although loss of life was not great, it destroyed 120 fishing vessels and twenty-one of the tourist zones, and left 29,000 homeless. Tourist visitors dropped by 36 percent, to 395,000 in 2005. Total damage to the islands is estimated at $470 million, more than 62 percent of its GDP. Impressive international support has helped the country to recover. Tourist centers have been rapidly rebuilt. But it will take years to restore the homes and trades of the devastated population spread through the inhabited islands.

Maldives has no institutions of higher learning, and medical facilities are limited. There are only four hospitals. But extended restoration and education programs and an emergency medical rescue service among the outlying islands rank Maldives just below Sri Lanka in the UN Human Resources Development Index. Adult literacy has grown to 97.3 percent. And the government continues to work to improve water supplies and to eliminate water-borne diseases through water purification, desalinization, and other public-health measures.

PUBLIC PROTEST FOR DEMOCRACY

Even with all of this beneficial support and growth, the people seek greater democracy. The initial government response was with acts of suppression. According to an Amnesty International report, an opposition candidate for president won 18 votes for nomination by the Majlis in 1993. He was subsequently charged with violating the Constitution and sentenced to banishment from the country for 15 years. Since 2001, five others have been detained for circulating articles critical of the government. On September 20, 2003, Evan Naseem, a political prisoner, was beaten to death in jail.

In November 1998, the Majlis amended the Constitution to guarantee citizens civil rights, along with decentralizing government administration among the many islands of the country. In 2003, it established a Human Rights Commission to look into reports of increasing prison abuses.

In August 2004, public demonstrations were held to protest the detention of political dissidents and to call for democratic reforms. The government responded by declaring a state of emergency. Hundreds of protesters were arrested, including several members of the Majlis committed to forming an opposition party peacefully, in a parliamentary process. Following parliamentary elections in January 2005, the Majlis amended the Constitution to allow for political parties. Four parties, Adhaalath (Justice) Party AP, Dhivehi Rayyithunge Party DRP, Islamic Democracy Party IDP, and Maldivian Democratic Party MPD were quickly registered.

All of these steps were not sufficient for a country impatient for political freedom. The Maldivian Democratic Party organized a political rally to be held on November 10, 2006, to push for further constitutional reforms. It was cancelled when the government threatened repressive measures on those taking part, in the name of maintaining order.

Based on his impressive record of developing economic and human resources, and in response to increasing public pressure, President Gayoom has called for Constitutional amendments to include limited terms for presidency, a strengthened parliamentary form of government, and an independent

(Courtesy of Shahee Ilyas/SI01)

Mali, the capital of Maldives, with a population of 80,000, sits on 7/10 square mile island.

Supreme Court, but all in a deliberate and orderly manner.

THE RISE OF THE OHCEAN

Because the islands offered little resistance to the tsunami on December 26, 2004, the waters simply rose about 12 feet and fell, causing fewer than 100 deaths. The force of the wave inundated most of the islands, submerging two-thirds of the capital city Malé.

And it contaminated most of the islands' groves and fresh water supplies.

But increasing population and a developing economy are having a longer-term impact on the islands' limited resources and fragile environment. The daily use of fresh water is drawing upon the aquifers faster than the annual rainfall replenishes the supply. And increasing human contamination threatens what water is available.

More critical is salt-water intrusion due to the breakdown of the protective corral reefs and

the rise in the level of the ocean through global warming. To restrain the short-term impact, the government is building an expensive, six-foot retaining wall around parts of the island of Malé, paid for by the Japanese government, with expensive restoration costs attached. The long-term outlook is overwhelming.

Maldives calls for an increasing international concern for the preservation of the global environment upon which its survival depends.

Nepal (Kingdom of Nepal)

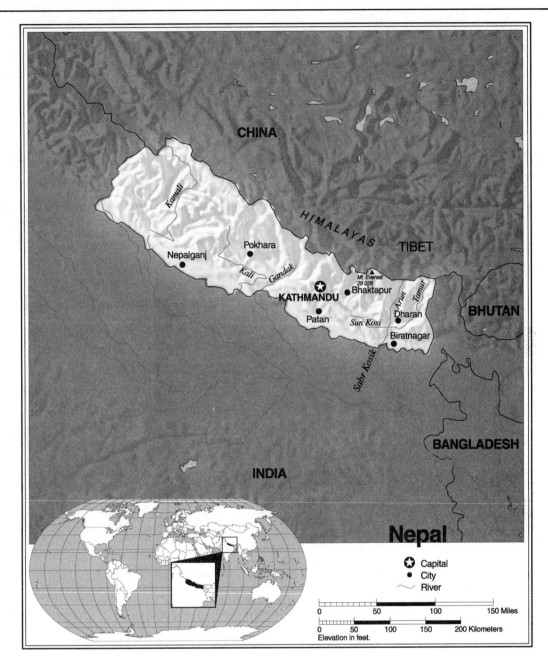

Nepal Statistics

GEOGRAPHY

Area in Square Miles (Kilometers): 56,812 sq. mi. (147,181 sq. km.)

Capital (Population): Kathmandu (1,203,100 metro area, 729,000 city proper)

Environmental Concerns: widespread defor- estation; wildlife conservation; water and air pollution

Geographical Features: flat river plain in south; central hills; rugged Himalayas in the north: landlocked

Climate: cool summers and severe winters in the north; subtropical in the south

PEOPLE

Population

Total: 28,287,147 (July, 2006 est.)

Annual Growth Rate: 2.17% (2006 est.)

Rural/Urban Population Ratio: 84.2/15.8 (UN 2005 est.)

Major Languages: Nepali; numerous other languages and dialects; English

Ethnic Makeup: 15.5% Chhettri, 12.5% Brahman-Hill, 7% Magar, 6.6% Tharu, 5.5% Tamang, 5.4% Newar, 4.2% Muslim, 3.9% Kami, 3.9% Yadav, 32.7% other (Gurung, Rai, Lumbu, Sherpa, and many smaller groups) (2001 census)

Religions: 80.6% Hindu, 10.7% Buddhist, 4.2% Muslim. 3.6% Kirant, other 0.9% (2001 census)

Health

Life Expectancy at Birth: 60.43 years
(male), 59,91 years (female) (2006 est.)
Infant Mortality: 65.32/1000 live births
Per capita total expenditure on Health: $64
(WHO 2003 est.)
Physicians Available: 1/15,777 people
HIV/AIDS Rate in Adults: 0.5% (2001 est.)

Education

Adult Literacy Rate: 48.6% (34.9% female)
(2000–2004 est.)
Compulsory (Ages): 6–11; free

COMMUNICATION

Telephones: 417,900 main lines (2004)
Cell Phones: 116,800 (2004)
Daily Newspaper Circulation: 8/1,000
people
Televisions: 12/1,000 people
Internet Users: 175,000 (2005)

TRANSPORTATION

Highways in Miles (Kilometers): 8,198
(15,905 km)
Railroads in Miles (Kilometers): 36 (59 km)
Usable Airfields: 48

GOVERNMENT

Type: parliamentary democracy and
contitutional monarchy
Independence Date: 1768 (unified)
Head of State/Government: King Gyanendra
Bir Bikram Shah; Prime Minister Girija
Prasad Koirala
Political Parties: Communist Party of
Nepal/Unified Marxist Leninist Party;
Nepali Congress Party; National
Democratic Party; Nepal Sadbhavana
(Goodwill) Party; Nepal Workers and
Peasants Party; others
Suffrage: universal at 18

MILITARY

Military Expenditures (% of GDP): $104.9
million (2.5%) (2005)
Current Disputes: dispute over Bhutanese
refugees in Nepal

ECONOMY

Currency ($ U.S. equivalent): 71,386 rupees
= $1 U.S. (2005)
Per Capita Income/GDP: $1,500 / $42.26
billion (2005 est.)

GDP Growth Rate: 2.5% (2005 est.)
Inflation Rate: 7.8% (October, 2005 est.)
Unemployment Rate: 42% (2004 est.)
Labor Force by Occupation: 76%
agriculture, 18% services, 6% industry
Population Below Poverty Line: 31%
(2003–2004)
Natural Resources: quartz; timber; water;
scenic beauty; hydropower; lignite;
copper; cobalt; iron ore
Agriculture: rice; corn; wheat; sugarcane;
root crops; milk; water buffalo meat
Industry: carpets; textiles; rice, jute, sugar,
and oilseed mills; cigarettes; tourism;
cement and brick production
Exports: $822 million f.o.b. (2005 est.)
(primary partners India, United States,
Germany)
Imports: $2 billion (2005 est.) (primary
partners India, China, UAE, Saudi Arabia)
Human Development Index (ranking): 136
(UNDP 2005)

SUGGESTED WEBSITES

http://rip.physics.unk.adu/Nepal/NPO.html
http://www.catmando.com
http://www.nepalnews.com

Nepal Country Report

Nepal is like a Tantric mandala: colorful and intense, leading to unexpected levels of awareness. The country is breathtaking, like the magnificent Mount Everest's peak, the highest in the world, which dominates a majestic row of 10 Himalayan Mountains over 26,000 feet high that mark the formidable boundary between Nepal and Tibet.

The land falls steeply from this arctic height into the lush Kathmandu Valley, some 20,000 feet below. It then rises again over the smaller, barren Mahabharat range, up to 11,000 feet, and drops once more through the foothills into a marshy plain along the Ganges River, about 900 feet above sea level.

Nepal is a land of immense natural contrast, with habitat for a wide variety of species, from the elusive snow leopards in the mountains to elephants, monkeys, tigers, and crocodiles in the Terai.

Nepal is also home to an immense variety of people. They are broadly divided by region, religion, and language into three distinct groups.

The mountainous regions to the north are sparsely inhabited, mostly by people of Tibetan descent and language who follow the Lamaist, or Tibetan, Buddhist tradition. Their dress and many customs are from Tibet. Some, for example, practice polyandrous marriage, wherein the wife of the eldest son is also married to his younger

brothers. In such families, their lands are not usually subdivided. Brothers also share in the few seasonal occupations that the frigid terrain allows: cultivating in spring, herding in summer, and trading in winter.

DEVELOPMENT

Most of Nepal's economy relies on subsistence agriculture and diminishing trade between Tibet and India. The successful ascent of Mt. Everest introduced a thriving tourist trade that has persisted through the ravages of a militant Maoist insurrection since 1996. It remains among the poorest nations in the world.

Even though arable land is scarce and trade has been drastically reduced by the Chinese takeover of Tibet, the people of the northern mountain region are more prosperous than those living in the more fertile valleys to the south. The alternative to family life presented by the Buddhist monastic tradition also restrains population growth in the northern mountains. Although their small, isolated communities span almost half of the total land area, they constitute only 3 percent of the total population of Nepal.

Almost a third of the population lives in the Terai, the low-lying, southernmost region

of the country in the Gangetic plain. They are mostly Hindu, although some are Muslim. They speak dialects of Hindi and are ethnically and culturally very close to their Indian neighbors. Because the land is flat, fertile, and nurtured by the snow-fed rivers flowing out of the mountains, agriculture is the primary activity. Although it is a narrow strip of land, only about 20 miles wide, and occupying 17 percent of the country, it produces more than 60 percent of Nepal's gross domestic product (GDP).

Two-thirds of the population of Nepal lives in the interlying hill region. It is also predominantly agricultural. Arable lands are scarcer than in the Terai and are terraced for farming. Because of the altitude, the growing season is shorter and the yields lower.

At the center of this region is the Kathmandu Valley, a lush alluvial plain 15 miles long and 12 miles wide. Nepal's three largest cities: Kathmandu, Patan, and Bhaktapur are in this valley, absorbing more of its land as they continue to expand. Wide arrays of ethnic and cultural identities as well as style and to fuse an overwhelming multiplicity of religious expression.

SOCIAL DIVERSITY

Nepali social diversity is partly due to the rugged terrain, which has kept many small groups isolated east to west in the several

(UN photo/Ray tlin/UNvitlin)

The festive custome on this child shows the continuation of distinct religious traditions in Nepal.

river valleys that descend down the steep southern slopes of the mountains. Also important, Nepal has long provided extensive trade routes from India north up the river valleys, through the high mountain passes into Tibet, and on into China. Nepali traders along these routes have maintained distinct ethnic identities, whether their primary interaction has been with the Tibetan culture to the north or with the Hindu culture to the south. The success of their mercantile activity with such distinct partners has reinforced the cultural contrasts between Tibet and India within the central region of Nepal itself.

The hierarchical social structure known as the caste system in India also contributes to Nepal's social diversity. This system, ranking rather than assimilating, maintains the distinctive customs and traditions of different communities. The Nepalese criteria for ranking appear more flexible than in India. The Gurkhas, for example, famous for their military prowess and courage, are recruited from three different Tibeto-Burman language communities from different parts of Nepal. They join together because of the opportunity for military employment that a shared identity as Gurkhas affords. Similarly, several distinct tribal groups in the Terai have claimed a single ethnic identity as Tharus in order to gain strength as

a political force not available to them as separate minorities. In contrast, Thaksatae villagers have distanced themselves from other Thakalis, with whom they share ethnic, linguistic, and religious identities, in order to maintain the trading privileges that they have achieved as a distinct community within that group.

POLITICS

The immense and confusing diversity of Nepal's population contributes to the country's struggle with democracy. For centuries, a strong, absolute monarchy held it all together.

Prithvi Narayan Shah, king of the western province of Gorkha forged the unity of present-day Nepal in the eighteenth century A.D. He conquered the surrounding kingdoms and established his dynasty in Kathmandu, the capitol of a defeated Newar ruler. His family's reign was circumscribed first by the British East India Company in 1815, and later, in 1845, by the Kathmandu Rana family, which established a powerful and hereditary prime ministry to rule the Shah domain.

In 1950, with the departure of the British Raj from the subcontinent, a national movement, modeled on the independence movement in India and led by the Nepali Congress Party, overthrew the Rana family. King Tribhuvan Vir Vikram Shah supported the anti-Rana movement and became a national hero. Upon his reinstitution as full monarch in February 1951, he worked to bring constitutional democracy to Nepal. He died in 1955, and his son, Mahendra, succeeded him. His initiatives still led to national elections in 1959, under a new Constitution that established a Parliament with powers that limited the role of the king. The Nepali Congress Party won 74 of the 109 seats in Parliament.

A year later, King Mahendra objected to his loss of power as absolute monarch. He dismissed the Nepali Congress Party government and banned all political parties. In 1962, he introduced a pyramidal process for electing representatives to the national legislature. Elections on the local level chose a village council (panchayat). Members of the local panchayats elected representatives to an 11-member district panchayat, which in turn elected members to the National Panchayat. The National Panchayat elected its own prime minister. But the king reserved the power to appoint all of the Council of Ministers, who oversaw the operation of the departments of government. This structure reinforced the traditional political power held by local landlords throughout the diverse regions of the country. The landlords, in turn, reaffirmed the authority of the king.

King Mahendras died in 1972, and his son Birendra became king. In 1980, in response to growing public agitation for greater democracy, King Birendra held a referendum to see whether the people wanted to continue the party-banned, tiered elections for membership in the National Panchayat or a multiparty, national election. The tiered panchayat system won by a 54.7 percent vote. Ironically, the majority of those elected to the National Panchayat in 1986 favored limiting the power of the king.

Encouraged by this result, leaders of the banned Nepali Congress Party (NCP) and the Communist parties organized public demonstrations to return to universal suffrage. They were joinged by a growing middle class, disaffected by economic hardship and the bungling, opportunistic leadership of the tiered-elected Panchayat. In response to the popular outcry, King Birendra worked out with the party leaders a new Constitution that limited his absolute sovereign power and established a multiparty, democratically elected, parliamentary government.

National democratic elections—the first since 1959—were held in 1991. Although the Nepali Congress Party won a majority in the new Parliament, its leadership struggled to hold the allegiance of its membership. In July 1994, 36 members of the party refused to attend the prime minister's annual address. Their absence led to a no-confidence vote in Parliament, its dissolution, and new elections, set for November.

In the 1994 elections, no party won a majority. The Unified Marxist-Leninist Party (UMLP) put together a fragile coalition that lasted for less than a year. The Nepali Congress Party then formed a coalition with two other parties to gain a majority. But two years later, this coalition also fell apart.

Still not wishing to face a new general election, the UMLP was then able to gather yet another coalition by giving its support to a monaschist, Lokendra Bahadur Chand, whose party held only 10 seats in the Parliament. Six months later he was ousted by members of his own party. They managed to

(UN photo 140, 484/Roy Witlin)

The geographic contrast in Nepal is dramatic. The Himalayas are the highest mountains in the world and act as an impressive backdrop for many of the populated areas.

form yet another coalition with the Nepali Congress Party. After a stormy six months in 1998, Girija Prasad Koirala, a longtime leader in the NCP, became the fifth prime minister of Nepal to serve since the 1994 elections.

In the 1999 elections, the Nepali Congress Party won enough seats to form a government on its own. Krishna Prasad Bhattarai was elected prime minister. But another revolt within the party a year later forced his resignation, and Girija Prasad Koirala became prime minister once again.

Two crises during this time of political instability in Parliament unsettled the country even more.

On July 1, 2000, Crown Prince Dipendra brutally murdered King Birendra. Not permitted by his mother to marry the woman of his choice, the distraught prince dressed in fatigues, grabbed an M-16 rifle, and shot his parents, his younger brother and sister, and an uncle and two aunts, before taking his own life. This episode shocked the country. The king's brother, Gyanendra, was hastily installed as king in his place.

HEALTH/WELFARE

In education and social services, the country struggles with limited resources, isolation, diversity, and insurgency. Adult literacy and life expectancy are both low. Malnutrition caused by a limited growing season and urban expansion has led to high levels of retardation and blindness.

A greater challenge to the government came from a dissident group of militant communist Maoists, strongly opposed to monarchy, corruption, and the oppression of the country's many poor. They drew their revolutionary inspiration from the Maos revolution in China, from the Naxalite movement in India, and the Shining Path, an extremist militant group in Peru. Their guerrilla agitation started in 1996, with the splintering of the communist parties in Parliament. They began by recruiting support among villagers in the remote and disadvantaged regions in the western part of the country, and demanding "fees" from trekking tourists for "protecting" them.

As their movement grew, a reign of terror ensued against those who resisted their cause. Abductions, maiming, and killing, matched in too many instances by abuses by the Royal Nepali Army, increased in intensity and violence throughout the countryside.

At the time of the regicide in July, 2001, when a Royal Army unit refused to fight against the Maoist insurgents, Prime Minister Koirala resigned. He was replaced by a rival Congress Party leader, who promptly negotiated a truce with the Maoists. It lasted only a few short months.

In November 2001, King Gyanendra declared a state of emergency. In response to the prime minister's request to dissolve Parliament and call for national elections, on October 4, 2002, the king dismissed the elected government and took over by royal decree. With foreign aid support, he mobilized the Royal Army of 95,000 to protect his rule. Then, in hopes of negotiating with the Maoists, he appointed one prime minister after another. None of them could function because they were opposed by a strong coalition of legislators who objected to the king's dissolution of Parliament. With increasing student activist support, they continued to call for the restoration of parliamentary government.

The conflict brought untold misery to a people already burdened with poverty, high population growth, and illiteracy. The Maoist movement cut deeply into tourist revenues and displaced more than 100,000 from their homes. More than 12,000 had been killed since the insurgency began in 1996. Caught in a deadly battle between monarchy and anarchy, the government, debilitated by continuing political struggles with the king and with itself, was unable to respond.

ACHIEVEMENTS

A ceasefire and election agreement between the Maoist insurgents and the 7 Party Alliance in November, 2006, has acknowledged democracy rather than war as the path to peace.

In June 2004, responding to a sense of conflict fatigue on the part of his people, the king tried once again to initiate discussions with the Maoists. But with continuing political infighting in Kathmandu, and with the Maoists now effectively in control of 68 of the 75 districts in the country, they were not interested, particularly not to give any legitimacy to the king, whose rule they opposed.

Things began to change dramatically in April 2006. Mass protests in the streets of Kathmandu forced King Gyanendra to end his control of the government, and to reopen Parliament, under the leadership of a Seven Party Alliance. Even more dramatic, with the king removed, the Maoists agreed to a cease fire in May, and to reenter into negotiations

toward their participation in parliamentary government.

This change came from an assessment by the Maoists that the path of violence was no longer a viable way to achieve their revolutionary objectives.

On November 22, 2006, after intense negotiations, Prachanda and the venerable Girija Prasad Koirala, now head of the Seven Party Alliance, signed a Comprehensive Peace Agreement that resolved many thorny issues to establish peace and effective governence for the people of Nepal.

CHALLENGES

First and foremost is the realization of the November agreement to achieve a stable and resourceful government to meet the many needs of the Nepali people.

Nepal's industrial potential has also long been restrained by trade agreements that tie the country's economy to India's development policies. And its commerce has been severely limited by the difficulty in traversing the trade routes to Tibet. According to the United Nations, 90 percent of the labor force is in agriculture, placing it among the least of the least-developed countries (LDCs). Unemployment is at 47 percent. According to a recent World Bank report, 42 percent of the people live in absolute poverty. The incidence of malnutrition-related retardation and blindness is high. Five thousand girls are trafficked every year to India. HIV/AIDS is beginning to take its toll. In education and medical and social services, the country struggles with limited resources and isolation among its diverse population.

The country seeks a consistent, stable, and purposeful government to confront and solve these difficult problems. With such overwhelming economic and social conditions

Timeline: PAST

A.D. 1742–1814
The Shah dynasty's expansion of the Kingdom of Gorkha

1815
The British East India Company reduces the Gorkha domain to the kingdom of Nepal

1845–1950
Rana family domination of the Shah dynasty

1949
The founding of the Nepal Congress Party

1959–1960
Constitutional monarchy

1960–1991
Absolute monarchy; constitutional monarchy established with a multiparty, democratically elected Parliament

1990s
The first national democratic elections in 32 years are held

PRESENT

2000–2005
Nepal continues to struggle with widespread and severe poverty

Crown Prince Dipendra murders the king and other family members

Rise of the Maoists insurgency that increases in terror and control of country

2006
Maoists agree to ceasefire, disarmament, and participation in parliamentary government free of royal interference.

among such an awesome diversity of peoples in such a rugged, breathtaking landscape, even the effort to grasp the incredible array of challenges leaves one with a sense of wonder.

Pakistan (Islamic Republic of Pakistan)

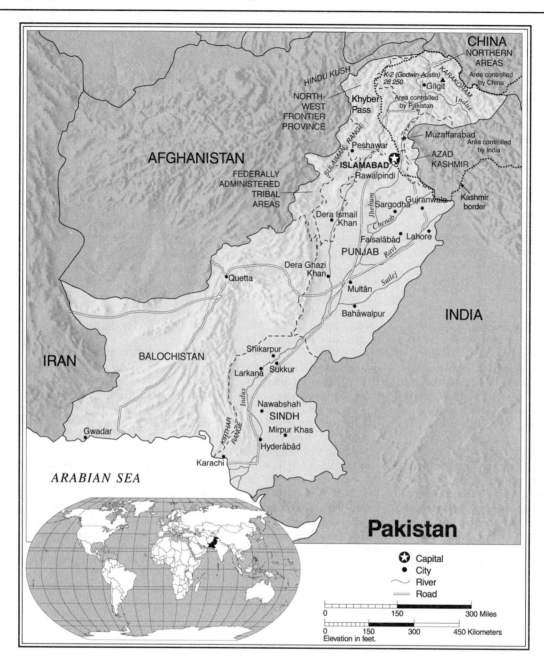

Pakistan Statistics

GEOGRAPHY

Area in Square Miles (Kilometers): 310,403
  sq. mi. (803,940 sq. km)
Captial (Population): Islamabad (601,600)

PEOPLE

Population

Total: 165,803,560
Annual Growth Rate: 2.1%
Rural/Urban Population Ratio: 65.2/34.8
  (UN 2005 est.)

Religion; 97% Muslims (77% Sunni, 20%
  Shia), 3% other

Health

Life Expectancy at Birth: 62.4 years (male);
  64.44 years (female)
Infant Mortality: 70.5/1000 live births
Physicians Available: 1/1,863 people
Per capita total expenditure on Health: $48
  (WHO 2003 est.)
HIV/AIDS Rate in Adults: 0.1%
  (2001 est.)

Education

Adult Literacy Rate: 48.7% (35.2% female)
  (2004 est.)

COMMUNICATION

Telephones: 4,502,200 main lines (2004)
Cell Phones: 5,022,900 (2004)
Daily Newspaper Circulation: 22/1,000
  people
Televisions: 16/1,000 people
Internet Users: 7.5 million (2005)

68

TRANSPORTATION

Highways in Miles (Kilometers): (254,410 km) (2004)
Railroads in Miles (Kilometers): (8,163 km) (2003)
Usable Airfields: 134
Motor Vehicles in Use: 1,100,000

GOVERNMENT

Type: federal republic
Independence Date: August 14, 1947 (from the United Kingdom)
Head of State/Government: President, Chief Executive (General) Pervez Musharraf; Prime Minister Shaukat Aziz
Political Parties: Pakistan Muslim League PML, PML/N (Nawaz Sharif faction), Muttahida Majlis-e-Amal, MMA, Pakistan Peoples Party, PPP, Muttahida Qaumi Movement (MQM), many smaller parties
Suffrage: universal at 18; joint electorates and reserved parliamentary seats for women and non-Muslims

MILITARY

Military Expenditures (% of GDP): $4.26 billion (3.9%) (2005 est.)
Current Disputes: border problems with Afghanistan; disputes over Kashmir and water-sharing problems with India; narcotics trade

ECONOMY

Currency ($ U.S. Equivalent): 59.515 = $1 U.S. (2005)
Per Capita Income/GDP: $2,400 / $384.9 billion (2005)
GDP Growth Rate: 6.9% (2005 est.)
Inflation Rate: 9.2% (2005 est.)
Unemployment Rate: 6.6% (2005 est.)
Labor Force by Occupation: 42% agriculture, 39% services, 20% industry (2004 est.)
Population Below Poverty Line: 32% (FY 2000–01 est.)
Natural Resources: land; natural gas; petroleum; coal; iron ore; copper; salt; limestone

Agriculture: cotton; grains; sugarcane; fruits; vegetables; milk; mutton; eggs; livestock
Industry: textiles; food processing; construction materials; consumer goods
Exports: $14.85 billion (2005 est.) (primary partners United States, UAE, United Kingdom, Germany, Hong Kong) (2004)
Imports: $21.26 billion (2005 est.) (primary partners Saudi Arabia, UAE, United States, China, Japan, Kuwait) (2004)
Human Development Index (ranking): 135 (UNDP 2005)

SUGGESTED WEBSITE

http://www.clas.ufl.edu/users/gthursby/pak/
http://www.dawn.com
http://www.pak.gov.pk
http://www.paktoday.com

Pakistan Country Report

Pakistan is the second largest nation in South Asia, about one-fourth the size of India, with one-seventh of India's population. It lies in the Indus River Valley, between the mountainous border with Afghanistan through which comes the famous Khyber Pass to the northwest, and the Great Indian Desert, and the Rann of Kutch, to the southeast. Long a land of transition between the rugged steppes of Inner Asia and the plains of India, it is today a new nation caught between the heritage of a glorious imperial past and the poetic image of an ideal theocratic future. The name, Pakistan, given by the Muslim poet Muhammed Iqbal in 1930, means "Land of the Pure."

The heritage of the people of Pakistan goes back to the earliest known urban culture in South Asia. Excavations of the ancient cities of Harappa and Mohenjodaro, discovered in 1922, reveal an impressive civilization that dates from 3000 to 1500 B.C. Distinctive are its knowledge of hydrology and its use of irrigation to cultivate the valley with the rich waters of the Indus River. Surplus agricultural production led to extensive commerce in cotton and grains throughout the ancient world.

Islam is a religious faith based upon the teachings of the prophet Muhammad revealed in the Koran in Arabia during the seventh century A.D. Arab traders and wandering Sufi mystics brought the religion into South Asia. The Sufis' spiritual discipline and religious teaching drew large numbers of indigenous peoples to submission to the will of Allah (God) as early as the eighth

century. The spread of this vibrant faith and subsequent rule of Islamic sultans and emperors led to the creation of Pakistan as an Islamic Republic in 1947. Today, 97 percent of the 166 million people in the country are Muslim. Of these, 77 percent belong to the Sunni tradition. There are also small minorities of Hindus, Christians, and members of the Ahmadiya Sect of Islam, whose faith is considered heretical by the orthodox.

DEVELOPMENT

Extensive investment in the cotton textile and food processing industries has kept Pakistan's economy growing. But it has not been matched by human resource development. Agriculture still employs half of the labor force, but contributes less to the GDP. The earthquake in October 2005 also had a devastating impact on human life and development.

Moghuls were militant Turks refined by the elegance of Persia and energized by their Islamic faith. The march of their conquering forces across the northern plains of South Asia to the Bay of Bengal in the sixteenth century, marked the period of greatest glory in the heritage of the Pakistani people. Akbar (1556–1605), the greatest of them, is remembered for the opulence and splendor of his court, for the far-reaching administrative control of his empire, and for his elaborate building projects which still stand as mas-

sive tribute to his commanding wealth and intellect.

Pakistan became independent at the departure of the British Raj in 1947, created especially for the 7.2 million people who migrated from central India (*mohsjirs*) to preserve the culture of a staunch Islamic and glorious imperial past. This heritage has been both an asset and an obstacle to its evolution as a modern nation state.

INDEPEFNDENCE MOVEMENT

The Muslim League was formed in 1906 to represent the interests of the Islamic minority, in the movement for freedom, convinced that Muslims would be oppressed in an independent India dominated by Hindus. In 1940, the League voted to demand a separate state for the Muslim population of South Asia.

The British Raj rewarded the persistence of the Muslim League's leader, Muhammad Ali Jinnah, by granting independence in 1947 to two nations instead of one. Its scheme to partition British India created a smaller, more populous East Pakistan, and a dominant Wet Pakistan, separated by nearly 1,000 miles of India.

This partition was disastrous. The Muslims in British India who most feared Hindu oppression were not those who had the security of living in Muslim majority districts, but those who lived in the Hindu-majority districts in north central India. They felt endangered in their own lands. Hindu and Sikh minorities in districts where the Muslims were in a majority also feared for their lives.

This mutual fear caused the migration of 14 million people, Hindus, Sikhs, and Muslims moving in opposite directions. Clashes in the border areas, especially in the Punjab, which was split in half between Muslim and Hindu districts, led to the killing of thousands of bewildered, anxious people. The consequences are still felt among the families that survived.

QUEST FOR POLITICAL STABILITY

The new Pakistan lacked adequate administrative services to cope with the disruption and bloodshed of the partition. Muhamad Ali Jinnah took upon himself the chief executive duties of governor general in the interim government In ill health at the time, he died 13 months later.

Liaquat Ali Khan, his successor as prime minister, was assassinated three years later, in 1951. The Muslim League, imported from British India, lost control of a unifying national agenda to the indigenous sources of provincial power: wealthy landowners and tribal leaders in the five distinct provinces in the country, each divided from the others by ethos and language.

The provincial identities of the people in the new nation accentuated rather than mitigated their differences on the national level. The political solidarity of the Bengali people in the province of East Pakistan was first realized by their opposition to accept Urdu, the language of the *mohajirs*, immigrants from north central India, as the national language of Pakistan. This opposition led to their split from Pakistan to form an independent nation, Bangladesh, in 1971.

Distinct languages in each of the four remaining states in West Pakistan also take precedence over Urdu, which is spoken by 8 percent of the population. In the early years of independence, Urdu-speaking immigrants made up 46 percent of the urban population in the country. Today, the Muttahida Quami movement (until recently the Mohajir Quami movement and now divided into two hostile camps), although limited to Karachi for its political base, is the fourth-largest political party in the country.

The Punjab is the granary of the country, with the most heavily irrigated and productive lands. Industrial development and wealth are also concentrated there. Lahore, its capitol city, was the administrative center for the region under the British Raj. All of these factors contribute to Punjabi domination in the ranks of the army and the civil services.

Sindh is the next-most-important state, sharing with Punjab about 90 percent of the industrial production of the country. Karachi, capitol of the state, with a population of over 9 million, is Pakistan's largest city and commercial center, and to date its only seaport. Yet only 12 percent of Pakistanis are Sindhi speakers.

Ten percent of the population live in the North-West Frontier Provinces, which lie along the rugged mountainous border with Afghanistan. The number of Pashtuns, who speak Pashto, increased by the influx of more than 3 million Afghan Pashtuns as refugees during the Soviet occupation of Afghanistan during the 1980s. Many of them who remain continue to cross the porous Durand Line. Pashtuns, in general, do not recognize it as a border between the two countries.

Balochistan, in the arid lands that border Iran and the Arabian Sea, is the largest state and the richest in natural resources. A seaport is being built with Chinese financing and labor at Gwadar on the coast. Yet the people who speak Balochi are less than 5 percent of Pakistan's population. A separatist movement started in 1973, based on many of the same issues which led to the break away of Bangladesh. It has been suppressed by military repression, which killed a respected tribal leader, Nawab Akbar Bugti in August 2006.

Pakistani Muslims are also significantly divided between a majority who seek a modern Islamic identity, and the more traditional Islamists, who have long felt their commitment to exclusive, coercive theocracy challenged by the quest for modern democracy. With the departure of Soviet forces from Afghanistan in 1989, the jihadis—ones who struggle for the faith—turned to free the Muslims in Kashmir from Indian military occupation. With the intrusion of western values by the defeat of the Taliban in Afghanistan in 2001, their cause has a new sense of urgency. A coalition of fundamentalist parties, called the Muttahida Majlis-e-amal (MMA), representing Balochistan and the North-West Frontier Provinces closest to Afghanistan in the National Assembly, has become a significant force in promoting their Islamist agenda in this region and in the nation as a whole.

Another challenge to a stable, democratically elected government in Pakistan is the wide division between the rich and the poor. A 1970 World Bank study found that 80 percent of the capital wealth in Pakistan was concentrated in just 22 families. A subsequent study in 1998 found 42.3 percent of the nation's wealth held by the top 20 percent of the population, with the lowest 10 percent having but 3.7 percent. The disparity between the industrial rich and the slum-dwelling poor in the cities continues to grow.

New wealth and a new class were created in Pakistan during the 1980s by jobs in the Persian Gulf oil fields. More than 2 million young people from all parts of the country sent home more than $4 billion a year, or about 10 percent of the country's gross domestic product. These monies stimulated conspicuous consumer buying, which led to a number of local enterprises using pickup trucks and video equipment. The loss of jobs during the Persian Gulf Wars had a doubly adverse impact on Pakistan's economy, cutting in half the remittances from overseas while increasing the number of unemployed within the country.

Amid all of these challenges to the formation of a single body politic, the military has been the strongest force for political unity, holding the country together under the fear of a life-threatening attack by India. Ironically, because of its dominant role in national government to maintain unity and stability, the military has also impeded the growth of democracy in Pakistan.

A constitution to establish a national parliamentary government was finally adopted in 1956, affirming the common sovereign identity of the two wings of Pakistan as an Islamic Republic. Yet this and each of the successive attempts to establish democratic rule—in 1971 and in 1988—occurred under the watchful eye of the military, and ended in a takeover: by General Ayub Khan in 1958, by General Yahya Khan in 1969, by General Zia-ul-Haq in 1977, and by General Pervez Musharraf in 1999. In all, the country has been under martial law for more than half of its years as an independent nation.

MARTIAL LAW: 1958–1971

General Mohammad Ayub Khan, commander-in-chief of the Pakistan army, became martial-law administrator in 1958, in hopes of stimulating economic growth among a people "not yet ready for democracy." He replaced the 1956 Constitution with a new Constitution, delegating extensive executive power to a president who would be elected only by those elected to local political offices. They also determined who would be elected to the National Assembly. In 1965, a limited electorate of "Basic Democrats," the 80,000 locally elected council members whom Ayub Khan accepted as prepared to vote, elected him president.

The use by the army of the imminent threat of war with India to unite a disparate and disengaged people under a single national banner proved to be a liability to Ayub Khan. For in the same year he was elected president, war actually broke out with India over their competing claims for the former princely state of Jammu and Kashmir, most of which India had occupied since 1947. When this war ended in military stalemate and a UN-observed ceasefire, an unfavorable peace settlement with India in the Tashkent Agreement of 1966 cost Ayub Khan his popular support.

Growing discontent over military rule during those years spawned two new political leaders, one in each of the wings of Pakistan. Mujibur Rahman, leader of the Awami League in East Pakistan, capitalized on the perception among the people of that region that they were treated as second-class citizens. His charismatic leadership won immense popular support for greater regional autonomy.

FREEDOM

The country has been under martial law longer than democratically elected government since independence. Popular elections were first held in 1971, and then suspended until 1988. Women are held to their traditional subservient role in Islamic society, even after the reform of the Hadood Ordinance in 2006.

At the same time, Zulfikar Ali Bhutto, a Western-educated diplomat from a large landholding family in the province of Sindh in West Pakistan, formed the Pakistan People's Party. Adopting the campaign slogan *Roti, Kapra aur Makon* ("Bread, clothes and shelter"), he mobilized a wide popular following in the western wing of the country toward a policy of democratic socialism. He did not attempt to generate a following of his own in East Pakistan. Nor did he anticipate the rise of the even more popular movement there by the Awami League.

President Ayub Khan was not able to contain either the Bhutto or the Rahman initiatives, and, in 1969, was forced to resign. General Yahya Khan, his successor, in a quest to bring order, declared the first popular national elections to be held in Pakistan since its independence, on December 7, 1970. In this election the Awami League won 160 of the 162 seats in the National Assembly assigned to the more populous East Pakistan. Bhutto's Pakistan People's Party won 81 seats of the 132 assigned to West Pakistan.

Bhutto felt that by winning a majority of the seats in the Assembly from West Pakistan, he was the rightful leader of the country. He therefore refused to join the newly elected national legislature until he was assured a position in the government. President Yahya Khan's suspension of the legislature in response to Bhutto's boycott, led to a vehement cry for independence in East Pakistan. President Yahya Khan sought to suppress this freedom movement by military force.

Millions fled for refuge in India. After several months of unrelenting bloodshed, the Indian government launched a military attack in support of the Bengali rebels. They won independence for their own country on December 17, 1971.

DEMOCRACY: 1971–1977

The separation of Bangladesh as an independent nation left the Pakistan People's Party with a majority in the National Assembly, and Bhutto became the president of Pakistan. He led what was left of the country toward a socialist state by nationalizing banking and such major industries as steel, chemicals, and cement. His policy created employment opportunities in an already cumbersome civil-service bureaucracy, but discouraged investment and led to a decline in industrial production.

Bhutto was more successful in restoring parliamentary government. He created a new Constitution—the third in 26 years—that was adopted in 1973. It established a National Assembly of 207 members, all of them elected directly for five-year terms. Bhutto then became prime minister, elected by majority of the National Assembly.

Bhutto called for elections in 1977 in hopes of getting endorsement for his leadership and his socialist economic policies. This call spurred an unexpected and virulent opposition of nine parties, which united to form the Pakistan National Alliance (PNA). Bhutto's Pakistan People's Party won the election. But the PNA, which won only 36 of 207 seats in the Assembly, charged that the elections had been fixed and took to the streets in protest. Bhutto called in the army to restore order and sought to negotiate with the PNA to hold new elections. Before any agreement was reached, Mohammad Zia-ul-Haq, chief of staff of the army, seized control of the government.

General Zia-ul-Haq promised to hold elections within 90 days, but then canceled them. He continued to hold out the promise of elections for the following 11 years, during which time he maintained firm military control. Part of that control was to bring charges against Bhutto of complicity in a political murder, which led to Bhutto's trial and execution on April 4, 1979.

MARTIAL LAW: 1977–1988

In the fall of 1979, Zia banned all political parties and imposed censorship on the press. The following year he removed the actions of his government and the decisions of the military courts from judicial review. Many of these measures were cloaked in a policy of "Islamization," through which his military

regime sought to improve the religious quality of the people's public life by an appeal to traditional laws and teachings of Sunni Islam. Once again, entrenched divisions and political turmoil led to repression more reminiscent of Moghul imperialism than the workings of modern representative government.

Zia's consolidation of power in Pakistan coincided with the collapse of the Shah of Iran, the rise of Saudi Arabia as a power in the Middle East, and the Soviet invasion of Afghanistan. The response of the United States to these developments gave Pakistan a strategic role in protecting western sources of oil and containing Soviet expansion. U.S. support for his repressive military rule not only set back the quest for democracy, but also ultimately weakened the authority of the Zia government itself.

DEMOCRACY: 1988–1999

A spirit of democracy did survive, if only partially, in a hasty referendum called in 1985 by General Zia to affirm his policy of Islamization by electing him an executive president for a five-year term. The Constitution of 1973 also survived, though altered by General Zia in an Eighth Amendment, to give the president executive power to dismiss the prime minister. He thus set the stage for legislative elections in November of 1988. He died in a plane crash in August, and the Supreme Court removed the ban on political parties. Bhutto's Pakistan People's Party, led by his daughter, Benazir Bhutto, won 93 seats in the 217-member National Assembly, and she was invited to become prime minister. Then just 35 years old, she was the youngest person and the first woman to lead an Islamic nation.

Benazir Bhutto's tenure, based on an uneasy balance within the legislature itself, was further complicated by competing claims outside the legislature by the other large power brokers in the nation—the army and the president. Even though General Beg, appointed army chief of staff in 1985, advocated restraint from involvement, the army remained a political presence.

In 1989, Benazir Bhutto tried to restore the full authority of the prime minister's office by having the Eighth Amendment of the Constitution repealed. She failed to get the necessary two-thirds vote. In the summer of 1990, her opposition in the National Assembly tried to defeat her, but did not have enough votes. President Ghulam Ishaq Khan asserted his authority under the Eighth Amendment to dismiss her government.

In the elections which followed her dismissal, Mian Nawaz Sharif, chief minister of Punjab and head of the Islami Jamhorri

Ittehad (IJI), or Islamic Democratic Alliance, brought his conservative party together with the communist-leaning Awami National party, dominant in the North-West Frontier Province, and the fundamentalist Jamiat-Ulema-i-Islam party. Their coalition won 105 seats in the 217-member National Assembly by winning 36.86 percent of the popular vote. Benazir Bhutto's People's Democratic Alliance (PDA) was reduced from 93 to 45 seats, even though it won 36.84 percent of the popular vote, Sharif, a member of a successful industrial family who migrated from Amritsar in East Punjab to Pakistan in 1947, became prime minister.

To fulfill a promise made during the campaign to form a coalition with the fundamentalist Islamic groups, Prime Minister Sharif introduced a law to make the Islamic code of Shari'a the supreme law of Pakistan. At the same time, he asserted that his Shari'a bill would not stand in the path of modernization. The Jamiat-Ulema-i-Islam party withdrew from the ruling coalition, objecting that the Shari'a bill that was passed by the National Assembly was too vaguely worded and not being implemented.

Even without their support, Nawaz Sharif still called upon Islam as a unifying force in holding the country together and in harmony with its neighboring countries to the west. His government enacted blasphemy laws and pushed to amend the Constitution to make the Koran "the supreme law of land." These acts were understood as efforts not only to divert attention from increasing economic instability and other political issues, but also to contain the potentially volatile force of religious fundamentalism as a threat to stability in the country.

HEALTH/WELFARE

Emphasis on the military budget has slighted government attention to human resource development in education and social services. The birth rate remains high, and infant mortality at birth is among the highest in South Asia. Adult literacy is low. Among women it is little more than half that of the male population.

Nawaz Sharif also tried to repeal the Eighth Amendment to the Constitution that granted the president the powers of dismissal. President Ghulam Ishaq Khan invoked it, for a second time, in April 1993, to dismiss the Sharif government on charges of corruption and nepotism.

This time, the Supreme Court overruled the president and reinstated the Sharif government. The army chief of staff, General Abdul Waheed, then brokered the resignation

of both the prime minister and the president. The National Assembly and state legislatures were then dissolved, and new elections set for October.

In the fall 1993 elections, Benazir Bhutto Pakistan People's Party won 86 seats, to 72 for Sharif's party. Her position was strengthened by the election a month later of Farooq Leghari, deputy leader of the PPP, to the office of president.

In her second term as prime minister, Benazir Bhutto pursued policies that destabilized the nation's economy, compromised foreign investment, and drove the inflation rate to 20 percent. In response, she imposed a sales tax that proved very unpopular. An image of rampant corruption in government, together with an attempt to appoint sympathetic judges to the high courts, also eroded her popular support. President Leghari dismissed her on charges of corruption and nepotism under the Eighth Amendment. New elections were called for February 3, 1997. To avoid any legal action against her, Benazir Bhutto fled the country.

ACHIEVEMENTS

Industrial growth and political stability has been achieved, largely through military domination. It demonstrated its nuclear capability in tests in 1998.

Even though voter turnout was low, Mian Nawaz Sharif and his Pakistan Muslim League Party won a two-thirds majority in the National Assembly. Benazir Bhutto's opposition party then joined his government to repeal the Eighth Amendment to the Constitution.

Reducing the power of the president did not place any restraint on the third element of political power in Pakistan, the military. In response to Prime Minister Sharif's repudiation of the military attack into the Kargil District of Kashmir in the summer of 1999, the army chief of staff, General Pervez Musharraf, staged a coup in October. He then brought charges against Sharif for treason and attempted murder. The courts found Sharif guilty, and sentenced him to life in prison, which General Musharraf commuted to a life in exile.

MARTIAL RULE: SINCE 1999

General Musharraf's coup overthrew the parliamentary government that had been elected in 1997. In June 2001, he took over the title of president from Rafiq Tarar, who had been elected to a five-year term in 1998.

Following the terrorist attacks in the United States on 9/11, the US began military op-

erations in Afghanistan to remove Osama bin Laden and al Qaeda bases. Pakistan became a necessary ally to provide bases and logistical support. Under strong American pressure, President Musharraf courageously withdrew support for the Taliban, which stirred strong opposition among a growing Islamic fundamentalist movement in his own country. At the same time he came under considerable international pressure to return Pakistan to a democratic form of government.

In response, President Musharraf set elections for a national legislature for the fall of 2002. In anticipation, he called for and won a national referendum on April 30 to extend his presidency for another five years, regardless of the outcome of the legislative elections. Then he promulgated amendments to the constitution, which included restoring to the president the power to dismiss the prime minister, the cabinet, and the legislature by decree. They also established a National Security Council that included cabinet members and chief provincial ministers, but was dominated by the military.

The election results in October did not yield the popular support that Musharraf had sought. A pro-Taliban, anti-United States coalition of Islamic fundamentalist parties, called the Muttahida Majlis-e-amal (MMA), won sufficient support in Balochistan and the North-West Frontier Province, closest to Afghanistan, to gain 60 of 342 seats in the National Assembly. Benazir Bhutto's PPP, with her in exile, won 81 seats. Musharraf's own PML(Q) won a plurality of 118 seats. He was not able to form a government for six weeks, until he had enticed enough members away from the PPP to gain majority support.

A simple majority did not provide Musharraf with enough votes to get legislative approval for his constitutional amendments. Nevertheless, he closely oversaw the activity of the Assembly under the leadership of his designated prime minister, Zafrulla Khan Jamali. In 2004 (after Manmohan Singh became prime minister in India), he replaced Jamali with the finance minister, Shaukit Aziz.

Through political maneuvering with the MMA, he got the Assembly to accept his presidency and constitutional changes, with the understanding that he would step down as chief of staff of the army by the end of 2004. Later he managed to remove constitutional constraints to his serving as both president and chief of staff. Pakistan's martial-law precedents keep him firmly in control of the government.

President Musharraf also managed to distance his government from any involvement in the proliferation of nuclear technology conducted by A. Q. Khan, the founder of Pakistans nuclear weapons program. In exchange for a pardon by the president, Mr. Khan took full responsibility for the illicit transfer of nuclear capability to other countries out of his research laboratories without authorization by the government. Musharraf was then able to assure the world that as long as he was in power in Pakistan, nuclear know-how would not get into the hands of terrorists, nor into the hands of an anti-American opposition in Pakistan itself.

Musharraf also asserted his military role in sustaining Pakistan's opposition to India's claim to Kashmir, which supports spending more than 20 percent of its annual budget on the military. It also required the testing of its own nuclear capability immediately following India's nuclear tests in May 1998, even at the high cost of international disapproval and U.S. economic sanctions. Musharraf supported the continuing tension and violent atrocities both by and on militant separatist groups in Kashmir to encourage resolution of the Kashmir issue under international auspices rather than continuing a military standoff with an intransigent India.

Recognizing the fragility of Musharrafs hold on power—he survived two assassination attempts in 2003—and the potential strength of his opposition in Pakistan, the international community has not been responsive to his plea.

The United States rejected Pakistan's support for infiltrators into Kashmir. It rather accepted India's refusal to discuss the Kashmir issue until President Musharraf brought an end to Pakistan's support of terrorism in Kashmir. In January of 2002, he outlawed two known terrorist organizations in Pakistan. And in May, he declared, "No infiltration is taking place across the Line of Control."

Bilateral negotiations between India and Pakistan picked up in the fall of 2006. "Greater autonomy" has gained currency in public discussion, and leaders of separatist movements in Kashmir are becoming part of the dialogue. Both of these initiatives give more promise for a peaceful solution to the Kashmir issue, which has taken the lives of 45,000 people since 1987.

President Musharraf also disclaims infiltration by Taliban fighters across the Durand Line into Afghanistan. In September 2006 he made an agreement with tribal leaders in Waziristan not to bring military force in the region if they restricted Taliban cross border activity. This agreement may have reflected the reality of his lack of control. It did little to assure the Afghan government and NATO forces assigned to reduce the growing insurgence of the Taliban in Afghanistan that Pakistan was an effective ally to establish stability there.

A deadly earthquake shook the mountains of northern Pakistan on October 8,

Timeline: PAST

3000–1500 B.C.
Harappan city culture

A.D. 1526–1857
The Moghul empire

1907
The founding of the Muslim League

1940
The Muslim League adopts the demand for the separate state of Pakistan

1947
The partition of British India; the creation of Pakistan

1948
War with India over Kashmir

1956
the first Constitution establishing Pakistan as an Islamic republic

1958–1969
Military rule of Ayub Khan

1965
War with India over Kashmir

1969–1971
Military rule of Yahya Khan

1970
First national popular elections: Mujibar Rahman's Awami League wins majority of National Assembly; Zulfikar Ali Bhutto's Pakistan People's Party wins West Pakistan majority

1971
War with India, the breakaway of East Pakistan to become Bangladesh, Bhutto becomes president of Pakistan

1973
A Constitution establishing parliamentary democracy is adopted; Bhutto becomes prime minister

1977–1988
Military rule of Zia-ul-Haq; national elections set; helicopter accident kills Zia; Benazir Bhutto becomes prime minister

1990s
Parliamentary democracy is restored, Pakistan tests it nuclear capability in the wake of Indian tests

1999
General Pervez Musharraf, army chief of staff, takes over government.

PRESENT

2000s
Military rule of General Pervez Musharraf Lack of human resource development and growing financial problems threaten the nation's economy.

2001
Pakistan becomes prominent in the aftermath of 9/11

2002
Parliamentary elections restored, but President and General Musharraf remains firmly in control of the government.

2005
Deadly earthquake kills 87,000, leaves 3 million homeless in northern part of country.

2006
Nawab Akbar Bugti is killed in military repression of Balochistan insurgency

Government withdraws military from Waziristan tribal areas in agreement for tribal leaders to stop support for Taliban insurgency in Afghanistan.

2005, killing more than 87,000 people. The remoteness of the region and the devastation made relief to the survivors very difficult. It took army units 3 days to cover 20 miles to get relief to Balakot, at the edge of the epicenter of the 7.6 quake. They found the town flattened, including 200 students crushed in their school building. Volunteers rushed from all over to rescue the survivors before lack of food and medical care, and

the onset of the arctic winter months threatened to add to the quake's toll.

The international community responded generously to President Musharraf's call for help, pledging $6.5 billion to meet the rescue and reconstruction costs. And private donations added another $200 million. He expects more than 600,000 housing units for the 3 million made homeless by the quake to be completed by the end of 2008.

A large question mark remains: does President Musharraf intend to continue to lead the country as a military state? It has been said that Pakistan is an army looking for a nation. The international community looks for that description to be reversed.

INTERNAL CHALLENGES

Many international forces and natural events have encumbered Pakistan's quest to become a democratic Islamic republic. But most of its challenges have their origin within the country itself. Areas of concern include a disproportionately high defense budget ($194 billion, or 21.5 percent of the 2004 federal budget), a high rate of population growth (2.1 percent), corruption in government, the loss of human rights through the imposition of religious blasphemy laws, and, most significantly, the lack of human resources development.

Human development factors such as poor working conditions, low wages, especially for women, lack of job security, but most importantly, lack of skill training and keeping abreast of fashion trends are identified as contributing most to the decline in Pakistan's substantial textile industry. Even with significant investments in production technology and textile machinery and indigenous cotton production, its exports have dropped 10 percent in a year. It is not able to compete with Bangladesh, which does not grow cotton.

A lack in human resource development is also evident in the limited—and elitist—opportunity for education in Pakistan. Literacy in the country is now at 48.7 percent, small improvement over the level, according to UNICEF, when Pakistan received its independence in 1947. Half of all secondary level students are educated in private schools, the only place they can get instruction in English, still the language of opportunity in the professions, technology, and trade.

Women are excluded even more from education: Their literacy is little more than half that of the men, (35.2 percent to 61.7 percent). Girls represent only a third of the student population. This lack of education opportunity for women reflects the traditional expectation of their subservience and seclusion in Islamic society.

General Zia-ul-Haq affirmed this attitude as national policy when he enacted the Hudood Ordinance in 1979, which places particularly poor and illiterate women in danger of being jailed when accused of adultery or report being raped. In 2006 General Musharraf introduced a Women's Protection Bill, which attempted to qualify some of the more blatant discrimination against women in the Ordinance. It transfers issues of rape from

Islamic law to Pakistan's penal code and makes accusations of adultery more stringent. The bill passed in the National Assembly over the strong objection of the fundamentalist Islamic parties. It was also opposed by human and women's rights groups, who wanted the Ordinance, which they claim has no basis in the Koran, repealed in its entirety.

Pakistan is committed to its survival as a unified, sovereign state, even though threatened by divisive political, social, and religious forces and by substantive economic and human development challenges. Affirming its integrity as an Islamic republic, its greatest challenge is to become a fully developed modern nation while remaining faithful to the teachings of Islam.

Sri Lanka   (Democratic Socialist Republic of Sri Lanka)

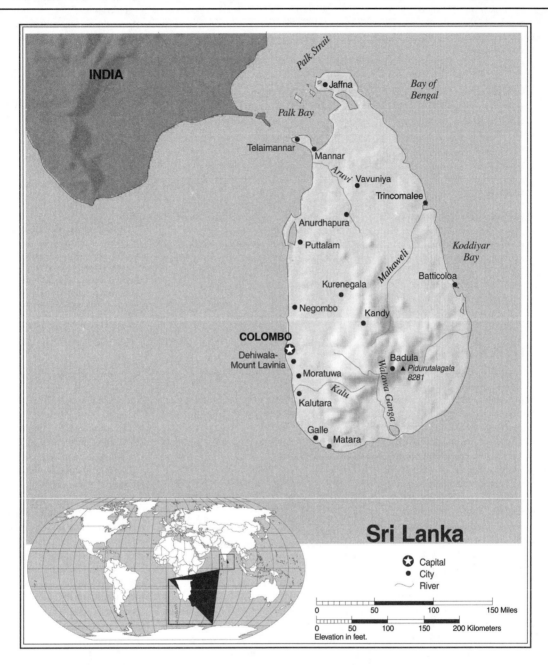

Sri Lanka Statistics

GEOGRAPHY

Capital (Population): Colombo (2,436,000 metro area, 656,610 city proper)

PEOPLE

Population

Total: 20,222,240 (July, 2006 est.)
Annual Growth Rate: 0.8% (2006 est.)
Rural/Urban Population Ratio: 79/21 (UN 2005 est.)

Major Languages: 74% Sinhala (Official Language), 18% Tamil, 8% other. English is commonly used in government and is spoken competently by about 10% of the population.
Ethnic Makeup: 73.8% Sinhalese, 7.2% Sri Lankan Moors, 4.6% Indian Tamils, 3.9% Sri Lankan Tamils, 10.5% other (2001 Census provisional data)
Religions: 70% Buddhist, 8% Muslim, 7% Hindu, 6% Christian, 9% other (2001 census provisional data)

Health

Life Expectancy at Birth: 70.83 years (male), 76.12 years (female)
Infant Mortality: 14.0/1000 live births
Per capita total expenditure on Health: $121 (WHO 2003 est.)
Physicians Available: 1/4,750 people
HIV/AIDS Rate in Adults: 0.1% (2001 est.)

Education

Adult Literacy Rate: 92.3% (2003 est.)
Compulsory (Ages): 5–12; free

75

Communication

Telephones: 1,130,923 (2005)
Cell Phones: 3,084,845 (2005)
Daily Newspaper Circulation: 25/1,000
  people
Televisions: 39/1,000 people
Internet Users: 280,000 (2005)

TRANSPORTATION

Highways in Miles (Kilometers): (97,287 km)
Railroads in Miles (Kilometers): (1,449 km)
Usable Airfields: 16 (2005)
Motor Vehicles in Use: 469,000

GOVERNMENT

Type: republic
Independence Date: February 4, 1948 (from
  the United Kingdom)
Head of State/Government: President Ma-
  hindra Rajapakse is both head of state and
  head of government.
Political Parties: Sri Lanka Freedom Party
  SLFP, United National Party UNP, Janatha
Vimukthi Perumuna VJP, Tamil National
Alliance TNA, National Heritage Party
JHU, Ceylon Workers Congress CWC, Sri
Lanka Muslim Congress SLMC.
Suffrage: universal at 18

MILITARY

Military Expenditures (% of GDP): $606.2
  million (2005 est.) (4.1% – 2006 est.)
Current Disputes: civil war, but hopes for
  peace

ECONOMY

Currency ($ U.S. Equivalent): 100.498
  rupees = $1 U.S. (2005)
Per Capita Income/GDP: $4,300 / $85.34
  billion (2005 est.)
GDP Growth Rate: 5.6% (2005 est.)
Inflation Rate: 11.2% (2005 est.)
Unemployment Rate: 8.4%
Labor Force by Occupation: 55.2% Services,
  27.1% Industry, 17.7% Agriculture
  (2005 est.)

Population Below Poverty Line: 22%
Natural Resources: limestone; graphite;
  mineral sands; gems; phosphates; clay;
  hydropower
Agriculture: tea; rubber; coconuts; rice;
  sugarcane; grains; pulses; oilseeds; spices;
  milk; eggs; hides; beef
Industry: rubber processing; clothing and
  textiles; cement; petroleum refining; tea;
  tobacco
Exports: $6.442 billion (2005) (primary
  partners United States, United Kingdom,
  India, Germany) (2004)
Imports: 8.37 billion (2005) (primary part-
  ners India, Singapore, Hong Kong, China,
  Iran, Japan, Malaysia) (2004)
Human Development Index (ranking): 93
  (UNDP 2005)

SUGGESTED WEBSITES

http://www.lanka.net/home/
http://www.cla.gov/cia/publications/factbook/
  geos/co.html
http://www.hinduonnet.com
http://www.eelam.com
http://www.saag.org/papers

Sri Lanka Country Report

Sri Lanka is a small island nation that hangs
like a pendant off the southeast coast of India.
Extending 270 miles from north to south, and
expanding to 140 miles in width toward its
southern end, it occupies just 1.5 percent of the
total landmass of the subcontinent. It was once
renowned for its pleasant tropical climate and
natural beauty. The Indian Ocean tsunami hit
Sri Lanka with devastating impact on December
26, 2004. But even more, for the past 20 years, it
has been ravaged by civil conflict. The country
once known as the "Pearl of the Orient" has become the "Lebanon of South Asia."

Sri Lanka is divided into two regions: a
low-lying dry zone to the north and a mountainous wet zone to the south. At the center
of the southern zone are the lush Kandyan
Highlands, whose extensive tea and rubber
plantations are watered by abundant rainfall,
especially during the southwest monsoon
season. Ceylonese tea, considered among the
finest in the world, has recently been replaced
by textiles as the country's leading export.

The northern plains are devoted mostly
to rice cultivation for domestic consumption.
Irrigation systems, necessary to support agriculture in this region, date from the earliest
record of settlers from India, in the fifth century B.C. Marauding forces from south India,
which destroyed the city of Anuradhapura in
the tenth century A.D., and malaria, borne
by mosquitoes bred in the still waters of the
irrigation lakes, drove the population of the
north-central region to the coastlands. Rede-

velopment of the blighted north-central region
started during the British colonial period.

DEVELOPMENT

Human resource development
and land and water reclamation
for agriculture and energy have
contributed most to Sri Lanka's
economic health. In spite of a decline in the
world tea market and, even more, the
devastation of civil war since 1983 and the
2004 tsunami, the country's largely
agricultural economy remains healthy.

In 1968 Sri Lanka undertook the Mahaweli
River Project to build five major dams and irrigation works along the 207-mile course of Sri
Lanka's longest river, from the central highlands to Koddiyar Bay on the east coast. This
development cleared, resettled and irrigated
900,000 acres. With substantial foreign investment, it was completed in 1983. The project
now produces 20 percent of the country's rice
and 45 percent of its power generation.

The Sri Lankan people are also divided,
north and south. Seventy-four percent of
Sri Lanka's population speak Sinhalese, 93
percent of whom are Theravada Buddhists.
Eighteen percent of the population is Tamil
speaking, two-thirds of whom are Hindu.

The Sinhalese trace their origin to fifth
century B.C. settlers from India. Legend describes their leader, Prince Vijaya, as of the

race of the lion, a Sinhal, a symbol of royalty
adopted from ancient Persian culture. Sent
from north India by his father, he arrived on
Sri Lanka on the day of the Buddha's death,
in 483 B.C. and established his kingdom in
the city of Anuradhapura in the north-central
region of the country.

Tradition also traces the origin of Buddhism on the island to Mahinda, the son and
emissary of the Indian emperor Asoka, in the
third century B.C. This Theravada tradition
reveres the teachings of the earliest disciples
of the Buddha—the elders (thera)—as contained in the Pali Canon. Itinerant monks
from India carried these sacred texts throughout South and Southeast Asia during the early
years of expansion of the Buddhist faith.

Portuguese, who arrived on the south
coast of Sri Lanka in the early 1500s, drove
many of the Sinhalese people of the south
into the mountains. There they established
a kingdom around the city of Kandy. Sinhalese Buddhists are divided today between
the Kandyans, who live in the Highlands, and
the "Low Country" people on the coastlands.
The latter are more numerous (60 percent)
and more prosperous, living in the more urban, coastal rim of the south.

The Tamils are also divided into two
groups: the Sri Lankan Tamils (70 percent)
and the Indian Tamils (30 percent). The Sri
Lankan Tamils are found mostly on the north
and east coastlands. Almost half of this Tamil
community lives in the northernmost district

of Jaffna, representing 95 percent of the district population. They share a long history on the island with the Kandyan Sinhalese, with whom they have the most in common culturally and ethnically.

The Indian Tamils were brought to Sri Lanka in the nineteenth century to work as field laborers on plantations set up by the British in the Kandyan Highlands. Their number was greatly reduced during the 1960s and 1970s by their repatriation to India. Those who remained, about 5 percent of the population of Sri Lanka, eventually received status as citizens of Sri Lanka.

Significant Christian and Muslim communities (8 percent and 7 percent), belong to both language groups. The Tamil-speaking Muslims live mostly along the east coast; a minority caught between the northern Tamils and Kandyan Sinhalese.

INDEPENDENCE

The British were the first to unify these peoples under a single government administration, in 1815. They introduced the rudiments of a national government in the port city of Colombo, on the southwest coast, and democratic institutions throughout the country. The first general elections were held in 1931, to select representatives to a National Assembly by universal suffrage under strict colonial control.

On February 4, 1948, Sri Lanka, then called Ceylon, received its independence as a parliamentary dominion in the British Commonwealth. In 1972, the government adopted a new Constitution as an independent republic, with a single legislature of 168 elected members. A further constitutional change, in 1978, endowed the presidency with extensive, independent executive authority. Junius Jayewardene, who had been appointed prime minister in 1978 after a sweeping victory of his United National party (UNP) in 1977, was elected president in separate national elections held in 1982.

His victory occurred at a time of great social unrest in the country. The vigorous pursuit of development, resettlement, and land reform projects had the unanticipated consequence of making many Kandy Sinhalese homeless. Their restlessness was expressed

by a militant, Marxist youth group called the People's Liberation Front (JVP), which began devastating attacks on villages throughout the south in 1971. These activities fed into an underlying conflict between the Tamil and Sinhalese populations that broke out into civil war in 1983.

CIVIL WAR

Soon after the independence of Sri Lanka, political leaders from the dominant Sinhalese community began to exploit a popular "Sinhala only" movement to eliminate advantages achieved by the Tamils during the Colonial period. S.W.R.D. Bandaranaike and his Sri Lanka Freedom Party, a coalition of leftist, pro-Sinhala groups, won the elections in 1956. He introduced then a bill to make Sinhalese the only official language of the country. The Tamil leaders responded with a nonviolent demonstration. Their protest incited an unchecked violent response by Sinhala extremists. Bandaranaikes attempt to restrain the anti-Tamil violence, and to find some accommodation for Tamil interests, led to his assassination in 1959 by an extremist Buddhist monk.

Adding fuel to the fire, the new constitution adopted in 1972, eliminated many of the minority protections adopted at the time of independence. In response, Tamil legislators formed a solid political caucus as the Tamil United Front to present their concerns in the national legislature. To diminish the appeal of a growing militancy among their youth, they also sought greater autonomy at the district level, to give them greater freedom and voice in those northern districts where they were in the majority.

The landslide victory of the United National Party in the 1977 elections took away the Tamil United Fronts leverage as a critical voting block at the national level. With the need to resettle some 130,000 families displaced by the new dams in the Mahaweli River Project, the UNP pursued policies that placed more Sinhalese in redefined districts in the northern part of the country. The Tamils then found themselves also losing political power at the district level.

The Tamils loss of political protection during the 1970s fanned the fires of some 36 militant student groups, youthful and eager for social and political change. Among them, the most ruthless and disciplined was the Liberation Tigers of Tamil Eelam (LTTE). It organized and carried out a sustained reign of terror throughout the northern regions of the country. In 1983, the LTTE ambushed a Sri Lankan army unit, inciting anti-Tamil riots in Colombo and across the south. Close to 2,000 Tamils were killed, 100,000 became internally displaced persons (IDP), and 130,000 fled to India as refugees. Civil war had begun.

Unable to control the violence, President Jayewardene invited the government of India in 1987 to send an Indian Peace Keeping Force (IPKF) to Sri Lanka. Faced with the IPKF's ineffectiveness and unpopularity, and with growing violence against the Tamils by the Sinhalese youth group JVP, Jayewardene did not seek reelection in 1988. His United National Party won the elections, and his successor, Ranasinghe Premadasa, asked the Indian Army to withdraw.

The Indian Peace Keeping Force left the LTTE weakened but no less resolved to seek independence for a separate Tamil state at any cost, including through drug trade and suicide bombing. This militant group was implicated in the assassination of President Premadasa on May 1, 1993, by a human time bomb, the same way Rajiv Gandhi, head of India's Congress Party, was killed while campaigning in south India in 1991.

The LTTE asserted its control in the northern Jaffna District by calling for a boycott of the 1994 national legislative elections. Less than 10 percent of the electorate in that district voted. In other parts of Sri Lanka, war-weary voters sought a political rather than military solution to the conflict between the Tamil insurgents and the Sinhalese majority. In hopes for peace, they elected a fragile coalition of leftist parties called the People's Alliance, led by Chandrika Kumaratunga.

Mrs. Kumaratunga was no stranger to politics. She was the daughter of S.W.R.D. Bandaranaike, the popular prime minister, leader of the Sri Lanka Freedom Party in the 1950s. Her mother, Sirimavo Bandaranaike, became leader of the SLFP after his assassination in 1959. She served as the nation's first woman prime minister from 1960 to 1965 and from 1970 to 1977, and as president from 1996 until her retirement in 2000. Mrs. Kumaratunga's husband, a popular film actor, was also active in national politics until his assassination, purportedly by a Sinhala nationalist group, while a presidential candidate in 1988.

Mrs. Kumaratunga initially proposed talks with the LTTE for a cease-fire. When

(Courtesy of Tamil Week/Tamil02)

Everyone standing around waiting at a distribution center in Jaffina for scarce food during the summer of 2006, when the Sri Lanka army cut off access to the city. This action caused the collapse of the Norwegian sponsored peace talks with the LTTE in Geneva in October 2006.

they did not materialize, the Sri Lankan army undertook a major offensive to remove the LTTE from its stronghold in the ravaged city of Jaffna. Her efforts to end the conflict by force did not bring peace.

Although weakened and further isolated from any political base, the LTTE continued to carry out guerrilla attacks in the northeastern coastal region of the country. It recaptured the town of Killinochchi on the vital highway to Jaffna in September 1998 and defeated the Sri Lankan forces in the Elephant Pass in April 2000. Its reign of terror included the assassination of two Tamil mayors of Jaffna to protest the attempt of a more moderate Tamil United Liberation Front to reestablish civil order there.

ACHIEVEMENTS

All are looking to achieve some normalcy and peace in a conflict that increasingly hardens the opposing forces, and makes resolution more difficult.

In 2001, the United National Party, campaigning to renew efforts toward peace in the national legislative People's Alliance. Prime minister Ranil Wickremesinghe picked up on initiatives for mediation by the Norwegian government to enter into a full ceasefire agreement with the LTTE in February 2002. In July, his government fulfilled a vital precondition of the LTTE to enter into peace

talks by withdrawing the ban placed on the LTTE as a terrorist organization. Formal talks with the LTTE then began with Norwegian facilitation in Thailand in September. At a later round of talks in December 2002, the Norwegian mediators offered a proposal called the Oslo Statement to explore an acceptable formula for limited autonomy for the Tamil people within a united sovereign Sri Lanka.

The Oslo Statement proved problematic for both parties, and the peace process stalled.

The LTTE did not want to discuss any proposal that presupposed a united, sovereign country. They wanted first to establish an Interim Self Governing Authority for the Tamil-speaking North Eastern Province. Once accepted as separate, then they would talk about assurances to make it possible for them to join in a shared governance of the island as a whole.

To push its agenda for self rule, the LTTE held "Heroes Week" demonstrations in the northeast region at the end of November 2004, to commemorate 17,800 Tamils who have died in their 30-year civil war. Alleged security force interference with the demonstrations led to a one-day strike in the northern cities of Trincomalee, Mannar, and Vavuniya. The cease-fire remained fragile, with UNICEF accusations of child recruitment by the LTTE, and fighting among factions within the LTTE as major concerns. On the other side, a roused Sinhala nationalist opposition defeated the United National

Party in the national legislative elections held in November 2003. It asserted that Prime Minister Wickremesinghe was making too many concessions in the Norwegian negotiations.

And then, on December 26, 2004, the Indian Ocean tsunami hit the east coast of the country from the tip of Jaffna in the north to city of Galle in the south. The immense power of its wave killed 30,240 people, and left 883,780 homeless. The survivors of Sri Lanka were overwhelmed by the indiscriminate devastation and heavy toll of the tsunami disaster and then by the incredible outpouring of relief provided by so many from all parts of the world.

Bickering over relief efforts, intensified by the LTTE's dominant control over the northern region of the country, quickly dissolved the hope that a shared national calmity might bring the warring sides together. The presidential election in November 2005, was won by Mahinda Rajapakse of the United Peoples Freedom Alliance. To increase his chance of victory he formed this coalition with Sinhalese nationalist parties which take a hard line for a unitary rather than federalist solution to the civil conflict. The LTTE, which saw more advantage to a hard line opposition in Colombo, enforced a boycott of the election in the region of the island under its control. That stance assured Rajapakse of success at the polls.

The Sri Lanka Monitoring Mission (SLMM) reported in August 2006 of an in-

Timeline: PAST

500 B.C.

Migration of Sinhalese Indians

247 B.C.

Mahinda introduces Buddhism

A.D. 1815–1948

British colonial rule

1948

The independence of Ceylon, as a British Commonwealth dominion

1972

A new Constitution establishes Sri Lanka as a democratic republic

1977

The United National Party wins elections by wide margin

1978

The Constitution is modified to establish an independent president

1982–1988

Junius Jayewardene serves as president; anti-Tamil nots break out; Indian Peace Keeping Force

1990s

Efforts to achieve a cease-fire between LTTE and Sri Lankan military forces and to negotiate a settlement in the dispute between the Tamil minority and Sinhalese majority tail

PRESENT

2000s

Sri Lankan economy hit by civil war and the Indian Ocean Tsunami

Tsunami death toll estimated at 38,000

The government and the LTTE achieve a cease-fire and hold talks facilitated by Norway to restore peace

India and South Asia—Sri Lanka

2001

The government and LTTE agree to Norway brokered ceasefire and to talks to restore peace.

2004

Indian Ocean Tsunami hits, leaving 30,240 dead and 883,780 homeless.

2006

With death toll of civil war rising to 67,000 since 1983, peace talks between government and LTTE break down.

creasing number of major violations in the Cease Fire Agreement in the North and East. United Nation's estimates report more than 3,000 deaths and 225,000 made homeless by terrorist and military action in 2006. And a meeting of both sides in Geneva to resume peace talks in October got nowhere.

To reaffirm its unitary position, the Rajapakse government has initiated a shared common policy with the United National Party toward firming a strong negotiating position in Norwegian sponsored peace talks. But with peace negotiations stalled and a move by President Rajapakse to lure members of the UNP away from their party by promising to appoint them as ministers in the UPFA government, the Memorandum of Understanding between the two parties collapsed.

President Rajapakse also created a multi-ethnic panel to recommend a form of genuine power-sharing which could accommodate minorities that have been side-lined and alienated from the state, while preserving the unity, sovereignty and territorial integrity of the state. A 37 page report of recommendations was issued in November, but with dissention among the 17 members who created it, there is little assurance that the affected minorities will see in it any avenue for recognition and peace.

Sri Lanka's experience in seeking an inclusive national identity as a democracy has taken a heavy toll among its people. Those who have been ravaged and displaced by civil war and by the tsunami do not see any assured end to their plight.

Five Years after 9/11

Shahid Javed Burki

That 9/11 changed the world is a time-worn cliche, now repeated countless times in books, magazine articles and newspaper columns. What is not said is how that change occurred. The fifth anniversary of that fateful day has come and gone with newspaper pages filled with stories about the families that lost loved ones and with analyses of how America and the rest of the world have fared since that morning, when three hijacked airliners hit the World Trade Centre at New York and the Pentagon near Washington.

That act of terrorism was carried out by 19 young men, most of them from Saudi Arabia, for reasons that are still dimly understood. A great deal has been written about their possible motives. The United States government spent millions of dollars in funding the work of a bipartisan commission of 10 members, five Democrats and five Republicans, in trying to understand what prompted these young men to act so desperately, and in the process, take nearly 3,000 innocent lives as well as their own. The 9/11 Commission gathered a great deal of information about the men who committed those crimes and also about those who motivated them. However, it did not reach a firm conclusion as to why these people hated the United States so much that they were prepared to give their lives to hurt some Americans, even those who were perfectly innocent.

Since that day, more innocent lives have been lost, some as a result of more acts of terrorism and some by the way the three countries that have led the charge against terrorism have acted. The leaderships of the three countries—America, Britain and Israel—have now concluded that what they are fighting is a dangerous ideology akin to those that produced so much havoc and misery in the 20th century.

The ideology has been given a name, Islamic fascism, and its objectives have been equated with those of fascism, Nazism and communism. These ideologies, all European in origin, attempted to overpower democratic-liberalism and reorder the industrial world. They were defeated either on the battlefield or by the sheer economic power liberalism was able to muster against state-controlled socialism. The same strategy is now being advocated by those who claim that the post-modern western world is once again challenged by another destructive ideology.

This time around, however, that ideology does not have its roots in Europe but in the sands of Arabia. It is being claimed that its origin lies in a religion that rose some 14 centuries ago in what is Saudi Arabia today and spread to all corners of the world. It now has 1.2 billion followers, a fifth of mankind.

There are many dangers in this new line of thinking for the entire Muslim world, not just the Arab countries. It threatens to turn the on-going conflict between a small group of Islamists who are not supported, let alone sponsored, by any Muslim state and some countries in the west into something much larger in scope: a clash between two cultures and two religions. By calling it an ideology, some Western leaders could turn this conflict into an all out confrontation between the Muslim world and the West. That would be a highly dangerous turn in events, brought about by a very deliberate attempt to misread what is actually happening in Muslim countries.

History, as has been proven time and gain, can be moulded into shapes that suit narrow interests. It is in the interest of the large majority of Muslims around the globe not to fall into this trap and mindlessly march towards a catastrophic confrontation. There is still time to halt this journey.

The Muslim community needs to do three things and do them urgently. In this context, the people and leadership of Pakistan as well as those of us who live abroad could play important roles. The first thing that needs to be done is to condemn all acts of terrorism, no matter where they are carried out and no matter which grievance motivates them. The message that must go out is that Islam does not condone violence of any form against innocent people. In fact, Islam teaches compassion, not mindless terrorism.

This message may resonate with those in the West who have open minds and are still prepared to listen. This message, even if it was communicated, has been done with a weak voice. It has given the impression that the majority of Muslims are content to move in the direction in which the extremists are pushing them.

That is certainly not the case but that sentiment should be openly and fearlessly expressed. Non-Muslims in the West must be made to believe that those who advocate and practise terrorism are indeed very small in number and do not represent Islam.

Second, the Muslim world and the Muslim countries around the world must be made to adopt political systems that are representative of all citizens and are not meant to serve the narrow interests of small elites. The resentment of the young is growing in countries where only limited political space is available to the people—especially the young—for expressing themselves and for having their grievances redressed. This is the case even in countries that have established and well-functioning democratic systems. Britain is one example of a country in which the political structure encourages Muslim exclusion and separation rather than their absorption. This has contributed to the expression of discontent through violence. The British approach to multi-culturalism—of allowing people with religious and systems of belief that are different from the majority to live separately from the mainstream—has not worked. It has created many islands of resentment to which the young men prepared to commit acts of terrorism belong.

Third, both the Muslim state and the Muslim communities that live in non-Muslim states must give the highest priority to human development. No additional analytical or statistical work needs to be done to underscore the important point that, in terms of human development, Muslims have been left behind; or, more accurately, they have allowed themselves to fall at the end of the queue that is moving towards development and modernisation. In its regional and country reports, the UNDP has clearly demonstrated how backward Muslims are, at this point in time, in educating themselves, training themselves and acquiring skills for themselves that are necessary to become productive participants in a fast moving world.

These three steps—raising a clear voice against extremism and terrorism, developing institutions that allow political participation to all segments of the citizenry, developing human resource—must be taken by Pakistan, the Muslim world's second largest country. But that is not the only reason why Pakistan must be at the forefront of this campaign against the small group of Muslim extremists who are determined to rock and disrupt the world. Because of the unhappy developments since America fought its first war against Afghanistan in the 1980s, Pakistan has become the epicentre of Islamic extremism. The only way to cure the country of this condition is to move resolutely in these three areas.

Those who believe in moderation must raise their voices. President Pervez Musharraf has spoken clearly on this issue but his administration shows less than total resolve when it comes to creating the environment needed to obstruct the advance of extremism. He has, at times, allowed himself to be intimidated by radical groups. He should have, for instance, taken a firm position that the Hudood laws don't belong to the law books of a modern society. They discriminate against women, something Islam never permitted. These laws should have been removed from the books a long time ago. But the hesitant moves in this direction have only emboldened the extremists and further tarnished Pakistan's already poor reputation.

On September 14, the New York Times carried a prominently placed story under the title "Pakistan bid to end abuse of women reporting rape hits snag." Wrote the newspaper: "Pervez Musharraf has sought to use the measure, the Women's Protection Bill, to burnish his credentials as a modern and moderate Islamic leader before his visit to the United States this month.

But the opposition has, temporarily at least, disrupted his well-orchestrated campaign."

Muslim societies must play a determined role in moving towards a situation in which they can fully participate in the rapidly changing world. They must not allow themselves to be isolated. This is happening and a part of the responsibility is that of the Muslim world. The other part is that of the West, in particular of some of the people who occupy positions of power at this critical time. For instance, the stance taken by the US president and the British prime minister continues to aggravate the situation in the Muslim world. The way the war in Iraq is being fought and the way Bush and Blair handled the conflict in Lebanon have further exacerbated the situation.

The way official Washington observed the fifth anniversary of the terrorist attacks of September 11, 2001 sent exactly the wrong message to the Muslim world. In a prime time speech delivered from the Oval Office, the American president sought to place the war in Iraq that he initiated in the context of an epic battle between tyranny and freedom, saying the conflict in that country was "the decisive ideological struggle of the 21st century and the calling of our generation." He continued: "if we do not defeat these enemies now, we will leave our children to face a Middle East overrun by terrorist states and radical dictators armed with nuclear weapons."

He equalled the task ahead of him to those faced by several of his predecessors, in particular Franklin Roosevelt who led the war against Adolf Hitler's Germany and the doctrine of Nazism. He also drew a parallel with presidents such as Harry S. Truman and John F. Kennedy who rallied America against another tyrannical ideology—European communism.

But in drawing these parallels and in settling down to explain the conflicts in Afghanistan, Iraq, Lebanon and Palestine as a war against yet another ideology, President Bush is treading on very dangerous ground.

This emphasis on a war with an ideology will push those who think otherwise into the arms of those who would like to portray it exactly in those terms. For the American president and the British prime minister it may be politically expedient to portray their wars in various Muslim countries in those terms.

This, they believe, would save them from admitting that the war in Iraq was a mistake, that the Palestinians should not be condemned to perpetual backwardness within the boundaries of an unviable state, that Israel should not have been allowed to hit Lebanon so mercilessly.

It was a mistake not to have stayed fully engaged in Afghanistan to the point where its diverse people were fully accommodated in that unfortunate country's fledgling economic and political system. Unfortunately, Afghanistan was left to its devices—in the hands of drug lords, warlords, and selfish tribal lords, while both Washington and London got engaged in an unnecessary enterprise in Iraq. Not recognising that a series of colossal mistakes were made and to portray them in the context of a war against an ideology would produce exactly what Osama bin Laden and Ayman al Zawahiri wanted all along: an all-out war with the West.

An Afghan Symbol for Change, Then Failure

DAVID ROHDE

It began last summer.

On a July morning, *Taliban* gunmen shot dead the province's most powerful cleric as he walked to the main city mosque to lead morning prayers. Five months later, they executed a teacher at a nearby village school as students watched. The following month, they walked into another mosque and gunned down an Afghan engineer working for a foreign aid group, shooting him in the back as he pressed his forehead to the ground and supplicated to God.

This spring and summer, the slow and methodical siege of this southern provincial capital intensified. The Taliban and their allies set up road checkpoints, burned 20 trucks and slowed the flow of supplies to reconstruction projects. All told, in surrounding Helmand Province, five teachers, one judge and scores of police officers have been killed. Dozens of schools and courts have been shuttered, according to Afghan officials.

"Our government is weak," said Fowzea Olomi, a local women's rights advocate whose driver was shot dead in May and who fears she is next. "Anarchy has come."

When the Taliban fell nearly five years ago, Lashkar Gah seemed like fertile ground for the United States-led effort to stabilize the country. For 30 years during the cold war, Americans carried out the largest development project in Afghanistan's history here, building a modern capital with suburban-style tract homes, a giant hydroelectric dam and 300 miles of canals that made 250,000 acres of desert bloom. Afghans called this city "Little America."

Today, Little America is the epicenter of a Taliban resurgence and an explosion in drug cultivation that has claimed the lives of 106 American and *NATO* soldiers this year and doubled American casualty rates countrywide. Across Afghanistan, roadside bomb attacks are up by 30 percent; suicide bombings have doubled. Statistically it is now nearly as dangerous to serve as an American soldier in Afghanistan as it is in Iraq.

Helmand's descent symbolizes how Afghanistan has evolved since the initial victory over the Taliban into one of the most troubled fronts in the fight against terrorism.

The problems began in early 2002, former Bush administration, *United Nations* and Afghan officials said, when the United States and its allies failed to take advantage of a sweeping desire among Afghans for help from foreign countries.

The Defense Department initially opposed a request by *Colin L. Powell*, then secretary of state, and Afghanistan's new leaders for a sizable peacekeeping force and deployed only 8,000 American troops, but purely in a combat role, officials said.

During the first 18 months after the invasion, the United States-led coalition deployed no peacekeepers outside Kabul, leaving the security of provinces like Helmand to local Afghans.

"Where the world, including the United States, came up short was on the security side," said Richard Haass, the former director of policy planning at the State Department. "That was the mistake which I believe is coming back to haunt the United States now."

The lack of security was just one element of a volatile mix. Twenty years of conflict had shattered government and social structures in Afghanistan, the world's fifth poorest country, where the average life expectancy is 43.

American officials said the country was more destitute than they had envisioned, yet the $909 million they provided in assistance in 2002 amounted to one-twentieth of the $20 billion allocated for postwar Iraq. Officials quintupled assistance to $4.8 billion by 2005, but then reduced it by 30 percent this year.

The Taliban leadership, meanwhile, found safe haven in neighboring Pakistan. And Robert Grenier, the *C.I.A.*'s former top counterterrorism official and Islamabad station chief, said Pakistani officials largely turned a blind eye to Taliban commanders, who later seeped back across the border.

The government of President *Hamid Karzai*, hailed as Afghanistan's eloquent new leader in 2001, has increasingly been criticized for indecisiveness, corruption and inaction.

In Helmand, the absence of security and government control enabled the province to become the largest heroin-producing area in Afghanistan.

By 2005, local Taliban fighters and drug traffickers had formed an alliance against the government. Today, the province's educated elite accuses local officials of engaging in drug trafficking, and impoverished farmers say they grow poppy to survive.

[Led by a 160 percent increase in Helmand's opium crop this year, Afghanistan's overall production grew by 50 percent to a record 6,100 metric tons, United Nations officials said Saturday. Afghanistan now produces 92 percent of the world's supply of opium poppy, the basis for heroin.]

Richard A. Boucher, the assistant secretary of state for South Asia, defended the pace of progress, saying expectations among Afghans and others that the war-ravaged country could be quickly rebuilt were unrealistic.

"Afghan development is a long-term project, even without the security problem," said Mr. Boucher. "Over all, I think it's pretty incredible what we've accomplished."

Despite an active insurgency, he said, 1.6 million Afghan girls are attending school, 730 miles of roads and 1,000 schools, clinics and government buildings have been reconstructed, and the country has its first democratically elected president and Parliament.

Bryan Whitman, a Pentagon spokesman, said that the recent surge in violence was the result of the Afghan central government and NATO exerting their authority in remote areas, prompting retaliatory attacks from the Taliban, drug traffickers and warlords.

The return of more than three million Afghan refugees and the arrival of some foreign aid turned the country's main cities into boom towns. But over time, the lack of construction in rural provinces fueled Taliban propaganda claims that Americans were enriching themselves and bringing only corruption to Afghanistan.

In impoverished southern rural areas, small numbers of Afghans are openly collaborating with the Taliban. Other Afghans, who say they are unsure of the American commitment and disillusioned with Mr. Karzai, sit by and dare not resist them.

Rauzia Baloch, a 33-year-old teacher, was one of a half dozen women elected to Helmand's provincial council last year. In December, the American government sent her on a study tour of the United States that included visits to Congress and a domestic violence shelter in Phoenix, and Thanksgiving dinner with a family in Indiana.

When Ms. Baloch returned to Helmand, she found the Taliban assassinating government officials.

"I learned a lot, but unfortunately the situation is not the same as in America," she said. "We cannot do anything."

Countering the Soviets

During the cold war years in the Helmand Valley, amid a flat, barren landscape of reddish soil and black boulders, dozens of American engineers and their families carried out a sweeping project designed to develop impoverished southern Afghanistan and wean locals from Soviet influence.

For more than three decades, the American government and Morrison-Knudsen, the firm that built the Hoover Dam, restored and expanded an ancient irrigation system. Its source of life, then and now, was the surging Helmand River, a finger of green that emerges from the mountains of central Afghanistan and snakes for hundreds of miles through the country's vast southern desert.

The project never irrigated as many acres as was hoped, but its training programs produced hundreds of American-minded Afghan engineers and technicians.

"Most of them have lived and worked and studied in the United States; some have married American wives," the British historian Arnold J. Toynbee wrote after visiting the area in 1960. "The new world that they are conjuring up out of the desert at the Helmand River's expense is to be an America-in-Asia."

Among the young Afghans who were transformed in the process was Ms. Olomi, the women's rights advocate. One of the first girls to attend the city's new co-educational school, she also went on to become one of Helmand's first women to graduate from college.

In a recent interview, Ms. Olomi, now 49, remembered only a handful of words in English. But she could still tick off the names of her American teachers and recite verses of "Twinkle, Twinkle Little Star" and "Puff the Magic Dragon." After school, she recalled, she played a game called basketball with American children.

"It was a very good time," she said, eulogizing the functioning schools, clean streets and tranquillity of Lashkar Gah in the 1960's and 1970's. "I was very happy."

But her good fortune, like that of Lashkar Gah's, would be short-lived. Americans abandoned the city just before the 1979 Soviet invasion. Twenty years of guerrilla and civil war ensued.

By the early 1990's, soldiers-turned-thieves roamed Lashkar Gah's streets and warlords encouraged local farmers to grow opium poppies, the raw form of heroin.

In 1994, residents welcomed the rise of the Taliban in Helmand's remote villages and applauded when thieves had their hands chopped off on a local soccer field. Crime plummeted.

For Ms. Olomi and other women, life fell apart. Her husband, who had gone to Russia to study medicine, never returned. Taliban religious police closed a girls' school she had opened to support herself. Ms. Olomi, who had chosen her husband at the age of 25, watched helplessly as her daughter was forced by her husband's brothers to marry a cousin at 13.

Hopes rose again in 2001, when American bombs drove the Taliban from power in Afghanistan. Residents like Ms. Olomi said they dreamed of another American-backed renaissance.

"At that time, we really felt so happy," she said. "We felt that we were free now."

Roads and Roadblocks

As expectations soared in Lashkar Gah and across Afghanistan, division emerged in Washington over what role the United States should play in rebuilding and securing the country.

During meetings in January and February 2002, Robert Finn, the first American ambassador to post-Taliban Afghanistan, proposed that the United States undertake ambitious construction projects as a way to cement the loyalty of Afghans. Top among them was rebuilding a pulverized ring road linking Afghanistan's major cities—a road Americans helped build during the cold war.

"I argued for them to build the road and all I got was 'no,'" Mr. Finn recalled. "It was just across the board in Washington: 'We don't do those kinds of projects anymore.'"

83

Andrew Natsios, then the administrator of the United States Agency for International Development, the government's main foreign development arm that had spearheaded the Lashkar Gah project years back, confirmed in an interview that he had opposed road building and other large construction projects.

He said he feared they would consume too much of his agency's limited budget and staff. Criticism of failed foreign projects and a drive to privatize aid work had shrunk the agency from 3,000 Americans posted abroad in the 1980's to 1,000 today.

In the end, the United States pledged $297 million in reconstruction money to Afghanistan in 2002. The *European Union* pledged $495 million. Japan gave $200 million and Saudi Arabia $73 million, but both were slow to deliver.

When aid officials arrived in Kabul in late 2001, they were shocked by the country's decrepit state. They had to build headquarters from scratch, they said, and contend with the lack of skilled Afghan workers. For remote areas like Helmand, it meant what assistance was available flowed in slowly.

At the same time, Secretary of Defense *Donald H. Rumsfeld* and Secretary Powell clashed over security issues, according to their aides.

In a response to written questions, Mr. Powell said that in early 2002 he called for American troops to participate in the expansion of a 4,000-soldier international peacekeeping force designed to bolster Mr. Karzai's fledgling government. Mr. Haass, the former State Department official, said informal conversations with European officials led him to believe the United States could recruit a force of 30,000 peacekeepers, half European, half American.

Mr. Rumsfeld and his aides were skeptical. They feared European countries would not provide enough troops, according to Mr. Whitman, the Pentagon spokesman. Defense Department officials believed it was better to train local security forces.

Over all, Pentagon officials hoped to minimize the number of American troops in the country to avoid stoking Afghans' historic resistance to foreign occupation, said Douglas J. Feith, the former under secretary for policy.

Ali Ahmed Jalali, the country's interior minister from 2002 to 2005, said Afghan resentment of foreign peacekeepers was "a myth." After 10 years of internecine civil war, he said, Afghans yearned for someone to step in.

"They could not help themselves," he said, referring to Afghans. "They were at war with themselves."

James Dobbins, then the administration's special envoy to Afghanistan, said Mr. Powell was ultimately unable to win support from Mr. Rumsfeld and other senior administration officials.

The 4,000-soldier international peacekeeping force would not venture outside Kabul. The United States deployed its 8,000 soldiers separately, but they focused on capturing or killing Taliban and Qaeda members, not on peacekeeping or reconstruction.

As an alternative, officials came up with a loosely organized system designed to empower Afghans to secure the country. The United States would train a 70,000-soldier army. Japan would demobilize some 100,000 militia fighters. Britain would mount an antinarcotics program. Italy would carry out judicial reform. And Germany would train a 62,000-member police force.

In April 2002, President Bush outlined his vision for rebuilding Afghanistan in a speech honoring George C. Marshall, the American general who led the rebuilding of postwar Europe.

Mr. Bush said the history of military conflict in Afghanistan had been marked by "initial success, followed by long years of floundering and ultimate failure." He vowed: "We're not going to repeat that mistake."

On the ground in Afghanistan, problems arose immediately.

When Mr. Finn, the ambassador, reviewed the first Afghan National Army troops trained by the Americans in the summer of 2002, he was dismayed.

"They were illiterate," he said. "They didn't know how to keep themselves clean. They were at a much lower level than people expected."

American military officials told him that local Afghan commanders sent them their worst conscripts.

Mr. Dobbins, the former special envoy to Afghanistan, said Defense Department hopes that Afghans could quickly take responsibility for their own security proved unrealistic.

"The reason we are there is that these are failed states," said Mr. Dobbins, who has also served as special envoy to Haiti, Bosnia and Kosovo. "The thought that this can be quickly remedied has proved unjustified in most cases."

The police were even more challenging. Seventy percent of the existing 80,000 officers were illiterate. Eighty percent lacked proper equipment and corruption was endemic. Afghan police did not patrol; they set up checkpoints and waited for residents to report crimes, with bribes often needed to do so.

Yet in 2002 and 2003, Germany, the country responsible for police training, dispatched only 40 advisers. They reopened the Kabul police academy and began a program designed to graduate 3,500 senior officers in three years. German officials said developing a core of skilled commanders was the key to reform, frustrating American officials who backed a large, countrywide training effort. Some American and European military units conducted ad hoc training around the country, but no comprehensive instruction occurred outside Kabul.

Shattered Judicial System

In Lashkar Gah, veteran policemen and judges who returned from living in exile during the reign of the Taliban were aghast at what they found. Only one-third of the province's 3,000 policemen were, in fact, trained. The rest, including the provincial police chief, were former guerrilla fighters who punished members of other tribes and turned a blind eye toward rogues from their own.

"They did not know about the law," said Abdul Shakoor, a veteran police lieutenant. "They had their tribal ideas."

Abdul Waheed Afghani, then a 67-year-old retired judge who had been in exile in Saudi Arabia, said the judicial system was no better. When he looked for judges to send to each of the province's 13 districts, he found only three people with judicial training. He asked for help from Kabul, but received no response.

"I have given reports to many branches of the government," he said. "But no one has helped me."

The only foreign troops to deploy in Helmand, a province twice the size of Maryland with a population of one million, were several dozen American Special Forces soldiers. They built a base in the center of the province in 2002, hired several hundred Afghan gunmen to protect them, and focused solely on hunting Taliban and Qaeda remnants, according to Afghan officials.

Helmand Province's voluble young governor, Sher Muhammad Akhund, was largely left to do as he pleased. The son of a famed local commander who fought the Soviets, Mr. Akhund entered Taliban-controlled Afghanistan in 2001 at Mr. Karzai's request and won control of Helmand with the help of the Special Forces. Rumors abounded about the governor. In interviews with journalists, Mr. Akhund said he was in his early 30's and a high school graduate. Afghan aid workers said he was in his late 20's and illiterate.

Whatever he may have lacked in administrative skills, he made up for in muscle. As the head of Helmand's largest and most influential tribe, the Alizai, he commanded several hundred gunmen.

As time passed, community leaders grew frustrated with Mr. Akhund. Haji Ahmad Shah, a wealthy local farmer, said Mr. Akhund initially refused to meet with him to discuss farmers' problems. When he finally did, he ignored the complaints.

"When I was sharing these problems with the governor, he didn't do anything," said Mr. Shah. "He was just working for his own benefit."

In 2003, Mr. Akhund confiscated 200 shops owned by a local minority group, according to a State Department report. Outside the city, the governor doled out parcels of land to his relatives and tribe, according to residents. Mr. Akhund denied the accusations.

At the same time, reports began to reach Kabul that Mr. Akhund was promoting the growth of poppy, according to an American official who spoke on condition of anonymity because of the sensitivity of the drug issue.

After the fall of the Taliban, poppy growth had exploded in eastern and southern Afghanistan, fed by poverty, weak law enforcement and an epic, five-year drought.

Mr. Akhund vehemently denied rumors that he took a cut of the poppy trade, but foreign officials remained skeptical. [On Saturday, Antonio Maria Costa, the executive director of the United Nations Office on Drugs and Crime, blamed Mr. Akhund specifically for Helmand's soaring poppy crop, saying there was evidence he encouraged farmers to grow opium poppies.]

While corruption grew in Afghanistan, the Taliban regrouped in Pakistan and changed tactics, according to American officials. After being decimated in open battles with American troops through 2002, the Taliban began ambushing small groups of American soldiers and unarmed aid workers in 2003. Over time, aid groups scaled back or suspended reconstruction projects in the rural south and east.

In March, a group of gunmen in Oruzgan Province pulled a foreign engineer out of a vehicle belonging to the International Red Cross, shot him in the head and back, and left his body in the dirt.

Two days later, in a remote riverbed in northern Helmand, gunmen ambushed American Special Forces as they drove past in a small convoy, killing two soldiers. When their comrades stopped to return fire, the gunmen vanished down a maze of gullies.

U.S. Shifts Course

In the summer of 2003, officials in Washington unveiled an overhaul of American policy in Afghanistan.

Until then, Americans had rebuilt the main highway linking Kabul and Kandahar, after initially rejecting the road proposal by Mr. Finn, the ambassador. Otherwise, Washington had shied away from large-scale projects like power plants.

Between 2003 and 2004, American assistance to Afghanistan increased from $962 million to $2.4 billion; the Afghanistan staff of the United States aid agency doubled; and Washington dispatched an aggressive new ambassador, Zalmay Khalilzad.

At the same time, the American military, expanding its role beyond combat, deployed eight new Provincial Reconstruction Teams, mostly to volatile southern and eastern Afghanistan. The units tried to win the loyalty of Afghans by equipping local government offices and mounting small reconstruction projects.

Mr. Feith, the former Defense Department official, said progress was made in Afghanistan in 2002 and 2003, but that the disappointing results of the allies' plan for training the police required an increased American effort.

Former United Nations and State Department officials said the weakness in the Afghanistan policy should have been apparent to the administration much earlier. "It was possible in early 2002 and late 2001 to have calculated more accurately the manpower and money needs," said Mr. Dobbins.

In Helmand, a field commander in the new development effort was Charles Grader. The 72-year-old Massachusetts native was the last American to head the Afghanistan program before the 1979 Soviet invasion. Twenty-five years later, he was back, managing a $130 million United States government contract to revitalize agriculture and slow the growth of poppy.

Mr. Grader was a marker of how the American approach to development had changed since the 1970's. No longer a government worker, he was now a private contractor paid $130,000 a year by Chemonics International, a for-profit consulting firm based in Washington. Instead of directing projects, the United States aid agency hired companies like Chemonics, which farmed out work to subcontractors.

In June 2004, Mr. Grader drove into Lashkar Gah with eight security guards and found a burgeoning city of 100,000 people that was a maze of new construction, shops and bustling open-air markets. But the prosperity was illusory. The boom was largely fueled by Helmand's opium trade, which by then had been spreading across the province for two and a half years since the Taliban was defeated.

On his first stop, Mr. Grader toured a demonstration farm bursting with cotton, pomegranates and other crops designed to show farmers they could make a legal living. Mr. Grader asked the Afghans who ran the farm what would persuade others to stop growing poppy.

Their responses had little to do with agriculture. They said the biggest problem was poverty and corruption. Farmers, they said, no longer believed the government would punish them for growing poppy.

"There is an inverse relationship between security and poppy growing," said Abdul Ghani Ayubi, an engineer trained by the Americans in the 1970's.

A local farmer was more blunt. "We don't have law. This is a warlord kingdom."

Mr. Grader promised to create public works projects that would repair the province's irrigation system and employ large numbers of farmers. Four months later he resigned after clashing with aid agency officials over the direction of the program. High turnover rates among both aid agency officials and contractors slowed the American effort, according to Afghan and American officials.

Some work did get under way, including repairs to the hydroelectric dam built by Americans during the cold war and an alternative-livelihoods program that put 37,000 Afghans to work cleaning hundreds of irrigation canals.

A dozen new or refurbished health clinics were opened and over 100 wells were dug or deepened. The aid agency reported spending about $180 million in Helmand since 2001. In addition, the reconstruction of Afghanistan's major highway included 90 miles in the province.

But local officials said these projects did not provide enough jobs to counter the lure of growing opium poppies for Helmand's 100,000 farmers.

In addition, a popular perception took hold that after foreign contractors and subcontractors took their cut of aid money, little cash was left for average Afghans. And local residents grew suspicious of the foreigners who lived in heavily guarded compounds with electric generators and satellite televisions while they lacked regular running water and electricity.

Aid agency officials defended their spending in Helmand, saying that foreign workers were needed to properly carry out the projects, train Afghans and prevent corruption.

In October 2004, one of the eight new American military Provincial Reconstruction Teams arrived in Helmand. Over the next two years, the team spent $9.5 million to build, refurbish or equip 28 schools, two police stations, two orphanages, a prison, a hospital ward and 20 miles of roads.

Just outside the American base, the United States built a women's job-training center for Ms. Olomi to run. The Americans provided dozens of computers and sewing machines and even set up a mock beauty salon so women could learn marketable skills. On one wall are pictures of *Laura Bush* visiting Afghanistan and meeting with the country's newly liberated women.

Brazen Attacks Increase

By the spring of 2005, the stepped-up American effort in Helmand was showing signs of being overmatched by the rising violence. On a May morning, gunmen stopped a vehicle carrying five Afghans working on the program to clean irrigation canals. In broad daylight a few miles outside Lashkar Gah, they shot the workers dead.

The following day, gunmen followed six relatives of one of the victims as they drove his body back to Kabul. Just off the main highway, they executed all six.

Days later, the canal cleaning project—perhaps the Americans' most successful undertaking in Helmand—was shut down over lack of security. Thousands of farmers were immediately out of work. Attacks also slowed repairs to the Kajaki dam.

Security had emerged as the largest single impediment to developing Helmand, but the country's nascent army and police force were unable to deliver it. The first units from the new, American-trained Afghan National Army arrived in Helmand in 2005, but they comprised only several hundred soldiers and carried out few operations, according to local Afghan officials. A new provincial antinarcotics force was created that year, but it consisted of just 30 officers.

The long-delayed Japanese-led program to disarm militia fighters began in Helmand in 2005, but only several hundred assault rifles and machine guns were collected, according to the local police. Officials said vast numbers of weapons remain in Helmand and are being used by the Taliban and drug traffickers.

Police training also continued to lag behind. After Germany failed to mount any training outside Kabul, the State Department hired DynCorp International, an Irving, Tex., firm, to recruit, train and deploy dozens of American police advisers in Afghanistan and build seven regional training centers.

By mid-2004, the centers were operating two- to four-week training classes across Afghanistan. European officials said the training should be at least three months long, and one derided the classes as "conveyor-belt courses."

"I had 15 days' training in Kandahar," said Mr. Shakoor, the police lieutenant. "The things that they were teaching me I already knew."

Corruption was also undermining progress. A 28-year-old police recruit who asked not to be identified because he feared retaliation said he was disappointed when he returned from training to his district in Helmand. His commander continued to take 50 percent of his salary, he said, and work with drug traffickers.

The United States, meanwhile, expanded DynCorp's police training contract, increasing basic courses from two to eight weeks, and sent two DynCorp contractors to important provinces to serve as advisers. Two retired American sheriff's deputies were sent to Lashkar Gah, to cover all of Helmand.

Jesse Valdez, 55, from Santa Cruz, Calif., had trained police officers in Bosnia, Indonesia and the Philippines. Steve Rubcic, 58, from Wyoming, had never been east of Wisconsin.

When they arrived in October, security was so bad they could not visit any of the province's 13 districts. In interviews, both said the Afghan police were eager for help and that they were making progress removing corrupt officials. Six weeks after they arrived, a small car bomb detonated outside the governor's office several minutes before they arrived for a meeting.

In March, two more DynCorp advisers joined them in Lashkar Gah. A month later, a suicide car bomb attack flipped their armored vehicle, but they survived. Both refused to leave.

In June, American officials dispatched an eight-man DynCorp "saturation" training team to Lashkar Gah. Brent

Thompson, a 33-year-old former police officer from Dallas who heads the team, said American officials calculated that six Afghan policemen were dying for every soldier in the National Army who was killed.

Half of the saturation team's two-week training course is devoted to teaching Afghan police military skills, like how to launch or survive an ambush. Mr. Thompson, who trained the police in Iraq for DynCorp, said the Afghan police were more poorly equipped than their Iraqi counterparts. In one recent Afghan class, he said, 40 police officers shared 15 rifles.

As of early July, the training segment that involved police firing their rifles was on hold. Security problems had delayed the delivery of ammunition to Lashkar Gah, according to Mr. Thompson.

During the training, Afghan officers pull the triggers on their rifles and pretend to fire.

Scorn from Locals

On July 10, Helmand's senior government officials, tribal elders and community leaders gathered for a public forum in Lashkar Gah entitled "Security, Reconstruction and Official Corruption." For the next hour, the locals heaped scorn on the Afghan government. Speaker after speaker talked of dashed hopes.

The leader of the newly elected provincial assembly said that "in a country where there is no security, there is nothing." A teacher who had received death threats from the Taliban warned that Mr. Karzai's government could collapse. An enraged tribal leader in a white turban said the police released the murderers of his sons and brothers after receiving bribes.

"Is this a government?" he thundered. "Anyone other than me would join the Taliban."

This spring, American forces handed over responsibility for Helmand to the British military. More than 3,600 British troops, 10 times the troops the United States deployed in Helmand, now patrol the increasingly violent province. This year, 15 British and 4 American soldiers have been killed there.

The violence has continued to hamper reconstruction. The canal cleaning project has resumed, but on a much smaller scale—and with many fewer local workers—than originally planned. Some road work is proceeding. But all repairs on the hydroelectric dam were suspended in July amid rising at-

tacks. Nationwide, 90 percent of Afghans still lack regular electricity.

Since early 2005, both Afghan and foreign officials had urged Mr. Karzai to remove Mr. Akhund as Helmand's governor. Last December, Mr. Karzai finally did. The Afghan leader's supporters argue that he was never provided with the resources needed to take on warlords.

The new governor, an engineer and former United Nations employee, accepted the assignment on condition he have his own 150-man security force. This spring, Mr. Karzai fired the province's police chief, but his replacement said he will make little headway stabilizing the province as long as the Taliban continues to have bases in neighboring Pakistan.

Mr. Afghani, the province's chief judge, said Taliban attacks this spring have shut down courts in 11 of the province's 13 districts. In June, he found an unexploded bomb in his car. In July, a suicide bomber killed four people in a Lashkar Gah court office.

"Nowadays, no one is taking care of judges in our government," he said. "We are helpless people. We don't have any power. We don't have any police."

Mr. Shah, the farmer, said he has given up on Mr. Karzai's government. After growing little opium since 2001, he grew large amounts this spring after his workers demanded higher pay. He and other farmers simply pooled their money and bribed a local official so that eradication teams drove past their village.

On a recent afternoon, Ms. Olomi gave a reporter a tour of her women's center, which was closed for security reasons after the killing of her driver in May. False rumors had been spread that the center's female students were being taken to the local American military base and forced to have sex with soldiers.

After the tour of the center, which had the feel of a museum, Ms. Olomi announced she was heading home and pulled out a burqa, the head-to-toe veil that became a symbol of Taliban oppression. Ms. Olomi shed her burqa after the group's fall in 2001, but began wearing it again after her driver's death to hide her identity from potential assassins.

As her car rolled out the center's front gate, Ms. Olomi pulled the burqa over her head and her face disappeared. In Little America in 2006, the former instrument of her oppression was her means of survival.

Pakistan Assessment 2006

Large tracts of Pakistan are now clearly conflict-afflicted with a wide array of anti-state actors and terrorists engaging in varying degrees of violence and subversion. A cursory look at the map indicates that the Federally Administered Tribal Areas (FATA), Balochistan and Gilgit-Baltistan are witnessing large-scale violence and subversion. Violence in parts of the Sindh, Punjab and North West Frontier Province (NWFP) has also brought these provinces under the security scanner. Islamabad's writ is currently being challenged vigorously—violently or otherwise—in wide geographical areas, and on a multiplicity of issues.

Crucially, where 648 persons (including 430 civilians and 137 terrorists) were killed in insurgent and terrorist conflicts through year 2005, by September 17, year 2006 had already recorded 1219 deaths (including 505 civilians and 443 terrorists). Given Islamabad's understated accounts, the suppression of the Press and erratic reportage, the actual numbers could be considerably higher.

The Balochistan province—accounting for approximately 44 percent of Pakistan's landmass—is now afflicted by an encompassing insurgency, as are most parts of North and South Waziristan in FATA—another three per cent of the country's total landmass. Gilgit-Baltistan has long been simmering, and

it is only the repeated cycles of repression and state-backed Sunni violence that have kept the restive population in rein in a region that accounts for another eight per cent of the country. 55 per cent of Pakistan-controlled territory, including Pakistan-occupied Gilgit-Baltistan, is, consequently, outside the realm of civil governance and is currently dominated essentially through military force. Further, sporadic acts of terrorist violence have been recurrent in parts of the NWFP, Punjab and Sindh, even as these emerge as safe-havens for a broad assortment of Jihadi and other anti-state actors.

The killing of tribal chief Nawab Akbar Bugti at Bhamboor Hills in the Dera Bugti district of Balochistan province on August 26, 2006, by the Pakistani security forces and the resultant violence across Balochistan and in some areas of Sindh province have exacerbated the military regime's problem. If Islamabad's repression does not succeed in Balochistan, Bugti's death will mark the beginnings of a greater consolidation of nationalist forces and a shift in tactics, from conventional guerrilla warfare—which is much more susceptible to detection and neutralization—to more decentralized and subversive means, including the targeting of infrastructure and assets outside Balochistan, and in urban concentrations, as well as an effort to bring in other groups, such as the Sindhis, the Seraikis, the

Year 2006

0	Civilians	Security Force Personnel	Terrorist	Total
January	114	29	22	165
February	88	16	2	106
March	91	19	221	331
April	96	144	53	193
May	43	39	5	87
June	26	29	47	102
July	12	52	49	113
August	22	43	64	109
September	13	0	0	13
Total	505	271	443	1219

*Data till September 17, 2006
Source: Institute for Conflict Management database.

Fatalities of Terrorist Violence—2005

0	Civilians	Security Force Personnel	Terrorist	Total
January	30	7	2	39
February	11	0	6	17
March	77	15	3	95
April	6	2	2	10
May	63	5	2	70
June	8	1	0	9
July	29	2	43	74
August	14	10	1	25
September	32	17	40	89
October	27	15	16	58
November	13	0	12	25
December	120	7	10	137
Total	430	81	137	648

Pashtun, and other disaffected political formations, into a broader insurgency. There is a danger, moreover, that the secular-nationalist Baloch movement may also see the influence of radical Islamist parties such as the MMA, which have, till now, remained restricted to the Pashtun areas of the North, growing in the Baloch areas of South Balochistan.

Notably, violence and the accompanying retreat of civil governance has occurred amidst the fact that Pakistan has committed approximately 80,000 troops in the FATA and 123,000 in Balochistan, with support from helicopter gun-ships, artillery and the Air Force. The writ of the state is increasingly fragile in these regions, with recurrent violence undermining official claims that the situation is 'under control.' Despite the 'intense' Army operations in FATA, sources indicate that frontline Taliban and Al Qaeda operatives still maintain a significant presence in the region adding to problems of the already-challenged US Coalition forces in neighbouring Afghanistan. Although the military regime has been claiming that most foreign terrorists have been evicted, there is mounting evidence that the Jihadi presence in FATA is strengthening, that Islamist extremists are regularly confronting the Pakistani state, and that they, in fact, control a substantial area in North Waziristan, and widening areas in South Waziristan, to an extent as to make a permanent military presence impossible.

That the local Taliban had gained immense influence in the FATA was officially acknowledged when the military regime entered into an agreement with them on September 5, 2006. The three-page agreement was signed by seven militants on behalf of the Taliban shura (advisory council) and by the Political Agent of North Waziristan, Dr. Fakhr-i-Alam, who signed on behalf of the Government. The agreement, mediated by a tribal Jirga (council), contains 16 clauses and four sub-clauses. Salient features include:

- There shall be no cross-border movement for militant activity in Afghanistan. On its part, the Government pledged not to undertake any ground or air operations against the militants and to resolve issues through local customs and traditions.

- The agreement will come into force with the relocation of the Army from checkpoints in the region. The Khasadar force (a local tribal force) and Levy personnel will take over the check-posts.

- Foreigners living in North Waziristan will have to leave Pakistan, but those who cannot leave will be allowed to live peacefully, respecting the law of the land and the agreement.

- Both parties will return each other's weapons, vehicles and communication equipment seized during various operations.

- Tribal elders, Mujahideen and the Utmanzai tribe would ensure that no-one attacked security force personnel and state property.

- There will be no target killing and no parallel administration in the agency.

- Militants would not enter the settled districts adjacent to North Waziristan.

- Government would release prisoners held in military operations and would not arrest them again.

- Tribesmen's 'incentives' would be restored. The administration is to resolve disputes in accordance with local customs and traditions.

- Government would pay compensation for the loss of life and property of innocent tribesmen during recent operations.

- There is no ban on display of arms. However, tribesmen will not carry heavy weapons.

- A 10-member committee—comprising elders, members of political administration and ulema (religious scholars)—is to monitor progress of the accord and ensure its implementation.

Islamabad has followed a strange mixture of carrot and stick in its strategy for FATA. Large-scale military operations, including targeted killings and strafing of population centres, have been a recurrent feature in the region over the past three years. On the other hand, the military regime has also sought to procure the allegiance of local leaders by doling out large sums of monies. Rising civilian fatalities have, in fact, deepened public alienation, and increased the likelihood that the disorder and instability gradually consume areas that are currently peaceful. Islamabad's attempts to restore order in Waziristan have, according to one estimate, led to 300 civilians and 250 troops being killed and about 1,400 persons wounded in 2005. According to open source information monitored by the South Asia Terrorism Portal, during January 1, 2005–August 31, 2006, 846 people, including 181 civilians and 176 soldiers, were killed. Once again, given the constraints on information flows from the region, these numbers may well be significant underestimates.

Sources indicate that the Taliban-led Islamist extremists are now in control of parts of the FATA bordering Afghanistan. The Dand-i-Darpa Khail region in North Waziristan, near the main town of Miranshah, is the focal point for Islamist extremists in Afghanistan, including former Taliban 'commander' Jalaluddin Haqqani, and his son Sirajuddin Haqqani. Maulana Abdul Khaliq, chief of the Gulshan-e-Ilm seminary in Miranshah, was declared the 'mastermind' of the March 2, 2006 incident in which the local Taliban occupied Government buildings, including a telephone exchange, in Miranshah. Sikander Qayyum, the Peshawar-based security chief for the tribal zones, told AFP on March 18, 2006 that the extremists had killed at least 120 pro-government tribal chiefs in recent months, even as the heads of sundry decapitated 'enemies of Islam' are flaunted on flagpoles in many areas. Federal Interior Minister Aftab Ahmad Sherpao admitted on March 11, 2006, that 'miscreants' were trying to wrest control of Government buildings and challenging the writ of the state in the region. He also warned of a spillover from tribal areas to settled areas while referring to two explosions in Dera Ismail Khan and three in Tank districts.

In a parallel and troubling development, there have been indications that the administration is under intense pressure from the Taliban to introduce Sharia (Islamic law) in Waziristan. In fact, clerics announced the enforcement of Sharia in South Waziristan on March 10, 2006 saying that disputes would now be resolved through Islamic laws instead of the tribal Jirga. An announcement to this effect was reportedly made during Friday prayer sermons in Wana and other towns of South Waziristan. The announcement came following letters from local Taliban commanders to all prayer leaders asking them to enforce the Sharia.

Comparable conditions of collapse prevail in Balochistan, where all 22 districts are reeling either under a sub-nationalist tribal insurgency or, separately, Islamist extremism. A crucial pivot of the insurgency in the Balochistan province, Nawab Akbar Khan Bugti, was killed along with 38 insurgents during a military operation in the Chalgri area of Bhamboor Hills in Dera Bugti District on August 26, 2006. At least 21 SF personnel, including a Colonel, two Majors and three Captains, were also killed in the intense clashes. The 79 year-old Nawab Bugti, leader of the dominant Bugti tribe and a former Chief Minister of Balochistan, went underground in 2005, and was since directing the armed insurgency, which has claimed more than 700 lives in 2005–06.

A small measure of the intensity of the Baloch insurgency is visible in the fact that approximately 1,500 rockets were fired in 40 attacks in January–February 2006 alone. According to official estimates, in the past two years, saboteurs have staged nearly 27,000 rocket attacks aimed at military personnel and outposts, Government installations and foreign nationals in Balochistan, the Karachi-based Newsline reported in its September 2006 issue. Attacks on critical installations have also led to power and gas shortages in the Punjab, the province whose domination over Baloch resources fuels the insurgency. The Pakistan Railways has reportedly stopped operating passenger trains at night all over Balochistan. Railways Minister of State Ishaq Khan Khakwani clarified to the Senate that night journeys were 'not safe' because of terrorist activities in the province, adding further that even at daytime, pilot engines were being operated on tracks to pre-empt terrorist activity. The state now engages 123,000 military and paramilitary personnel in the ongoing operations in the province, expending Rupees Six billion a month, according to Senator Sanaullah Baloch. Some 600 check posts have been set up in Balochistan in an effort to contain the movement of insurgents. Structural and constitutional biases prevailing against the provinces feed popular anger and the insurgencies, and militate against any possible solution, particularly given Islamabad's track record of intransigence. Adding to the Baloch insurgency are the Pashtun Islamist extremists concentrated in and around Quetta, tied closely to the Taliban, and engaged in a campaign of terror on both sides of the Afghan border in their areas of domination. Most of the violence in Balochistan is, however, 'nationalist' and there is no cooperation between Islamist terrorists in pockets in the North and the Baloch insurgents. There is, moreover, little love lost between the mullahs and the Sardars (Baloch tribal Chieftans).

FATA, NWFP, Balochistan and Gilgit-Baltistan are areas of long-term neglect and of recurrent insurrections. However, the Pakistani 'heartland,' Sindh and Punjab—particularly the politically and militarily dominant Punjab province—are now also passing progressively into the ambit of violence by anti-state actors. There were as many as 34 terrorist incidents in Punjab in 2005, and another eight in 2006 (till July); Sindh witnessed 50 incidents in 2005. Among the significant incidents in 2006 was the suicide car bomb attack near the U.S. Consulate in Karachi, in which American diplomat David Fyfe and two others were killed, and 54 persons injured, on March 2, a day before President George W. Bush visited Pakistan.

Pakistani insecurities on the Afghan front are directly related to the contested nature of the Durand Line. Most Afghans (and Pashtuns) believe that the Durand Line should rightly have been drawn much further South, at Attock, and this is what the Afghans will inevitably press for when their country is strong enough. Within this context, it is useful to note that, south of the Durand Line, in what are currently the Pakistani NWFP and FATA, land records, police, legal and administrative records still refer to the people as 'Afghan.'

The Taliban, as has been documented extensively, exists on both sides of the border. While they have obviously been weakened, they retain substantial subversive capacities. With Islamabad's strategy to quieten the chaotic Waziristan region along the Afghan border having failed, the mountainous terrain along the Durand Line provides a secure pathway and safe hideout for the Taliban and Al Qaeda. On February 17, 2006, Afghan television channel Tolo broadcast video recordings of men beheaded in Pakistan because they opposed the presence of Taliban and Al Qaeda terrorists there. The macabre images showed the heads of three men being held up in front of a crowd, which chanted "Long live Osama bin Laden" and "Long live Mullah Omar." "The footage . . . shows half a dozen dead bodies being dragged by a vehicle through the streets of Mandrakhel [in Waziristan]—while a uniformed Pakistani military officer drives past without interfering," Tolo stated.

Afghan officials have consistently asserted that Taliban and Al Qaeda operatives are coming in from Pakistan, where they are reportedly based in areas of the NWFP, FATA, and also from Balochistan. Afghanistan has given Pakistan detailed information about members of the Taliban who, Kabul says, are orchestrating an insurgency from Pakistani soil. On February 18, 2006 President Hamid Karzai told a news conference at Kabul, "We gave our brothers a lot of information, very detailed information about individuals, locations and other issues," referring to the intelligence handed over to the Pakistani authorities. Karzai, according to noted Pakistani journalist Ahmed Rashid, handed over extensive intelligence dossiers to Musharraf, containing details of how suicide bombers who attack targets in Afghanistan are being recruited, trained and equipped in Pakistan. The dossiers reportedly include the names and addresses of Pakistani recruiters, trainers and suppliers. "In places like Karachi, Pakistani extremist groups working on behalf of the Taliban for a fee carry out the recruitment and then bring them to safe houses in Balochistan for training and equipping with the (suicide) vests," said a senior Afghan official who accompanied Karzai. The official said that all top Taliban 'commanders,' including Mullah Mohammed Omar, are known to be living in Pakistan and the issue had been repeatedly raised with Pakistan.

Taliban have regrouped rather well along the Afghan countryside, particularly in provinces along the Pakistan-Afghanistan border. Unsurprisingly, violence is significant near the Pakistan border. The subversion that targets Afghan provinces close to Pakistan, like Paktika, is a reality despite the fact that Islamabad has deployed approximately 80,000 troops on their side of the border. The burden of evidence suggests that the Taliban/Al Qaeda have in fact been provided space by the military to operate in the Pakistani areas along the border. Notably, the Muttahida Majlis-e-Amal, an Islamist alliance with close links to the Taliban, governs Balochistan and the NWFP.

Assisting the Pakistani and Taliban strategy is the regrettable reality that the Karzai regime has little control over southern and eastern Afghanistan. The end-game that Islamabad seeks to achieve, while reframing its quest for 'strategic depth,' is to prevent the Kabul regime from stabilizing without a pre-dominant Pakistani role. Anything contrary to this would mean an increase in the dissent on the Durand Line, and a further destabilization of North Balochistan, the NWFP and FATA.

A look at the current security and socio-political matrix of the region suggests that the state has suffered a significant retreat. Islamist extremist forces, evidently, provide a semblance of what is denied by the legitimate state structure. There has been a stream of reports indicating that clerics were replacing chieftains in all committees in South Waziristan. The Taliban has reportedly opened recruiting offices in the Wana, Makeen and Barwend areas of South Waziristan. The state's retreat has also meant that the Taliban now also assumes a role in the political administration in certain areas of Waziristan.

The social sphere has for long been the focus of radical Islam in Pakistan. The Taliban was a state of mind even before it became a regime in Afghanistan. In a mirrored evolution, moral policing and social edicts are now an accepted reality in Waziristan: shopkeepers are debarred from trading in music or films in any manner, barbers have been ordered not to shave beards, and women have been told not to go to the market or other public places.

Taliban-linked operatives have reportedly opened offices and set up check-posts at the main marketplace in Wana, collecting toll from vehicles. They have also set up a court to conduct summary trials. Bringing back memories of the gruesome Taliban executions in Afghanistan, a man 'convicted' of killing his son was shot dead in front of a crowd of 150 people in late March 2006. Earlier in December 2005, at least seven alleged bandits at Miranshah in North Waziristan were killed and their mutilated corpses hung from an electric pole. A DVD of the macabre incident was widely circulated subsequently. The state, meanwhile, preferred to overlook these incidents and did nothing to stop these public executions. Nor has anything been done to encumber the movement of the 'local Taliban' who continue to consolidate their presence, encouraged by the state's inaction.

Despite occasional successes, Pakistani troops, with a fair measure of assistance from the U.S. military across the border in Afghanistan, have largely been unable to move out of their fortified positions to carry out area domination exercises, with the result that a large expanse of territory continues to remain under the influence of the Taliban-backed terrorists.

On December 17, 2005, the Pakistani Army and paramilitary launched an operation against the Baloch insurgents in the Kohlu, Dera Bugti, Noshki and Makran Districts, as well as other parts of the Balochistan province. The subsequent and escalating violence, including the indiscriminate bombing and strafing of civilian populations, and repeated and widespread clashes with suspected Baloch insurgents and dissenting tribesmen has led many to describe this as the 'fourth rebellion' in the Province since the creation of Pakistan.

The province is of critical importance to Pakistan, both strategically and otherwise. There are four major cantonments, 59 'mini cantonments,' six missile testing ranges and three nuclear testing sites in Balochistan. Pakistan Air Force has six bases and the Navy another three in the troubled province, which is dotted with over 600 military check posts. Baloch nationalists describe the entire province as a 'mega-cantonment.'

Contrary to General Musharraf's position that only three of the 78 tribal chiefs in the province were "troublemakers," the truth is that insurgent attacks have left no part of the province unaffected. There has also been a continuous series of bomb and rocket attacks on gas pipelines, railway tracks, power transmission lines, bridges, and communications infrastructure, as well as on military establishments and governmental facilities and enterprises since the beginning of 2005.

Official data indicated that 187 bomb blasts, 275 rocket attacks, eight attacks on gas pipelines, 36 attacks on electricity transmission lines and 19 explosions on railway lines occurred in the year 2005. According to open source information monitored by the South Asia Terrorism Portal, at least 182 civilians and 26 security force personnel died in the Province during 2005. However, given Islamabad's understated accounts, the suppression of the Press and erratic reportage from this poorly covered region, the actual numbers could be much higher.

It is useful to recall in this context that a report of the Balochistan Inspector General of Police in January 2005 had indicated that in 2002 a total of 7 cases of rocket firing were reported in A areas in which only two persons were injured, while in the B areas 13 cases of rockets firing were reported in which two persons were killed and 12 injured. In 2003, 43 rockets were fired in A areas in which 4 persons were killed and 8 injured and in B areas, 58 rockets were fired in which three persons were killed and four injured. In 2004, 117 cases of rocket attacks were reported in A areas, in which two persons were injured. In B areas however, 553 cases of rocket attacks were reported killing four and injuring 17 people.

The year 2005 saw a marked decrease in the fatality index of sectarian violence. Approximately 160 persons were killed and 354 others injured in 62 incidents of sectarian violence in 2005 as compared to 187 persons killed in 19 incidents during the year 2004. Among the major incidents of sectarian violence in 2005 were:

October 7, 2005: Eight persons are killed and 19 others were injured when unidentified assailants opened fire in an Ahmadiyya place of worship at Mong village near Mandi Bahauddin in the Punjab province.

May 30, 2005: Six people, including two of the three assailants, among them a suicide bomber, are killed and 19

persons sustain injuries during an explosion in the courtyard of a Shia mosque at Gulshan-e-Iqbal in Karachi.

May 27, 2005: At least 25 people, including a suspected suicide bomber, are killed and approximately 100 others sustain injuries during a powerful explosion at the Bari Imam shrine of the Shia sect located in vicinity of the diplomatic enclave in capital Islamabad.

March 19, 2005: At least 50 people are killed and over 100 others sustain injuries during a bomb explosion at a crowded gathering near the shrine of a Shia saint at Fatehpur village in the Jhal Magsi district of Balochistan province.

January 8, 2005: At least 15 people are killed, including six members of a family who were burnt alive, and 14 were injured during sectarian clashes at Gilgit in the Northern Areas of Pakistan occupied Kashmir (PoK) where a curfew was imposed and troops deployed to restore law and order.

More than six years of General Musharraf's authoritarian rule have pushed peripheral movements of political dissent into full-blown insurgencies, and the widening trajectory of violence demonstrates that the military regime is failing to shape an appropriate strategy of response in the face of multiple insurgencies and a rising trend of terrorist attacks across the country. Past experience in South Asia has, moreover, shown that the recovery of geographical spaces, once anti-state violence escalates beyond threshold levels, is extraordinarily difficult. The preceding and extended narrative is a clear indication that Gen. Musharraf has opened far too many fronts, his security forces are overstretched, and there has been a comprehensive and augmenting failure to contain the widening insurgencies, sectarian strife and Islamist terrorist violence that now envelope large swathes of the country.

Related Links

- *Waziristan: Deal with the Devil—Kanchan Lakshman, SAIR*
- *Balochistan: The Army Blunders On—Amir Mir, SAIR*
- *Balochistan: Musharraf's Pyrrhic Victory—Kanchan Lakshman, SAIR*
- *Balochistan: After the 'Triumph'—Kanchan Lakshman, SAIR*
- *Terrorists and their Fellow Travellers—Ajai Sahni, SAIR*

The War in Balochistan: A Backgrounder

Praveen Swami

Indian television viewers and newspaper readers could be forgiven for not knowing it exists. South Asia's most violent low-intensity conflict has garnered just a few column-inches of print and barely a few minutes of airtime.

Using combat jets, helicopter gunships and artillery, Pakistan's military has been pounding tribal insurgents in the gas-rich and strategically crucial province of Balochistan since the middle of December. Hundreds are believed to have died in the fighting, mainly civilians. The veteran Baloch leader Sardar Sherbaz Khan Mazari, a moderate, told the *Daily Times* that the situation was similar to that which preceded the 1971 Bangladesh war of liberation.

For a conflict that threatens to become a crisis for South Asia, the fighting in Balochistan had relatively innocuous origins. In January 2003, four Pakistan soldiers were alleged to have raped a doctor employed by Pakistan Petroleum at the Sui gasfield. When the authorities failed to file a case, Bugti tribesmen attacked the gasfield. Other tribes joined in, hitting the port at Gwadar as well as railway lines and military facilities. Pakistani forces responded in strength.

Enormous Stakes

For both sides, the stakes were enormous. Tribal leaders saw the conflict as a last opportunity to get what they considered a fair share of Balochistan's enormous gas resources; Sui has among the largest reserves in the world. The Government, in turn, saw the fighting as an intolerable challenge to its authority and as a spark that could set off similar fires in other provinces.

In an article in August 2005, the eminent journalist Najam Sethi blamed the crisis on "the social and electoral engineering engineered by the military regime." By sidelining mainstream parties in favour of Islamists, he said, President Pervez Musharraf alienated both "the old non-religious tribal leadership as well as the new secular urban middle classes of Balochistan, who see no economic or political space for themselves in the new military-mullah dispensation."

By contrast, Gen. Musharraf has sought to present himself as a modernist whose developmental successes have provoked reaction from the powerful tribal 'sardars'—the hereditary rulers of the dominant Bugti, Marri and Mengal clans.

Whatever the truth, Gen. Musharraf's polemic hasn't helped his own case. In one interview, he said that if the Baloch insurgents continued fighting, "I will hit them so hard they won't know what hit them," language that outraged many.

Attack on Rally

The current military assault was provoked by a rocket attack on a rally held by Gen. Musharraf in the town of Kohlu in December. A day later, insurgents opened fire on a helicopter carrying the Inspector General of the Frontier Corps, Balochistan, Major General Shujaat Zamir Dar, and his deputy. Soon after these attacks, Frontier Corps paramilitary and regular Army units, backed by helicopter gunships, launched full-scale attacks on the insurgents.

To those with a sense of history, it isn't hard to see what could lie ahead. In February 1973, Pakistan's Inter-Services Intelligence discovered a consignment of arms allegedly shipped by Iraq's Embassy to members of the Marri tribe. President Zulfikar Ali Bhutto promptly dismissed the provincial government; Baloch nationalists responded by launching a full-blown insurgency. For the next five years, a 55,000-strong Baloch irregular force fought six Army divisions, backed by air strikes.

Huge Casualties

By the time fighting ended, an estimated 5,000 insurgents and 3,000 soldiers had died, along with tens of thousands of civilians. On that occasion, India chose not to use its considerable post-1971 leverage in Pakistan to end the carnage. Unlike in Bangladesh, its covert services did not respond to the insurgents' appeals for help. While New Delhi has now taken the unusual measure of expressing concern on the situation in Balochistan, no evidence has so far emerged that it is actually financing the insurgents.

India Assessment—2006

Two thousand two hundred twenty-one people have died in terrorism-related violence in India during year 2006 (till October 1). A review of the data indicates that nearly 45 per cent of all such fatalities occurred in Jammu and Kashmir (J&K) alone as a result of the separatist proxy war in that State. 23 per cent were accounted for by insurgencies in the Northeast. Approximately 32 per cent of fatalities resulted from Left Wing Extremism (Maoist/Naxalite) in some areas of the States of Chhattisgarh, Andhra Pradesh, Maharashtra, Orissa, West Bengal, Uttar Pradesh, Jharkhand, Bihar and Karnataka.

In comparison to the year 2005, when 3236 people had died in terrorism-related incidents across the country, there is a definite decrease in the fatality index of year 2006.

Approximately 192 of the 608 districts are currently afflicted, at differing intensities, by various insurgent and terrorist movements. Terrorism in Jammu & Kashmir (12 districts), in different States of the Northeast (54 districts) and the challenges posed by left-wing extremism (affecting at least 126 districts in 14 States) continue to pose serious challenges to the security framework. In addition, wide areas of the country appear to have 'fallen off the map' of good governance, and are acutely susceptible to violent political mobilization, lawlessness and organized criminal activity.

Jammu and Kashmir

Since 2002, terrorism-related fatalities have demonstrated a secular decline in Jammu and Kashmir (J&K). Although the State continues to suffer from a substantial degree of violence and subversion, the military regime in Pakistan which was forced to scale down its proxy-war under intense international scrutiny momentarily has shown no indication of dismantling the vast terrorist infrastructure on its soil. Amidst the hype on people-to-people contacts and confidence-building measures (CBMs), the fact remains that the reduced levels of violence is primarily tactical. In the India-Pakistan calculus, there always exists a possibility of Islamabad seeking to up the ante in order to extort concessions from India.

There were 1732 terrorism-related deaths in J&K during 2005. Continuing with decline in violence, 873 people have died in year 2006 (till October 1). More than 40,000 people have lost their lives in the conflict since 1989, and even at present, an average of 100 lives is lost each month in J&K.

Even as talks between India and Pakistan continue under the aegis of the Composite Dialogue, terrorist violence in J&K, and sporadically in other parts of the India continue, even as Pakistan complains bitterly about the slow pace of 'progress' towards the goals it seeks to secure on the negotiating table, having failed to achieve these through a vicious campaign of terrorism over 17 years.

In realistic terms, it is clear that the process is headed nowhere and there is every likelihood of an eventual breakdown, transient or permanent. The reasons are not far to seek. First, the peace process remains, in substantial measure, tactical rather than substantive, with Pakistan in particular treating the negotiations as a parallel instrument to terrorism to exert pressure on India. Further, the hiatus between the rival positions on Kashmir is unbridgeable, and it is unsurprising, consequently, that

Fatalities in Terrorist Violence–2006

0	Civilians	Security Force Personnel	Terrorist	Total
2001	1067	590	2850	4507
2002	839	469	1714	3022
2003	658	338	1546	2542
2004	534	325	951	1810
2005	520	216	996	1732
*2006	285	125	463	873

*Data till October 1, 2006
Source: Institute for Conflict Management database.

the two sides are yet to commence substantive discussions on this issue. The restoration of communication links, people-to-people exchanges, Track Two diplomacy and a range of confidence building measures have all gone smoothly and have largely been successful. The Indian High Commission in Islamabad, for instance, issued 90,000 visas to Pakistanis in the year 2005 in comparison to 60,000 in 2004, a reflection of rising popular bonhomie. In particular, the bus services (Srinagar-Muzaffarabad and Amritsar-Lahore) and coordinated relief efforts in the aftermath of the October 2005 earthquake have been received well by people of both the countries. The ground situation in J&K, however, remains a cause for concern, with terrorism related killings and a continuous stream of infiltrators across the Line of Control (LoC) and international border, though the secular decline in levels of violence, which commenced after the 9/11 attacks in the US, has been sustained—albeit only marginally between 2004–2005.

Worse, terrorist attacks by Pakistan-backed groups have occurred in places as far as Mumbai, Delhi, Bangalore and Varanasi. Furthermore, arrests and seizures connected with Pakistan-backed terrorist groups across India, outside J&K and the Northeast, numbering at least 76 modules during the 2004–06 period indicate the level of penetration and subversion. These modules have been neutralised in locations that extend from Uttaranchal in the North, to Andhra Pradesh in the South, and from Gujarat in the West to West Bengal in the East. These terrorist modules were tasked to target security and vital installations, communication links, and commercial and industrial centres, as well as to provoke instability and disorder by circulating large quantities of counterfeit currency and by drug trafficking.

Meanwhile, the Prime Minister, Dr. Manmohan Singh, announced on May 25, 2006, the formation of five Working Groups to discuss various issues relating to Jammu and Kashmir. Addressing a press conference at the end of the two-day Roundtable Conference in Srinagar, he said that setting up of the Working Groups was the "best way to move forward and ensure that the views of different segments are incorporated." The Groups will deal with improving the Centre's relations with J&K, furthering the relations across the Line of Control (LoC), giving a boost to the State's economic development, rehabilitating the destitute families of militants and reviewing the cases of detainees and ensuring good governance. The Prime Minister also declared his Government's readiness to talk to terrorist groups if they gave up the path of violence. "Anybody who shuns violence and gives up the path of terror, we are willing to find ways and means to interact with all such groups," he said. On the issue of alleged human right violations by the security forces, he said, "our armed force is not an armed force of occupation . . . . They have a proud record, though there could be some aberrations, but these aberrations cannot be allowed. There should be zero tolerance for human rights violations for all our security forces."

Insurgencies in the North East

Certain states of the northeast have shown remarkable signs of recovery in recent years in their fight against insurgency. Tripura, once considered to be one of the most violent States of the country, recorded less than 75 insurgent-related fatalities in 2005. In 2006 (till October 6), there have been 48 insurgency-related deaths in Tripura. Similarly, the fight against insurgency in Meghalaya and Arunachal Pradesh has been largely successful. At the same time, Manipur and Assam continue to remain affected by militancy, despite operations by the security forces. Nagaland, where both the militant outfits are in cease-fire agreements with the Government, continues to witness fratricidal clashes, large-scale extortion and abduction. Indeed, Governments in such States have been held hostage to the diktats of the outfits.

The demands of various groups engaged in violence in the Northeast have varied from autonomy to secession. In view of the chronic nature of the violence in the region, largely exacerbated by external manipulation and support, the society and politics of the region have been victims of a sustained culture of violence. This culture of violence has assumed an autonomy of its own and a subversive style of politics. In spite of the Government's efforts in bringing the militant outfits to the negotiating table, the region continues to remain disturbed.

The militant outfits operating in this region in various provinces have usually found refuge in the neighbouring countries like Bangladesh and Myanmar. Fencing along the 4096.7 kilometer long border with Bangladesh, suggested as a remedy to the problem of militancy, has not been completed and that provides easy entry and exit points to the militants. Similarly, a number of the militant outfits in Assam, Nagaland and Manipur have taken shelter in Myanmar.

Manipur remains the most violent state in the region next only to Jammu and Kashmir. According to the Annual Report 2005–06 of the Ministry of Home Affairs, 410 fatalities were recorded in 2005 in militancy-related activities in Manipur, a huge leap over the corresponding figure of 258 in 2004. While a number of other States in the Northeast have or are being reclaimed from protracted insurgencies, Manipur's rendezvous with militancy appears to be an unending affair. According to the Institute for Conflict Management data, sustained terrorist violence in 2006 has claimed 235 lives in the State (till October 6). Unabated extortion and its impact on ordinary lives, as well as those of people at the helm of affairs are symptomatic of the complete administrative breakdown in the State. Assam too remains a disturbed state with 398 militancy related incidents in 2005 compared to 267 such incidents in 2004.

Left-Wing Extremism

From nearly a sixth of the total fatalities in J&K in 2002, Maoist fatalities had risen above the half-way mark by year 2005. Maoists, today, exercise dominance over a huge spread of the country's territory, carry out attacks on security forces and symbols of governance at will. Chhattisgarh has now emerged as one of the principal centres of a coordinated movement of left-wing extremism. While the number of Maoist-affected States in the country is currently pegged at 14, the movement has demonstrated the intent and potential to spread across the length and breadth of the country, constituting what Prime Minister Dr. Manmohan Singh rightly remarked is the "single biggest internal security challenge."

Fatalities in Left-wing Extremism, 2006

States	2005				2006*			
	Civilian	SFs	Terrorist	Total	Civilian	SFs	Terrorist	Total
Assam	149	10	83	242	51	30	28	109
Nagaland	9	0	31	40	8	1	51	60
Meghalaya	2	1	26	29	7	0	16	23
Manipur	138	50	143	331	83	35	117	235
Tripura	34	8	31	73	11	10	27	48
Total	332	69	314	715	160	76	239	475

* Data till October 6, 2006. (Source: Institute for Conflict Management)

Fatalities in Left-wing Extremism, 2006

States	Civilian	SF	Naxal	Total
Andhra Pradesh	13	7	96	116
Bihar	16	5	19	40
Jharkhand	10	33	28	71
Chhattisgarh	176	48	99	323
Maharashtra	13	3	26	42
Orissa	1	4	13	18
West Bengal	9	6	2	17
Uttar Pradesh	0	0	1	1
Total*	238	106	284	628

* Data till October 1, 2006

The Maoist threat appears to have overtaken all other insurgencies in the country—at least from the geographical spread point of view. At least 165 districts in 14 States, out of a total of 602 districts in the country, are currently affected by various levels of Maoist mobilisation and violence. Terrorism in Jammu & Kashmir affects 12 districts, while the combined influence of the multiple insurgencies in India's Northeast afflicts, in various measures, 54 Districts. Over the past years, moreover, while fatalities in various other insurgencies have tended to decline consistently (with the exception of Manipur) fatalities as a result of the Maoist conflict have continuously been augmented.

A total of 628 persons have died in Maoist-related violence across the country in 2006 (till October 1).

Maoists increased their activities dramatically in 2005, with 717 persons killed (281 civilians, 150 police personnel and 286 Maoists), compared to 566 deaths in 2004. Chhattisgarh in 2005 emerged as the worst affected state after Andhra Pradesh—displacing Bihar and Jharkhand—and Dantewada district is by far the worst off in the State.

The threat of the Maoists is not limited to the areas of immediate violence, nor does this threat vanish if violence is not manifested at a particular location for a specific period of time. It is in the complex processes of political activity, mass mobilisation, arms training and military consolidation that the Maoist potential has to be estimated.

The Maoist menace continues to expand, except where it has been confronted by coherent use of force—as is presently and substantially the case in Andhra Pradesh, where area domination exercise under the leadership of the local Police, backed by the armed reserve forces and the Grey Hounds, and a well-developed intelligence network has succeeded in beating back the Naxalites to a large extent, and has forced their leadership into flight. The Andhra Pradesh Police has long prepared for this confrontation and has consistently developed its capacities to engage with the Maoists in their 'strongholds,' though it has been repeatedly inhibited by political constraints from effective action. These constraints appear, for the moment, to have been lifted.

Other states, however, remain far from prepared. Indeed, a consistent feature across all the major Maoist-affected States is that they have extraordinarily poor policing capacities. As against a national average of 122 police personnel per 100,000 population, and some peaceful States with ratios as high as 854/100,000 (Mizoram) and 609/100,000 in Sikkim, Bihar has just 57, Jharkhand—85, Chhattisgarh—103 and Orissa—90, and even Andhra Pradesh, just 98 per 100,000 population. Worse, there is ample evidence that large proportions of the Central allocation for police modernisation and up-gradation remain unspent or are being diverted or mis-spent. Utilization of funds is particularly poor in Uttar Pradesh, Bihar, Madhya Pradesh, Chhattisgarh and Jharkhand.

The rampaging Maoist movement has violently drawn attention to itself with a succession of daring and bloody attacks that go to the very core of governance, the credibility of administration, and the sagacity of political leadership across extended areas of the country. The growing audacity of the Maoists has been reflected in actions involving hundreds, and occasionally thousands, of cadres in operations that increasingly mimic the now-established tactics of their Nepali counterparts, involving coordinated attacks on police stations and posts, as well as on administrative headquarters and well-guarded Government establishments.

Terrorism Outside J&K and the Northeast

According to data compiled by the Institute for Conflict Management, at least 76 Inter-Services Intelligence-Jihadi modules have been disrupted just over the years 2004–2006, leading to hundreds of arrests across India—outside Jammu and Kashmir and the troubled Northeast—in locations that extend from Uttaranchal in the North, to Andhra Pradesh in the South, and from Gujarat in the West to West Bengal in the East. Further, official sources indicate that, between 1998 and 2003, security agencies had neutralized more than 180 ISI-backed terrorist modules across the country (excluding J&K and the Northeast), who had been tasked to target security and vital installations, communication links, and commercial and industrial centres, as well as to provoke instability and disorder by circulating large quantities of counterfeit currency and by drug trafficking.

Terrorist attacks in places like Mumbai (July 11, 2006), Varanasi (March 7, 2006) Bangalore (December 28, 2005) and New Delhi (October 29, 2005) are only the more visible evidence of a long-term war of attrition by Pakistani state agencies and their Jihadi surrogates, intended to undermine India's political stability, increasingly by attacking its economic, scientific and technological strengths. These incidents only confirm the strategic continuity of Pakistan's broad orientation towards India, and its sustained enterprise of encirclement, penetration and subversion, with an objective to do as much damage as is opportunistically possible, under the cover of (no doubt diminishing) credible deniability. The objective is to gradually undermine India's capacities for growth, as well as to weaken international confidence in the country and to create an atmosphere of pervasive terror over wide areas that would dampen the country's capacity to attract foreign investment.

The frequency, spread and, in some cases, intensity of these operations has seen some escalation in the past years, as international pressure on Pakistan to end terrorism in J&K has diminished levels of 'deniable' engagement in that theatre, and as violence in that State demonstrates a continuous secular decline since the events of September 11, 2001 in the US.

It is important to note, however, that despite occasional and inevitable 'successes,' this relentless strategy—which has targeted virtually every concentration of Muslim populations in India for decades—has overwhelmingly failed to secure a base within the community, beyond a minuscule radical fringe. Further, the record of intelligence and security agency successes against such subversion and terror, although lacking the visibility and drama of a terrorist strike, is immensely greater than the record of the successes of this strategy.

Related Links

- *Punjab: Another 'Module' Implodes*—K.P.S. Gill, *SAIR*
- *A Prime Minister Speaks: Finally, a Clear Voice on Terror*—K. P. S. Gill, *SAIR*
- *Maoist Insurgencies: The Eclipse of Governance*—Ajai Sahni, *SAIR*
- *Naxalites: While We Were Sleeping*—Ajai Sahni, *SAIR*
- *"Food for Thought"*—Ajai Sahni, *SAIR*
- *Salvaging a Relationship*—E.N. Rammohan, *SAIR*
- *Bad Medicine for a Red Epidemic*—Ajai Sahni, *SAIR*
- *The Chasm between Rhetoric and Reality*—G. Parthasarathy, *SAIR*

Article 6

Inside India's Hidden War

RANDEEP RAMESH

Forty young men and women in ill-fitting army fatigues, clutching flintlocks and pistols, stand in the shade of a mango tree. Beside them flaps a red flag emblazoned with a hammer and sickle.

In a show of strength, the soldiers creep up on imaginary enemies through long grass. Armed with weapons and the opinions of the doctrinaire left, these guerrillas, or Naxalites as they are known, are part of a hidden war in the middle of India's mineral-rich tribal belt.

The Naxalites are heirs of the revolutionary ideology of Mao Zedong. Unlike their ideological cousins in Nepal, the guerrillas are not prepared to consider exchanging the bullet for the ballot box. Across a wide swath of India, from Andhra Pradesh in the south to the Nepalese border, there are daily reports of underground armies hijacking trains, mounting audacious jailbreaks and murdering local politicians.

Last month the prime minister, Manmohan Singh, described the rebels as "the single biggest internal security challenge ever faced by our country." Nowhere is this conflict more acute than in the dense forests of southern Chhattisgarh state, the scene of violent land disputes and social clashes. In the past year the state has armed thousands of villagers with guns, spears and bows and arrows. Child soldiers are often ranged against opponents of similar age. In Chhattisgarh a battalion of Indian paramilitary forces has backed this militia, known as Salva Judum (Peace March), against the Naxalites, turning the forest into a battlefield.

Entire villages have been emptied as tribal communities flee from the burnings, lootings and killings. The civil conflict has left more than 50,000 people camping under tarpaulin sheets without work or food along the roadsides of southern Chhattisgarh.

Campaigners say that the reason why the government has opened a new front in this battle lies beneath Chhattisgarh's fertile soil, which contains some of the country's richest reserves of iron ore, coal, limestone and bauxite. Above live some of India's most impoverished people: semi-literate tribes who exist in near destitution.

India's biggest companies have moved stealthily into the forest areas, buying up land and acquiring the rights to extract the buried wealth. Last year the Chhattisgarh government signed deals worth 130bn Indian rupees (£1.6bn) with industrial companies for steel mills and power stations.

The Naxalites have begun a campaign against such industrialisation, which the state sees as necessary to create jobs and provide the raw materials for economic growth.

Watching his "troops" conduct military exercises is Gopanna Markam, company commander in the People's Liberation Guerrilla Army, whose rank is denoted by the AK-47 in his hands. He says the "exploitation" needs to be stopped. "The government is bent upon taking out all the resources from this area and leaving the people nothing."

These are no idle threats. Police estimate there are 4,500 armed left-wing guerrillas in Chhattisgarh. In recent months they have attacked mines, blown up electricity pylons and torched cars used by contractors. They have set up "people's courts" to punish, and in some cases execute, those deemed to be capitalist collaborators.

The guerrillas' aim is violent revolution. Their political wing, the Communist party of India (Maoist), operates underground and has an armed presence in almost half of India's 28 states. The cadre fervently believes that India's feudal traditions, ingrained caste hierarchy and skewed land ownership provide fertile ground for rebellion. "The path ahead will become more difficult for us but we know history is with us," said Commander Markam.

The Naxalites argue that they have brought order if not law to the area—banishing corrupt officials, expelling landlords and raising prices at gunpoint for harvests of tendu leaves, used to wrap bidi cigarettes. They finance their operations by levying "taxes" of around 12% on contractors and traders.

In the tribal areas, officials estimate half the population supports the Naxalites, through choice or coercion. Two-thirds of the forests have been off-limits to government staff. In many districts 40% of police posts are unfilled and a quarter of doctors' positions are vacant.

Mahendra Karma, a state politician of tribal heritage, said the Naxalites have "collapsed the social, economic and traditional administrative structure" and tribes now are "backward people who want to go forward with industry."

Although Salva Judum is widely seen as his brainchild, Mr. Karma says the movement was a result of "spontaneous anger bursting through."

The first signs of this anger were seen last June, when thousands of villagers marched with police in the village of Kortapal, where the Naxalites had abducted several government supporters. A fierce gun battle followed, with many running for cover in the forest. The village today is deserted and many of the houses have been vandalised.

This policy of emptying villages where there is support for Naxalites has been implemented across southern Chhattisgarh, with the attacks becoming bolder and bloodier. The response has been equally devastating. In February the Naxalites blew up a truck carrying Salva Judum workers back from a rally, killing more than 50 people.

In March a series of lightning raids led to tit-for-tat disappearances, beheadings and shootings. Ten days ago the bodies of 13 villagers who had protested against the guerrillas were found dead. Human rights groups say the conflict has claimed more than 150 lives this year.

"[Naxalites] have developed sophisticated strategies. We have recovered rocket launchers, mortar shells and machine guns recently," said the state police intelligence chief, Sant Kumar Paswan.

In the areas controlled by the Salva Judum, teenagers with bows and arrows guard roadblocks and Indian paramilitary forces patrol the refugee camps.

While the soldiers say villagers come seeking refuge from the violence, the tribals tell a different story. They claim that the camps are, in reality, prisons.

The guards in Bhairamgarh camp brought out captured Naxalite political agents, known as Sangam, for the Guardian to interview. Each told a story of state-backed terror. A mob of government supporters invaded their village backed by armed soldiers who opened fire on "Naxalite houses." A battle ensued and the guerrillas, outgunned, fled.

Once an area has been "cleansed," the homes of those used by leftwing guerrillas are destroyed and their owners brought to the camps.

"I was a Sangam. People were getting shot and homes burnt every day. I had no choice but to come here," said Buddram, who used to farm around Kortapal.

In the camps, fear stalks the inhabitants. The men have to report daily to the police station. Twice a day they queue up for a roll call and a drill.

Families are supposed to build their own makeshift houses. Without the state providing food or medicine, the displaced villagers say, anyone who can work is forced to do so for 50 rupees a day digging roads through the forest.

Caught in the crossfire are thousands of innocent villagers. Clutching her baby to her chest, Jamli recounts how the Salva Judum militia kidnapped her and seven friends as they travelled to a market. "We were told we had to come to the police station. Once we reached there we were kept overnight and driven to this camp where we were told if you leave you will be killed," she said. "I was alone until my husband arrived a week later and he is trapped here too. We are not Naxalites. We have no homes here, just these tents."

A third of Chhattisgarh's 21 million people are aboriginals, mostly from the Gond tribe. Experts say that the situation is in danger of turning into an "African-style" conflict over minerals, with refugees herded from one camp to another, dying of illness, hunger and thirst.

Pradeep Prabhu, a tribal campaigner, said the basic problem was one of land rights. In India everything below the ground belongs to the state, not the people who live above it.

"States like Chhattisgarh are seething with anger over this issue. The issue came up in parts of Africa where it has caused so much mess."

Backstory

The **Naxalites**, a name taken from Naxalbari district in **West Bengal** where the movement began in **1967**, have spread to 160 of India's 604 administrative districts. In the 1960s they won the approval of **Beijing**, but China has since denounced the guerrillas.

The Naxalites functioned outside the parliamentary system, organising uprisings among **landless workers** in **West Bengal, Bihar** and **Andhra Pradesh**. They spread to the mineral-rich areas of **Orissa, Chhattisgarh** and **Jharkhand.** The two armed wings, **People's War Group (PWG)** and the **Maoist Communist Centre**, combined 18 months ago to form one front: **Communist party of India (Maoist).**

With a force of **15,000 soldiers**, it controls an estimated fifth of India's forests. The eventual aim is to capture the Indian state.

Lashkar-e-Taiba's Network

Top Lashkar-e-Taiba operative Shabbir Bukhari's story offers unprecedented insight into the organisation's working—and raises disturbing questions about the threat it holds out to the India-Pakistandétenteprocess.

PRAVEEN SWAMI

Early in the autumn of 2003, Shabbir Bukhari delivered an impassioned speech defending Jammu and Kashmir's accession to India and condemning terrorist violence. Among those in the audience at Srinagar's Gandhi Bhawan who applauded the young Kashmir University law student's speech were the State's Director-General of Police, Gopal Sharma, and a host of senior bureaucrats and politicians.

At the Lashkar-e-Taiba's command headquarters in Muzaffarabad, however, top operatives knew another Bukhari. Known to his handlers by the code-name 'Abu Sumama,' Bukhari had worked as a Lashkar courier, propagandist, and recruiter since 2002. In 2004, he would rise to command a unit that would carry out a series of *fidayeen* suicide-squad attacks in which dozens of security force personnel and civilians would die.

Over the last week, an intelligence-led operation by the Jammu and Kashmir Police has delivered the most vivid picture so far available of the Lashkar's operations in the State. Investigators have found that even as terrorist activity in Jammu and Kashmir went into decline after the India-Pakistan near-war of 2001–2002, the Lashkar focussed its energies on building up successive rings of highly-organised covert skills, drawing on individuals with high levels of education and technical skills.

In the wake of the great earthquake that destroyed much of Pakistan-administered Kashmir in October, the formidable capabilities of the Lashkar's covert cells have been unleashed. Its legitimacy revived by its well-funded and highly-organised earthquake relief efforts, the Lashkar now seems prepared to renew its operations against India in and outside Jammu and Kashmir. "Everyone thinks the *jihad* is drawing to a close," Bukhari says quietly, "but they are wrong. Just plain wrong."

To those who knew him well, Bukhari's 2003 speech was no surprise. His father, Syed Ghulam Mohiuddin Bukhari, was a well known Sufi mystic, a living repository of a religious tradition hostile to Islamists and their pro-Pakistan political project.

His peers believed Bukhari's upbringing was the reason why he had maintained a studied distance from campus Islamists and Kashmiri nationalists, the two main ideological currents amongst the largely bourgeois student body.

In 2002, however, Bukhari began to evolve a life-transforming relationship with a north Kashmir-based Lashkar operative. Abdul Wahab, a resident of Multan in Pakistan educated at the International Islamic University in Islamabad, had abandoned his career as a chartered accountant to serve as a Lashkar operative in Jammu and Kashmir. "I was impressed," Bukhari says, "by the fact that he was willing to sacrifice so much for a cause larger than himself—to fight for something other than just a career or wealth."

Over months, Bukhari and Wahab built an intellectual relationship, forged over extended readings of Islamist tracts and through discussions of theology and religious issues. To Wahab, Kashmir's Sufi traditions were a failure. Quiescent Islamic practices, he argued, had led to wars of oppression against Muslims across the globe, from Kashmir to Chechnya and Palestine, and to the ascendance of the West. *Jihad*—not the kind of traditionalist piety represented by Bukhari's father—was the answer.

Although Bukhari never embraced the external manifestations of the Lashkar's Salafi-school ritual practices—"I never had the courage to fold my hands across my chest as they do during *namaaz*," he says, "for fear of my father's wrath"—he was persuaded by the arguments. Bukhari was slowly assigned low-level tasks. He wrote leaflets and newspaper articles under a pseudonym. On one occasion, in late 2003, he carried a defective satellite phone for repair to a Lashkar unit near Anantnag.

Bukhari's most abiding contribution to the north Kashmir Lashkar, however, was to provide it a steady flow of useful local intelligence. In 2003, after the Jammu and Kashmir Police's crack Special Operations Group established a unit in Kreeri, Bukhari helped organise efforts to have it removed. Pressure was brought to bear on an influential local People's Democratic Party leader, Basharat Bukhari, a distant relative of the Lashkar operative, by threatening to kidnap his brother. While the efforts did not yield results, Shabbir Bukhari had proved his utility.

Wahab's death in a 2003 encounter finally motivated Bukhari to join the Lashkar full-time. "He was buried like a dog," Bukhari recalls, "without even a headstone to mark his grave. I wanted to do something for the cause for which he gave his life." Operating under the command of the then-north Kashmir Lashkar divisional commander, still known only by his aliases 'Khalid' and 'Sierra-7,' Bukhari was told to build contacts among political activists and journalists in Srinagar, and establish an overground structure that could provide infrastructure for the terrorist group's armed activities.

Abu Sumama's Cell

Bukhari's decision to join the Lashkar full-time could not have come at a better time for the organisation. In 2003, 22 Lashkar operatives had been arrested as a consequence of an Intelligence Bureau operation that decimated the Lashkar's operational infrastructure. Its main city commander Abdul Rehman 'Mota,' a joking reference to his obesity, had been forced to shift to northern Kashmir. Under pressure from the United States, Pakistan had also begun to put pressure on the Lashkar to scale back its operations.

Drawing on the lessons of the 2003 debacle, the Lashkar set about building multiple cells under strong protective cover. For example, Bukhari recruited Shakeel Ahmad Sofi, a longstanding Youth National Conference activist who had been given secure official accommodation in 2002. Apart from allowing the use of his quarters for Lashkar work, Sofi provided party identification cards for Lashkar terrorists moving in and out of the city. Bukhari also purchased a white Maruti jeep, of the type used by the Jammu and Kashmir Police, allowing for the easy transport of weapons and Lashkar operatives.

Funds and operational instructions for Bukhari's cell were provided by the Lashkar commander who had replaced Abdul Rehman, a Pakistani national still known only by the multiple aliases 'Bilal,' 'Haider,' and 'Salahuddin.' 'Salahuddin' whose police dossier records that he is over 6 feet 6 inches tall and wears size-14 shoes, had earlier served under 'Khalid' in northern Kashmir, and knew Bukhari well. By the end of 2004, the group executed several sensational *fidayeen* operations, shipping in cadre to execute an attempt on the life of Prime Minister Manmohan Singh in November 2004 and the recent assassination of Jammu and Kashmir Minister of State Ghulam Nabi Lone.

Mirroring the activities of the Bukhari cell, other Lashkar cells run by ethnic Kashmiris were also set up in Srinagar, each under the command of a senior Pakistani operative. Abdul Rashid Khanday, a Srinagar resident who spent two years in jail after he was arrested in connection with an abortive *fidayeen* attack in 2000, ran what was code-named the 'Dar' cell. Operating under the command of Pakistani national Abdul Ahad, who used the code name 'Dawood,' the cell was responsible for several *fidayeen* attacks before the elimination of the terrorist and the subsequent arrest of its key members in August this year.

Abdul Rahman 'Mota' himself, meanwhile, activated a third cell, code-named 'Iqbal.' Little is known about the mechanics of the 'Iqbal' cell, which police sources believe carried out several high-profile *fidayeen* attacks in 2004. Although Abdul Rehman was eliminated earlier this week by the Jammu and Kashmir Police, the local ethnic-Kashmiri support structure of the 'Iqbal' cell still seems to be intact—evidence of the redundancies built into the Lashkar's new structures. "We are under no illusion," says Inspector-General of Police K. Rajendra, "that the Lashkar has been wiped out."

Challenges Ahead

To analysts of terrorism in Jammu and Kashmir, the unravelling of Bukhari's cell and the intelligence that has emerged from it hold several instructive lessons. First, the Lashkar has demonstrated the ability to recruit ethnic Kashmiri cadre—individuals, moreover, with significant educational and technical skills. Even if Indian policy-makers do arrive at an accommodation of the mainly ethnic-Kashmiri Hizb-ul-Mujahideen, this suggests groups like the Lashkar can pose an independent threat.

Secondly, the Lashkar has demonstrated both that its infrastructure is still intact and that its *jihadist* agenda remains in place. The Lashkar's renewal of pan-India operations after the October earthquake, illustrated dramatically through the Deepavali serial bombings in New Delhi, make clear just how ineffective Pakistani President Pervez Musharraf's promises to act against terror groups have been. Indeed, General Musharraf's failure suggests the Lashkar has powerful allies within Pakistan's military establishment—allies whom the Pakistani President is either unable or unwilling to confront.

Given that Indian counter-infiltration positions along the Line of Control have been disrupted by the earthquake, and the fact that newly inducted Central Reserve Police Force formations in Srinagar have yet to demonstrate an independent operational capability, the challenges to the peace process are significant. A series of major terrorist operations will make it increasingly difficult for the Manmohan Singh Government to push ahead with the *détente* process, something organisations like the Lashkar will be delighted by.

With the credibility of the Musharraf regime undermined by its dismal earthquake-relief performance, though, it is far from clear if Pakistan can act to stop a renewed *jihadist* offensive. Indian policy makers will have to grapple with the difficult task of defending the *détente* process as the Islamist siege of the Pakistani state strengthens.

India Fears Some of Its Muslims Are Joining in Terrorism

Somini Sengupta

The bomb attacks last month on seven Mumbai commuter trains did more than raise Indian hackles against Pakistan for failing to rein in terrorist groups operating on its soil.

They also underscored a gathering threat for India: a small but increasingly deadly cadre of young and often educated Indian Muslims who are being drawn directly into terrorist operations.

The scale and coordination of the July 11 attacks, a senior Indian government official said, suggest that at least one terrorist cell, made up of fewer than a dozen local people and probably directed and financed by militants based in Pakistan, carried out the bombings, which killed 183 people.

In the past, the official said, Indian operatives have aided foreign militants in what he called a benign fashion, sometimes providing little more than shelter or food. "The change is that some of them really know what they are up to," the official said, speaking on condition of anonymity because the investigation was in progress.

The emergence of more sophisticated homegrown terror cells carries grave repercussions not only for national security, but also for domestic politics, Hindu-Muslim relations and diplomacy with Pakistan.

Perhaps most important, it touches on India's idea of itself as the world's largest secular democracy, capable of including a multitude of peoples and faiths.

"A small section of the Indian Muslim community has been radicalized," said C. Raja Mohan, a columnist for the daily Indian Express and a member of the National Security Advisory Board. "That's what makes it that much more challenging for the country as a whole to deal with."

The police have arrested eight men from Mumbai, formerly Bombay, in connection with the attacks, though no specifics have been disclosed about their possible links to the bombings. Among them are a doctor of traditional Islamic medicine and a largely self-taught software worker who the police said had landed a job with the American database and software company Oracle.

Six of those arrested are said by the Indian authorities to have trained at terrorist camps in Pakistan run by the militant group Lashkar-e-Taiba. Several have been linked to a radical homegrown outfit, now banned, called the Students Islamic Movement of India.

For all the finger-pointing across the border, the attacks have forced India to confront a worrying disquiet among Muslims at home, who have overwhelmingly resisted calls to join in Islamic radicalism.

"That is still true to a very, very large extent," India's national security adviser, M. K. Narayanan, maintained. "But what has happened is that a very, very manifest attempt to recruit Indian Muslims is now being done."

Those efforts, he said in an interview on CNN-IBN television, are increasingly directed at educated Indian Muslims and, more troubling, at elements within the military.

Senior Lashkar officials interviewed in Rawalpindi, Pakistani, said no more than 50 Indians attended military and religious training camps in Pakistan and the Pakistani-controlled part of Kashmir on average each year.

But they confirmed that an active recruitment drive was under way in India.

It is impossible to pinpoint to what extent the still apparently small number of recruits are motivated by essentially Indian grievances—especially the pogroms in 2002 against Muslims in the state of Gujarat, which left 1,100 dead—or by the ideology of global political Islam.

But increasingly, many here fear, the two are at risk of merging.

In fact, Mr. Narayanan said, a reminder of anti-Muslim violence in India is a powerful recruitment tool. "Quite often," he said, "the motivation is 'You know what happened in Gujarat.'"

The Business Standard, an English-language daily, urged India in an editorial last week to start looking inward at what it called a "homegrown jihad," suggesting that blaming Pakistan alone for attacks on Indian soil was no longer sufficient.

"The national effort should make sure that even if Pakistan does its damnedest to plant evil seeds in this country, it must not find hospitable soil," the editorial concluded.

Just how hospitable India, home to roughly 140 million Muslims, may be as a breeding ground for extremism remains a matter of debate.

Some analysts in India maintain that were it not for the efforts of Pakistan-based militants, Indian Muslims would lack the resources to carry out large-scale terror attacks.

"The entire leadership that is creating violence in India is in Pakistan," insisted Ajai Sahni, an intelligence analyst in New Delhi who runs a Web site called the South Asia Terrorism Portal. "If you extract Pakistan from the problem and the flow of funds, the subversive cadres, there would not be this problem in India."

But visiting the Muslim neighborhoods of Mumbai in the aftermath of the July 11 bombings, what can plainly be felt is fear and resentment, fueled more than anything by police suspicion.

In the last two weeks the police have combed these neighborhoods in search of clues and suspects. They have knocked on doors demanding that parents produce their sons for questioning, unleashing even more bitterness.

"It has become now very difficult to live as a Muslim in this country," Aslam Ansari, 58, grumbled in the hallway of a dilapidated largely Muslim apartment block in a central city neighborhood called Mominpura. "We have to bear. We cannot go anywhere."

Among those arrested was one of Mr. Ansari's neighbors, a doctor named Tanvir Ansari, 32, who according to the police traveled to Pakistan for arms and explosives training. The two are not related, and Aslam Ansari insists that his neighbor is innocent.

Also taken into custody were two brothers from Mira Road, a largely Muslim northern suburb of Mumbai.

Faisal Shaikh, 30, the elder brother, is described by investigators as a crucial Indian liaison to Lashkar-e-Taiba. It was his younger brother, Muzamil, 23, who was hired by Oracle in Bangalore. The police say he followed his brother into the arms of Lashkar, and to Pakistan, via Iran, for training.

Sleeper cells connected to Pakistani-based organizations came on the Indian intelligence radar at least 10 years ago. Since then, bombings, arrests and weapons seizures have offered tiny peepholes into their suspected scope and strength.

In 2003, a Mumbai couple with suspected links to Jaish-e-Muhammad, a banned Pakistani-based group, was charged in connection with a pair of powerful car bomb attacks, including one in front of the iconic Gateway of India monument in Mumbai that killed more than 50 people.

The police said at the time that the couple was accused of planting the bombs in the trunks of two taxis as part of a local outfit calling itself the Gujarat Revenge Force.

Last year, the Delhi police arrested a mechanical engineer on charges of conspiring to attack military and financial centers on behalf of Lashkar.

And in May a large haul of guns and military explosives exposed what the police called a sleeper cell of roughly a dozen people operating out of Aurangabad, a provincial town about 200 miles northeast of here.

As in the past, the arrests in the last three weeks have largely homed in on the Students Islamic Movement of India. The police say several of those arrested in connection with the July 11 blasts were once members. Its leaders deny any involvement with the attacks.

"Some such modules have been unearthed here," said Mumbai's commissioner of police, A. N. Roy. He said former members of the organization "form a fertile ground for providing local foot soldiers."

Founded 30 years ago to promote Islamic teaching among Indian youth, the group began to espouse armed resistance more than a decade ago after a band of Hindu radicals tore down the 400-year-old Babri Mosque in the north Indian city of Ayodhya in 1992, unleashing an orgy of Hindu-Muslim riots across the country.

The lingering tensions in this city are deeply worrying. Since the July attacks even career-minded young Indian Muslims complain that they are under constant glare.

The ones who sport beards and skullcaps worry about how many times they will be frisked at the train station. Those who live in Muslim enclaves see the police knocking on doors.

One young man recalled a banner that went up in his neighborhood, exhorting enemies of India to leave the country. "Our identity is the main problem," said Abdul Hannan Khan, 21, a college student who plans a career in advertising.

It is the same routine after every act of terror, said Sheik Abdul Qayyum, 20, recalling the Gujarat riots, which broke out after fire engulfed a train carrying Hindu pilgrims, killing 59. Whether the fire was deliberate or accidental is still disputed, and embroiled in political feuds.

In Mr. Qayyum's mind there is no disputing the lesson of Gujarat, where he lived at the time. He says the violence there was the most important event in his life.

"I learned that as minority Muslims we are unprotected," he said, and then quickly added, "According to the current situation, Muslims in the whole world are not protected."

From *The New York Times*, August 9, 2006, pp. A3. Copyright © 2006 by The New York Times Company. Reprinted by permission.

Gauging Terror—Part II, India

Despite suffering substantial losses from terrorism, India resists initiating military strikes.

MICHAEL KREPON

When you have a hammer, every problem can look like a nail. But when a hammer is used to deal with the problem of terrorism, the nails can multiply. The US is learning this painful lesson in Iraq, and Israel seems to have relearned it in Lebanon, where Israeli military campaigns first created Hezbollah and now greatly empowered it. The development of power projection capabilities takes hard work and considerable expense. But it takes real wisdom to know when and how to use military power to combat terrorism. Without wisdom, power projection can be negated, while producing adverse, unintended consequences.

One dog has yet to bark in what President George W. Bush calls the "global war on terror." Since 1994, India has suffered almost 20,000 fatalities as a result of acts of terror, losses that dwarf those suffered by the US and Israel. Despite these losses, New Delhi has been very reluctant to initiate cross-border military strikes against targets based in Pakistan, where supporters and perpetrators of acts of violence directed against India have found safe haven.

Pakistan is an essential partner in fighting terrorism, but is also an incubator of terrorists. This paradox, which has long confounded US and Indian leaders, is most evident in Kashmir and the Pashtun belt along Pakistan's border with Afghanistan. If or when the Indian government feels compelled to retaliate militarily against acts of terror, it is likely to do so across the Line of Control that divides Kashmir. Prediction in such matters is hazardous, given New Delhi's record of prior restraint, which also makes the element of surprise more likely. Cross-border military operations would open another "front" in the war against terror, one in which both adversaries possess nuclear weapons.

A face-off involving India and Pakistan would therefore be quite different from the military campaigns waged by the United States and Israel. To begin with, the use of force would presumably be far more glancing and circumspect. Prior wars between these two rivals, which were joined at the hip until partition in 1947, have been limited in scope. But choreography in warfare is a tricky business, and any new front in the global war against terror—especially in South Asia—poses huge risks, including risks for the Bush administration.

The Bush team has prided itself on improving bilateral relations with both India and Pakistan. This significant accomplishment could be destroyed in the event of military hostilities on the subcontinent. As the victim of terrorism, India would naturally expect the sympathy and support of the Bush administration. If, instead, Washington seeks to play an evenhanded, honest-broker role, the vaunted strategic partnership sought by the Bush team would be placed at risk. And if Washington aligns with another democracy under threat by Islamic extremism, its relations with Pakistan would plummet, with potentially far-reaching consequences for the war against terror, domestic politics in Pakistan, Afghanistan's future, proliferation and India-Pakistan relations.

Any use of force between India and Pakistan, both nuclear powers, would presumably be glancing and circumspect.

The initiation of another limited war between India and Pakistan would also test the "stability-instability paradox." This academic construct—an offshoot of deterrence theory—holds that two nuclear-armed rivals will rile each other, but will avoid crossing the nuclear threshold. So far, both elements of

Pakistan is an essential partner in fighting terrorism, but is also an incubator of terrorists.

the stability-instability paradox seem very much in place on the subcontinent. India and Pakistan have experienced a succession of crises and one limited war since acquiring nuclear weapons—without producing mushroom clouds. But academic theories are neat and tidy, whereas crises and warfare can take unexpected and unwanted turns.

Clearly, much could go wrong if successive acts of terror lead to skirmishing between India and Pakistan, which means that much is riding on New Delhi's state of mind regarding its chronic difficulties with Pakistan. The US has served as the crisis manager in previous nuclear-tinged confrontations, a role that was greatly facilitated by the reluctance of Indian leaders to go to war, even after grievous acts of terror. In the last such effort, the Bush administration brokered a climb-down from a 10-month-long military mobilization triggered by an attack on the Indian parliament building in December 2001.

India and Pakistan have experienced a succession of crises since acquiring nuclear weapons–without producing mushroom clouds.

The Bush team is not well positioned to play this role again. The White House and State Department have their hands full in dealing with wars in Iraq, Lebanon, Palestine and Afghanistan, as well as with the nuclear ambitions of Iran and North Korea. The administration has waged wars in Iraq and Afghanistan predicated on the imperative to root out distant dangers before Americans again suffer the consequences of terrorist acts at home. Having embraced a proactive role in fighting terror, and having backed Israel's military campaign against Hezbollah in Lebanon, the Bush administration is in no position to counsel New Delhi to exercise restraint.

The last crisis between India and Pakistan was defused by then-Deputy Secretary of State Richard Armitage, who in 2002 extracted a pledge by Pakistani President Pervez Musharraf to "permanently" end cross-border violence directed against India by Islamic extremists. This pledge and others like it from Musharraf make it more difficult to defuse another crisis preceded by heightened infiltration across the Kashmir divide and by bomb blasts at sensitive locations in India.

Since the last exercise of US crisis management, Pakistan's list of grievances with the United States has grown considerably, while India has become the Bush administration's most favored up-and-coming regional power. Most recently, New Delhi has been gifted with a nuclear cooperation agreement that Bush pointedly declined to offer Islamabad. This deal was strongly supported on Capitol Hill by US business interests and by the Indian-American community, which views the "Jewish lobby" as its model. With Republicans unwilling to undercut the White House, and with Democrats unwilling to offend the Indian-American community in an election year, the Congress shunted aside substantive concerns to endorse this deal overwhelmingly.

India's leaders understand that military power is not well suited for combat terrorism.

If, after this sequence of events, India suffers horrific acts or terrorism, New Delhi has every reason to expect US support if it decides to strike "terrorist camps" and other targets across the Line of Control. And if New Delhi gets that backing, Pakistan could well explode.

The Bush administration has long wanted to "de-hyphenate" India-Pakistan relations. If this dreaded scenario plays out, de-hyphenation could be shunted aside by a stark either/or choice. President Bush's famously simple formula—are you with me or against me in the war on terror?—could conceivably be played back at him. Then the Great Simplifier would face an excruciating choice: whether to lose one strategic partner or two.

Because this scenario is sufficiently grim and plausible, preventive action in India and Pakistan is worth taking in the form of heightened domestic security against extremist groups and renewed diplomacy. A disproportionate share of this burden falls on India because its leaders understand far better than their counterparts in the US and Israel that military power is not well suited to combat terrorism. But at some point, reaching for the hammer could become New Delhi's unwelcome choice.

MICHAEL KREPON is the co-founder of the Henry L. Stimson Center, the editor of *Nuclear Risk Reduction in South Asia,* and the author of *Cooperative Threat Reduction, Missile Defense and the Nuclear Future,* both published by Palgrave Macmillan.

Acting Tough

At long last the Bangladesh government takes some action against Islamist militancy by arresting two of its top leaders.

HAROON HABIB

Islamist militancy in Bangladesh apparently suffered a setback in the first week of March with the arrest of two of the movement's most important leaders. On March 2, the elite Rapid Action Battalion (RAB) arrested Shaikh Abdur Rahman, the founder of the Jamaat'ul Mujahideen Bangladesh (JMB) who is considered the spiritual guide of Islamist militants in the country. The organisation is allegedly responsible for several bomb attacks that have occurred in Bangladesh over the past few years, especially the countrywide bombings of August 17, 2005. The RAB also arrested Siddiqul Islam, known as 'Bangla Bhai,' the 'operations commander' of the Jagrata Muslim Janata Bangladesh (JMJB), a sister outfit of the JMB.

The Shaikh's arrest from a house in north-eastern Sylhet followed a 31-hour-long operation that involved peaceful negotiations. 'Bangla Bhai,' on the other hand, suffered injuries in the operation to capture him from a remote village in northern Mymensingh. Both were arrested along with their wives and children and a few associates. Huge quantities of arms and ammunition were recovered from them. Although Shaikh and 'Bangla Bhai' demanded interaction with mediapersons and a few government leaders including Ministers, the authorities did not allow it.

On March 13, the RAB raided another hideout of the militants in Comilla, some 160 km from Dhaka, and killed Shakil, said to be a bomb-maker. The wife and two children of Shakil, also known as 'Mollah Omar,' died in the operation. During the operation, the RAB caught Shaikh's son Nabil Rahman and some others.

Both Shaikh and 'Bangla Bhai' fought in the war against the Soviet intervention in Afghanistan in the 1980s, were closely associated with the Jamaat-e-Islami, the main coalition partner of Prime Minister Khaleda Zia's Bangladesh National Party-led ruling alliance, and were sentenced to 40 years in prison *in absentia* in February 2006. 'Bangla Bhai,' nearly 40, is also one of the seven members of the JMB's highest decision-making body, Majlis-e-Shura. The JMB and the JMJB have been working underground for the past six years to establish a Taliban-like government in Bangladesh. The JMJB's operational base was the northern region of Rajshahi and the organisation allegedly enjoyed the protection of a section of the ruling alliance and the local administration.

During interrogation, Shaikh confessed to the RAB that the bombing of cinema halls and attacks on the country's leading intellectuals were carried out by his men. "He has taken all responsibility for the August 17 attacks and for the attacks on the professors," Gulzar Uddin Ahmed, RAB Intelligence Director, told mediapersons. "We have been questioning him about the motive behind the attacks and initially he was saying that it was to establish Islamic law."

The JMB chief admitted links to various jehadi leaders and organisations, and his organisation's plans to establish Islamic rule both in and outside Bangladesh. He said that he had received huge amounts of money from them and invested it to increase his organisation's strength, but refused to disclose their names. "I travelled all over the world, mainly Islamic countries, to establish relations with some Islamic leaders, who encouraged me to establish Islamic rule in Bangladesh, by providing mental and financial support," a leading Bangladesh daily quoted Shaikh.

The capture of Shaikh and Bangla Bhai may have weakened the JMB and the JMJB, but the jehadi networks have not yet been dismantled. News reports indicate that thousands of JMB activists, especially members of its suicide squad, remain beyond the reach of the police and are planning to carry out more attacks.

An Unholy Nexus

Within hours of Shaikh's arrest, Khaleda Zia addressed the nation and claimed that "Bangladesh [had] proved before the world that it could successfully combat terrorism in the name of Islam." She said that her government, by arresting the militants, had achieved what powerful nations had failed to do. However, a close look at the rise of Islamist fundamentalism in Bangladesh, reveals that her claims do not stand up to scrutiny. In fact, it reveals a connection between a section of government leaders and the militant leadership.

Even at the height of militant violence in the country, the Khaleda Zia government refused to blame the JMB or the JMJB. Instead it interpreted the violence as part of an "anti-Bangladesh campaign" and suggested that foreign nations were behind it. For instance, the government appointed a one-man Justice Zoinul Abedin Commission to probe the attack on the Awami League headquarters on August 21, 2004 in which former Prime Minister Sheikh Hasina narrowly escaped death but over two dozen of her party workers died. The commission's conclusion was that local hoodlums in collaboration with a foreign country's intelligence agency was behind the attack.

Moreover, there is ample evidence for the Jamaat-e-Islami's link with the JMB and the JMJB, though the party, which opposed Bangladesh's war of liberation from Pakistan, has refuted the charge. At the height of the militancy, a senior Minister in the Cabinet and the ameer (leader) of Jamaat-e-Islami, Maulana Matiur Rahman Nizami, claimed that there was no one by the name of 'Bangla Bhai' and that he was a creation of the media.

The confessional statements and the backgrounds of captured JMB activists, including Shaikh and 'Bangla Bhai,' have pointed to a close link with the Jamaat. Works of Maulana Sayedi, a Jamaat theoretician, and a few books written by Golam Azam, the founder of the Bangladesh chapter of the Jamaat were recovered from the captured militants. Jehadi books written by Maulana Matiur Rahman Nizami were also recovered from the JMB's Comilla hideout. But it is alleged that the government agencies did not include the Jamaat literature in the list of items seized from the militants.

The covert links between the Jamaat and a section of the government were first made public by a BNP leader. Abu Hena, a Member of Parliament elected from Bagmara, Rajshahi, said he had informed the Prime Minister and the State Minister for Home about the dangers posed by 'Bangla Bhai' but nothing was done. "It is unlikely that 'Bangla Bhai' has risen to the top without any knowledge of the administration," Hena said.

Behind the Scenes

Why did the Khaleda Zia government crack down on the JMB leadership now? Some analysts say that since the general elections are approaching and the ruling alliance knows there is a perception that the government was behind the emergence of Islamist militants, it had to act. The Opposition parties and a large section of society consider the arrests of Shaikh and 'Bangla Bhai' "a drama." They believe the Khaleda Zia government arrested them when it realised that they were no longer safe. Some political observers allege that the government timed the arrests to coincide with George W. Bush's visit to South Asia in order to persuade him to include Bangladesh in his itinerary. The Bush administration had been putting pressure on the government to crack down on militancy.

Another reason could be the government's need to improve its image. An abnormal hike in the prices of essential commodities, acute shortage of power and the politicisation of administration had alienated the people from the government.

Civil War Returns to Sri Lanka

Still recovering from the December 2004 tsunami, Sri Lanka is once again enmeshed in a civil war. With the world's major powers choosing to look the other way, the victims of the island's latest round of violent clashes have only international aid organizations to turn to for help.

RÜDIGER FALKSOHN AND PADMA RAO

On a rainy evening in the Sri Lankan capital, Colombo, Kethesh Loganathan hears a knock on his front door. It's late and he isn't expecting visitors. Nevertheless, Sri Lanka's acting peace coordinator gets up and opens the door.

He peers out into the dark, and perhaps he even notices a minibus nearby with its engine idling, but what he doesn't notice is a group of shadowy figures who seem to emerge out of the earth in front of his house. The men are his murderers, the last people Loganathan, a Tamil intellectual who sought to achieve reconciliation between the island nation's warring factions, will see before he dies. The killers fire five rounds into Loganathan's body, jump into their minibus and speed away into the night.

Violence flares up again two days later on a busy shopping street in downtown Colombo, not far from Liberty Plaza. Although his Mercedes is guarded by a military escort in a white Land Rover, this doesn't stop Pakistani Ambassador Bashir Wali Mohammed's would-be assassins, who have rigged one of the city's ubiquitous covered moped taxis with explosives and parked it inconspicuously between trash bags set out on the curb. When the ambassador's small convoy passes the moped taxi at 1:25 p.m., his killers detonate two Claymore mines by remote control.

The diplomat remains uninjured, but his bodyguards are not as lucky. The full force of the exploding three-wheeled vehicle throws their SUV against a nearby wall, killing four bodyguards and three bystanders. The 15 injured on this gloomy Monday include young schoolchildren who, still in a state of shock from the explosions, are rushed to a nearby emergency room.

The attack was apparently the work of the Tamil Tigers, or Liberation Tigers of Tamil Eelam (LTTE), separatists who, as the self-appointed representatives of Sri Lanka's 3.5 million Tamil minority, have been waging a war to establish their own state for more than two decades. The Tigers launched their armed resistance movement in 1983, when suppression and persecution of the Tamils by the ruling Singhalese became unbearable and began escalating into pogroms against the minority group.

Tsunami and Civil War

The LTTE has controlled the north and the eastern edge of this tropical paradise for some time. And although the group signed a peace treaty with the Sri Lankan government in February 2002, that agreement is now worth less than the paper on which it was written. The latest round of violence began when the country's foreign minister was assassinated—exactly one year before Loganathan was shot to death two weekends ago. Since then, old animosities between the two rival ethnic groups have flared up again in the form of political murders in Colombo and government military reprisals on the fringes of the Tiger belt. "We must respond in a language they understand," barked government spokesman Keheliya Rambukwella in the wake of the most recent Tamil Tiger attacks. "Attack is our best defense!"

Rambukwella's threats were apparently serious. A short time later, a handful of the Sri Lankan air force's Kfir jets took off for the Tigers' strongholds in the north, where they promptly flattened a building in the town of Vallipunam. According to government sources in Colombo, the target was a barracks building where they claimed the LTTE was training child soldiers who, in the government's eyes, are just as culpable as their adult counterparts. The Tigers promptly retorted that the building was a school for orphans, and that the children were in the midst of a first aid course when the bomb struck. But United Nations Children's Fund (UNICEF) observers who quickly arrived on the scene corroborated the Tigers' story.

One of the basic truths about this civil war, a conflict characterized by its brutality and by the two sides' ongoing reciprocal assignments of guilt, is that both sides play dirty. It's also true that 16 bombs rained down on Vallipunam last Monday at 7 a.m. local time. At least 51 girls were killed and 155 wounded. The air attacks became yet more intense on Thursday. Perhaps the saddest of truths facing the island nation is that those who have been forced to bear the brunt of this vicious conflict—in which neither the LTTE nor the government's army, the SLA, has managed to gain the upper hand in more than two decades of fighting—are ordinary Sri Lankans, still reeling in the aftermath of the deadly 2004 tsunami.

The suffering being visited on this spice island and popular holiday destination, where ongoing flare-ups of terror form a jarring contrast to the Sri Lankans' famously broad smiles, hasn't attracted much international attention. Far from stepping in to help resolve the conflict, the world's major powers have instead chosen to witness the slaughter from afar, content to periodically issue boilerplate statements of consternation.

While China and Pakistan supply weapons to the SLA (which explains the attack on the Pakistani ambassador), the country's powerful neighbor to the north, India, concerned about a possible arms buildup in its backyard, limits itself to providing logistical support, including the delivery of radar systems. U.S. President George W. Bush has shown no interest whatsoever in this small island nation. Germany, for its part, threatened last week to cut off development aid if the violence continues.

Northern European mediators have been working for years to help bring peace to the region, either in the form of autonomy for Tamil-controlled areas or at least an interim solution both sides can accept. But after the European Union banned the Tigers as a terrorist organization in May 2006, furious LTTE officials demanded the withdrawal of EU observers by Sept. 1. The Europeans have been quick to comply, fearing retribution from rebel leader Velupillai Prabhakaran and his rival Karuna, who controls the eastern portion of the island. The EU contingent, which consists of Finns, Swedes and Danes, is expected to leave Sri Lanka by the end of this month.

The only international officials who will remain on the island after Sept. 1 to help minimize the damage are the nongovernmental aid organizations, or NGOs, that have been active in Sri Lanka since the December 2004 tsunami, and a handful of about 20 Norwegian and Icelandic "observers." Since both Norway and Iceland are not members of the EU, the Tigers consider them—and their observers—neutral.

"The international community was ultimately a total failure here," says Norwegian chief mediator Jon Hanssen-Bauer, staring gloomily from behind his thick glasses. Hanssen-Bauer is visibly exhausted from a job that is both hectic and stressful. He negotiated unrelentingly with the Tigers when they recently sealed off and then mined a small group of canal locks in the east of the island. The effects of the Tigers' move were devastating.

Fifteen thousand farmers were cut off from their water supply for weeks, and some lost their harvests. The campaign was so spectacular that even the global press took notice, highlighting the LTTE's reputation for perfidious ingenuity. Although Colombo sent a force of 3,000 troops to the region, it remained ineffective, as is so often the case in Sri Lanka, and ultimately resorted to shelling the locks on the Maavilaru canal.

President Mahinda Rajapakse had to do something, and bombing the locks was ultimately little more than a PR campaign to show the public that he was in fact doing something against the Tigers. Ulf Henricsson, the Swedish head of the observer mission, was almost killed by artillery fire while accompanying the Tigers to the locks on August 6. Two days later, after almost three long weeks, the rebels finally opened the locks and released the water.

The Battle for Trincomalee

The east is Sri Lanka's trouble spot. Although the government still controls the city of Trincomalee, no one knows how much longer it can hold out. The Tigers are intent on capturing "Trinco" as a crown jewel and as the capital of a state they would call Tamil Eelam—or at least an autonomous region with practically full sovereignty.

Hanssen-Bauer compares the region—populated in almost equal parts by Muslims, the Buddhist Singhalese and the mostly Hindu Tamils—to a spotted leopard skin in which the government and LTTE struggle for territorial dominance. Holding or capturing Trinco is a matter of prestige for both sides, while being forced to abandon it would be deeply humiliating. Caught between the poorly delineated fronts in recent days and weeks, tens of thousands have already fled to camps run by the NGOs. At least 800 rebels and government soldiers were killed in the space of only one week.

Merely driving into the crisis zone is a highly dangerous endeavor. Two-thirds of the 280-kilometer (174-mile) route, up to the city of Habarana, are still relatively safe and well traveled, but then the road crosses into new terrain and a critical dividing line. The jungle gives way to a charred, bush-like topography. SLA roadblocks—many of them little more than rudimentary barbed wire barriers nailed to branches, interspersed with impromptu corrugated metal checkposts that are reinforced with sandbags—become increasingly frequent on what is now a lightly traveled road. As nervous travelers hand over their documents, uniformed soldiers patrol open stretches of road between the checkpoints. The A6, the east coast's main highway, is dotted with observation posts perched like sore thumbs on earthen mounds.

The army's rickety reconnaissance vehicles, some clad with corrugated metal as armor, look as if they could barely withstand an overly enthusiastic elk, not to mention enemy fire. Like the naïve young faces emerging from a wide range of uniforms, these vehicles merely highlight the SLA's fundamental inadequacies.

Like rebels the world over, the supposedly liberating Tigers recruit their human cannon fodder from within the very population for which they claim to be fighting. With no support from any foreign government, the guerillas buy their weapons on the world's black markets, partly with contributions from overseas Tamil exiles. In an effort to put a legal plug on this flow of cash, the EU placed the separatists on its list of terrorist organizations at the end of May.

Though LTTE has only a handful of aircraft in its arsenal, the "Sea Tigers" operating off the coast of Trincomalee are highly effective. They already appear to have made up for the destruction the 2004 tsunami inflicted on their fleet, as evidenced by the thousands of east coast residents who have now fled from their attacks.

A Growing Refugee Crisis

The scene behind a railroad embankment in Kantalai, where the area's largest refugee camp stretches along a canal, reveals the full scale of the region's misery. Camp Perathuvelee, where 7,334 newcomers were registered last Tuesday, is populated exclusively by Muslims. Less than a week earlier, the camp was home to as many as 13,000 IDPs, the aid workers' acronym for "internally displaced persons."

According to the official count, by last Tuesday 52,501 Sri Lankans had chosen to endure the hardships of life in a refugee camp, the jostling for food and the lack of privacy, over the prospect of returning to their homes on the coast. Although refugees have been given the option of returning home, and some have done so, aid officials are reluctant to send anyone home and possibly into harm's way.

Those who choose often do so to escape the madness of camp life, where three to four families share crude tents fashioned from blue or gray tarps and the entire camp must make do with a dozen latrines.

Forty-year-old Fatima stands in front of her tent watching her children. The youngest play with dark red stones on a sheet of cardboard spread out on the ground in front of the tent flap—their only toy. Inside the tent, the grandfather dozes on a grass mat, surrounded by cardboard boxes, tin bowls and a plate of five tomatoes—a meal for the family of seven.

This isn't the first time the war has driven Fatima from her town, Muttur, where her husband runs a small pharmacy. But in the past Fatima and her family sought shelter in SLA camps. This time Muttur came under fire from both warring parties, prompting the family to flee inland. "The government would prefer to load us onto buses and send us home now," says Fatima in a deep, raspy voice, "because they claim it's quiet there now. But no one believes them."

Indeed, "Samadhanam," the Tamil word for peace, is a long way off for Sri Lanka. On Aug. 6 Muttur, on the southern edge of the large bay surrounding Trincomalee, became the scene of an outrageous act of bloody violence and the epitome of the horrors of the Sri Lankan civil war. Fifteen local employees of French aid organization Action Against Hunger (Accion Contre la Faim) were found lying face-down on the ground, executed

with shots to the head. Two others were found dead in a nearby car. All but one were Tamils.

No one has claimed responsibility for this taboo-breaking massacre, with each side claiming it was the work of the other. The lack of a plausible motive made the incident all the more shocking.

"If the SLA loses Muttur, it will lose the war," says Amjad Mohamed-Saleem, head of the British organization Muslim Aid's Sri Lankan operation. Judging by the amount of effort the government has put into holding on to little Muttur and larger Trinco, he may be right. Trinco, where soldiers almost outnumber civilians, has the air of a ghost town. Two soccer fields on the seashore are deserted and the adjacent playground is empty. "Club Oceanic," a resort, is offering a 15 percent discount "on everything" and, in an effort to shield its guests, prefers not to tune its TV sets to the news.

Only a year ago, the hotel was booked solid and the remains of a 40-foot dugout canoe lying off the hotel's beachside deck, ripped apart by the tsunami, were practically a tourist attraction. Today the shattered canoe is testimony to the double burden that's been hoisted on the Sri Lankan people, both by the devastating force of the giant wave and one of the world's longest-lasting civil wars. A hotel employee nicely sums up this double whammy against Sri Lanka when he says: "I hate myself for having been born in this part of the world."

In the evening, heavy clouds hang over the Bay of Trincomalee. The good people from the NGOs and the UN gather around a large table for supper in the dining room at the Club Oceanic. This evening they're discussing a warning that has just arrived by text message. The LTTE announced its first-ever attack on the city and encouraged everyone to leave Trinco by no later than the next morning.

The news hasn't stopped Katey, a cheerful employee of the UN's Trincomalee mission, from spreading her good spirits. Sullen Damian, who works for an NGO in Kantalai, pensively rotates his wine glass back and forth. Lars, a German who runs a medicine project, constantly harps on the bad luck that brought him to this place and the even worse luck that will take him to Sudan next year. The assembled aid workers talk and fiddle with their electronic organizers and mobile phones, as if communication technology were the only salvation in their current, difficult situation.

The power suddenly fails at 9 p.m., bringing conversation to an abrupt end. It's pitch-black inside the hotel, as black as the night over the bay. And it's silent, so silent that everyone in the room hears the Tigers setting of an explosion in Trinco.

Getting India Right

PARAG KHANNA AND C. RAJA MOHAN

For those who missed the symbolism of Indian flags draped from the White House's Old Executive Office Building, President George Bush's words on the morning of July 18, 2005, while standing next to Indian Prime Minister Manmohan Singh, drove home an emerging reality with trademark pithiness: "The relationship between our two nations has never been stronger, and it will grow even closer in the days and years to come." Combined with the Bush administration's visible push to strengthen Japan's hand in managing Asian security, the Indian prime minister's visit to Washington cemented a growing de facto strategic partnership between the United States and India.

Numerous American officials already used the term "irreversible" to describe the course of Indo-U.S. relations. No U.S. president visited India between January 1978 and March 2000, when President Clinton made a historic trip to the Subcontinent. Cabinet-level exchanges have since become routine, and President Bush's planned visit in early spring 2006 will reflect an agenda that has come to encompass shared global interests and concerns ranging from Iran and China to nuclear cooperation and biotechnology. Some have begun to see Bush's visit to India as similar, in both intent and consequence, to that of Richard Nixon to China in 1972—which transformed Sino-U.S. relations and the global balance of power for the next three decades.

Given the bilateral tensions over nuclear proliferation in the 1990s, such strong relations are in themselves remarkable. When viewed through the prism of geopolitical shifts, however, Indo-U.S. alignment is if anything long overdue. American military and diplomatic movements from the Middle East through Central Asia to the Pacific Rim are in a state of flux for reasons ranging from the Iraqi insurgency to the Iranian nuclear crisis to the rise of vocal new regional institutions such as the Shanghai Cooperation Organization and East Asian Community. Asia, where two-thirds of the world's population resides, is the new geopolitical stage. It is the principal source of the global power shift and will also face most of the political consequences. Yet the constantly shifting loyalties and alliance patterns in Asia confound both historians and experts in geometry. There is the patron-client dyad from Beijing to Islamabad, routine Russian-

Chinese-Indian summitry with declarations affirming the need for multipolarity, joint Russo-Japanese and Sino-Russian military maneuvers, talk of a three-cornered nuclear calculus in the U.S.-China-India triangle, and America's attempt to transcend its historical "tilting" between India and Pakistan. The only clear inference from these asymmetrical configurations is that most Asian states continue to subscribe to an adage common to their cultures: to be polite especially to one's enemies. While all Asian powers are wary of American preponderance, they have also sought good relations with Washington. None of them was at the forefront of the worldwide criticism (led by Europe) of the American occupation in Iraq.

Historically, the U.S. has viewed the Middle East and Pacific Rim theaters as separate policy realms, with India falling in between and viewed through the exclusive prism of South Asian politics. But India lies at the crossroads of Asia, a factor which was at the heart of British policy towards the East. Only after the Second World War and the partition of the Subcontinent was India's position weakened, a shift accentuated by India's socialist and inward-looking policies. Yet as India's weight grows in the international system, it can become a strong anchor in support of America's ambition to pursue a liberal order across Eurasia. Indeed, if the U.S. should welcome the emergence of any one Asian power, it should be India, which shares America's concern over the spread of Islamic fundamentalism, sub-state nuclear proliferation, and China's ambitions. Furthermore, each Indian election entrenches its status and credibility as the world's largest democracy, and its growing economic clout and diaspora presence in the U.S. are tying the two societies on opposite sides of the world together as never before. Indeed, there is not a single area in which India's rise threatens America's interests.

When President Bush visits India, he will surely reiterate his administration's support of India's emergence as a great power. But America cannot itself make India great, nor can it guarantee that India's emerging power will be used to the benefit of American interests. Indeed, plausible scenarios for U.S.-India relations still range from having India as stable democratic ally in the heart of Asia to India as a reluctant partner in the Sino-Russian anti-hegemonic coalition. As Manmohan Singh declared on the eve of his July visit to Washington, "We are an independent power; we are not a client state; we are not a supplicant. As two equal societies, we should explore together where there is convergence of interests and work together."

A broad, integrated American policy towards India should therefore begin by asking how America can promote—rather than interfere in or manipulate—the complementarity of Indian policies and American interests. For the hopes of an enduring alliance on the scale of America's relations with Japan to materialize, U.S.-India relations will have to be constantly nurtured and the competing sets of priorities jostling for influence in both Washington and New Delhi mastered. Building a strategic partnership with India will test America's ability to engage an independent democracy that has had no record of security or economic dependence on the United States.

Nonaligned No More

According to the latest report of the CIA's National Intelligence Council, *Mapping the Global Future*, by 2020 "India's GNP will have overtaken or be on the threshold of overtaking European economies," potentially making it the world's third largest economy. As the report concludes, "Barring an abrupt reversal of the process of globalization or any major upheavals, the rise of these new powers [China and India] is a virtual certainty. Yet how China and India exercise their growing power and whether they relate cooperatively or competitively to other powers in the international system are key uncertainties."

India on its own has begun the journey from its self-perception as an anti-imperialist power to a great power in its own right and is already defying the axiom that large states tend to be conservative about foreign policy. Though not a systemically revisionist power, it has pursued an increasingly activist foreign policy agenda, seeking to become not only South Asia's dominant power, but an eminent Asian power.[1] Many in the U.S. might want India to become a Britain or Japan, mainly following where Washington leads. Others, like Jean-Luc Racine of the National Center for Scientific Research in Paris, believe "India has basically a Gaullist vision of the world" and want India to become a France to the United States. But there are good reasons to believe India will be none of the above. Indo-U.S. strategic engagement will have to be constructed on an entirely different basis.

The perceived distinction between India's nonaligned past and alliance-oriented future is a complex one. At one level, India continues to cling to a cherished Nehruvian ideal of autonomous action based on democratic right and self-defined interest. At the same time, India has shown increasing flexibility in engaging the major powers and has expanded cooperation with the United States even in areas of prime security concern to itself. All of this makes India what political scientist Stephen Krasner calls a "modified structuralist" state, seeking to maximize its interests and power but also to opportunistically transcend individual calculations of national interest. In India's case, this position is actually based as much on an ideology of nonalignment, interpreted as an independent foreign policy that seeks to maximize India's weight in world affairs. As Manmohan Singh has stated, "We should develop friendly relations with as many major powers as possible. This will help in securing wider international support when we need it most."

While there is no guarantee that India will become more allied or aligned, there has been a continuous trajectory toward a diplomatic posture which is perhaps best described as "neo-Curzonian," after the British imperial viceroy and player of the "Great Game" Lord George Curzon. Ironically, India's neo-Curzonian worldview is the logical heir to one of the nation's strategic ur-texts, Kautilya's fourth-century B.C. *Arthashastras*, which locates India at the nucleus of concentric rings of potential friends and foes. A neo-Curzonian foreign policy is premised on the logic of Indian centrality, permitting multidirectional engagement—or "multi-alignment"—with all major powers and seeking access and leverage from East Africa to Pacific Asia. Such a forward foreign policy emphasizes the revival of commercial cooperation; building institutional, physical and political links with neighboring regions to circumvent buffer states; developing energy supplies and assets; and pursuing multistate defense agreements and contracts. Today, India has recovered this 360-degree vision, looking west to boost investment from Europe and the Persian Gulf, north to secure stable energy supplies from Central Asia (including Iran), and east for partnerships and free trade agreements with South Korea and Australia. It engages actively in regional fora such as the South Asian Association for Regional Cooperation (SAARC) and the Association of South East Asian Nations (ASEAN) while not shying away from potential strategic competition with neighbors such as Pakistan and China. Furthermore, it has transitioned from demanding respect on the basis of its nuclear status to proving greatness on the basis of its political and economic accomplishments.

Since injecting nationalism into its foreign policy and simultaneously making it more pragmatic, India has experienced a marked improvement in its global visibility. Interestingly, the traditional sympathies for the Third World in New Delhi are slowly being morphed into a search for markets and influence in such regions as Africa and East Asia. India is steadily expanding the scale and scope of its foreign assistance programs, which now have reached an annual level of nearly U.S. $350 million.[2] India's aid program also has the features of great power aid policies of the past, such as support to domestic industry and penetration of foreign markets. India no longer reactively asks what others would like it to do, but rather takes the lead in defining its own goals.

From Estrangement to Partnership

It has become the norm to speak of India as a "natural ally" of the United States, and in the first years of the Bush administration, India transacted more political business with the United States than in the previous 40. That public attitudes in India toward the United States have begun to shift in a fundamental manner was evident in a recent Pew Research Center Global Attitudes Survey. Of all the countries surveyed, pro-American sentiment was strongest in India, where 71 percent of respondents reported a favorable view.

Yet bilateral relations have continued to carry some of the baggage of historical antagonism. India lost its independence when America gained its own, and when India did become free, it placed itself essentially on the opposite side of the Cold War from the U.S., leading to decades of mutual suspicion and mistrust. Though in the 1950s the U.S. had pledged to pursue a "non-zero sum" relationship with India and Pakistan, American weapons found their way into Pakistan's arsenal during the two countries' second major war in 1965. Though Jawaharlal Nehru himself believed that the U.S. and India should be natural democratic allies, and though India's shared commitment to the ideals of the European enlightenment is evident in its secular democracy, it was only with the passing of both colonialism and the Cold War that India and the U.S. could undertake a systematic and lasting rapprochement.

On the whole, the 1990s saw a number of missed opportunities for deepened strategic engagement with India. Though respectful of India's democratic character, the Clinton administration saw India primarily as a nuclear proliferation threat; India's troubled relations with Pakistan and the violent insurgency in Kashmir also topped America's diplomatic agenda with India. At the time, it was not even clear whether the U.S. considered the emergence of a strong, liberal and democratic India in its interest. Reflecting on this period, influential Congress Party minister Jairam Ramesh remarked, "We find the Americans over-bearing, preachy and sanctimonious . . . insensitive to our needs, aspirations, challenges and threats."

This was to change rapidly. A succession of events—India's nuclear tests in 1998, the Kargil war of 1999, and the Musharraf coup in Pakistan—created the circumstances for putting relations on a new, more even keel. It may seem ironic that this rapprochement occurred only after India conducted its nuclear tests. Though India proved that it would not buckle under the pressure of American economic sanctions and sign the Comprehensive Test Ban Treaty (CTBT), the Clinton administration, in India's view, continued its policy of condoning Chinese missile and nuclear technology transfers to Pakistan.[3] Through an intensive year-long dialogue between then Deputy Secretary of State Strobe Talbott and then Indian Foreign Minister Jaswant Singh, the U.S. came to a de facto acceptance of India's nuclear capability and posture. Simultaneously, Pakistan's Kargil misadventure in 1999, followed by the Musharraf coup—the first in a nuclear-armed nation—validated India's concerns over its volatile Western neighbor. By the time Clinton visited India in March 2000, he praised India as history's greatest melting pot in a speech before parliament and signed a "vision statement" for future cooperation. By contrast, he scarcely left Air Force One when it landed in Islamabad for six hours. He lamented the return of military rule in Pakistan and admonished those who "struggle in vain to redraw borders with blood." Clinton's personal intervention in the Kargil escalation and his subsequent visit convinced many Indians for the first time that the U.S. could indeed play a constructive role in the region. Yet the Clinton administration could not bring itself to transcend the nonproliferation dilemmas and consider the geopolitical importance of strengthening India's power capabilities; that had to wait until the advent of the Bush Administration.

The terrorist attacks of September 11, 2001, produced a rare opportunity and a difficult challenge. On the one hand it aligned India and the United States in the war against terrorism. Simultaneously, however, it also brought back into focus the centrality of Pakistan on the front line of the campaign. While India offered full support to the U.S. in the war against the Taliban, Washington turned again to Pakistan. India was deeply disconcerted by the fact that Pakistan had returned to the affections of the United States. Traditionalists in the Indian establishment were concerned about renewed American arms supplies to Pakistan. As Pakistan became America's most intimate ally in the "war on terror," India chose to keep a low profile even as Pakistan's President General Pervez Musharraf won his country the designation of a "major non-NATO ally" and began collecting hundreds of millions of dollars in military assistance. To its credit, the Bush administration prevented a return to the zero-sum game of the Cold War in its relations with the Subcontinental rivals and persisted with a solid engagement with New Delhi. Indeed, it is said that India and Pakistan are now "America's two new best friends."

Just as the renewed focus on Pakistan did not disturb new trends in Indo-U.S. engagement, neither did domestic political change in India undermine it. While many believed the return of the Congress Party to power in May 2004 would undercut the new bonhomie between Delhi and Washington, Prime Minister Manmohan Singh brought even stronger commitment than his BJP predecessor Atal Bihari Vajpayee to building a stronger relationship with the United States. Few expected that a Congress government supported by Communists would sign a path-breaking bilateral defense framework with the United States in June 2005 and a nuclear pact in July 2005, as well as vote with the United States against Iran at the International Atomic Energy Agency (IAEA) in September 2005. Clearly, the progress in Indo-U.S. relations has been due more to structural factors than the political preferences of the ruling parties.

The July 2005 "Joint Statement" on civilian nuclear cooperation represented the most decisive step on the part of the United States in demonstrating its readiness to treat India differently—from a nuclear pariah to a partner. In working bilaterally with a de facto nuclear power such as India, the Bush administration has won praise for outlining principles for responsible nuclear behavior beyond the moribund principles of the Non-Proliferation Treaty (NPT), which excluded India from the nuclear clubhouse because it failed to conduct a nuclear test before the treaty came into force. The Bush administration broke the mold by finding a nuclear modus vivendi with India. In return for full civilian nuclear cooperation from the United States, India agreed to separate its civilian and military nuclear facilities, declare such facilities to the IAEA and put them under IAEA safeguards, uphold the moratorium on nuclear testing, accede to the Fissile Material Cut-Off Treaty (FMCT), refrain from the transfer of nuclear enrichment and reprocessing technologies, and comply with the guidelines of the Missile Technology Control Regime (MTCR) and Nuclear Suppliers Group (NSG).

China has strongly criticized U.S.-India nuclear cooperation as a "nuclear exception," potentially creating a domino effect of proliferation and competition. So have many in the U.S. Congress, who continue to chide India's non-NPT status. Both positions are ironic. Given that India is already a model of nonproliferation behavior in its foreign relations—particularly when compared to China, Pakistan, and Russia—India's limited ambitions set a positive example to ambiguous nuclear states like Iran and North Korea. Furthermore, dogmatic advocates of nonproliferation in the U.S. Congress have done little to reinforce the NPT regime and should see the pragmatic virtue in India's emphasis on nuclear safety and compliance with its important safeguard clauses. Indeed, even IAEA head Mohamed El-Baradei has endorsed the deal; it at least brings India into an active monitoring framework rather than none at all.

Nuclear cooperation alone will not make or break the Indo-U.S. relationship. American policymakers must take into account the full range of India's security and commercial interests. Yet by putting one of the most contentious bilateral issues aside, the Bush administration has opened the door for wide-ranging strategic cooperation with India. The implementation of the nuclear pact is likely to end the deepest suspicions in Delhi that America is not ready to accept India's power potential. U.S. nuclear cooperation will allow India to consider hitherto unacceptable propositions on defense cooperation and strategic coordination in Asia with Washington.

As India sets its own course, the U.S. cannot afford to be ambivalent, which only begets ambiguity in return. Furthermore, given the history of mutual suspicion, the lingering U.S. fear that India seeks to subvert American interests will only lead to a self-fulfilling prophecy. The U.S. must therefore be proactive and willing to take risks to support India in its geostrategic context. Like such other U.S. allies as Turkey and Israel, India is located in a turbulent neighborhood but has a robust military capable of affecting the outcomes of potential conflicts in Southwest and Central Asia.[4] It also has a strong sense of national identity based on secular ideology, despite its tremendous ethnic and religious diversity. As a state with a large Muslim minority and heavy dependence on Middle Eastern oil, there are structural limits to India's cooperation with any aggressive American activity in the Gulf region. Like Turkey, it will not respond favorably to heavy-handed American pressure.

At a time when the U.S. is making promotion of democracy a national strategic objective, India too has begun to echo the Bush doctrine from its own perspective. While other democracies are either scornful or dismissive of American emphasis on democracy, India has seen the value of freedom in transforming its neighborhood. As Katrin Bennhold put in the *International Herald Tribune* (December 7, 2004), "India has been a beacon of democracy and stability in a region where both are the exception." Prime Minister Singh has begun to define India's self-identity in terms of democracy, replacing the traditional primary self-perception of anti-imperialism. As he said in his *India Today* Conclave speech in New Delhi (February 25, 2004), "If there is an 'idea of India' that the world should remember us by and regard us for, it is the idea of an inclusive and open society, a multi-cultural, multi-ethnic, multi-lingual society . . . . Liberal democracy is the natural order of social and political organization in today's world. All alternate systems,

authoritarian and majoritarian in varying degrees, are an aberration. Democratic methods yield the most enduring solutions to even most intractable problems." This is not very different from President Bush's focus in his second term on the "transforming nature of liberty," although Singh articulates it more cautiously. The convergence between Bush and Singh was reflected in their joint declaration on July 18, 2005, on a global democracy initiative and in their joint support for the United Nations Democracy Fund in September 2005. In a significant departure from its traditional focus on north-south issues, this was the first time India supported the notion of promoting democracy at the United Nations. On China and the Asian balance of power, not only do Indian and American interests converge, but both sides also recognize that an emphasis on democracy in Asia is a useful template to deal with long-term challenges in the region.

In their quest for greater energy security, both India and the U.S. share a keen interest in developing ties with the Caspian Sea region to diversify oil and natural gas supplies. India currently relies on the Persian Gulf for 90 percent of its oil supply. Indian Petroleum Minister Mani Shankar Aiyar has pursued the creation of an "Asian energy grid," recently persuading Bangladesh to participate in a natural gas pipeline from Burma to India and investing over $5 billion in exploration from Russia to Vietnam. The Bush administration should recognize that even Pakistan sees the 25-year, $20 billion liquid natural gas purchasing deal between India and Iran as win-win, given its potential revenues as the transit state. The U.S. must therefore trust New Delhi's ties with Tehran, and could also leverage the greater knowledge and access Indians have in Iran.

The Question of China

China presents the biggest geopolitical test for both the U.S. and India, and relations with China have always been more decisive for the making of Indian foreign policy than the U.S. has appreciated. Though China currently views Russia, Japan, and India as peer competitors, it seeks to be second to none. After the 1950s-era fraternal mantra of "Hindi-Chini bhai-bhai," India suffered a humiliating military defeat at China's hands during their 1962 border clashes, ceding the Aksai Chin region of the Himalayas (though it remains disputed still). A 20-year cold war ensued with the glacial process of normalization hampered by the upswing in New Delhi-Moscow relations after the Sino-Soviet split, as well as China's broadening relations with Pakistan.

Chinese defense ministry white papers do not refer to South Asia as a region of strategic interest, but China's accelerating effort to build a sphere of influence in Central Asia through the Shanghai Cooperation Organization (SCO) make it a de facto part of India's calculus as it seeks to capitalize on a stabilizing Afghanistan to improve trade ties with post-Soviet nations. Furthermore, India feels increasingly encircled by Chinese naval activity in the Bay of Bengal, both through its client Burma and through its massive investment in deepening the Gwadar port in Pakistan's Sindh province. Despite its current limited resources, India has been determined to engage in quiet competition with China in Southeast Asia even as the region is increasingly drawn towards Beijing. Whether it is growing political cooperation with Singapore, Vietnam, Indonesia and Japan or deeper involvement in Burma, India will not simply cede primacy to China in Asia. Chinese efforts to keep India out of the core group directing the creation of an East Asian Community and Beijing's attempts to undercut India's primacy in South Asia will remain important spurs to a complex Indian engagement with China.

As the U.S. makes parallel overtures to both China and India, it needs to better understand the subtle dynamic governing their ties. The U.S. sees India as an ally in balancing China but must also appreciate that beyond this, growing Indian trade and interdependence with China are a principal vehicle for changing Chinese behavior and calculations in the long run. For New Delhi, therefore, there is no contradiction between stronger military ties with the U.S. and the pursuit of an Asian energy grid linking Iran to China via Pakistan, India, and Burma—an effort the Bush administration currently opposes.

Seeking to prevent India from cozying up too closely to the U.S., particularly in their talks on missile defense, China is playing to India's insecurities in broadening bilateral cooperation. India also has an interest in resolving its long-standing bilateral problems, such as the boundary dispute. New Delhi has thus accelerated the effort to break out of its two-front problem on its land borders. During Chinese Premier Wen Jiabao's visit to India in April, Manmohan Singh declared that "India and China can together reshape world order." Both have much to gain from developing stronger economic and political ties multilaterally around the region. Just as New Delhi hopes it can prevent China from being too one-sided in its relations with Pakistan, reconciliation with India is also part of China's broader strategy of "cooperative security," which aims to build ties based on mutual economic and security interests with states from Central to Southeast Asia. Counterterrorism is an area of emerging cooperation, particularly as both China's west and India's northeast are underdeveloped and restive. India increasingly sees its northeast as the "gateway to ASEAN," but to further expand trade and transport links eastward, India requires a stable and open Burma. It is China, however, which pulls the strings in Rangoon. China has also made a strong appeal to India's desire to become a leading destination for international capital and has begun negotiations on a bilateral free-trade agreement. Sino-Indian trade is galloping at a fast clip, touching nearly $20 billion in 2005.

Yet there remain areas of competition between the two sides, and India remains wary of continuing Chinese assistance to Pakistan's strategic programs. Even as New Delhi and Beijing launch a strategic dialogue, they will continue to compete for power and influence in Asia. Some in India have always hoped for an alliance with the United States against the growing challenge from China. Yet with no invitation to a containment party from the United States, it would be imprudent for India not to further develop its relations with China. While the Bush administration seems more concerned about the rise of China in its second term, it is likely to follow a cautious policy towards Beijing. In such circumstances India and the U.S. should be looking for ways to expand their defense and security cooperation to ensure a stable balance of power in Asia. Washington should also encourage the fledgling strategic engagement between India and Japan and remove the remaining restrictions on high-technology and military transfers to India.

Given that India is currently hemmed in militarily by a combination of the Himalayan mountains and failing states from Pakistan and Nepal to Bangladesh and Burma, it is in the area of naval modernization where the U.S. can best address India's geopolitical needs. As China pursues a "string of pearls" strategy to develop deep-water ports and stronger diplomatic and military relations with Pakistan, Burma, and Indonesia, boosting the capacity of the Indian navy (through Project Seabird) to police and even deny access to the Indian Ocean sea lanes becomes more important than the strengthening of its army. Furthermore, India occupies a critical position for patrolling major transport sea lanes from the Arabian Sea to the Straits of Malacca, where both countries fear the growing specter of naval or "containerized" terrorism by groups such as al Qaeda. While important regional players such as Malaysia, Singapore, and China have reservations about the U.S. pushing its geostrategic objectives in the name of maritime security, and thus object to joint U.S. patrol of the region's strategic waterways, India can serve as an important surrogate.

Stabilizing South Asia

Though india has achieved its cherished goal of de-hyphenation, U.S. policy towards Pakistan still plays a decisive role in both countries' interests. Like the U.S., India remains deeply concerned about the possibility of Pakistani nuclear weapons or related material falling into the hands of terrorists. According to Stephen Cohen, Pakistan has already become "perhaps the leading center of proliferation in history, having shared its nuclear technology with a variety of states, all of which are hostile to America."

Yet despite not allowing either American or International Atomic Energy Agency inspectors to interrogate A.Q. Khan, Pakistan's nuclear mastermind, General Musharraf has been less than shy about manipulating America's largesse in the war on terror to gain ground technologically on India. In addition to the planned sale of F-16s to Pakistan early next year, the recent $1.3 billion arms package (paid for out of the agreed $1.5 billion in military aid from the U.S. over five years) includes eight P-3C Orion naval reconnaissance planes with anti-submarine missiles, 2,000 TOW-2A heavy anti-armor guided missiles, and Phalanx Close-In weapon systems for ships. In the context of the war on terror, it is hard to imagine terrorists with the kind of "Explosive Reactive Armor" the TOW is designed to penetrate. On the other hand, it is well suited to neutralize Indian T-90 tanks. Indeed, Larry Pressler, the former Senator whose eponymous amendment forbade the previous sale of warplanes to Pakistan a decade ago, remarked, "You don't fight terrorism with F-16s. F-16s are capable of nuclear delivery. That's about the only reason Pakistan wants them." Including these freebies from the U.S., Pakistani defense spending is touching a staggering 8 percent of GDP.

115

The U.S. must be careful about assuming that it can succeed in satisfying both India and Pakistan simultaneously by way of what it views as incremental and mutually exclusive bilateral armament. Though the U.S. increasingly sees Pakistan as a necessary front in dealing with Iran, it is the U.S. that is losing out by allowing the Pakistani military's gravy train to continue. Arms sales to Pakistan no doubt buttress Musharraf's position within his own army, but likely at the cost of an already long-overdue return to democracy and with no positive impact on the war on terror.

The U.S. clearly needs Pakistan to be more forthcoming and productive in its contributions to global counterterrorism and make clear that F-16s are not the way for it to achieve this. As prominent defense experts warn, the F-16 deal threatens to reintroduce militarism on the Subcontinent. Indeed, every time the military has been in power in Pakistan, there has been war with India. If Musharraf becomes overconfident due to his perceived American carte blanche, we might witness a return to the misplaced logic of ultimatums and escalation that led to the Kargil debacle. In the meantime, Pakistan's performance in capturing Taliban and al Qaeda agents has been dismal. Furthermore, General Musharraf recently called off the hunt for Osama bin Laden in South Waziristan, that operation having yielded the only intelligence reports indicating that he remains alive and at large. From inside Pakistan, Taliban fighters still train and conduct anti-U.S. attacks in Afghanistan. Pakistan is thus both part of the problem and part of the solution. The Bush administration should therefore change course and make F-16 sales to Pakistan conditional on access to A.Q. Khan for questioning.

Indian criticism of the F-16 deal was largely muted, in part because of the larger stakes in the U.S. relationship. While India is open to defense cooperation with the U.S. and is willing to consider major defense purchases from Washington, success will depend on the American willingness to offer advanced defense technologies to Delhi and possible coproduction of key components. Any attempt by Washington to limit high-technology defense cooperation with India citing Pakistani concerns would, however, limit Indo-U.S. defense cooperation. The Indian defense industry is well-positioned to become an industrial partner of the U.S., though some political heavy lifting in both capitals is necessary. The U.S. has also begun to expand its nascent dialogue on missile defense with India. With $15 billion earmarked for defense spending over the coming decade, India is a potentially lucrative acquisitions market for American contractors providing the PAC-3 anti-missile system, C-130 transport aircraft, and P-3C Orion surveillance planes as well as the Multimission Maritime Aircraft the U.S. is currently developing. The U.S. failure to develop a bold initiative on defense industrial collaboration with India will only reinforce Delhi's traditional defense links with Russia, France, and Israel.

Developing a common approach to Pakistan remains the single most important obstacle in the prospects for Indo-U.S. strategic partnership. While many in Delhi and Washington have begun to see the importance of creating a shared template to think about the future of Pakistan and integrating it into the cooperative dynamics of the region, there is considerable hesitation in both capitals even to discuss Pakistan's problems bilaterally, let alone work together. The importance of moving in this direction cannot be overstated, for there is little evidence that nuclear weapons have ameliorated South Asia's security dilemma. In the 1980s, Pakistan became increasingly assertive as its atomic program developed, and its surprise infiltration across the Line of Control in Kashmir's Kargil region happened only a year after the 1998 nuclear tests, the largest military engagement between the two sides since the 1971 war. Pakistan's calculation—that the nuclear shield would restrict India's response, but that the move would raise international concern and lead to rapid mediation—was tactically brilliant but the strategic failure led to a military coup in Pakistan.

Furthermore, Indians are concerned that if Pakistan fails, the region stretching from Iraq through Iran, Afghanistan, and Pakistan could become a "belt of terror," unleashing waves of multipronged attacks in its direction. Pakistan remains home to at least four State Department-designated terrorist groups: Hizbul Mujahadeen, Haraku-ul-Mujahadeen, Jaish-e-Muhammed, and Lashkar-e-Taiba. The first three have been banned, but Lashkar remains active in Pakistan-occupied Kashmir and coordinates al Qaeda's International Islamic Front out of Karachi. India requires a stable Pakistan as its bridge to the energy supplies of Iran and Southwest Asia, but it is the U.S. which must recalibrate its policies to move Pakistan in that direction. Ultimately the stability of Pakistan cannot be ensured without cooperation between India and the United States.

After Iraq, India suffers from the greatest number of terrorist incidents per annum, according to the State Department's annual *Patterns of Global Terrorism* report. Most attacks against civilians and military facilities in India's Kashmir province are linked to Pakistan-backed terrorist groups infiltrating from across the Line of Control, as well as a brazen attack on the Indian parliament on December 13, 2001, and the spate of bombings across crowded New Delhi bazaars during the busiest and holiest weekend of Diwali in October 2002. To date, however, Kashmir has not appeared significantly on America's terrorism radar screen. Though Singh and Musharraf made a joint statement at the United Nations in September 2004 pledging to "explore possible options for a peaceful negotiated settlement of the Jammu and Kashmir issue," the U.S. needs to anticipate Pakistan's fear of losing internal Kashmiri dissatisfaction as a pressure point in altering the province's political dynamic. Only through stronger U.S. pressure on Pakistan can the seasonal cycle of infiltration, violence and political tension be reversed. The U.S. thus has an indirect role in pressing Pakistan to keep levels of violence low and, ultimately, in creating a set of incentives for Pakistan to accept a reasonable final settlement of the Kashmir problem.

Despite the second round of "cricket diplomacy" between the nuclear-armed neighbors in 2005, infiltration was in fact rising across the Line of Control until the devastating October earthquake centered in Pakistan-occupied Kashmir. Since that time, measures aimed at General Musharraf's plea to "make the Line of Control irrelevant" have been halting but promising, much like the steps taken by distressed Kashmiris crossing the rickety bridge separating the two Kashmirs to search for lost relatives. Indian families and relief workers have delivered significant amounts of humanitarian assistance, and during the current winter phase, India provides an important land bridge to reach the thousands of victims the Pakistani military was unable to reach before being cut off by the region's heavy snowfall.

Additionally, the U.S. must encourage India to devise a plan for stabilizing Nepal. Over 12,000 casualties have been suffered in the past decade as Maoist rebels have advanced around the country, threatening to take over the capital and depose the king. The situation is most sensitive to India, as the Maoist advance has emboldened India's own Naxalites, who have stepped up their bombing campaigns and attacks against both civilian and military targets in India's northeastern provinces. Bearing in mind that an Indian military intervention—beyond its present support for the king and army—would disturb China, India needs to apply far greater pressure on King Gyanendra to restore constitutionalism and more actively consider a multinational peacekeeping effort. That India and the U.S. are already working together on Nepal presages a whole new dynamic for the future of the Subcontinent.

Global India

India's billion-plus hands are working hard at catapulting India from its present $500 billion economy to a multitrillion-dollar marketplace—to make it, according to a widely cited Goldman Sachs study, the world's third largest economy by 2050. Typically, India is employing a melting pot of homegrown and foreign strategies to get there.

No country has watched China's utterly spectacular economic rise as closely and jealously as India. China began its economic reform process 15 years before India. Since 1978, China has averaged 9.4 percent growth and in the last six years has invested over $30 billion in infrastructure. Only now, with the architect of India's early 1990s reforms elevated to the prime minister's office, is India taking its infrastructure deficit and crippling underdevelopment seriously. Manmohan Singh has promised a hassle-free environment to investors in the hope of attracting $150 billion over the next 10 years to develop the country's roads and power supply and modernize its manufacturing and agricultural base. At the same time, he hopes to retain the option of a China-like "state nationalist" response to globalization run rampant. Under the leadership of former IMF official Montek Singh Ahluwalia, India's Planning Commission has pledged to spend far more of its record $120 billion in foreign exchange reserves on national development. With more arable land than China, planned investments in rural credit could double agricultural productivity.

Since the 1998 nuclear tests, however, intermittent prospects of war and terrorism have hurt India's investment profile. Amidst Indo-Pak mobilization in 2002, the U.S. put out a diplomatic warning on travel to India, hurting India's bottom line. Such incidents have forced it to take a more assertive approach to regional economic integration despite continuing political divisions. Learning from the ASEAN model, India has realized that it must turn the moribund South Asian Association for Regional Cooperation (SAARC) into a South Asian Free Trade Area (SAFTA). A "good neighbor" trade policy, combined with a second generation of economic reforms, could be sufficient to increase foreign direct investment, boost exports, and encourage dynamic private industries. If 8 percent growth continues, the National Intelligence Council predicts that India's per capita income will double by 2020.

In India, entrepreneurs in the private sector, not the government, are taking the lead in transforming the economy. India has succeeded in branding itself as the world's leading destination for business process outsourcing (BPO), and even high-end operations such as GE medical labs and Hewlett-Packard research facilities are contributing to make India a leader in technology innovation. Four hundred of the *Fortune* 500 already have operations in India. Already one of the world's largest producers of vaccines, India's biotech sector is set for even greater growth and has rapidly outpaced both China and South Korea in the filing of biotech patents. The potential in food processing and storage, telecommunications, financial services, and insurance is similarly vast. Microcredit enterprises have become stable business propositions, even in the area of agriculture, sparking hopes for a second, private-sector-led Green Revolution.

These developments hint at some of the unique aspects of India's economy which must be understood to grasp its potential. No other developing country has such a postindustrial economic structure, with 50 percent of GDP derived from the services sector and manufacturing and agriculture comprising a quarter each. As a result of the outsourcing revolution, India has emerged as a major hub for international technology products and services, already accounting for 20 percent of world software exports. The information technology sector has boomed because the government got out of the way; it literally had no plan. If the new government can get serious about structural reform, horizontal growth could start to affect a greater share of India's enormous population. As the distinguished economist Lord Meghnad Desai of the London School of Economics argues, India's businessmen must take charge of the country: "The argument that the government will look after the poor should be abandoned. Governments don't look after the poor; the poor look after themselves if obstacles are removed from their path in terms of services and credit."[5]

India is staking its economic future on the quantity and quality of its human resources. As one industrialist has put it, "What oil is to Saudi Arabia, human talent is to India." Demographically, its mobile and ambitious youth will be the world's largest working-age population segment by 2015, at which point it may even provide surplus labor to an aging China. Indeed, India is aging gracefully while China is heading towards an unprecedented challenge of getting old before it gets rich. But India can maximize this demographic dividend only by improving education, establishing innovative vocational training, and retraining its workforce to fill gaps in the global economy. This is difficult for a government running deficits close to 10 percent of GDP—among the highest in the world. At present, India ranks only 50th out of 117 economies surveyed in the World Economic Forum's Growth Competitiveness Index based on an evaluation of its macroeconomic environment, public institutions and technological penetration.

As it works to create the conditions for a long investment-employment cycle, India must find a balance between educating its workforce and keeping costs competitive. Some see a division of labor emerging, with China and India dominating global manufacturing and information technology services, respectively. In other words, China will be the world's workshop, India the world's laboratory.

What India has also learned from China is that trade is a critical lever in American foreign policy decision-making. For all the heated rhetoric and debate during the 2004 presidential election about the outsourcing of jobs to India, India has yet to enter the same league as Mexico, Canada or South Korea in terms of volume of trade with the U.S. Currently, around $20 billion of merchandise trade flows annually. The recently negotiated U.S.-India Free Trade Agreement in services would allow Indian health and information technology professionals unrestricted access to the U.S., and in exchange American firms would have the freedom to open financial service, banking, telecom and retail operations in India, increasing India's visibility as a global market. A bigger trade deal should be in the works over the next four years but will require the U.S. Congress to overcome entrenched interests preventing liberalization of benefit to both countries. Trade disputes could also elevate India's attention level in Washington. Together with the European Union, Brazil, Japan, and Canada, India won a World Trade Organization (WTO) ruling permitting retaliatory duties on American products to counter continued American anti-dumping practices under the Byrd Amendment. American exports to India, now well below potential, could increase markedly in coming years. The key to this rests in raising the volume of high-technology goods, especially aerospace and military. The Bush administration's recognition of India as a responsible nuclear power is a positive sign in this regard.

Though India has some distance to go in achieving economic or military parity with China, it has stepped up the effort to match it in terms of diplomatic status. Though its efforts to gain a permanent seat on the UN Security Council have stalled in the broader deadlock over UN reform, the U.S. has welcomed a greater role for India in the nascent but effective G-20 and has encouraged India to take a leadership role in cultivating a Community of Democracies within the UN General Assembly. Both the U.S. and India seek to modify the Yalta security system, which India believes is antiquated as much as the Bush administration argues it is ineffective, particularly concerning core mutual interests such as nonproliferation and counterterrorism. Though historically India has butted against the U.S. in important United Nations votes, today there is hardly a better ally to advocate democracy promotion, secular governance, pluralism, and the rule of law. While the UN Security Council seat is important for India, New Delhi is under no illusion that it will change everything. Like the Bush administration and unlike the Europeans, India is wary of giving too much say to the UN in the management of global security, seeking instead to transform the global security order.

India's quest to go global has not only reached the United States; in many ways it originates here. Numbering almost two million, Indian-Americans are now the wealthiest ethnic minority in the country, boasting a median income of $60,000 and 200,000 millionaires. Fifteen percent of Silicon Valley start-ups have been launched by Indians, many of them first-generation immigrants who have chosen to make the U.S. their home. Indian-Americans are also leaders in the medical and financial professions and—following in the footsteps of the Jewish diaspora—are increasingly seeking to match their rising economic and social status with political clout. Though India has yet to learn the ropes of lobbying hard for its interests in the areas of steel, agriculture, pharmaceuticals, and weapons, it has pushed membership in the bipartisan India Caucus of the House of Representatives to over 130 congressmen. Furthermore, a half-century after Dilip Singh Saund, the first Asian to serve in the U.S. Congress, the savvy young Bobby Jindal was elected a Republican member of the House from Louisiana in November 2004. Jindal's fast-track academic career is also but one example of Indians' amazingly disproportionate representation on Ivy League campuses. Given the Indian diaspora's contributions to American economic and cultural life, the more than 50 percent decrease in H1-B visas for Indian professionals has been extremely disturbing to Indians in both countries, and the 25 percent drop in MBA applicants from India is similarly worrying. If the U.S. does not allow Indian nationals to become Indian-Americans—in a demonstration of American pride, many prefer this term to be de-hyphenated as well—it ignores the Asia Foundation's advice that the Bush administration should "continue to take advantage of Indian-Americans as a bridge" between Washington and New Delhi.

Towards the end of the Cold War in 1989, the Pentagon commissioned the Rand Corporation's George Tanham to report on India's strategic thinking; he famously concluded that there was none. This is no longer the case. India is beginning to rediscover the enduring elements of its own traditional geopolitical thinking and actively considering partnership with America, if only to advance its own interests. Within a constellation of shifting regional alliances among major states and powers such as the U.S., EU, Russia, Iran, Pakistan, China, South Korea, and Japan, India's relevance to the future of international power balances is assured. India's strategic canvas is broadening, as is its thinking in the military, economic, diplomatic, and cultural realms. America's trade with China will eclipse that which it has with India for years to come, but democratic India is sure to be a more reliable partner.

Better relations, however, create rising expectations. As American and Indian interests naturally come into closer alignment, both countries must recognize that their noisy democracies will examine every minute detail in the agreements that the two governments negotiate. Preventing these noises from overwhelming the long-awaited strategic signals of greater engagement will be the most difficult challenge that Washington and Delhi have to overcome.

Notes

1. As a recent Asia Foundation report, *America's Role in Asia*, notes, India is "unwilling to cede a dominant role to any outside power in its neighborhood, is eager to expand commercial ties with all countries, and determined to play a larger role in global trade negotiations."

2. Gareth Price, "India's Aid Dynamics: From Recipient to Donor," Chatham House Asia Program Working Paper (London: Royal Institute of International Affairs, September 2004).

3. Not surprisingly, then, India was further peeved that Clinton enlisted China's Jiang Zemin in June 1998 to publicly bash India's "irresponsible" nuclear tests even though, as then Prime Minister Atal Bihari Vajpayee explained in a letter to President Clinton, China was the motivating concern for the Indian tests, with Pakistan's counter-tests being an unfortunate by-product.

4. As Christine Fair writes, "India stands out in the landscape of potential partners. It has the largest army of any democratic country, a highly regarded, well-trained, and professional army that has operational flexibility and niche warfare capabilities. . . . Notably, India has a well-honed and exceptional high-altitude warfare capability, of which few countries can boast." C. Christine Fair, "U.S.-Indian Army-to-Army Relations: Prospects for Future Coalition Operations," *Asian Security* 1:2 (April 2005).

5. Meghnad Desai, "India business surrendered 20th century," *India Abroad* (December 3, 2004).

PARAG KHANNA is a fellow at the New America Foundation and author of *The Second World*, forthcoming from Random House. **C. RAJA MOHAN** is strategic affairs editor of the Indian Express in New Delhi.

From *Policy Review*, February/March 2006. Copyright © 2006 by Hoover Institution/Stanford University. Reprinted by permission of Policy Review and Parag Khanna and C. Raja Mohan.

Article 13

India's Nuclear Albatross

New Delhi deluded itself that it scored a coup by signing the July nuclear deal with Washington. It must now confront the bitter truth: 'normalising' its nuclear weapons status will entail erosion of its policy independence in different fields. The crisis over Iran's nuclear programme is the starkest example.

PRAFUL BIDWAI

When Prime Minister Manmohan Singh embarked on his mid-September visit to the United States, he must have desperately hoped that he would not be confronted with an "either you are with us or you are against us" choice from Washington over joining the U.S.' escalating effort to isolate Iran and have its nuclear programme referred to the United Nations Security Council for possible sanctions. He must have also hoped that President George W. Bush would somehow delink the Iran issue from the commitments he made in the July 18 nuclear deal to make an exception for India in the matter of loosening the nuclear control regime.

The hope can only be called desperate because the signals emanating from Washington in recent weeks were loud and clear. The U.S. would be insistent that India join it in its confrontation over Iran. Secretary of State Condoleezza Rice made the point explicitly on September 9 when she said: "Now we need leadership on this. The European Union-3 [the United Kingdom, France and Germany] led on this issue. The United States supported the E.U.-3 . . . But Iran needs to get a message from the international community that it is a unified message. And by this I mean not just the E.U. and the U.S., but also Russia, China and India."

Recent reports in the U.S. media unmistakably pointed to the connection Washington would make between the nuclear accord with India, and the "responsible" role that India must play on such global issues as the U.S. considers important. The debate in a U.S. Congressional Committee over the Indo-U.S. nuclear deal, in which Representative Tom Lantos targeted India's "pro-Iran" stance, highlighted this.

Just a few days earlier, Foreign Secretary Shyam Saran had "reiterated" India's stand on Iran with "no ambiguity": Iran, he said, should adhere to its international obligations. Any questions about Teheran's nuclear programme should be resolved through

discussion, not confrontation. (*The Hindu*, September 10). This was a subtle shift from India's oft-stated position that the International Atomic Energy Agency has found no evidence that the Iranian uranium enrichment programme has a weapons component; and that Iran has every right to enrich uranium for peaceful purposes subject to its obligations under the Nuclear Non-Proliferation Treaty (NPT).

In New York, Manmohan Singh faced a choice, or what has been called the "litmus test," to demonstrate the independence and principled basis of India's foreign policy. If and when pressed by Bush, would he defend Iran's right to enrich uranium, in keeping with the stand of the Non-Aligned Movement (NAM) group in the IAEA's Board of Governors, or cave in to the U.S. in some measure?

Manmohan Singh's response was equivocal. He reiterated India's "consistent" and "principled opposition" to any kind of nuclear proliferation and said Iran must fulfill all its international obligations and commitments. According to Saran, he indicated India's preference—to let "diplomacy" produce a "consensus" in the IAEA. India would "constructively" contribute towards finding a "consensus."

This obviously did not satisfy the U.S. administration, which takes a dim view of what it regards as India's "demurring." According to senior officials quoted in *The New York Times* ("India Balks At Confronting Iran, Straining Its Friendship With U.S.," September 15), the U.S. does not want the IAEA Board to take its decisions by "consensus." It is keen to change the IAEA's decision-making procedure, by pressing for a majority vote. "With India's help, they can obtain a majority vote . . . to refer Iran to the Security Council," the officials said.

The message given to Manmohan Singh was that India has "to make a basic choice." An official said: "Indians are emerging from their non-aligned status and becoming a global power, and they have to begin to think about their responsibilities." Washington believes India "is in the middle between the West and Iran, with which it has tried to foster a close relationship." "In effect," reports *The Times*, "Bush administration officials say India must now choose who is the best partner to meet its surging energy needs—Iran with its natural gas resources, or the West with its ability to help in developing Indian civilian nuclear power."

India's position on the Iran issue is shot through with anomalies, four of which are noteworthy. First, the U.S. is prejudiced against Iran. It has demonised Iran since the Islamic Revolution of 1979, regardless of its changing domestic realities; just as Iran emerged from the shadow of Ayatollah-style extremism, Washington declared it a "rogue state." The U.S. has now unilaterally decided that Iran is—like Iraq under Saddam Hussein—acquiring nuclear weapons. It wants to act unilaterally and is threatening multilateral agencies with irrelevance if they do not fall in line. It would be tragic if India were to legitimise U.S. unilateralism.

Second, not even a remotely plausible case has been made that Iran has nuclear weapons or, that its nuclear programme is military. True, Iran hid a part of its programme from international eyes for many years. But it has opened it to the IAEA since 2003, when it "temporarily" suspended enrichment preparations and activities as part of a negotiated deal with the E.U.-3.

The IAEA has repeatedly given Iran a clean chit. Its recent reports conclude that the traces of enriched uranium detected two years ago at Iranian facilities are attributable to equipment imported from Pakistan. Inspections have found no evidence of Iran running a clandestine nuclear weapons programme. But the U.S. dismisses these conclusions and ignores Iran's cooperation with the IAEA.

Independent assessments suggest that Iran may be five to 10 years away from acquiring nuclear weapons capability. A recent report by the London-based International Institute for Strategic Studies estimates that Iran would need more than 10 years to build an industrial-scale centrifuge plant at Natanz. At the moment, Natanz is basically a "pilot plant," with a relatively small number of centrifuges. India is being pressed to disregard these facts.

Third, India has failed to differentiate itself adequately from the inconsistent position of the E.U.-3. The E.U.-3-Iran talks started off well. Both sides made, and improved on, offers. The E.U.-3 offered political, economic and nuclear cooperation with Iran, as well as security guarantees. Iran agreed to suspend its nuclear programme and place it under the IAEA's inspections.

Things changed when Iran's presidential election was announced and Mahmoud Ahmadinejad, a supposed "hardliner," emerged as a contender. While waiting for his installation, the E.U.-3 missed the agreed deadline (July 31) to propose a promised improved deal with Iran. The E.U.-3 had prepared a package on the assumption that the "moderate" Ali Akbar Rafsanjani would win the election. When he lost, the E.U.-3 hardened the deal's terms, ignoring Iran's broad domestic nuclear policy consensus, which cuts across "moderate-extremist" lines. The E.U.-3 demanded that Iran permanently renounce uranium enrichment.

Iran refused, arguing that no self-respecting state could permanently surrender a right available to it under the Non-Proliferation Treaty (NPT) and international law. Iran suspected that the E.U.-3 were "playing into the hands of the U.S.," and decided to resume conversion of uranium oxide into uranium hexafluoride gas at Isfahan. (The gas is meant to feed enrichment centrifuges at another facility, in Natanz. Iran has not started enrichment yet.) The Iran-E.U.-3 talks collapsed.

In early September, the IAEA reported that Iran had produced seven tonnes of uranium hexafluoride. This gave the U.S. an opportunity to raise its anti-Iran campaign to a high pitch. The E.U.-3 caved in to U.S. pressure to have Iran referred to the Security Council. The IAEA alone can make that reference. (Its Board of Governors is scheduled to meet on September 19, three days before this column is being written.) The E.U.-3's record casts doubts on the quality of the "consensus" that might emerge. Yet, India is putting all its eggs in the "consensus" basket.

Fourth, the IAEA is divided on the Iran issue. About two-thirds of its 35-member Board—including Brazil, South Africa, Pakistan and India, besides 11 other non-aligned countries—are reluctant to refer Iran to the Security Council. Russia and China are even more reluctant. The NAM group, currently headed by Malaysia, forms a solid bloc in the Board and acts unanimously. Its stated position is that Iran has a 'right' to enrich uranium for peaceful purposes. Malaysia declares this right as "basic and inalienable."

It is hard to fault the NAM position—irrespective of one's stand on the desirability and sustainability of nuclear power. So long as the NPT exists as an international treaty, legal rights and obligations under it cannot be revoked. Legally, it is equally futile to argue that Iran has plenty of oil/gas and will not need nuclear power. Russia and the U.S. too have plenty of oil or gas, but no one questions their substantial nuclear power programmes on similar grounds.

India thus risks splitting the NAM group in the IAEA by pleading for a bogus "consensus." Matters will worsen if India toes the U.S. line. This will have serious consequences. The Iran issue has become a symbol of Third World defiance of unreasonable Western pressure. India will be on the wrong side of the divide.

India may not face a critical test over its stand on Iran just yet. On available indicators, the U.S. has not managed to gather enough support in the IAEA Board to win a vote on Iran. It is likely to delay discussion beyond September 19. Rice admits as much: "The world is not perfect in international politics. You cannot always get a 100-percent solution." But this test could come very soon. Washington seems determined to force the issue. It is even examining the possibility of an armed attack on Iran.

The respected U.S. magazine, *The Nation*, has reported: "Bush has given the Defence Department approval to develop scenarios" for an attack "if Teheran proceeds with uranium-enrichment activities viewed in Washington as a precursor to the manufacture of nuclear munitions." According to *The American Conservative*, U.S. contingency plans may use conventional and even nuclear weapons against over 40 targets in Iran.

The present situation is similar to what happened in 2002–03 over Iraq. The international community did not favour invading Iraq. The U.S. mounted an energetic campaign to mobilise opinion in the Security Council for a "second resolution" authorising military intervention. Despite its efforts at bribery and coercion, it could not get the required support of two-thirds of the Council's 15 members. It was not just France, Germany, Russia and China, but even small states like Cameroon, Angola, Chile and Pakistan that did not yield. Yet the U.S. went ahead and invaded Iraq.

The real issue is this. What will India do if confronted with a division in the IAEA? Will it behave like the refuseniks of 2003 and chart out an independent, dignified course? Or will it abandon all principle and abjectly capitulate to U.S. pressure, as many "realists" (read, defeatists) in our strategic community are urging it to do in the name of "strategic partnership" and a "historic" nuclear deal with the U.S.?

Besides principle, does India set any store by relations with a friendly country like Iran, with which it has important economic, especially energy, transactions, which are likely to grow with the Iran-Pakistan-India gas pipeline project to the collective benefit of all three nations? Does it take regional economic integration seriously, or merely pay lip-service to it? Does India see itself a part of the developing world and the non-aligned concept, or does it delude itself that it has graduated—despite its appalling poverty, and its rank of 127 in the Human Development Index—to the Big League led by a hegemonistic America in search of a global Empire?

Another question arises. Indian supporters of the nuclear bomb claimed that nuclear weapons would help India expand its room for independent manoeuvre in global politics. The opposite has happened. India's effort to get its nuclear status accepted and "normalised" has drawn it into awkward compromises with the Great Powers, especially the U.S. India has had to offer a bargain to Washington in which it would become a "partner" or friendly power—within a deeply asymmetrical relationship. Partnership is no free lunch. The dominant power will lay down the terms of "partnership" and "responsibility";

the subordinate power must contortedly strive to adjust to the terms, sometimes at enormous harm to its interests in some field or other.

Besides, the U.S. is not the kind of power that practises parity or even equitable consultation with its allies. It treats them with disdain, contempt, even hostility—remember Donald Rumsfeld's dismissive remarks about "the old Europe" after France and Germany deferred to the democratic urges of their peoples and refused to join Iraq's invasion?

India's search to maintain and extend its nuclear weapons status will make it extremely vulnerable to all kinds of pressure from the U.S. Right now, the pressure is centred on Iran: choose between Iran with its natural gas, or the West with its nuclear power. As *The New York Times* reported: "Administration officials have warned India that if it fails to cooperate on Iran, the civilian nuclear energy agreement . . . could be rejected by Congress."

However, Washington can, at any time, threaten to block or suspend the implementation of the nuclear deal, or cite resistance from Congress, to drive unequal bargains on trade, agriculture, intellectual property, services, foreign investment. There is not even a remotely reasonable or credible assurance that India can successfully resist such pressure, or indeed that it wants to do so.

As this column has argued right since the Pokhran-II tests, nuclear weaponisation was a historic blunder and a remarkably bad bargain. It has eroded India's security, lowered its global stature, damaged its credibility and turned its image from a pro-disarmament force to a cynical, hypocritical power. It has distorted internal social priorities, and promoted militaristic and macho ideologies. It will also impose huge economic burdens as the nuclear weapons programme proceeds apace. To this must now be added the burden of the July 18 "historic" nuclear bargain, which has further raised India's vulnerability. The need for undoing and reversing Pokhran-II has never been more urgent.

India's Energy Dilemma

India's rapid economic growth has made it the second fastest–growing energy market in the world. Its domestic strategy for dealing with this raises painful questions about efficiency and fiscal soundness. Its international strategy involves a relentless push to diversify suppliers, increase India's equity stake overseas, and try to avoid destructive commercial competition with China. In some cases, this has produced foreign policy differences with the United States that will require careful management on both sides.

VIBHUTI HATÉ

The Indian economy has clocked an average growth rate of 7 percent in the last decade. To maintain this pace, experts believe that the country will have to increase its energy consumption by at least 4 percent annually. This relentlessly increasing demand is a massive challenge for India, affecting not only the domestic economy but India's foreign policy.

India is the world's eleventh-largest energy producer, with 2.4 percent of energy production, and the world's sixth-largest consumer, with 3.5 percent of global energy consumption. Domestic coal reserves account for 70 percent of India's energy needs. The remaining 30 percent is met by oil, with more than 65 percent of that oil being imported. Demand for energy is expected to double by 2025; by then, 90 percent of India's petroleum will be imported.

India's Energy Sector

Of the three major energy sources—coal, oil and gas—coal is India's major source of energy. With 7 percent of the world's coal India has the fourth largest coal reserves. The Carbon Sequestration Leadership Forum (CSLF) estimates that at the current level of consumption and production, India's coal reserves will last for more than 200 years. Unfortunately, in addition to environmental concerns (coal is one of the dirtiest hydrocarbon fuels), coal cannot meet all of India's energy needs. The transportation industry requires oil, and much of India's coal is not of the type needed in steel and other industries. In spite of India's coal reserves, the Indian government's flagship steel company, the Steel Authority of India Ltd. (SAIL) imports 60 percent of its coal needs.

India's oil and gas reserves are not sufficient to meet its rapidly growing energy needs. Oil is the life-blood of the rapidly expanding transportation sector. Barring a major new oil discovery, India will have to increasingly rely on imports to meet future demand for oil.

Most of India's gas is now used for the electricity sector, although the expanding use of compressed natural gas (CNG) for urban transport makes this a growing market segment. Most of India's current gas needs are met from domestic sources. Liquefied Natural Gas (LNG) has not figured prominently in the energy mix, but is slowly increasing. Experts estimate that by 2012 India's LNG imports will be on par with Japan's current LNG imports of 60 million tonnes per annum. Although the Gas Authority of India Ltd. (GAIL) has already begun work on a National Gas Grid, there is considerable technological progress that has to be made in terms of extraction, transportation and delivery of LNG. It is estimated that once the grid is fully functional, LNG could offset a significant portion of India's energy demand.

India's energy sector is dominated by the public sector. Within the electricity supply industry, there are some private electricity generating operations, but almost all are required to market through the State Electricity Boards (SEBs), owned and controlled by individual states. The petroleum industry and gas industry are currently dominated by the Oil and National Gas Corporation (ONGC), the Gas Authority of India Ltd (GAIL), and the Indian Oil Corporation (IOC). Private sector involvement has been restricted to the refining section of the energy industry. ONGC, the government's oil exploration and production enterprise, is one of the most profitable companies in India and is responsible for 77 percent of crude oil production and 81 percent of natural gas production. A majority of India's refineries are owned by IOC, which is one of the 20 largest petroleum companies in the world and features on the Fortune 200 list. GAIL is the leading gas transmission and marketing firm in India and is one of the 10 most profitable companies in the country. Together ONGC, IOC, and GAIL form three of the nine crown jewels, or *navratnas*, of the Indian government's public sector undertakings.

Need for Reform

Many observers believe that the most effective way to meet this growing demand is to reform the energy sector. Leaving aside the need for technical modernization of the industry, discussions of reform tend to revolve around three policy areas: bringing prices closer to world market levels; putting the energy industry, and especially the State Electricity Boards, on a sound fiscal basis; and making greater space for the private sector in the industry. Each of these will meet with ferocious resistance from constituents accustomed to subsidized energy, politicians who fear the consequence of reducing subsidies, and those who currently have the responsibility for running the public sector energy organizations. And especially with today's high oil prices, the government will be seriously concerned about the impact of market prices on poverty in the country.

Expanding the energy sector to meet India's future needs will also be expensive. The IEA (International Energy Agency) estimates that India will need to spend approximately $800 billion dollars on its energy sector by 2030. Additionally, the rising price of oil will make it difficult, if not impossible, for the Indian government to maintain the current subsidized prices. In 2006, volatile oil prices in the international energy market led to a substantial increase in kerosene and domestic LPG prices. Almost 85 percent of this price increase was borne by the Indian government and its oil companies. India has expanded the role of the private sector in a number of other fields that had traditionally been public sector preserves. In almost every case, this was done by creating space for private sector operators to come in alongside the public sector, often starting with carefully defined, value-added operations. In all likelihood, if India expands the role of the private sector in energy, it will follow this same pattern.

Oil Diplomacy

India's basic approach to energy diplomacy—both oil and gas— has been to develop as many potential supply arrangements, with as many potential suppliers, as it possibly can, and to try to neutralize its potential competitors (principally China) with cooperation agreements. It has made considerable progress in diversifying its sources of supply, but as a result has been moving into some tough markets where frustration was an almost inevitable by-product.

India currently imports 60–70 percent of its oil needs, mainly from countries in the Middle East. Experts estimate that by 2025, India will be the third-largest importer of energy, with 90 percent of India's supply being imported from abroad. ONGC Videsh, the international arm of ONGC, has been actively pursuing foreign energy sources for energy supply contracts, and exploration and drilling rights. In Central Asia, ONGC has made significant inroads into Iran, Kazakhstan, Turkmenistan, and most recently in Tajikistan. It has formally bid on Tengiz and Kashaugan oil fields and the Kurmangazy and Darkhan exploration blocks in Kazakhstan.

The Indian government has also ventured into Africa. India has acquired shares in oil exploration ventures in Indonesia, Libya and Nigeria, and made substantial investments in Sudan's hydrocarbon sector. It has also announced plans to invest approximately $1 billion dollars in the Ivory Coast for offshore drilling. Furthermore, Reliance Industries, India's largest private-sector oil firm, is currently negotiating energy partnerships in Angola, Cameroon, Chad, Congo, and Nigeria.

Importing Gas

India has also been energetic in seeking out long-term gas deals. India has a number of active LNG supply contracts with countries, including Iran, Qatar, Australia, Malaysia, Oman, and Turkmenistan. It tried for years to arrange for the supply of gas from Bangladesh to the north Indian market, and later explored the idea of a pipeline from Burma to India via Bangladesh. Neither of these ideas materialized, partly because of domestic political pressures in Bangladesh, and partly because of apparently competing arrangements between Burma and China.

The Indian government has signed a $40 billion dollar gas deal with Iran which guarantees India 7.5 million tons of LNG over a 25 year period. It also gives India development stakes in Iran's largest offshore oil field, Yadavaran, and in the Jufier oilfield. For close to a decade now, India has been discussing the possible construction of a transnational gas pipeline from Iran's South Pars field to India via Pakistan. If this "IPI" pipeline becomes operational, it will be able to transport 90 to 90 million standard cubic meters of gas per day. This pipeline involves difficult issues of security, pricing, and above all political risk. For India, it would involve importing a strategic commodity across the territory of Pakistan, with which it has often had hostile relations, and both countries would need to find ways of protecting against supply interruptions. Pakistan has decided that it is prepared to move ahead despite its general aversion to normalizing economic relations with India before it has made significant progress on the Kashmir issue, but the politics of the pipeline will be affected by the general tenor of India-Pakistan relations. But the size of Iran's gas resources, its proximity, and its willingness to provide other strategic benefits to India (such as land access to Afghanistan and Central Asia) make it a particularly attractive partner for India's energy diplomacy.

India has also started negotiations with Turkmenistan in the past on a gas pipeline, commonly known as the "TAP line" that will run from Turkmenistan to India through Afghanistan and Pakistan. In addition, ONGC has established partnerships in Southeast Asia with investments in Vietnamese offshore fields.

Possible Complications in U.S.-India Relations

India's choice of energy partners like Iran, Libya, Syria and Sudan has occasionally led it to work at cross-purposes with the United States. Iran has been the clearest and most difficult example. U.S. Secretary of State Condoleezza Rice publicly said, during a March 2005 visit to New Delhi, that the United States had serious problems with the proposed pipeline. This statement led to some Indian concern about whether Washington would try to undercut India's other strategic interests in Iran. The U.S. has not focused thus far on India's energy purchases in Iran or even on India's work on the Iranian port at Chabahar. And India has voted with the United States when Iran's nuclear program came up in the International Atomic Energy Agency. India probably hopes Washington will be willing to live with the pipeline, if it ever comes to fruition, provided India's policy on Iran's nuclear program remains reasonably compatible with Washington's. But the two countries have very different visions of how to deal with Iran.

Other areas where India's energy-driven policies may be out of step with U.S. goals include Nigeria, where India announced in 2005 that it would help Nigeria modernize its military capabilities.

The United States is sympathetic to India's energy needs, and has established a high-level energy dialogue to find ways of cooperating and using the scientific know-how of both countries to benefit India's energy market. The proposed India-U.S. agreement on civil nuclear cooperation also has potential energy benefits. From India's point of view, however, these are supplements, not alternatives, to a policy of aggressively diversifying energy supplies.

The China Connection

China's demand for energy is growing even faster than India's, and China is pursuing a similar strategy of diversifying its sources of supply through energetic business and political diplomacy. China is well ahead of India in acquiring new sources of energy. The China National Petroleum Corporation (SINOPEC) has invested approximately $45 billion dollars in efforts to establish new energy partnerships. By contrast, ONGC has invested a modest $ 3.5 billion dollars in its global energy partnerships. Although India and China have jointly bid on oil assets in Syria, and Colombia, and signed several memorandums of understanding on energy issues in 2006, this has not prevented them from direct competition over energy deals. In 2004, SINOPEC outbid ONGC Videsh and acquired an oil-exploration block from Shell Oil in Angola. Chinese companies have also outbid ONGC and IOC on energy deals in Nigeria and Ecuador. Similarly, the competition between India and China for new energy sources in Central Asia is also clearly well underway. So far, the collaborative efforts between India and China regarding new energy sources have been minimal. It is fair to assume that as far as energy is concerned, Sino–Indian relations will continue to be competitive.

Future of Energy Policy

Energy is the area where India's independent foreign policy has the most immediate connection with its economic growth plans. Efficiency, fiscal reform, expanding the possibilities for private sector involvement in energy, and energy diplomacy are all different facets of the same basic requirement to service India's growing market. The United States remains India's most important external friend, and the area of overlap between Indian and U.S. strategic interests continues to grow. But many of the areas where they are not in harmony have an important energy dimension.

India's Coming Eclipse of China

Hugo Restall

Economic comparisons of India and China inevitably start with the two nations' obvious strengths. India punches above its weight in the service sector, particularly information technology and IT-enabled services. China is the undisputed leader in attracting foreign direct investment, and it is remarkably open to trade for a large developing country, with imports and exports accounting for more than 50% of GDP. With these starting points, both countries appear to have bright futures.

But in fact their strengths are symptoms of underlying weaknesses. Indian capital and talent is drawn to the IT sector largely because it is one of the few new fields which has not yet been stifled by government regulation. Service companies, especially in fields that export their product over a fiber-optic line, also stand out because they are less vulnerable to the country's infrastructure bottlenecks.

Likewise, China's dependence on FDI stems from the weakness of the country's banks and capital markets. With a savings rate of more than 40% of GDP, there is plenty of capital around, but few domestic institutions to allocate it efficiently. Moreover, high trade figures are symptomatic of a shortage of innovative companies able to create new products and build global brands. So far, China is stuck as the world's low-cost workshop, importing components, snapping them together and shipping them out again, adding little value.

This analysis means that it would be foolish to extrapolate the future of these two giants from the consensus view of their strengths. Rather, both are going to change dramatically as they address these weaknesses. That will take them in new directions with new growth trajectories.

Today India and China are racing at breakneck speed, with as little as one percentage point difference in their growth rates, and in theory they could sustain this pace for decades. Because China embarked on its economic reform program 13 years before India, it currently enjoys a healthy lead in per capita GDP. But India's challenges are more conventional for a developing country, and more easily addressed. China, by contrast, faces several perilous transitions which will slow its growth. As a result, India is set to steal the spotlight as leader of the developing world.

Miracle or Mirage

Let's stipulate that China is not willfully fooling the world with outrageously inflated statistics as it did during Mao Zedong's time. But some part of its latest economic "miracle" will also turn out to be a mirage. This growth is driven by levels of savings and investment the world has never seen in a market economy. Even though China has largely abandoned state planning, it still resembles Stalinist Russia in this one respect: Mobilization of capital, labor and raw materials provides the bulk of its growth, not productivity gains.

In fact, given the amount of investment, the biggest surprise of China's growth is how slow it remains. As a recent World Bank study said, "[T]he growth outcome, while high in comparison with other countries, is not commensurate with the input of resources." During their high growth phases, both Japan and Korea grew faster than China today, with a lower level of investment.

All this makes many economists nervous about the quality and sustainability of China's growth. Before the 1997 Asian financial crisis, East Asia's fastest growing economies were dependent on this kind of mobilization of resources rather than productivity growth. The result was that when faced with overcapacity, companies could not make the profits necessary to service the debts they had incurred in order to build their factories.

China's squandering of capital will have long-term consequences. While some believe that future growth in demand will take care of overcapacity problems, it is more likely that Chinese companies will have to export their way out of trouble. Given that trade tensions with the U.S. and Europe are already running high, this sets the stage for a crisis in the global trading system.

Moreover, the banking system's nonperforming loans are officially estimated at about 25% of total loans, but most experts put the real figure at around 40%. At that level, they are bankrupt. Because of the high savings rate, new deposits continue to flow in, keeping the banks liquid and allowing them to go on lending. But when the flow of savings slows, as it must some day, the government will have to recapitalize the banks and add their losses to the national debt. At current levels that is still manageable, but for how much longer nobody knows. Occasionally there are small bank runs in China, but so far the government has been able to maintain confidence by standing behind the banks.

China's incremental capital-output ratio, a measure of the amount of investment needed to create a given amount of GDP, is high and rising. According to the World Bank, the ratio has steadily risen to 5.4 in 2002 from 3.96 in the first half of the 1980s. The crisis in 1997 was preceded by a similar phenomenon in East Asian countries.

The FDI Champion

Much attention is paid to the fact that China pulled in some $60 billion of FDI last year, while India attracted an estimated $5 billion. In part this is due to measurement problems. If India used the standard definition of the International Monetary Fund, its FDI figure would be closer to $10 billion. And a large portion of China's FDI, perhaps one-third, is really domestic capital leaving and then re-entering the country, so-called "round-tripping," in order to receive the preferential treatment given to foreign-invested enterprises.

Even so, China remains a bigger destination for investments by multinational companies. But is this a sign of strength or weakness? Many argue the latter.

Despite its abundant savings, China's most dynamic companies often struggle to get funding. That's because the banking system is almost entirely state-owned, and the banks are reluctant to lend to private companies. As Yasheng Huang and others have written, entrepreneurs access finance by partnering with foreign companies. The more entrepreneurial state companies which want to escape government interference also sell stakes to foreign firms. Since foreign-invested firms get all sorts of preferential treatment compared to locals, such as tax holidays and exemption from troublesome regulations, the incentive is all the greater to find a foreign partner.

Why does China treat foreign businessmen better than its own people? One answer is politics. The Communist Party is afraid of nurturing a class of local entrepreneurs which could form an independent power base. It is more comfortable with foreigners, especially overseas Chinese, because they generally have no interest in challenging the power of the party.

This explains why the foreign-invested sector of China's economy accounts for most of its productivity gains and about half of its exports. These companies have brought in management and production techniques perfected elsewhere and combined them with cheap Chinese labor. But there is little local innovation in such enterprises—research and development, design, branding and other such high value-added activities have up until now been kept in the headquarters abroad.

Truly private businesses have contributed to China's growth, but they have to keep a low profile. The typical entrepreneur raises his start-up capital from friends, family and underground banking institutions. He reinvests his profits, and when his business reaches a moderate size, he stops growing that enterprise and uses his profits to start from scratch in other industries, creating a mini-conglomerate. Therefore private enterprises, while very entrepreneurial, never have a chance to achieve real efficiency through economies of scale and concentration on a core business.

So what Chinese companies do get loans from the banks? Mostly state-owned enterprises, which are protected by officials at various levels of government. They account for only 25% of output, yet they receive 65% of lending.

True, state companies are not as hopeless as a decade ago. Between 1998 and 2003, the government undertook massive lay-offs of 50 million workers, or more than one-third of the state-sector workforce. It also sold off most of the small- and medium-sized SOEs. Today we are told that the remaining large SOEs are profitable on the whole.

But there is good reason to be skeptical. "Reforming" SOEs without changing ownership makes little difference in their performance. We know that these companies do not face a hard budget constraint, meaning it is possible for them to use new borrowing to cover up past losses.

Incredibly, Beijing harbors dreams of creating state-owned conglomerates that will become world-class like Japan's keiretsu or Korea's chaebol. Conveniently ignored is the fact that these companies, while receiving much government support, remained private. While it dithers over privatization, vested interests that will resist future reforms are becoming more entrenched.

By handicapping its own entrepreneurs, China has largely confined itself to being an assembly center.

Together these phenomena explain why there is so little total factor productivity growth in China, so little innovation. China is not developing world-famous brands because its big companies are not nimble or savvy enough. By handicapping its own entrepreneurs, China has so far largely confined itself to being an assembly center for the world's multinationals.

India Shining

India's approach has been almost exactly the opposite of China's—it nurtured its own entrepreneurs and held multinationals at arm's length. Its largest private firms are about 10 times the size of China's. The problem was that they were sheltered behind a high wall of protectionism until a decade ago, so they didn't have to compete with world-class companies. In a hangover from colonialism, Indians worried that if multinationals were allowed in, they would exploit Indian workers and consumers, strip the country of profits, and drive local companies out of business.

That attitude is largely history, although vestiges persist. India's trade barriers are still high, with peak tariff levels at 20%, compared to China's 10.4% and a developing country average of 13.4%. Nevertheless, it has been gradually opening and finding that its companies not only cope with competition, they thrive. Success in the IT sector has been the catalyst, showing Indians that they can be world-beaters.

India has a huge advantage in its financial institutions and capital markets. Its banks are largely privately owned, and while their levels of nonperforming loans are relatively high at around 15%, they conduct credit risk analysis on their borrowers and are run along commercial lines, in contrast to China. India also has a functioning stock market.

As a result, Indian companies use capital more efficiently. The country's incremental capital-output ratio is generally lower than China's, and in recent years it has actually been falling. As is normal for a developing country, its savings rate, currently around 25% of GDP, is not sufficient to finance its investment. This reflected in higher interest rates: India's prime lending rate is consistently over 12%, compared to 8% in China. But now the vast pool of global capital is discovering India. The country is set to reap the benefits of higher levels of investment as FDI and portfolio investment increases in the coming years.

That will be combined with a huge wave of new and trainable workers. Demographically, India is a young country, with more than 40% of the population under the age of 20—that's 450 million people, as compared to 400 million in China. More important than their ability to work is their ability to think: The generational divide in India is pronounced, with the young by and large uninterested in the zero-sum socialist ideas of their elders. It's also revealing that they are pursuing advanced education with a zeal that was formerly thought of as a Confucian trait—American universities enroll 80,000 Indian students, compared to 62,000 Chinese.

Finally, India is attractive to multinationals because it has a commitment to the rule of law and protecting intellectual property. Not that either is always well implemented, but the contrast with China, headquarters of the world's IP pirates, is striking. This explains why India has home-grown, innovative companies, and is becoming a base for multinationals to conduct research in high-tech fields. Many came initially to arbitrage lower wages on routine work, but are now pressing into cutting edge fields.

Even the notion that business gets done more quickly in China needs to be re-examined. Narayana Murthy, founder of Infosys, was shocked it took months just to conclude a land agreement for a 15,000-employee facility in Hangzhou. Of Chinese officials, he complains, "Sometimes you can get confusing signals." Getting money out of Chinese clients is not easy either; Infosys gets paid in 56 days on average in India, but in China it must wait 120 days.

Politics in Command

To China's credit, it is addressing many of its problems. But here is where the contrast between Indian democracy and Chinese authoritarianism really comes into play. China has done well by picking the low-hanging fruit, the easy reforms in which there were many winners and few losers. For instance, by freeing farmers to produce their own crops 25 years ago, rural incomes rose and the supply of food in the city improved. Allowing prices to fluctuate with supply and demand corrected gross misallocations of resources. But more recently reforms have required difficult choices, such as laying off state workers.

So far, Beijing has continued to press ahead. But it is facing a rising tide of discontent, with about 75,000 public demonstrations a year. The benefit of authoritarianism was supposedly that China could make decisions for the greater good without

being stymied by the objections of a minority. Yet it is becoming increasingly unclear whether the Chinese government can retain the consent of its people.

China's embrace of globalization was never built on a solid foundation, and thus a public backlash against the government could bring the whole edifice down. Andy Xie, Morgan Stanley's chief Asian economist, recently released a report entitled "Time to Change," which concluded: "Rising internal tension over inequality and external friction over China's trade success suggest that China's government-led and export/investment-driven development model may be reaching its limits."

Meanwhile, India's politics are as tumultuous as ever, but the caravan of reform moves on, regardless of changes of government. That's because under its strong democracy, India has worked through dissent rather than sweeping it under the carpet. Now the country is finally getting a fillip from the phenomenon that has kept China afloat all these years: When a rising tide is lifting most boats, disputes over necessary reforms become less acrimonious. At or above the current level of 8% growth, some believe, India is able to pursue reform and use its increased revenues to compensate sectors of the population who are temporarily left behind.

So can India learn anything from China? Certainly China has done better at providing necessary infrastructure, but that is already well understood. More critical is the problem of excessive labor r egulations, which China eliminated first in special economic zones and then nationwide. In Chennai, the editor-in-chief of the Hindu, N. Ram, borrows the old Chinese term "iron rice bowl" to describe jobs at his newspaper—nobody can be fired, no matter how little work they do. "It's better than a government job," he says.

This especially hurts India's ability to attract investment in manufacturing. And it is manufacturing, not services, that can provide employment for the hundreds of millions of low-skilled farmers who will leave the land. This is also the key to raising productivity and incomes—at present, the roughly 60% of the population engaged in agriculture produces just 22% of GDP, and output is growing at less than 2%.

Yet so far, parliamentarians are reacting to a spate of farmers' suicides by approving money for make-work schemes in the countryside, instead of clearing the way for a manufacturing boom that could offer life-saving opportunity. Changes in labor regulations are the No. 1 policy change that could unlock faster growth.

A close second is opening up the retail sector fully to foreign competition, and here again India could learn from its neighbor. By allowing in firms like Wal-Mart and Carrefour, China has benefited consumers, stimulated demand, helped to develop a host of other industries and fostered the creation of distribution networks. Until now, both moves have been blocked by left-wing parties in the ruling coalition.

Nevertheless, the incremental steps being made show that these changes are within reach. For more than a decade, China has been the darling of the global business community, which fawns over its "miraculous" growth. Now India is poised not only to shine, but even to eclipse China.

India's Promise?

Conflicting prospects for the world's most populous democracy.

Devesh Kapur

Things have never been as good for India as they appear to be today. Its economy has grown by nearly 6 percent annually for the past quarter-century—virtually unprecedented for any sizable democratic polity. In contrast to the near-famine conditions of the mid 1960s, the country sits on a mountain of grain surpluses and poverty levels have almost halved since that time. Fertility rates, too, have nearly halved during the past few decades, while literacy and health indicators have steadily climbed from their erstwhile dismal levels. This sharply improved economic performance is rooted in a burgeoning middle class, estimated to be almost one-quarter-billion people.

During the 1990s, India's democracy faced severe challenges from the forces of Hindu nationalism, but that threat, too, has ebbed in recent years. Following its loss in the 2004 general elections, the Hindu nationalist Bharatiya Janata Party (BJP—Indian People's Party) is in disarray. While the events of the 1990s engendered trepidation in India's religious minorities about the country's commitment to secularism, current political conditions appear to allay those fears. Today, for the first time, this country in which four-fifths of the population is Hindu has a Sikh prime minister, a Sikh head of the army, a Muslim president, and, as its most powerful political personality, a Catholic-born Italian Indian.

Internationally, the nation is thriving as well. India is being courted by the world's major powers—a sharp contrast to the pariah status that it earned following the nuclear tests of 1998. China's spectacular growth has raised apprehensions among other countries in the region, thus leading both the United States and Japan to court India more assiduously. In turn, China has tried to strengthen its relations with India to preempt Indian involvement in any alliance against it. Trade with China has grown exponentially—from less than $1 billion a decade ago to nearly $14 billion in 2004. Chinese premier Wen Jiabao's recent visit to India was a remarkable testimony to improved relations between the two neighboring giants, given their strained relations since India's humiliating defeat by China in 1962. Even

neighboring Pakistan has been forced to rethink its relationship with India. In 2002, the countries' dealings were at such a low ebb that almost one million troops faced off against each other. But with the larger powers courting India, and facing a very different international environment, this long-strained relationship has begun to thaw. The cross-border movement of people across divided Kashmir that commenced this April has raised cautious hopes of progress on an issue that has bedeviled the region for nearly six decades.

There has been a singular change of attitude within India as well. Its elites, basking in the glow of international attention, are convinced that their giant nation's time has finally arrived. The unprecedented self-assuredness extends beyond the business class to a large number of the young urban educated, who are riding a wave of self-confidence generated by India's information-technology (IT) boom.

The exceptional confluence of good news—economic, political, international, internal—might seem to indicate that India's moment has finally arrived. Or has it? Is India's future akin to an Asian European Union—a liberal, democratic, multinational polity (albeit with lower levels of income)? Or is Brazil the more likely model—a giant system that has become wealthier but remains extremely unequal, and is afflicted by high levels of endemic violence? Or could India go the bleak way of Indonesia—a sprawling but weak polity led by governments with ostensible power but little authority; one that, despite its size, is likely to continue to languish in the minor leagues?

It has long been claimed that everything one can say about India is true—and so is the opposite. Indeed, India, a land of severe paradoxes, straddles several centuries simultaneously. While parts of rural India have agricultural practices akin to those of medieval Europe, its globally competitive IT firms are at the cutting edge of technology. Today, India produces more engineers than Europe and the United States combined, yet the country has the world's largest number of illiterate citizens. It has a growing and sophisticated nuclear-missile arsenal, yet a mounting Maoist insurgency poses a serious security threat in nearly one-quarter of India's 600-odd administrative divisions (districts). Despite substantial food-grain surpluses, India harbors the world's largest concentration of undernourished people. Even as "health tourism" is flourishing, driven by relatively cheap world-class tertiary-care facilities, India's health indicators are little better than those of sub-Saharan Africa. Although cheap, Indian-manufactured AIDS-cocktail drugs are now widely available in Africa, they are scarcely accessible to the more than five million AIDS patients in India itself—now the largest number in any one country. India's intellectuals and politicians rail against the evils of privatization, yet the country is, de facto, one of the most privatized economies in the world: virtually anything connected to the government—from state jobs to ministerships, from officials' transfers to access to subsidized state services—can be bought. The Indian state resembles a gigantic eBay—anything that can be sold, is. Even as minorities are found at the pinnacles of political power, neither accountability nor justice has been rendered for bloody state-directed anti-minority riots—whether against Sikhs in 1984 or Muslims in 1992–93 and 2002.

Perhaps the biggest paradox about India—one that goes virtually unnoticed today—is that the country has remained democratic despite overwhelming odds. India's democratic endurance, reaching back to its founding as an extremely poor multinational polity that was overwhelmingly rural and largely illiterate, is one of the political miracles of the twentieth century. That miracle is a testimony to the institutional foundations laid by the country's nationalist movement. But these foundations have been corroding in recent years. The sheer venality of contemporary India's political class cannot be exaggerated.

There are several reasons for this worrisome state of affairs: a lack of accountability and sanctions for even the most egregious behavior is perhaps the most critical factor. The principal mechanism of accountability is elections—an instrument with inherent limitations in any democracy. In India elections provide an even slighter check for several reasons.

First, despite having one of the highest turnover rates of any democracy (incumbents have a less than even chance of being re-elected), the pool of candidates, many with criminal cases, offers voters a choice between Tweedledum and Tweedledee. Second, the rising salience of identity politics in recent decades has privileged caste or religion over all other attributes of a candidate. Third, the sharp political cleavages between Hindu nationalists and secular political groups since the early 1990s have led the latter to accommodate and indulge the actions of any political faction, however venal, as long as its adherents claimed to be secular—paralleling the deeply deleterious effects of similar accommodations made by governments around the world in the struggle against terrorism. Fourth, there has been a deep decline in political parties as institutions. Most are run as family holding companies, epitomized by India's Congress Party. Virtually all of the scores of political parties in the world's largest democracy have the most anti-democratic internal practices. The exceptions are the two parties at the polar extremes of the ideological spectrum: the Communists and the Hindu nationalists. These factors, when combined with India's British-style parliamentary system,

have enhanced the power of individual elected representatives and led to a profusion of political parties in an era of coalition governments. Candidates for elections often buy tickets for electoral contests from party leaders—and if they are unsuccessful, shop elsewhere or start their own parties.

The Indian state has been described as having the engine of a bullock cart and the brakes of a Rolls Royce.

As a result, politics in India is a thriving business. Even the most obvious and blatant cases of corruption are not punished by voters, largely because of the force of identity politics. Despite the fact that India's courts, in particular the Supreme Court—one of the most independent and powerful courts in the world—have pressed for investigations of high-level corruption, politicians virtually never go to jail. Even if they do, they continue to run their activities with impunity. In states such as Bihar, politicians used to hire criminals to strong-arm rivals and herd voters to the polls. Now criminals have instead decided to get into politics themselves and have become members of parliament, thereby obtaining official police security to boot! India's police forces are under the same politicians' complete control. Little wonder that they are so demoralized and brutal. While Indian elites become indignant about the horrors of Abu Ghraib, similar practices occur in their own country daily. The state of affairs in the Central Bureau of Investigation—the key federal agency charged with pursuing corruption—is an emblem of the deep disarray in Indian institutions. The bureau has become so politicized that it is unable to prosecute successfully even the most blatant legal transgressions by India's politicians and bureaucrats.

From courts that take decades to settle cases, to police and prison systems that are brutal and corrupt, to lawyers who periodically go on strike and shut down the courts, the process of justice in India is itself the most potent punishment. Big business buys itself protection (when journalists cannot be bought off, they can be physically threatened), so it is rare for white-collar crime to be successfully prosecuted. In an atmosphere where everyone is deemed corrupt, state functionaries prefer to drag out and lose cases rather than try to arrive at a settlement, because the latter course leaves them exposed to accusations of bribery. For the same reason, honest officials are reluctant to make decisions lest they be accused of acting in "undue haste"—resulting in a state that has been described as having the engine of a bullock cart and the brakes of a Rolls Royce.

At the core of the problems that plague India lies the Indian state itself. India's elite bureaucracy, once a bastion of probity, has become politicized to such an extent that a minister reportedly claimed recently that, compared to the past, bureaucrats have become so complaisant that when they are simply asked to bend, they now crawl. Transfers to undesirable postings are the key mechanism to ensure bureaucratic pliability: if honest officials continue to be a "problem," false charges are launched against them. This behavior has adversely affected both the quality of recruitment and the capabilities of the bureaucracy, even as the demands of the economy have become more complex. The problems stemming from an unaccountable polity and bureaucracy are, of course, compounded by a citizenry whose social divisions hamper collective action.

India's statist model of development created vast patronage possibilities, pursued by powerful coalitions among politicians, bureaucrats, big business, and the rural elite. This dominant nexus was supposedly an important target of the economic liberalization launched in 1991 by the Congress government. Yet the resulting economic dynamism notwithstanding, systemic corruption has, if anything, increased. The economic prominence of the state does not necessarily decline with liberalization: its locus simply shifts from production to regulation. From taxation to land-development decisions in a rapidly growing, land-scarce economy, from state jobs to agricultural subsidies, and even through the process of obtaining a passport, possibilities for patronage and graft are ubiquitous. What is deeply disturbing in the Indian case is the shift in state corruption from "grease money" to outright extortion, paralleling what occurred in Indonesia in the waning years of the Suharto regime.

India's policymakers and politicians of all hues and stripes have learned—like many of their counterparts around the world—the virtues of a Janus-faced posture toward reforms. Essentially, this entails presenting a friendly persona to foreign investors, who will then perceive the Indian leaders as "reformists," thereby ensuring them much greater leeway in domestic matters. Indian politics has become much like options trading: politicians can undertake reckless and egregious behavior to achieve or retain power. If they succeed, they gain personally; if they don't, the losses are inflicted on society at large. Certainly the Congress Party acted this way, starting with Indira Gandhi's emergency suspension of civil rights in 1975, followed by the anti-Sikh riots in Delhi in 1984, and including electoral fraud in Kashmir over the decades. The BJP simply continued this tradition in such actions as the destruction of the Babri Masjid mosque in 1992–1993 and the horrific Gujarat riots in 2002. (Although there have been moves within the BJP to remove the chief minister of Gujarat, widely regarded as the architect of the 2002 riots, the motivation is not shame but mere self-interest: he is regarded as one of the politicians least open to bribes, so fellow party members feel he has made it more difficult for them to make money.)

Even after unexpectedly regaining power in 2004, the Congress Party has not desisted from constitutional improprieties. Contravening all constitutional norms, it precipitated crises by trying to topple opposition-led governments in state elections. Although these were averted at the last minute, they underscored the larger systemic risk that brinkmanship and partisanship could easily reach a point of no return. That this happened under a prime minister whose integrity and intellectual acumen are considered beyond reproach is particularly remarkable—if Manmohan Singh did not know about the unconstitutional intrigues of his own party, it only underscores his own political weakness; and if he did, then the integrity of India's political system is even more suspect.

The challenges arising from such a hollowing out of the Indian state should not be underestimated. As the quality of public services stagnates and in many cases declines, elites have de facto seceded from the state. From education to electric power, from phones to transport, from security to the postal system, from water to sanitation, India's growing middle class is exiting public services—and democratic politics as well. As a consequence, a powerful voice for systemic reform and change is being lost. With India's income inequalities increasing, as one part of society confidently integrates into a global economy while the other, much larger, part limps along, India is exchanging one set of inequalities—historic, deep-rooted, and caste-based—for another that is class-based and equally as troubling. These inequalities increase the support for populist demagoguery. At the same time, the state's weakness in providing essential services has created space for more extremist groups to fill in the gap, whether the Maoist Naxalites on the left or the Hindu nationalist Rashtriya Swayamsevak Sangh on the right.

Critics of liberalization in India incessantly harp on the necessity of increasing national government expenditures on health and education. They are loath to admit that primary education and health are principally the responsibilities of the state authorities. Even the Marxist government in power in the state of West Bengal for more than a quarter century has failed to make much progress in providing universal primary health and education (the one realm where communist governments have had relative success). The reason is simple: an unwillingness to enforce the basics of public administration by ensuring that well-paid government employees—from health workers who don't show up at clinics to teachers who don't show up to teach—do their jobs, because those same civil servants are an intrinsic part of the ruling party.

The inability of the political system to grapple with long-term challenges bodes ill for India's future.

The inability of the Indian political system to grapple with the many long-term challenges facing the county bodes ill for its future. Despite its high economic growth rate, India continues to run one of the world's largest fiscal deficits more than a decade after liberalization. This fiscal "overgrazing" is a classic tragedy of the commons, as individual parties and politicians benefit while the costs are shared by future generations. These expenditures are largely directed to a pampered government bureaucracy, rather than to long-term investments or social supports for the poor. India's human-development indicators continue to be abysmal for a country aspiring to become a great power. Growing water scarcities foreshadow greater internal conflicts, yet politicians continue to insist on free irrigation for water-guzzling crops such as sugarcane and rice. India's urban infrastructure is creaking due to low public investment—and this in a country that is one of the least urbanized in the world.

But instead of investing in urban public-transport systems, investments facilitating private automobiles are favored. Although India has very low per-capita consumption of electric power, shortages are frequent—and yet free power continues to be promised to farmers. Amid all these alarming trends, there is little indication that the political class's preoccupation with grabbing and maintaining power will change, provoking further dangerous neglect of India's real challenges.

It could be argued that fears concerning the troubling state of Indian governance are misplaced. After all, in the nearly six decades since independence, analysts have frequently underestimated India's resilience. The diverse face of the current national leadership can be taken as an encouraging sign, for example. The rapidly growing economy is creating new interest groups. Just as, a century ago, the excesses of patronage politics and raw capitalism created a groundswell of support for change in the United States, India has many actors who could do the same. Both a vibrant civil society and a dynamic private sector are promising. Indian politics is also likely to be invigorated as constitutional amendments passed a decade ago, reserving one-third of all elected seats in local governments for women, gradually create a new and potentially transformative political leadership.

But Indonesia is a sobering reminder that even decades of growth are no guarantee against sharp and debilitating reversals. Even given the resiliency of democracies, beneath the veneer of India's middle-class success and international recognition, its governing systems are severely stressed. Hundreds of millions of its citizens continue to be marginalized. India cannot emerge as a major power unless it urgently addresses state reforms, in particular by holding all state functionaries much more accountable for their actions than is currently the case. When the very source of the problem is its solution, the challenge is that much more difficult. Reform is possible, but self-reform—the requirement here—is always the most difficult to effect.

Can India fulfill its democratic promise, its destiny as its founding fathers saw it, in the years ahead? If that happens, it will affect not only the fate of one-sixth of humanity, but will also address one of the most challenging issues facing the global polity: whether poor, multinational, multiethnic states can emerge as liberal, prosperous democracies in the twenty-first century.

DEVESH KAPUR, Danziger associate professor of government through the end of the 2004–05 academic year, is moving to the University of Texas at Austin this summer as associate professor of government and Asian studies.

Leading by Example

Rani Sathappan's two terms as panchayat president were not without hurdles but she managed to overcome them.

RAMYA KANNAN

It seems irrelevant now to talk of the metamorphosis of Rani Sathappan from housewife to leader. After two terms of serving as the president of K. Rayavaram Panchayat in Pudukottai district, Tamil Nadu, she seems a natural leader.

No doubt, she has had two terms to get her act together and the villagers, who elected her with a margin of 194 votes, did see her potential; but two state awards and additions to infrastructure were beyond their imagination. K. Rayavaram is ahead of other villages in the area. "We are a small *panchayat*," Rani begins, apologetically, "So it is probably easier for us to do things."

First Task

Though Rani makes it sound as if she has had an easy run, clearly her journey has not been without its hurdles. She does not flinch at saying her engineer-husband guided her initially, fresh as she was to administration, but insists that she has, since then, learned the ropes and taken over the reins. Orientation sessions at the political studies department of Gandhigram Rural Institute, Dindigul, were a great help, she admits.

As she rolled up her sleeves, she discovered that her first task was to get the traditional village leadership (comprising only men) with the *ambalam* at its head on her side. With her husband's help, she managed to win them over and assured herself the support of the committee. This had a huge influence on the villagers. Once she cemented this relationship, it was time to begin the "real work" she says.

Desilting the village *ooranis* and *kanmais* was Rani Sathappan's first step. Armed with the will of the people and their commit-

ment to actively participate, Rani set about clearing encroachments, removing trees and overgrowth in the local water bodies. It was not without its share of problems, with red tape and long-winded government procedures. But at the end of a three-year battle, Rani managed to finish what she set out to do. The tanks are now brimming with water and the villagers are happy to see the fruits of their efforts.

She does not take any travel allowance or meeting allowance that presidents are eligible for. Rani spends her own money for travelling and for small administrative expenses. Inspired by her example, the other members on the committee too plough back their allowance into the panchayat kitty.

Achievements

Over two terms, Rani has also focussed on building women's self-help groups, improving sanitation facilities in the village, planting trees and ensuring immunisation targets were met. An added bonus was declaring the village a plastic-free zone. "Well, it is not entirely plastic-free, but unless we declare it, we will go nowhere," she says. The theme is to discourage the use of non-recyclable plastic in the village and reuse any available plastic item. Force will never work, she says, explaining in précis the reason for her success. "A leader must be convinced about the project, spread awareness among the people, ensure their participation and mobilise funds." Rani is clear she will not contest another time, even if it were possible. Besides, she will, after 10 years, have more time to make the *rava ladoos* she is famous for.

Article 18

An Interview with Amartya Sen on Alternative Radio

DAVID BARSAMIAN

Tell me about your family background.

My maternal grandfather Kshiti Mohan Sen was also called Sen, as it happened. He was professor of Sanskrit in Santiniketan. In India, the first child was often born in the mother's parental home. So I was born at their house. My parents lived in Dhaka. My father was a professor of chemistry there. My paternal grandfather was a judge, a lawyer. So there was a very spread-out background. My mother, who is close to 90, edits a literary magazine in Bengali. She was also a dancer and played the lead role in several of Rabindranath Tagore's (1861–1941) dance dramas in Calcutta. It was relatively uncommon, for middle-class women to actually dance on the stage. She was quite good at it.

When did Tagore establish the school at Santiniketan?

It was established in the very beginning of the twentieth century. My mother was a student there. I have one sister, Supurna, who now lives in Santiniketan and she also went to school there. We've all been there.

Would it be fair to say in the shadow of Tagore?

To some extent. He was clearly the strongest influence. Later on, thinking about it, I thought that I agreed much more with Tagore than I recognized then, because his presence was so strong there. There wasn't enough contrast. But only when I was thinking about other people who influenced my thinking, like Mahatma Gandhi, John Stuart Mill, Karl Marx and Adam Smith, I did think that Tagore had a very particular role which I wasn't fully aware of at that time.

He was not only a Nobel Prize winner but a Renaissance man, a musician, a writer, a playwright. He did so many things.

A great essayist, too. A visionary man in addition to being extremely talented. And his painting, which was originally thought to have just been a hobby, of course now is very highly prized.

He won the Nobel Prize in 1913. He was celebrated in the West. Then he went into a bit of an eclipse a few decades later.

The appreciation of Tagore was very peculiarly slanted in England and through England elsewhere in the West. It empha-sized his religious side. It overemphasized his mystical side, which was not all that strong in reality, and underemphasized his secularism and his interest in science, reason and social equity. It made him into more of a guru figure from the East than he could be fairly described as. While Gitanjali, the book that won the Nobel Prize, is a very fine collection of poetry, many people wouldn't regard that as being his best work in any sense. Those poems are quite often written in a religious style, but in many of them there was a great deal of ambiguity as to whether the addressee is God or a lover.

That's true of much of Tagore's love poetry, either it's a gentle love poem or a devotional poem. That ambiguity is very important because the language is used in a way that transcends that. It's part of one of the schools of Hindu thought that the relation with God is like the relation to a lover. That's certainly not a Christian thought. It's part of the Bhakti movement and the Bauls. The Bauls are kind of the wandering minstrels of Bengal. They are strongly influenced by the Islamic Sufi tradition. But in the rigid hands of W.B. Yeats, possibly the greatest English poet of the twentieth century, Tagore's poems took something of a turn. Yeats was pretty merciless in eliminating all those ambiguities as much as possible and making Gitanjali distinctly mystical and devotional. To a Bengali reader something was lost because ambiguity is a very important part of that poetry. The religious was only one aspect of one side of Tagore. Another aspect was this rather mystical experience with God rather than the fearless, warm friendship; that is a characteristic feature of his religious thought and is also absent. There's no God-fearing devotion there. There isn't very much in Gitanjali either. But some of the affectionate closeness with God is gone. I say that with some hesitation as a non-religious person. It's an intellectual subject one can react to. Something of Tagore's religion is also reduced. He gave a wonderful set of lectures called "Religion of Man" at Oxford in 1930. He also made use of a lot of Baul and Bhakti poetry, from a collection that my grandfather K.M. Sen put together. He was a great collector of songs. I think he did the first modern collection of Kabir's and Dadoo's songs. Kabir and Dadoo were mystics who combined elements from Hinduism and Islam, from the Sufi and Bhakti movement. Tagore used that extensively in his Oxford lectures.

What was your personal contact with Tagore?

I was very young. Up to the age of three I was in India, mainly in Dhaka. Then we moved to Burma. My father taught at the Agricultural College in Mandalay. During that period when I was in Mandalay, we went to Santiniketan regularly in my father's vacations. During those visits, I must have been four or five then, my grandfather thought that the time had come when I should not only speak Bengali but also start doing a little bit of Sanskrit. I was very grateful that I was introduced to a classical language very early in my life. But I didn't start doing that very seriously until at the age of six I came back to Dhaka. For about a year I was a student at St. Gregory's School in Dhaka. Then I went to Santiniketan. But by the time I got there in 1941, Tagore had just died. I had met him a number of times as a child, but I didn't have any real communication with him. I remember him as a benign, friendly presence.

There was an interesting split between Tagore and Gandhi. It's kind of ironic, because it was Tagore who popularized the term Mahatma, "great soul."

Faith was more important for Gandhi. Reason was more important for Tagore. That's one contrast. Being free to determine what you want to do rather than being guided by tradition, received wisdom, was much more important to Tagore than it was for Gandhi. These are matters of somewhat fine distinction. In some ways Gandhi was also interested in reason and freedom, indeed, much of his life was concerned with that. But there was more constraint on what is an appropriate field of reason for Gandhi than for Tagore. Emperor Akbar, whom I cited in the New York Review piece I did called "Reach of Reason," said that there's nothing that we can accept without first reasoning about it. To some extent that was true of Tagore, even though he wouldn't deny the immediate role of raw sentiments and unexamined affection. But the point comes when you have to decide what you want to do.

In his novel The Home and the World, *there's a very sharp division on the issue of the swadeshi movement. Tagore had strong opinions about that.*

That's the third distinction vis-à-vis Gandhi, other than the greater focus on reason and freedom, and not unconnected with that. Tagore was very keen on traditional Indian culture. He also felt that the civilization of every country was a personal inheritance from which he himself had benefited, and so does everyone. He insisted that any idea or any cultural contribution which I enjoy instantly becomes mine for that reason, no matter where it has its origin. I don't think that would have been Gandhi's attitude. There was a clear distinction between the nation, its own contribution, and other nations. He was respectful of other nations. He was very tolerant of diversity in the world, but there wasn't a great pride in world civilization as such, even though he himself was influenced by Tolstoy and by English legal thinking, Ruskin, as well as Thoreau and Emerson. The concept of the Other was much less sharp in the case of Tagore. There's a kind of seamless wholeness to world civilization. And I grew up in that culture.

Didn't Tagore feel that the burning of British-made clothes would exacerbate communal feeling, particularly in Bengal?

There were two things here. He thought that burning any useful product seemed a negative and basically unattractive gesture. One could say that Tagore was not being sufficiently political. Gandhi was capturing the high ground of politics by burning British made clothing by showing how it had brought about the decimation of the Indian textile industry. I think Gandhi was making his point, which Tagore, being not such a political person, may not have attached importance to and could actually have missed. But there's a second aspect of it connected with your question, namely that it so happens that a number of people involved in the cotton trade were Muslims, so that the burning of these clothes would be particularly detrimental to the interests of that community. Tagore foresees in *The Home and the World* that the Muslim traders' resistance to the swadeshi movement and reluctance to join it, for which they had good economic interests, would actually exacerbate tension between Hindus and Muslims, which in effect it did. Here Tagore was being a more far-seeing statesman than the followers of Gandhi who are portrayed in the novel. Tagore was careful not to make it a criticism of Gandhi himself, and I think that's fair.

What impact did the first partition of Bengal have in the early 1900s?

The partition was clearly politically motivated. Like any decision you take, there are several reasons. But one of them was the political agitation. Bengal was certainly the hotbed of political revolt at that time. Virtually all of what the British would say were terrorist activities at that time was coming from Bengal. Throughout the nineteenth century the British found the Bengalis particularly difficult to control. A distinguished member of my college, Macaulay, was very explicit on the failings of the Bengalis. In Kipling's stories there is often the caricature of the Bengali babu. Hence there is often the dislike of Bengal, which was resisting British rule more and more. Oddly enough, much of the administration of the British Indian Empire was basically based in Bengal and the capital was in Calcutta until past the 1905 partition. The Bengalis had produced a new urban middle class to a great extent connected with the Raj. They served as the junior boys in the administration, but by the middle of the nineteenth century the rebellious element is beginning to get strong. By the beginning of the twentieth century it had become very strong. That political consideration must have played a part in the thinking of the Viceroy Lord Curzon and others involved in that partition.

And the shifting of the capital from Calcutta to New Delhi, to build a new imperial city in 1911, what was that about?

There are at least three good reasons for moving it. First of all, Delhi had been the capital of Mughal India for a long time and therefore held a position such that even when there was a rebellion against the East India Company and British rule in 1857 in the so-called Sepoy Mutiny, while the British headquarters remained in Calcutta, the rebels wanted to have their headquarters in Delhi. Second, Delhi offered a much greater opportunity of expansion, more open land than Calcutta could offer. A place like New Delhi, which was built as it were almost like the ninth city of Delhi. There were seven Islamic cities, and then there was an earlier Indian city, near Hastinapur, and at last comes the British city. The third reason was that Delhi was much more central in the days before partition, as it no longer now is because it's so close to the Pakistan border. At that time it was very central. On top of that, the irritation of the occasionally sharp-shooting Bengali must have been quite strong also at that time. All these contributed to that. I don't want to insist on a purely political (narrowsense) explanation. But it would have been a matter of relief for the British that they were moving out of Calcutta to safer ground elsewhere.

Today the position that Gandhi and Tagore occupy in the Indian imagination, some people have said they have been deified. They're icons. The content of their work has largely been vacuumed out.

To a certain extent that is true. That statement is often made, and you can see why. They are both respectfully remembered, Gandhi more and much more often than Tagore, and yet Gandhi was very concerned that his model of self-sufficient village economy, his opposition to technology, his skepticism of international trade, these have not really survived in today's India. But after having said that, one also has to recognize that this cannot be a just criticism of modern India, partly because many of Gandhi's ideas were very difficult to relate to a program of economic and social development. I don't just mean things like opposition to big dams. It's not clear exactly what Gandhi's position on that was. Certainly it was less clear than Nehru's. But these are not issues that seemed that big. Dams looked very good in Nehru's time, too. At that time the analysis seemed to indicate that that would raise living standards, like the Tennessee Valley Project. They looked promising, but they often proved to be creating more problems than they solved. But the general hostility to modern technology and to modernity as such wasn't such an easy thing to deal with. Gandhi was opposed to railroads. He was opposed to modern medicine. One of his children suffered from illness and in fact died without getting the benefit of modern medicine. There are many aspects of Gandhi which are not the reasons we remember him. We remember him because of his message to love humanity, because of his perfecting of the technique of nonviolence, because he was able to show that to fight evil you don't have to be evil yourself. You can fight evil with good. All these are major thoughts. Those, too, are often not remembered sufficiently. That I would complain about. But the neglect of some of his other ideas, including the self-sufficient village economy, opposition to railways and other modern technologies and modern medicine, that I don't lament.

There are more thoughts needed about his attitude about our position in the world. I am very opposed to the Indian nuclearization. There is something to be learned from Gandhi here, since he was so opposed to militarism. But at the same time, I don't think there the analysis has to be primarily Gandhi-oriented. We have to see what India gets from the nuclear bomb. All Indians lose by insecurity and diversion of resources. Rational economic and political analyses show that we have good reason to reject militarization. There Tagore has more to offer. That's Tagore's territory. You ask yourself why you are doing it, what do you get out of it? You ask yourself, Am I being sufficiently self-critical? Am I asking the right questions? Is this right for

me? What will it do to other people, because we also belong to a world community? What do we owe to others and what do others owe to us? How do we relate to each other? One could say that Tagore's ideas, not so much ideas but techniques of analysis are more relevant than Gandhi, who was less concerned with reason in a very broad sense. To take into account affection and sentiments and emotions but at the same time subject them all to reasoned scrutiny. That is quintessential Tagore territory.

Tagore had been knighted by the British. After the Jallianwala Bagh massacre in Punjab in 1919, he renounced his knighthood. What kind of impact did that have on the nationalist struggle?

He denounced the British action and that made dramatic headlines. As a political act it drew attention to his renouncing an honor that the Rajhad given to him, and that was quite important. The beastliness of that massacre was so great that it would have been very hard for somebody as sympathetic to humanity in general to live quietly with the kind of distinction that the Raj had offered him in the form of the knighthood. So it was a natural act to undertake. I don't think Tagore undertook it as a political action. Gandhiji, who was much more a political person, would have probably seen the political consequences much more clearly than Tagore. For him it was a gut reaction. He did not want to associate with murderers. But it so happened that it was a politically important step. I personally don't think he thought of it as a political step at all, but it proved to be one.

Tagore is the only composer in the world who wrote the national anthems of two countries, India and Bangladesh.

I mentioned that in my New York Review article. I kept on thinking and searching to see whether there was anybody else who might have that distinction, but I didn't find any. I think it's remarkable. Both the Indian anthem "Jana Gana Mana" and the Bangladesh anthem "Amar Sonar Bangla" are not only poems of Tagore, but they had been very well-known poems before they were adopted in the two countries as the national anthem. I have a very strong association with Bangladesh myself. I come from there and to a great extent grew up in Dhaka. If somebody asked me where is my home I would have to say Dhaka and go more deeply into the village in the Dhaka district where I come from, Manikganj, and a small village called Matto, that sense of belonging is very strong. I've visited it recently also. Given that sense of attachment, it's particularly pleasing for me that somebody whom I knew, namely Tagore, who also happened to have given me my name, is also remembered in Bangladesh not just through his rich artistic output, but also in having one of his poems as its national anthem. The other one is similarly a very powerful song on India and its diversity. That's what the song is about, a celebration of India's diversity. Nevertheless there is an attempt to stick together. That's the main theme of the Indian national anthem. That comes through very well. The two songs are in a very different spirit, but they both work respectively, one for a large federal country like India, and the other as a culturally integrated country like Bangladesh. Both nations chose their anthems very well.

You had an early childhood experience in Dhaka involving a man named Kader Mia. Can you tell that story and the influence it had on you?

I was very small then. I think it happened when I was ten. I was playing alone in the garden of our home in Dhaka, "Jagat Kutir," which means world cottage. I was suddenly made aware of the presence of somebody. I looked up and there was a person profusely bleeding from his stomach. He had clearly been knifed. He came through the door wanting help and some water. I had never seen somebody knifed like that before. I shouted for help while trying to make him lie down on the ground. There was a little cement seat where I helped to place him. While my father, who was upstairs, came down, I brought him a glass of water. I was chatting with him. He was a Muslim daily laborer who had come for work in this largely Hindu area called Wari. He had come despite knowing that these were troubled times, where in Hindu areas Muslims were getting butchered and in Muslim areas Hindus were getting butchered. He came with great reluctance, but he was poor. His family had very little to eat. He wanted to come and earn some income. He was offered a job. He was on his way there when he was knifed. He kept on telling me then, as well as when I went to the hospital with my father in the car, that his wife had said not to go to such a dangerous area. But he felt economically compelled to do so in order to have an income. The penalty of that economic unfreedom proved to be death. It had a tremendous impact on me. First of all, it was incredible to me that members of one community could be killing members of another community not for anything personal that they hold against the person other than the identity of the person as a member of another community. That's a very difficult thought. People get used to it because of experiencing that kind of event so often. It's still a hard thought for a human mind to comprehend, why you should try to take the life of someone who has done you no harm, whom you don't even know, just because he belongs to some group. I found that terrifying and utterly perplexing, both from an ethical point of view and intellectually. What kind of thought process can lead to such an act? Secondly, it also had the impact of making me deeply skeptical of community-base identities. Even to this day, I remain instinctively hostile to communitarian philosophy and communitarian politics. Part of that hostility is based on some analyses, which I've tried to present in my writings. But I think the instinctive revulsion is connected with having seen some of the ugly sides of community identity. That was a very strong thing. I knew that there were riots going on, but until I held somebody in my own arms who was bleeding to death, and he did finally die in the hospital, it wasn't as real to me. I think nothing could have made it as real as an experience of that kind. Thirdly, of course, what he told me, and that he particularly told me about his decision to risk it, which was the second sentence after I had given him some water. He said that his wife had told him not to come. It's difficult for me even to recollect those moments now. The lack of freedom in his life, if he was to be a good father and feed his children, he had to take every opportunity that came his way, even at great personal risk. He took the risk and lost his life and the earning power for his family. I was overwhelmed even to think about it. It also made me take a view that I've tried to develop in my book *Development as Freedom*. Different kinds of freedoms interrelate, lack of economic freedom, could be a very major reason for loss of liberty, in this case,

liberty of life. The fact that freedom of different kinds interrelate was a central notion for me. The beginning of that idea was those moments. It stayed with me in my student days in Santiniketan and at Presidency College in Calcutta, where I was politically quite active, and later at Trinity College in Cambridge. Over those years, Kader Mia's explanation of why he could not listen to the wise counsel of his wife, was a strong presence in my thinking. It was a very important experience for me.

In 1943 the Bengal famine occurs. Three million Bengalis die. Your call as a child handing out a tin of rice to starving refugees as they passed your grandfather's house in Santiniketan. There was no evidence that there was a shortage of food supplies, even though it was during World War II. What did you later learn about this horrific event?

First a comment on the tin of rice. It's true that I remember that, but that's not my strong memory. Somehow in one of the interviews that was done of me, I did mention, among many other things, that my grandfather allowed me to take a cigarette tin and from the large jar of rice we had I was allowed to give one tin to any family that came for help. But it's not a big thing. I sometimes dislike the focus on that because it makes it look like too much of a charitable activity. The main memory that I have of that period is not of my trying to help in a tiny little way, but the opposite. The bewilderment as to why suddenly people were dying in such numbers. Where did they come from? I didn't know any of them. Like all famines, this was a rigidly class-based one. Depending on which occupation group you belonged to, which class you came from, you either got decimated or you had no problem whatsoever. Ninety to ninety-five percent of Bengalis' lives went on absolutely normally, while three million died. Three million, by the way, was my estimate. The official estimate was much lower, a million, perhaps a million and a half. That was far too low, but it is possible that my number, three million, overestimated it somewhat. On the basis of later statistics it would seem that a more acceptable number is somewhat lower than that, like two and a half million. It was a large number, but they all came from a small community, a small class. Famine is a kind of subject in which class-based analysis is very helpful. The people who died were primarily rural wage earners working and cultivating fields, but also wageworkers working in river transport, minor trade, minor services like barbers and craftsmen producing crafts to sell, for none of which there was a market once the famine hit. They belonged to a small group of people who were economically most vulnerable. They got drowned by the famine. I had not met anyone of that kind. They didn't come to the school that I went to, not a rich person's school, but primarily a middle-class school. I don't think there was any fee worth mentioning, but you had to be moderately well off to be able to send your children to a school. There was a very nominal fee. So I think the class basis was a very strong memory of that. Later I would find studying famine that that's true everywhere. Hardly any famine affects more than five percent, almost never more than ten percent of the population. The largest proportion of population affected was the Irish famine of the 1840s, which came close to ten percent over a number of years. But mostly this is a small proportion of the underdogs of the society.

Secondly, there's also considerable evidence which I already knew, as a child, from my parents and others that the crop hadn't been bad in any sense, so it was surprising that there would be a famine. The Famine Inquiry Commission appointed by the Raj later reported that the food statistics must have been wrong. But in fact, when I studied it much later, it was clear that the food statistics weren't really very wrong. They needed only minor correction, and that wouldn't explain the famine. One must see it plainly in terms of a fuller economic analysis of how people earn a living and how they can use their wages and income to buy food. Just to give an example, sharecroppers and cash wage laborers in normal circumstances are almost equally poor, but the famine hit the wage laborers much harder than the sharecroppers. It happened during World War II. The Japanese were in Burma and the British army was in Bengal. There was war-based production. Prices shot up. When prices shot up, the wage earners, with fixed money wages, started going down right away, whereas sharecroppers, since they get their income in the form of part of the food, didn't suffer in the same way. Indeed, I found on the basis of indicators of mortality as well as indicators of occupational distress on which we had data that sharecroppers were not distressed at all in the way that cash wage laborers were. This indicated that I was on the right line. So the kind of economic analysis, the complexity of the entire economic system could be brought into the story. This is a simple example; there were more complex issues as well, such as the effect of government procurement and of speculation by traders. The recognition that the story was not just about food was already clear when I watched the famine and its class-based nature, its suddenness and its contrariness.

In Development as Freedom, you write that "No famine has ever taken place in the history of the world in a functioning democracy."

It became increasingly clear to me by the 1970s that both empirically famines have actually not occurred in functioning democracies and also that that didn't seem like a fluke but there was a good reason. My first book on famines, Poverty and Famines, came out in 1981, by then I thought I understood something about how famines operate and how easy it is to prevent them. You can't prevent undernourishment so easily, but famines you can stop with half an effort, without difficulty. Then the question was, Why don't the governments stop them? The first answer is that the government servants and the leaders, whether they be military or non-military, are upper class. They never starve. They never suffer from famine, and therefore they don't have a personal incentive to stop it. However, if the government were vulnerable to public opinion, then famines are a dreadfully bad thing to have. You can't win many elections after a famine, and you don't like being criticized by newspapers, opposition parties in Parliament and so on if you are in a democratic country. Democracy gives the government an immediate political incentive to act.

Given that political incentive, and taking note of the economic analysis that famines are easy to prevent, you would expect that in a democracy there will be no famine. Whereas in the absence of a democracy you may avoid famine if you are lucky. A famine may not develop. On the other hand, if one were to develop, there's no guarantee that the government will try to prevent it. Some time there will be a visionary leader who will actually do it without needing the political incentive, but you don't have the guaranteed reaction by the government which you would expect in a democracy if there is no democracy but a dictatorship, either of an alienated kind, like a colonial administration, like the British Raj in India or for that matter in Ireland, or military dictators in one country after another, like Somalia, Ethiopia and many other countries. Also, the one-party states like we had in the Soviet Union and China, despite the fact that the governments were generally committed to the interests of the underdog, indeed, that's how they had come to power, they were so dominated by theory that they were not in a position to react. Often they were particularly inhumane in not feeling the manifest suffering that they saw around them, thinking that somehow in the long run this would turn out to be right. The Chinese had the failure of the Great Leap Forward, which led to a famine between 1958 and 1961 in which nearly thirty million people died. While tens of millions were dying every year, the disastrous policies of the government were not revised for three years. This would be unthinkable in a democracy. Similarly, while the famine was going on, there were also starving of information for the government. This is an additional factor, the informational connection as opposed to the political incentive connection. This is because each commune in China, each collective, obviously saw that they were not doing very well themselves but they read in the papers that everything was fine in the rest of the country. That's what censorship does. They all came to the conclusion respectively that they alone were failing. So rather than admitting failure, they cooked the numbers and reported higher food output than was true. When Beijing added these up at the height of the famine, they thought that they had a hundred million more metric tons of rice than they actually had. So the censorship of the press which often goes with lack of a democratic system had the effect not only of hoodwinking the public but ultimately hoodwinking the state. Something similar happened in the Soviet Union. They were partly deluded and partly theoretically arrogant and overconfident of their policy. But in the case of the Ukraine and the Soviet famine, there was also a kind of dislike of one group, the Kulaks, so there was somewhat of a basic lack of sympathy for the rural areas. But on top of that, the lack of democracy, of political incentives that go with democracy and the lack of information added to the story. So I think the one-party state in the Soviet Union or China (or Cambodia, or North Korea) or the military dictatorship as in many of the African countries or the colonial rule like in the British Empire and the French Empire bring out plentifully the penalty of political unfreedom, the lack of democracy.

Talk about what you've described as "subcontinental nuclear adventures." In May 1998, India conducts nuclear tests. A month later Pakistan follows. Within a year, the largest military confrontation in decades occurs in the Kargil sector of Kashmir.

I thought this was a disastrous development. India of course had exploded a nuclear device in 1974. That was a regrettable event. The Indian government didn't admit that this was actually a nuclear bomb, but said that they would not manufacture nuclear bombs. To some extent, there was some consolation in that because it did seem that after having established its capability to do so, India wasn't keen on taking it further. But all that was changed by 1998, when the new government came into office. There was pressure in that direction anyway by the scientific community involved in the nuclear military research. Part of the army also had been interested.

The new government being the Bharatiya Janata Party, BJP.

Yes, the BJP led the Hindu nationalist-led government which came to office in the early months of 1998. While there was strong support for nuclearization of the military on the part of the military and a part of the research establishment connected with military research, given the nature of Indian democracy, that could not sway the government easily. There was no way the military could impose a policy unless the civilian government agrees. The previous governments had been tempted but restrained in this respect. It was part of the BJP's agenda when they were elected that they would develop a nuclear bomb and carry forward the nuclear program, and this they did. A lot of the writing in the West has underestimated the extent to which it divided the country and how much there was opposition to it. It's very easy to capture pictures of jubilant people on the street after the nuclear bomb. But if you approve of an event, you're much more likely to come out on the streets and be jubilant than if you are opposed. There are no pictures of morose people sitting in their kitchens and living rooms. But immediately after the partial euphoria was over, mainly in urban areas, when one looked at the real numbers, it was quite clear that the government got nothing in terms of popular support for nuclearization, so much so that when the government fell later on and had to go to the polls again within the year, they decided not to put nuclearization as part of the electoral manifesto of the BJP. To me it's a very important lesson, that the nuclear program which they thought was a success had the effect of taking it out as a political vote-getting issue. That to me is worth emphasizing. India, being a democratic country, it does make a difference what people ultimately think. The rural population never showed a great enthusiasm for the nuclear weapons at all.

In effect, the tests contributed very little to India's well-being. It made the entire subcontinent less safe. It was predictable that Pakistan would retaliate. Everybody knew that Pakistan had the capability to produce the bomb. It doesn't matter that its capability is much less than that of India because with a nuclear holocaust you get hundreds of millions dying anyway. It made the situation much less stable. The argument that that would prevent conventional war, which is a kind of quick wisdom from the Cold War days between the Soviet Union and the U.S., was often aired in India. That was given a lie by the Kargil confrontation that occurred in the summer of 1999 which indicated that it didn't have that effect at all. If anything, just the opposite. The Indian view, which is probably right, is that the intruders came in from Pakistan to India. Pakistan, which could be now quite certain that India would hesitate to do what would be the standard thing to do. Since Pakistan was occupying the high ground in Kashmir and coming down into the valley, they had reason to try to cross over on the Pakistan side of the border in retaliation. But the fear of a nuclear holocaust was a deter-

rent, so that India had to fight the battle in most adverse circumstances in going uphill. So it didn't stop the war and didn't make the Indian case easy.

As far as taking India more seriously is concerned, I think there's deep confusion in Delhi about the effect. It's true India is taken somewhat more seriously now. But that's much more to do with economic development, with the fact that in information technology India is a relatively big player. There is a big presence of India in America and in Europe. India is the second-largest producer of computer software in the world. And India is a big economy which is moving in a way Pakistan's economy has not been. So because of these factors we would have expected greater recognition of the presence of India in the world among the bigger powers. To attribute that recognition to the nuclear bomb is a great mistake. Nuclear bomb is something that India and Pakistan have in common. If that had made the crucial difference, then Pakistan would have exactly the same greater recognition as India has. But it hasn't. The reason is that what differentiates India from Pakistan is a more solvent and dynamic economy and a functioning democracy. I'm full of sympathy for Pakistan as a neighboring nation, because of the stagnant nature of its economy and its polity. Because of the absence of the same kind of interaction in the world economy as in the Internet and information-technology and computer software, Pakistan does not get the attention that India does. I think the whole reading that India got some advantage, either diplomatic or political or military, is mistaken. On top of that, from an economic point of view, it diverted a lot of resources which could be much more productively used for economic and social development, for which India badly needs money. It is a disastrous policy.

On the other hand, I have to say that at least the bulk of the Indian population was not taken in by the argument that this is a great thing and in India's interest. The voters have not voted in that direction. It hasn't done much for the ruling party. In fact, in some ways, the part of the BJP government which is on the economic side which has continued the policy of more market orientation and more intercourse with the world probably has done more to expand India's standing and political and social role in the world than the nuclearization of the military which government did with the hope of achieving these results.

India is often hailed in the Western press as the world's largest democracy. Yet paradoxically, it's being led by a nationalist, Hinduformation with quite frankly some very fanatical elements. What has led to that kind of "jihadization" of politics in India?

First of all, I don't think that India is much celebrated for its democracy. Democracy has been a very neglected commodity at home and abroad. In India it did not get much praise from many in the left because there is a tendency to dismiss democracy as bourgeois and a sham. It was very strong in my student days and it remained strong until very recently. The idea that democracy is something that is in itself important and even if you don't achieve much economic development is something which is relatively new. I remember crying hoarse on this at Presidency College in the very early 1950s when I was a student there. I was very active in left-wing politics. Many others who were active in politics thought it was an amiable eccentricity on my part to regard democracy to be such a big thing. Similarly, in the West people have taken relatively little interest in Indian democracy. The governments and the hard-headed military establishment and the general conservative part of America have never taken much interest in democracy anyway. But also on the left there is a deep skepticism: what does democracy mean if you are hungry and poor? The celebration in that context of China, which of course had many reasons to be celebrated but not for its lack of democracy, did actually act as a kind of barrier to see that India was doing something major. So I want to correct that impression, that even now the importance of democracy in India I don't think is adequately recognized anywhere in America.

My second point is that I regret of course the fact that the BJP is in power. I've never voted for it and never will. However, in a democratic country it could easily happen, especially with coalition politics, that you might end up being in office. It has to be said that the BJP has not been opposed to democracy as such. There has never been a proposal to suspend the Constitution, to change voting rights or to dispense with elections. So in that respect you couldn't say that it is a contradiction, an anti-democratic party had been elected to run the government. That's not the case. But their interest, of course, is much more in favor of one community in a multi-community country. India, I believe, is quintessentially multi-community, multi-religious, multi-cultural, with Hindus and Muslims and Sikhs and Christians and Jains and others making up the population. It's unfortunate that they have gone in that direction. The BJP has tried to argue that they have Muslim members. I don't take that terribly seriously. They're not very powerful. In fact, the political underpinning of the BJP lies very much in Hindu sectarianism. But it's interesting that even with that sectarian base, given the nature of Indian polity, they have to claim that they are somehow multicultural themselves, which to me is a kind of backhanded tribute to the constitutional democratic secularism that we are lucky enough to have in India.

The third point to make is that the BJP gets about a quarter of the vote. Its share of the vote has not grown for many years now. To some extent they have been able to capture the ground of nationalism in a way that other parties have not, and to some extent the dissension within Congress has made it easier for BJP to capture that ground. Since Hindus are a very large majority in India, it is possible to utilize the Hindu rhetoric as a kind of Indian rhetoric, which I regret, but I can see its feasibility. But the fact is that the voters have never given them a mandate to run a government of their own. They are in a coalition government, and they have made good electoral alliances, more skillfully than Congress or the left coalition in the form of the Janata group managed to do. As a good democrat, I think it's only right that they should run the government. I'm certainly in favor of accepting that. To a certain extent, in a number of fields they have done relatively better than I feared. On the other hand, I would have expected them to move even more in the multicultural direction and restrain the hotheads on the Hindu sectarian side of the base of the BJP, which they haven't done. Persecution of minorities, while not intense, is present and occasionally takes a beastly form, like the killing of a Christian

missionary. In those cases, the government should come down with a much stronger and heavier hand than it has done. It tries to establish itself as being a mainstream party, which has been one of the reasons why they have been quite restrained, relatively speaking, in economic and social affairs. So you have to take the rough with the smooth, and the BJP is part of the rough edge, in my judgment, of Indian politics.

What is the nature of a democracy when forty percent of the population, as in the case of India, that's 400 million people, is illiterate?

There's no question that literacy increases the effectiveness of democracy. But I would certainly dispute the claim that democracy makes no sense if you don't have literacy. That has been the argument that dictators have used again and again. This is a classical argument that the ruling elites always used in order to keep out the masses from having a share of power. In a wonderful play of Tagore, *Raja o Rani*, there is a great discussion about how the palace is skeptical of the masses who cannot think of anything high because they're illiterate and only think of such things as food and clothing. Defranchising the illiterate would be a terrible crime.

It's a reactionary argument. I'm not saying your question is reactionary. But if it had been a rhetorical question it would be reactionary. Democracy can be used as a means to expand people's social opportunities if it's properly used. The fact that in India education did not become until very recently a politically active issue is very unfortunate. But for that you have to look not at current illiteracy, but to the classist nature of Indian society, of which caste is one manifestation, but not the only one. In some ways the leadership of all the parties has tended to come from the same group, with some exceptions. In Kerala, the Communist Party may have been led by the underdogs of society, namely those coming from what used to be untouchable castes, but in my part of the country in West Bengal, where the Communist government has won elections for a longer stretch than any other place in the world, the leadership has tended to be always middle class, often Hindu, often Muslim, but basically middle class. That again contributed to the skepticism about education until recently. It's changing now, both among the left parties as well as in Indian politics in general. But it took some time. Properly used, it could be a great means of expanding demand for education and the circumstance in which you find yourself, whether in India or Africa.

It's not the case that illiterate people don't worry about their political and civil rights. When we're talking about democracy, we're looking not only at an instrumental virtue, but something which is intrinsically important, the right to participate. The Indian population, even the illiterate Indian population, takes that quite seriously. So when in the middle 1970s Indira Gandhi's government suspended electoral rights and basic political liberties and also habeas corpus and then she still went to the polls, she was resoundingly defeated because poor, illiterate Indian population still felt very strongly that democratic rights were important. So the scepticism about the voting rights of illiterates would be not only reactionary, but also wrong. It overlooks the possibility that democracy opens up and the fact that illiterate and poor people still value political liberty. After all, human beings, even in the most reduced circumstances of poverty as well as in articulateness that illiteracy produces have a desire for freedom that is quite strong. That is what makes human beings what we are.

Perhaps to get beyond the conventional notion of literacy, I've met rickshaw drivers in Delhi who were technically illiterate but who could recite "shers" (couplets) or "ghazals" (poems).

This is a double-edged sword. On one side, it's important to recognize that even illiterate people have other sources of wisdom and sometimes you have illiterate people who resent the fact that they're illiterate and later on in life still achieve something. Perhaps the most spectacular example is the Mughal emperor Akbar. He was one of the greatest emperors that India ever had. He was a great defender of reason, of intellectual scrutiny of every subject, but he was formally illiterate. He was on the run because his father, Emperor Humayun, was being hounded out of India by Sher Shah. He didn't acquire the letters. He resented it, but he insisted on things being read to him. He wanted to chat with people like Abul Fazl, one of the learned members of his court. Akbar achieved tremendous wisdom and knowledge and acquired a level of intellectual judgment which is breathtaking.

One must emphasize that while literacy is not all there is in education, it is in fact extremely important. It's a great opportunity. It's quite remarkable that even sometimes you can quote great people in India, including Mahatma Gandhi, being quite skeptical of "mere literacy." I think that's a mistake. Literacy makes a big difference. We talked earlier about Tagore and Gandhi. It's interesting that when Tagore goes to Russia in the 1920s, the thing that he separates out for special praise is the expansion of education across the territory in the Soviet Union, including Soviet Asia. The thing that he was critical of, in an interview that he gave to Pravda that was not published in Pravda but appeared in The Manchester Guardian, was the lack of democracy. It was quite interesting that in terms of getting his perspectives right, he did emphasize what personally I believe to be the important part of the Soviet achievement, namely its education. At the same time he was already very aware of the penalty that the Soviet Union was paying and would pay more in the future by not having a democracy and not allowing criticism and open public discussion. Since you began by asking a question about Gandhi and Tagore, if I may come back to that to say that to me there was a great sense of depth and wisdom in Tagore's attitude to these issues. He was really at his best in his writing and art. But also when it comes to international affairs, the penetrating nature of his analysis, whether it was the Soviet Union or China or Japan, there's a lot of learning, even in today's world, from Tagore's ideas.

You are a strong advocate for women's rights. You talk about the centrality of gender equity and link it to economic freedom.

The differential treatment of women in education, health care and sometimes nutrition are striking facts which one can see in many parts of the world today. It exists in many countries in Asia and Africa. There is a reason to rebel against it, just on grounds of equity even if it didn't have any other bad effects. But it soon also becomes clear that the penalty of gender inequality is paid not only by women but also by men. The neglect of women's

education tends to reduce the voice of women in family affairs and fertility decisions. That has the effect of increasing child mortality rates. There's a strong connection between reduction of child mortality and women's literacy and women's empowerment. There's also a clear and strong connection between fertility reduction and women's literacy and empowerment, including women's gainful employment. If you look at the more than three hundred districts of India, the strongest influence in explaining fertility variations are women's literacy and gainful economic employment. No matter what the effect of the rapid rise of the population may be in the long run for the environment, the immediate impact of constant bearing and rearing of children is on the lives, liberty and freedom of young women. Anything that increases the voice of young women tends therefore to reduce the fertility rate. There is another connection which I've been working on recently. It turns out that women's maternal undernourishment often leads to fetal distress. One effect of that is seen not just among the children when they're born, neonatal or older children, but decades later in the lives of people in their being more vulnerable to cardiovascular diseases. This is a connection which has emerged from the works of a number of English doctors in particular, led by Professor D.J.P. Barker of Southampton University. It's not surprising that for example the South Asian population, where maternal undernourishment is high, where women's neglect of health care and nutrition is also quite high, also happens to have the highest case of cardiovascular diseases, even after correcting for the economic and social factors that might influence it. This shows that the reach of gender inequality often penalizes men, because it's men who are much more vulnerable to cardiovascular diseases than women are. I don't believe in God, but if I did, one could see almost a divine retribution that you neglect women and they ultimately hit back on men in terms of contributing to greater cardio vascular ailments in late life. The recognition that the interests of men and women have great interdependence is very strong, both on grounds that it's unjust and inequitous for women to have a worse deal than men as well as in terms of the interconnection that ultimately affects the interests of men, too, as well as children immediately. That seems to me to be kind of an inescapable thought that one has to be interested in the issue of gender and gender equality. I don't really expect any credit for going in that direction. It's the only natural direction to go in.

What are your views on globalization? Advocates hail it as a great economic force that is going to liberate the world's poor. Critics see the rise of transnational corporations with concentrated power as a new form of colonization.

Globalization is a complex issue, partly because economic globalization is only one part of it. Globalization is greater global closeness, and that is cultural, social, political, as well as economic. I think the whole progress over the last two or three millennia had been entirely dependent on ideas and techniques and commodities and people moving from one part of the world to another. It seems difficult to take an anti-globalization view if one takes globalization properly in its full sense. I'm beginning in this high ground because it's also hard to be opposed to just economic globalization while you want globalization in everything else. David Hume noted in the 1770s, shortly before he died, in one of his essays, that if you have global commerce and come in touch with people whom you did not know before, you cannot but take an interest in their lives. They become real as part of your life in a way that in the absence of commerce they wouldn't be. So commerce in that early globalization would have the effect of making people take an interest in each other. It is also true that there would be no ability to have such a well-organized protest movement against globalization in the absence of globalization. The anti-globalization movement is one of the biggest globalized events of the contemporary world, people coming from everywhere, Australia, Indonesia, India, Poland, South Africa, to demonstrate in Seattle or Quebec. What could be more global than that? We are beginning to have a world community, and economic contact has partly contributed to that. It's also the case that economic opportunity opened up by economic contact has helped to a great extent to reduce poverty in many parts of the world. East Asia's success is in that direction. Going further back, the escape from poverty in Western Europe and Europe generally and North America is also connected with the use of economic opportunity that international trade helped.

But the American experience was built on genocide and expropriation of an entire continent, and Europe's wealth was directly connected to its colonial empires.

I think one has to separate out the different factors in it. It is certainly correct to say that America was very lucky to get a large amount of land, and the native Indians were extremely unlucky to have white men coming over here. But to say that the whole of the American prosperity was based on exploiting the indigenous population of America would be a mistake. To a great extent it was based on productivity of modern industries which Karl Marx in particular saw very clearly. When Karl Marx discusses in Kapital volume 1 what is "the one great event of the contemporary world," he separates out the American Civil War. What is the Civil War about? Replacing a non-trade-based relationship, namely slavery, by a wage-based relationship, which in other contexts Marx described as wage slavery. But nevertheless, in this context it is the one great thing happening in the world. He doesn't talk about 1848 and the Paris Commune as "the one great event." Marx as a realist saw that industrial capitalism was producing a level of wealth that was never achievable earlier and which could be the basis of a prosperous society. In this respect, Marx was a great follower of Adam Smith and David Ricardo in seeing that a market economy had enormous opportunity of expanding wealth across the nation and making people escape poverty. You needed to go "beyond it," but you needed it first. Similarly, there might have been genocide, but the history of the world is full of mixed stories. To say that it was the genocide that made Europe or America rich is a mistake.

In Europe it was the direct expropriation from the colonies. Bengal itself was stripped of its wealth, pauperized. Bengal got a very raw deal. Its development was put back. There's no question that Bengal suffered enormously from colonialism. But to say that Europe would not have had any industrial revolution but for the colonies is a mistake. I don't think that's the analysis you get. Ultimately, imperialism made even the British working classes suffer. This is a point which the British working classes found quite difficult to swallow, but they did, actually. The labor movement did emphasize that ultimately it's not that poverty is removed in Britain by exploiting the colonies. To say that the whole of the industrial experience of Europe and America just shows the rewards of exploiting the Third World is a gross simplification. Look at some other country, like Japan. It became an imperialist country in many ways, but that was much after they had already made big progress. I don't think Japan's wealth was based on exploiting China. Japan's wealth was based on their expansion in international trade. One has to be realistic. One's concern for equity and justice in the world must not carry one into the alien territory of unreasoned belief. That's very important.

To continue to engage in some of the points you raised, I'm in favor of globalization in general. I'm generally in favor even of economic globalization. Having said that, economic globalization doesn't always work and does not immediately work in the interest of all. There are sufferers. It's a matter of statesmanship to see how to deal with those who are displaced from jobs or who may work in very unsavory conditions. They may still prefer them to starving and not having a job, but nevertheless there is a question to be asked. Do we need these sweatshops? Why is it not possible to have the productivity of modern industries without these extraordinarily unfavorable circumstances?

What we have to look at is not a kind of wholesale denunciation of globalization, which gets us nowhere. This is like King Kanute trying to discipline the sea. Quite aside from the importance of globalization, it's inescapable. It's a question of how to make it more humane and just. That requires paying attention to the underdog. I believe that virtually all the problems in the world come from inequality of one kind or another. And what we're looking at is inequality. Globalization tends to benefit most people, but not all. Some benefit greatly and others benefit relatively little. We have to see how we can make it more equitable. That requires a great deal of attention being paid to particularly labor conditions. It requires much more activism by the labor movement. It requires more reviving of cooperative attempts, and they have been successful in some countries. Bangladesh is a good example. We need more of that. It requires revision of the financial architecture of the world, because as it emerged in the 1940s it reflected a reality which is no longer true. The Bretton Woods conference in 1944 set up the IMF, the World Bank and GATT. The WTO was the one late addition to that, but basically it's the same architecture. In the 1940s, half of the world was colonial territory. Most people were living in colonies. Democracy in the Third World was unknown. Human rights wasn't an active issue. The prospect of rapid economic growth for any poor country, especially in Asia, was unknown. The fact that people could agitate for their rights and defend the environment and demand global equity was unknown. One of the great realities today is the positive influence of the anti-globalization movement. Even though I'm pro-globalization, I have to say thank God for the anti-globalization movement. They're putting important issues on the agenda. The themes that the anti-globalization protesters bring to the discussion are of extraordinary importance. However, the theses that they often bring to it, sometimes in the form of slogans, are often over-simple. But just because the theses may be easy to reject and a skillful economist or even a skillful financial journalist will be able to shoot it down, does not mean that the process itself is valueless. The process is basically putting certain items on the agenda. My attitude to globalization is that one has to recognize first of all its inevitability, secondly its importance as an intellectual, social, political force, even as an economic force, but recognize that it can be very unjust and unfair and unequal, but these are matters under our control. It's not that we don't need the market economy. We need it. I would certainly reject the view that we don't need the market economy, but I would equally strongly reject the view that the market economy would have priority or dominance over other institutions. We need democracy. We need political activism. We need social movements of various kinds. We need the NGOs. I'm proud of the fact that I'm an honorary president of OXFAM, which has done a lot of good in the world. We live in a world where there is a need for pluralistic institutions and for recognizing different types of freedom, economic, social, cultural and political, which are interrelated. It's that complexity which would seem to me quite central which cannot be captured either being anti-globalization or being pro-globalization without qualification.

You mentioned the need for statesmanship. One study indicates that of the one hundred largest economies in the world, fifty-one are corporations. States seem to be receding in terms of power.

States have sometimes overextended in the wrong direction. So some of the recessions I don't mind at all. When I wrote my first book on India in 1995, with Jean Drèze, called *India: Economic Development and Social Opportunity*, I was very struck by the fact that the government was overactive in controlling industry and making it almost impossible to get a licence to introduce and expand competition. It provided great protection to domestic bourgeoisie which could make a good deal of profit in the absence of international competition and make the life of the small entrepreneurs particularly difficult through bureaucratic red tape. At the same time the government was doing very little on basic education, basic health care, land reform, expansion of microcredit movement and so on. So I don't think the attitude is one of wanting more government or less government. It's a question of seeing what the proper role of government is. I think the proper role involves many supportive things, improved expansion of social opportunity, especially through education and health care. It also requires making sure that the benefits of the market expansion are more widely shared. But if you're illiterate, if you haven't gone to school, if you don't have any credit facilities, if you have no collateral to borrow money on and there are no microcredit movements, you don't own land because there hasn't been any land reform, you can't even enter the market economy. One of the criticisms I would like to make of the pro-market people is that they don't take the market sufficiently seriously, because if they did they would make it easier for people to enter the market. For that you often need state action, through land reform, microcredit, education and basic health care. These are very important areas for state action which make the market economy itself more efficient

and more equitable. So I would tend to think of the problem in terms of what the complementarities are between the different institutions and not judge it in terms of whether, taking everything into account, the state is increasing or coming down.

The issue of corporations is a different issue. That is a matter of competition, a matter on which one could be a very pro-market person and be very anti-corporation. Indeed, trust-busting is a very old capitalist virtue, that is, a virtue of a pro-market economy where you want competitive capitalism. A kind of Smithian pro-marketing person would want some restraint on the corporations. That's a different question. One has to separate out the question of inequality within the market economy in the form of corporations at one level, which is the highest level, and inequality at the other end, whereby a lot of people are prevented from entering the market because they can't borrow money, they are not educated enough and skilled enough to enter the modern economy. That is one kind of issue. There is the other issue of the state and the market. The market is after all only an instrument. To be anti-market, pro-market, anti-state, pro-state, I think that's not the right way of thinking about the issue. One has to take it in terms of what it does to the lives and freedom of the human beings that make up society. We need different institutions, not choose "between" them to get exclusiveness.

What drives you?

I wish I knew. We live for a short stretch of time in a world we share with others. Virtually everything we do is dependent on others, from the arts and culture to farmers who grow the food we eat. We live in an interdependent world. Given that fact, the idea that somehow a person could feel very comfortable being enormously ahead of others seems to me to be ultimately a mistake. Quite a lot of the differences that make us rich and poor are matters just of luck. To somehow revel in one's privilege would be a mistake. An even bigger mistake would be trying to convert that into a theory that the rich are so much more productive than the others. That's at the one end. But the other end, if one thinks about the people who live in a world in which they need not be hungry, in which they need not die without medical care, in which they need not be illiterate, they need not feel hopeless and miserable so much of the time, and yet they are, that seems to be scandalous. But this is not just a matter of poverty. There are some people who say that they're concerned only with poverty but not inequality. I find that very difficult for the reason that Adam Smith discussed a long time ago in The Wealth of Nations. He pointed out that the same thing that everyone likes doing, talking with others, appearing in public without shame, taking part in the life of the community, if you live in a community that's relatively rich, you need a much bigger income to be able to do these elementary things. If you are a villager in rural Bangladesh or Uganda, you might be able to meet with people very easily even if you're not schooled or if you don't have a car or if you're not clothed in a way that's regarded as obligatory in some cultures. But in, say, America, if you don't have a television at home your kids might find it hard to converse with each other in school. The income that we need in order not to be poor is much higher in a richer society. So that relative poverty, which is really a matter of inequality, in terms of income can be the cause of absolute poverty, the inability to do the basic things which Adam Smith noted we all like doing. The idea that we can be interested only in poverty but not in inequality I don't think is a sustainable thought. A lot of poverty is in fact inequality because of this connection between income and capability. The same capability to take part in the life of the community requires a much bigger basket of commodities and therefore a much bigger income in a rich society. So you have to be interested in inequality. And since we live in a global village, events in different parts of the world influence each other. The Internet begins to penetrate in my country. Indians begin to find out how other people live in the rest of the world. Given these circumstances, the issues of inequality and the issue of poverty are not separable even globally. They're very closely linked, both in terms of the need to ask the moral question, Is it right that I should enjoy my privileges, and not feel I owe anything to others? As well as the other level, Do I have a right to be content living in a world with so much poverty and inequality? Both these questions motivate us to take these issues to be central to human living. Ultimately, the old Socratic question, How should I live? has to include a very strong component of awareness and response to inequality.

Transcript of "An Interview with N. R. Narayana Murthy"

Nayan Chanda: We have with us in the studio Mr. Narayana Murthy. He is the founder and mentor-in-chief of Infosys, India's second largest software company. Infosys was founded in 1981 with capital of $250, and today market capitalization is about $22 billion. Mr. Murthy, welcome.

N.R. Narayana Murthy: Thank you very much.

Chanda: It is a great pleasure to have you on our campus and to answer some questions about the developments in India. First of all, Infosys has become an iconic institution in India. In the course of a very short time, it has risen to the top. How do you account for this meteoric rise of Infosys in the context of India?

Murthy: Well, you're right. We celebrate our 25th year this year. On 2 July of 2006, we will have completed 25 years. First of all, I must say that God has been very kind to us because, as Louis Pasteur once said, that when God decides to announce his presence, he comes in the form of chance. Having accepted that, let me say this, right from day one, when we founded the company, when we sat for four hours to discuss what we should seek in this journey, we were all unanimous that we would seek respect. We would seek respect from customers, from our employees, from our investors, from our lender departments, from the government and from the society. And we said, if we seek respect from each of these stakeholders, we will do the right thing for them. And if we do the right thing for them, then everything will fall into place. So I'm happy that the company has not swerved from that part of taking respect right from day one to now. And that is perhaps the reason we have had what little success we have had so far.

Chanda: But in 1981, India was not at all friendly to enterprise, from the type of place you set up. From what I recall, you had difficulty getting your first computer, getting your first telephone line. And how do you work on those obstacles?

Murthy: Well, you know that entrepreneurship is all about courage, it's all about thinking about a powerful idea and then converting it into wealth. When we founded the company in 1981, we had tremendous friction to business. But there were two important paradigm changes taking place at that time. First, of course, there was the PC revolution. Microsoft had started in 1976. Many computers and super min-computers had come into existence. Borland was about to announce the first 100,000 software—

In other words, we realized that the power of software would be unleashed in the years to come, and number two, that software would become more and more demanded because the cost was going down and people were realizing the power of software. That was the first paradigm. The second is the paradigm of globalization. I define globalization as sourcing capital from where it cheapest, sourcing talent from where it is best available, producing where it is most cost effective and selling where the markets are without being constrained by national boundaries.

Now, this we realized was a unique opportunity for countries like India, to release the power of the availability of English-speaking technical talent to produce powerful software for the global market. And thanks to these two paradigms, I think, Infosys took off, though the first ten years we had tremendous friction to business. And thanks to the economic reforms of 1991, Infosys took off from 1992. Just to give you a data point, between 1981 to 1992, we grew our revenues from $130,000 in 1981–1982 to about $1.6 million in 1992, but from between 1992 and 2006 we went from $1.6 million to $2.15 billion. In other words, we grew by a factor of approximately 1300 times in the second half, that is the last twelve, thirteen years, as against 10 times in the first ten years.

Chanda: In fact, you mentioned the 1991 reform. The 1991 crisis in March 1991, India was left with a total foreign reserve of $1.2 billion, which is worth two weeks of imports, and that's exactly the amount you're worth today, yourself, according to Forbes magazine. And so it shows the kind of journey that you have made in these 25 years. And the question is, apart from the availability of Indian technical talent, apart from the existence of markets, you needed something to link the markets to the Indian technical talent. And from what I recall, you initially took your engineers to the client site as well as what is called body shopping. And that kind of model changed with the availability of satellites and then fiber optics, am I right?

Murthy: You're right, because in the beginning, we had no access to data communication lines. It took us a year for us to get a telephone line. It would take us two years, to get a license from Delhi to import a computer worth $50,000. In other words, everything was stacked against us. So we realized that if we want to have a growing business, then it was best if the talented teams of Infosys went to customers' offices, to give the software to them, install it in support of them, rather than doing it from India.

But you know, I must say all of that changed in a dramatic manner with the economic reforms of 1991, because Dr. Manmohan Singh, at that time the finance minister and now the prime minister, he did a few things that were remarkable: One, he removed licensing, which meant that we did not have to go to Delhi and wait in the corridors to import anything. Today, government is not a bottleneck. It's just we have to finalize what we want to buy and we buy quickly. Second, we introduced current accounts convertibility. Until 1991, we couldn't set up offices abroad, we couldn't travel easily, we could not hire consultants and quality brand equity from abroad, etc. All of that got changed when he introduced current accounts convertibility. Third, he abolished the office of the comptroller of capital issue. This was an officer who determined at what price we would have our IT loan. And this officer had no idea of capital markets. And he would rarely allow you to list your stock at anything better than your par value, which meant there was very little incentive for entrepreneurs to list because then you would use so much of equity and raise so little funds. On the other hand, Dr. Manmohan Singh said, "Look you can decide the price at which you want to have your IT loan in consolidation with your investment banker, then officers realized we would get the fair price from the market—the market's world was going to be the determinant—and that was another important thing he did to encourage entrepreneurship.

And finally, he allowed 100 percent equity for multinationals. IBM and Coca-Cola had walked out of India in 1977, and when he allowed these companies to have 100 percent equity, then what happened was, we had tremendous competition in India, not so much for market, because the market hardly existed, but for talent, and because there was tremendous competition for talent in India and these multinationals had great names, prestige, a lot of money, etc., we had to fight for talent in competition against these great multinationals, and that's exactly what made India's companies stronger because that's when we realized that we had to create a good infrastructure, we had to give good salaries, we had to give a good work environment, if we want to attract good people. So I would say that these are the four things that India did.

Chanda: Since India has now become the leader of outsourcing in the world, what are the challenges you see for Infosys in maintaining its tradition?

Murthy: Well, there are many, many challenges. First, we have to move up the value chain, which means you have to enhance per capita productivity. I always say that just as the per capita GDP is a good index of the development of a nation, per capita productivity is a good index of the growth of a corporation. So we had to enhance per capita productivity. To do that we had to become more and more relevant to our customers' businesses and we had to have greater and greater impact on that—which means we have to learn to provide more

and more end-to-end business solutions, innovative technology. In other words, we have to do more consulting, we have to do more business assistance integration, etc. Second, we have to handle scalability, scalability in terms of the number of customers, scalability in terms of the number of employees, scalability in terms of physical infrastructure, technological infrastructure, etc., etc. For example, today, we have about 52,000 employees. We have about 55,000 known networks. We have to train about 20,000 people in a year. You know, we have recruited 300 students, people from the colleges in the US.

Now we are taking them for a nine-month long training program. It's the first time in the history of India that a set of 300 employees who will work in the US are going to India for a training of nine months. So scalability is another challenge. Third, I think the ability to work in multicultural teams is another important challenge. Fourth, we need to create better infrastructure in the cities, because that's where all our operations are. Fifth, I'd say we have to enhance our brand equity, because we have to get to more and more get hundreds-of millions-dollar projects, maybe a billion dollars or more for outsourcing projects, etc.

Chanda: Because so far, India—Infosys is somewhat apart—but a lot of other IT companies are using basically cheap labor—educated cheap labor—to leverage India. Is that sustainable?

Murthy: No, I have a slightly different view on that. At that end of the day, business is all about bringing better value to money. As economists say, price is what you pay and value is what you get. So if for a dollar, we can give our customers better value for money. One way of looking at it is better value for money and another way of looking at it is cheaper. So be it. As long as we are able to satisfy our customers' needs better and better and better, it doesn't matter. So, I don't look at it as providing things cheap, I look at as providing better value for money.

Chanda: No, what I meant was that, that cheap labor, other countries could offer as well.

Murthy: No, I think India has some unique advantages. We are a nation of a billion people. We produce anywhere from 3.5 to 4 million graduates every year. We produce 450,000 engineers. We produce about 300,000 master's IT and applications graduates. And all of that is getting enhanced year after year after year. And at the end of the day, let's remember, if we have to solve the problem of poverty in India, the only way we can do that is by creating more and more jobs. And if you want to create more and more jobs with good disposable income, then you need to expand in sectors like this.

Chanda: But there again the population of India, especially in the villages, and the education is still very poor, still 40 percent illiterate. So what do you see looking down from your own IT domain, for India as a whole, what do you think should be India's strategy?

Murthy: Well, you know, I believe we have to do more of many things. We have to expand the software industry because there is considerable opportunity in the global market. Second, we have to focus on low-tech manufacturing because that's how we can create a large number of jobs for the masses of Indians who are semi-literate or in some cases illiterate. So, we have to focus on low-tech manufacturing and create anywhere from 10 to 15 million jobs per year for the next 10 years. And that cannot be done by the software industry alone, it has to be done, reinforced by focusing on low-tech manufacturing.

Chanda: Your company has moved to China. What is happening with China, what are you doing there?

Murthy: Well, you know, if you want to be a high-aspiration corporation today, if you want to be in the top five in any sector of the economy—for example in the software services, we are in the top five in the world, you have to have a presence in China for multiple reasons. One, China is a fast growing market. It is growing at 10 percent or so. There are lots of things happening out there. So, we have to have presence there. Second, like India, China too has a large population. There is good technical talent out there. And as we keep growing in revenue, we have to leverage the talent in China. Third, there is a large Chinese diaspora in East Asia and Southeast Asia etc. And Japan is very near. So you can service Japanese clients from the northern part of China. So looking at all these things, I think China is an important piece in the jigsaw puzzle.

Chanda: The rapid growth of outsourcing is very good news for a country like India or China. But one sees an increasing concern in Europe and the US about white-collar jobs leaving the country and going outside. Do you see that this could be a drag on your business?

Murthy: You know my view is that people in glass houses should not throw stones at others. After all, what we are doing is what we were preached to do by the rest of the nations. My European friends, my American friends, told me umpteen times in the 1980s how India should become more and more open, how India should open up its borders, how India should reduce its tariffs, how India should allow competition from multinationals, etc. I agreed with all of them. All we've been doing is implementing the ideas that they have been propounding. So, at this point in time, just because the shoe pinches a little bit, I don't think we should go back on those principles.

So my view is, at the end of that day is that we're making corporations in the US, in Europe, in Japan, in other countries, more competitive, not just for selling in their own countries, but in other countries. So just as we accepted liberalization, just as we opened up our borders, I believe that western nations, too, would gain from such open access.

Chanda: Globalization has become a very contested word. A lot of people are turning anti-globalization. To me, India seems to be one of the more pro-globalization countries, is that right?

Murthy: I would think so. Because, remember that we have a coalition government, which is supported by communists. Now in spite of that, our government has made many, many moves forward. We increased foreign holding in the banking sector to 74 percent. We introduced foreign participation in the

weakest sector. We have liberalized in the civil aviation sector. So in many areas we have brought in liberalization. So when you do it in the context of the coalition government, supported by the communists, I think it's not a bad record.

Chanda: And finally, the outsourcing which started as essentially software services or back-office work sent outside of western Europe and America, is now becoming a global model. I just read an article in "Foreign Affairs" by the former CEO of IBM, he talks about MNCs being replaced by new model which he calls globally integrated enterprises. And is this a trend that you see from your perspective going to touch other sectors of industry?

Murthy: Absolutely, absolutely. For example, I think since Excel, we have a program called M3 +, Infosys phase two. And what they're trying to do is bring the power of globalization, that globally integrated model into areas outside just software—accounting, systems integration, equity research, customer service. In all these areas, we are bringing the power of globalization. We are liberating the strength of talent in India. Now, for example, a friend of mine is starting an enterprise to maintain aircraft. He thinks that India will be the right place to maintain aircraft, where people can get the best value for money. And aircraft from all over, Asia, perhaps from some parts of Europe and the US, too, could be maintained from India or from some other part of the world too—but focused from the talent available from India.

Chanda: And that's one of the things that I think Infosys has done, not just write codes, but for business purposes, but many other industrial operations, they are coming to you for solutions to their problems.

Murthy: Sure.

Chanda: So your employees include not just code writers, but experts from other fields.

Murthy: Oh yes. Because if we want to become more and more relevant to customers' businesses, if we want to have greater and greater impact in the areas of business relevance, then we have to be the main expert. We have to understand the business of the customer. So our focus has been to enhance the market readiness of our people in the domain knowledge. In fact, we have several initiatives in this area. We encourage our people to get certified by industry associations at different levels. For example, we have retail 101, retail 201, retail 301, banking 101, etc., etc. We do it so our people, over a period of time, have become more and more business domain knowledge-ready.

Chanda: You have become more and more of a consulting company—

Murthy: Absolutely.

Chanda: —than just a software provider. Well, Mr. Murthy, thank you so much for your time.

Murthy: Thank you, thank you.

From *YaleGlobal Online*, June 5, 2006. Reprinted by permission from YaleGroup Online, (http://yaleglobal.yale.edu) a publication of the Yale Center for the Study of Globalization. Copyright © 2007 Yale Center for the Study of Globalization.

Article 20

260 Million Indians Still Below Poverty Line

Aarti Dhar

A large proportion—26 per cent or about 260 million (193 million in rural areas and 67 million in urban areas)—of Indians are still below the poverty line, according to India's first Social Development Report released in New Delhi on Friday.

The spatial map and social base of poverty have significantly changed over time and poverty is increasingly concentrated in a few geographical locations and among specific social groups. Among the States, Punjab has the lowest incidence of poverty (6.16 per cent as per 1999–2000 figures), followed by Haryana with 8.74 per cent, and Kerala with 12.72 per cent. Orissa has the highest number of people living below the poverty line (47.15 per cent), followed by Bihar (42.60 per cent), and Assam (36.09 per cent). While poverty levels have shown a decline, there is huge disparity among the social classes with the percentage of the poor among the Scheduled Tribes being 43.8 per cent, Scheduled Castes 36.2 per cent, and Other Backward Classes 21 per cent.

Bihar, Uttar Pradesh, Madhya Pradesh, and Rajasthan, which account for 45 per cent of the country's population, also account for two-thirds of the infant mortality rate in the country (26 per cent in Uttar Pradesh alone), and two-thirds of the maternal mortality rate. Less than 25 per cent of the children in these States are immunised.

Rural Kerala tops the States in social indicators followed by Himachal Pradesh. Punjab, Jammu and Kashmir, and Haryana figure among the best-performing States while Bihar, Jharkhand, Uttar Pradesh, Madhya Pradesh, and Orissa are at the bottom. The 21 indicators taken into account while grading the States included demography, health care, education, unemployment, poverty and social deprivation.

In the urban scenario, Kerala has been pushed to the third rank. Himachal Pradesh tops the list followed by Punjab, Karnataka, and Assam. At the bottom are Bihar, Uttar Pradesh, Jharkhand, Chhattisgarh, and Orissa.

The report, brought out by the Council for Social Development and Oxford, says Kerala has the lowest infant mortality rate of 11 deaths per 1,000 births, followed by Mizoram and Goa at 16. Orissa has the highest IMR of 83 deaths per 1,000 births, Madhya Pradesh has 82, and Uttar Pradesh 76.

Among the disadvantaged classes, the IMR is higher among Scheduled Castes (83). It is 85.2 among the Scheduled Tribes, and 76 among the other disadvantaged classes compared to the rate of 61.8 among the rest of the population. A similar trend is witnessed with regard to the mortality rate of children under five, underweight children, children and women with anaemia.

The report brings out the need to harness the nation's social energy to ensure a fair and equitable process of development, identifies key concerns, and proposes possible intervention measures.

Kerala has the highest literacy rate of 90.92 per cent, followed by Mizoram at 88.49 per cent, and Goa at 82.32 per cent. Bihar has the lowest literacy rate of 47.53 per cent, Jharkhand 54.13 per cent, and Jammu and Kashmir 54.46. However, Mizoram tops the States with the lowest gender gap in literacy with a difference of only 4.56 percentage points.

In Meghalaya it is 5.73 percentage points and 6.34 percentage points in Kerala. Rajasthan has shown a large gap in gender literacy of 32.12 percentage points, Jharkhand 28.56 percentage points, and U.P. 27.25 percentage points.

Ironic as it may sound, Punjab ranks high in the urban social indicators but has the lowest child sex ratio of 798 girls to 1,000 boys. Haryana is slightly better at 819 and Gujarat is at 883. The traditional societies, including tribal communities, have an impressive sex ratio of 975 girls to 1,000 boys (Chhattisgarh), 973 (Meghalaya), and 966 in Tripura—much higher than the national figure of 906.

He Lives To See Justice Done

All Bhaiyalal Bhotmange, the Dalit whose family members were killed by some of his fellow villagers in on September 29, wants is the culprits brought to book.

MEENA MENON

Police pickets are everywhere on the approach road to Khairlanji in Maharashtra's Bhandara district. In the village itself, the ramshackle house where Bhaiyalal Bhotmange and his family once lived has been sealed off. Armed police keep watch over it.

Bhaiyalal's thatched hut looks like a loose collection of bricks piled one on top of the other. The black door is locked now. All this security means nothing to 48-year-old Bhaiyalal, a partial witness to his entire family being bludgeoned to death by a mob from his village on September 29. The bodies were loaded on to a bullock cart and dumped in a canal near the village. While the body of his 17-year-old daughter Priyanka was found the next day, the bodies of his wife and two sons were found on October 1. The incident sparked violent protests in various parts of the State and the Government finally handed over the probe to the Central Bureau of Investigation.

Bhaiyalal, the lone survivor, is a tired man. He now lives with relatives in Varti near Bhandara. Hounded by the media and politicians, he finally took refuge at the Bhandara civil hospital last Sunday where he was admitted for a couple of days. Doctors say he could be suffering from shock and trauma. Various well-meaning activists almost always surround him. "I am not taking any money from the government and I don't want the job it is offering me," Bhaiyalal told The Hindu after being discharged from hospital. "What I want is quick justice. I want the accused to be hanged. Will the lakhs of rupees I am being offered bring back the dead?" Now it had all become political, he admitted.

On September 29, returning home from a day's work in his field, Bhaiyalal saw a mob going towards his house. He saw people dragging out his wife, Surekha, 40, two sons, Sudhir, 21, who is partially blind, and Roshan, 19, and daughter Priyanka. Terrified, he ran away and tried to get help. He has named several people he saw that evening. The mob allegedly stripped the victims, and assaulted them with axes and other weapons and killed them. The post-mortem report says they died of head injuries. While 44 people, including two women, have been arrested, Bhaiyalal feels some of the main people are still at large. Seeing the condition of the bodies of the women, Bhaiyalal suspected rape. Unhappy with the first post-mortem, which did not follow due procedure, he asked for a second one. This too did not establish sexual assault.

History of Discrimination

There is a history of discrimination in this village. About 100 km from Nagpur, Khairlanji has about 125 houses; a majority of the residents belong to the OBCs, mostly from the Kunbi and Teli communities. One of the three Dalit families in the village, the Bhotmanges, came to this village from Ambagad in the Tumsar taluka about 16–17 years ago. Bhaiyalal does not have a legitimate housing plot and lives in a single room hut. There is no electricity either. He owned five acres of land. A dispute arose over it when villagers wanted a road to go through it. "I agreed to this and the problem was solved two years ago," he said. However, he said an incident on September 3 when a relative of his wife, Siddharth Gajbhiye, was attacked created tension. Gajbhiye, a police patil from nearby Dhusala, was a frequent visitor to the Bhotmange house and a well-wisher. Bhaiyalal said Siddharth was helping him and other villagers resented this.

Surekha and Priyanka were witnesses to this attack and on September 29, 12 persons from Khairlanji were arrested in connection with the case. As only a case of assault was registered, they got out on bail. That evening, they went looking for Gajbhiye. As he was away, they turned their anger on the Bhotmange family, according to the police.

The villagers have always resented the fact that the Bhotmange children were educated. Priyanka was on the merit list in the tenth standard examinations two years ago. "She had dreams of joining the police," said Bhaiyalal. Roshan was also studying in college. Villagers of Khairlanji are tight-lipped.

Sarpanch Upasrao Khandate claimed he was not there on September 29. However, he said there was a fight between Gajbhiye and another villager, Binjewar, on September 3 as a result of which Gajbhiye was admitted to hospital. He claims he was not aware of the attack on the Bhotmange family till late in the night when he called the police.

Panchshila Shende, an anganwadi worker, says she was at home that day and did hear shouts but never thought things could be so bad. She heard people running around but heard no women shouting. "Maybe their mouths were closed," she said. She said Bhaiyalal worked hard and his children were studious. "He was a simple man and that's why they did this to him," she said. Now she and her brother, Durvas Khobragade, are afraid. "Yes, there is so much police but they are not here for our security."

Horrifying as the events of September 29 were, what followed was even worse. The lack of response from the police who were informed when the massacre was taking place and the inept handling of the post-mortem of the four persons who were killed have resulted in four policemen and a medical officer being suspended, and another being dismissed.

Activists are now demanding that criminal proceedings be initiated against them for negligence of duty.

On India's Farms, a Plague of Suicide

SOMINI SENGUPTA

Here in the center of India, on a gray Wednesday morning, a cotton farmer swallowed a bottle of pesticide and fell dead at the threshold of his small mud house.

The farmer, Anil Kondba Shende, 31, left behind a wife and two small sons, debts that his family knew about only vaguely and a soggy, ruined 3.5-acre patch of cotton plants that had been his only source of income.

Whether it was debt, shame or some other privation that drove Mr. Shende to kill himself rests with him alone. But his death was by no means an isolated one, and in it lay an alarming reminder of the crisis facing the Indian farmer.

Across the country in desperate pockets like this one, 17,107 farmers committed suicide in 2003, the most recent year for which government figures are available. Anecdotal reports suggest that the high rates are continuing.

Though the crisis has been building for years, it presents an increasingly thorny political challenge for Prime Minister Manmohan Singh. High suicide rates and rural despair helped topple the previous government two years ago and put Mr. Singh in power.

Changes brought on by 15 years of economic reforms have opened Indian farmers to global competition and given them access to expensive and promising biotechnology, but not necessarily opened the way to higher prices, bank loans, irrigation or insurance against pests and rain.

Mr. Singh's government, which has otherwise emerged as a strong ally of America, has become one of the loudest critics in the developing world of Washington's $18 billion a year in subsidies to its own farmers, which have helped drive down the price of cotton for farmers like Mr. Shende.

At the same time, frustration is building in India with American multinational companies peddling costly, genetically modified seeds. They have made deep inroads in rural India—a vast and alluring market—bringing new opportunities but also new risks as Indian farmers pile up debt.

In this central Indian cotton-growing area, known as Vidarbha, the unofficial death toll from suicides, compiled by a local advocacy group and impossible to verify, was 767 in a 14-month period that ended in late August.

"The suicides are an extreme manifestation of some deep-seated problems which are now plaguing our agriculture," said M. S. Swaminathan, the geneticist who was the scientific leader of India's Green Revolution 40 years ago and is now chairman of the National Commission on Farmers. "They are climatic. They are economic. They are social."

India's economy may be soaring, but agriculture remains its Achilles' heel, the source of livelihood for hundreds of millions of people but a fraction of the nation's total economy and a symbol of its abiding difficulties.

In what some see as an ominous trend, food production, once India's great pride, has failed to keep pace with the nation's population growth in the last decade.

The cries of Indian farmers—or what Prime Minister Singh recently described as their "acute distress"—can hardly be neglected by the leaders of a country where two-thirds of people still live in the countryside.

Mr. Singh's government has responded to the current crisis by promptly expanding rural credit and promising investments in rural infrastructure. It has also offered several quick fixes, including a $156 million package to rescue "suicide prone" districts across the country and a promise to expand rural credit, waive interest on existing bank loans and curb usurious informal moneylenders.

But pressure is building to do more. Many, including Mr. Swaminathan, the agricultural scientist, would like to see the government help farmers survive during crop failures or years of low world prices.

Subsidies, once a linchpin of Indian economic policy, have dried up for virtually everyone but the producers of staple food grains. Indian farmers now must compete or go under. To compete, many have turned to high-cost seeds, fertilizers and pesticides, which now line the shelves of even the tiniest village shops.

Monsanto, for instance, invented the genetically modified seeds that Mr. Shende planted, known as Bt cotton, which are resistant to bollworm infestation, the cotton farmer's prime enemy. It says the seeds can reduce the use of pesticides by 25 percent.

The company has more than doubled its sales of Bt cotton here in the last year, but the expansion has been contentious. This year, a legal challenge from the government of the state of Andhra Pradesh forced Monsanto to slash the royalty it collected from the sale of its patented seeds in India. The company has appealed to the Indian Supreme Court.

The modified seeds can cost nearly twice as much as ordinary ones, and they have nudged many farmers toward taking on ever larger loans, often from moneylenders charging exorbitant interest rates.

Virtually every cotton farmer in these parts, for instance, needs the assistance of someone like Chandrakant Agarwal, a veteran moneylender who charges 5 percent interest a month.

He collects his dues at harvest time, but exacts an extra premium, compelling farmers to sell their cotton to him at a price lower than it fetches on the market, pocketing the profit.

His collateral policy is nothing if not inventive. The borrower signs a blank official document that gives Mr. Agarwal the right to collect the farmer's property at any time.

Business has boomed with the arrival of high-cost seeds and pesticides. "Many moneylenders have made a whole lot of money," Mr. Agarwal said. "Farmers, many of them, are ruined."

Indeed, one or two crop failures, an unexpected health expense or the marriage of a daughter have become that much more perilous in a livelihood where the risks are already high.

A government survey released last year found that 40 percent of farmers said they would abandon agriculture if they could. The study also found that farming represented less than half the income of farmer households.

Barely 4 percent of all farmers insure their crops. Nearly 60 percent of Indian agriculture still depends entirely on the rains, as in Mr. Shende's case.

This year, waiting for a tardy monsoon, Mr. Shende sowed his fields three times with the genetically modified seeds made by Monsanto. Two batches of seed went to waste because the monsoon was late. When the rains finally arrived, they came down so hard that they flooded Mr. Shende's low-lying field and destroyed his third and final batch.

Mr. Shende shouldered at least four debts at the time of his death: one from a bank, two procured on his behalf by his sisters and one from a local moneylender. The night before his suicide, he borrowed one last time. From a fellow villager, he took the equivalent of $9, roughly the cost of a one-liter bottle of pesticide, which he used to take his life.

Those like him with small holdings are particularly vulnerable. A study by Srijit Mishra, a professor at the Mumbai-based Indira Gandhi Institute of Development Research, found that more than half of the suicides in this part of the country were among farmers with less than five acres of land.

But even those who are prosperous by local standards are not immune. Manoj Chandurkar, 36, has 72 acres of cotton with genetically modified seeds and sorghum in a neighboring village called Waifad. Every year is a gamble, he said.

Each time, he takes out a loan, then another and then prays that the bollworms will stay away and the rains will be good. On his shoulders today sit three loans, bringing his total debt to $10,000, a vast sum here.

The study by Mr. Mishra found that 86.5 percent of farmers who took their own lives were indebted—their average debt was about $835—and 40 percent had suffered a crop failure.

The news of Mr. Shende's death brought his wife, Vandana, back home to Bhadumari. Relatives said she had gone to tend to her sick brother in a nearby village. By the time she arrived, her husband's body was covered by a thin checkered cloth.

A policeman had recorded the death—the eighth in six months for the officer.

Ms. Shende, squatting in the narrow village lane, shrouded her face in her cheap blue sari and wailed at the top of her lungs. "Your father is dead," she screamed at her small son, who stood before her, dazed.

Islands of Despair

Rural misery and the crumbling infrastructure in smaller towns take the sheen off Maharashtra's success story.

KALPANA SHARMA

In every State in India, no matter how prosperous, there are islands of deprivation. Maharashtra is no exception. It stands almost at the top of the list in terms of prosperity. It fails miserably when it comes to equity.

Rural misery has been written about and noted, exemplified by the continuing suicides of farmers in Vidarbha and Marathwada. The Bombay High Court has also, once again, warned the Maharashtra Government that it must do something about the high incidence of malnutrition among children between the ages of one and six. In the last three years, over 24,000 children have died of malnutrition.

Economic Neglect

What is not so well known is the pathetic state of some of the smaller towns of Maharashtra. This became evident when three bombs exploded in the powerloom centre of Malegaon in North Maharashtra on September 8. Not only did the bombs shatter the uneasy peace in this town of around 8,00,000 people, of whom the majority is Muslim, but they exposed the pathetic absence of civic infrastructure and economic neglect.

Thirty-one people were killed and over 200 injured on that Friday afternoon when the devout were almost through with their prayers. It was a big day, the Shab-e-barat, when prayers would be said at the Bada Kabristan through the night to remember the loved ones who had moved on. Instead, it became a night for multiple burials, as some of the dead were interred in the same graveyard.

Few Options

But unlike the July 11 serial bomb blasts on Mumbai's commuter trains, where the injured could be rushed to any one of several public hospitals within easy reach of the railway lines, the injured in the Malegaon blasts had few options. The only public hospital there is poorly equipped and was simply unable to cope.

People had to rush about trying to find help. They found this in a good Samaritan, Dr. Saeed Ahmed Farani, who threw open his private nursing home and treated over 100 of the injured. Others had to travel 55 km over bad roads to the nearest decent hospital in Dhule in the neighbouring district. The district headquarters at Nashik does have a referral hospital but it is over 100 km away.

If this is the state of a town that is not remote, that has been an important powerloom centre, and even boasts of a local film industry, one can imagine the state of some of the other towns in Maharashtra.

Fortunately for Malegaon, the bomb blasts have heralded a change in its fortunes. Or at least that is what its residents hope. For the disaster brought to the town's doorstep people like Congress Chief Sonia Gandhi. She saw the state of the town. She also heard its angry residents turn down compensation cheques. They told her to keep the money and instead ensure that the town had medical and civic facilities.

As a result, within 10 days, the State Government cleared an investment of Rs. 22 crores for a 200-bed hospital in Malegaon. Although State Government norms permit a hospital of this size only at district headquarters, an exception has been made. With 274 staff posts, the hospital will have an intensive care unit (ICU), a paediatric ICU, a burn ward, CT scan, trauma care and a psychiatric department. The Malegaon municipal corporation is giving nine acres of land for the hospital.

But a hospital alone, when and if it is finally built, cannot cure Malegaon's malaise. Its roots lie in the absence of commitment to ensure that development is for everyone and not just for those who live in the metropolitan cities. When you drain the countryside, concentrate industry and infrastructure around places that are already well served, and have no plan to bring other parts of your state on par, you end up with what we have in Maharashtra—dead lands that are noticed only when there is a disaster. No one, least of all the Government, understands the permanent disaster that has visited these towns.

Like Malegaon, there are towns scattered across the state, where there has been little new investment. Civic infrastructure is crumbling. There are few jobs. People have no option but to migrate—join the millions looking for work and hope in the "golden triangle" of Mumbai, Thane and Pune where most of Maharashtra's industry and investment are concentrated.

Additional Label

If these towns also happen to have a Muslim majority, as Malegaon or Bhiwandi, then they are strapped with the additional misfortune of carrying the "terrorist" label. Hard line groups of all persuasions flourish in urban centres where the young have no opportunities. But in these days of the global "war on terror," it is the Islamic groups who are under constant scrutiny. As a result, towns like Malegaon and Bhiwandi do get special attention but not the kind they need.

You cannot wish away alienation if you deliberately allow parts of your state to fester and rot while a few islands flourish. That should be the real lesson the Maharashtra Government should draw from Malegaon. Unfortunately, it has yet again failed to do so. As in the past, its response is short-term—give people a little something and then hope they will forget.

But they will not forget.

Afghanistan: Qanooni's Moment of Triumph

With Yunus Qanooni's election as Parliament Speaker, a complex calculus of power is forming. Though they are seen as rivals, Mr. Qanooni's political platform is far from irreconcilable with that of President Hamid Karzai.

M.K. BHADRAKUMAR

The 13th century Italian theologian and philosopher, Saint Thomas Aquinas, said that in order for a war to be just, the three things needed would be the "authority of the sovereign," a "just cause," and a "rightful intention." By that moral compass, the war in Afghanistan could probably be on its way to becoming one-third "just."

Whether the Afghan war concerned a "just cause" would be debated long and hard. Some believe the Bush administration viewed Afghanistan as a backwater along the road to Iraq—a sort of detour during which high-tech warfare and the anatomy of "terrorism" were put under scrutiny. Some others say the war itself created an enemy, which the U.S. needed in the post–Cold War world and took an interest in preserving.

As for its "intention," the war transcended Afghanistan and took protean forms. It made an appearance in the Ferghana Valley. It has crossed over to Pakistan's Balochistan province, and may be lurching toward Iran—another turf of Balochi subnationalism in a strategic swathe of land with an impressive waterfront facing the Arabian Sea. Indeed, the Afghan war resonates with ancestral voices prophesying war, as Coleridge's *Kublai Khan* would have heard amid the tumult of the steppes.

Meanwhile, the "authority of the sovereign" largely escaped attention. It is in this respect that Yunus Qanooni's election as Speaker of the newly elected Afghan Parliament inspires contemplation. The election was genuinely contested. Mr. Qanooni won narrowly defeating Abd al-Rabb al-Rasul Sayyaf. For the first time in the post-Taliban period, a political equilibrium was allowed to develop without manipulation by American viceroys.

Mr. Qanooni was a key aide to Ahmad Shah Masood. He comes from the Afghan *jihad* and the anti-Taliban resistance. A gifted politician, Mr. Qanooni revealed his skill in the three critical weeks following Masood's assassination on September 9, 2001, by negotiating an Afghan government-in-exile to be headed by former King Zahir Shah. Afghans preferred a national front to challenge the Taliban Government in Kabul rather than a foreign invading army. Hamid Karzai made it a point to sideline Mr. Qanooni.

Mr. Sayyaf, on the other hand, has a pedigree going back to Zahir Shah's rule, as an Islamic scholar of high repute in Kabul. He headed the Mujahideen group with Wahhabi leanings (Ittehad), whose cadres subsequently moved in and out of the Taliban movement.

An impression prevails that Mr. Karzai preferred Mr. Sayyaf to Mr. Qanooni. But appearances can be deceptive in Afghanistan. Mr. Sayyaf is an enigmatic and mercurial personality. Where exactly he stood at any given time through the past quarter century *vis-à-vis* Pakistani and Saudi intelligence or the Taliban and Al-Qaeda, no one could tell.

Pakistan seems to have suffered a huge setback in Mr. Qanooni's reappearance in the top echelons of power. With Mr. Sayyaf as Speaker, new vistas would have opened for Pakistan in Kabul's corridors of power.

The Afghan Parliament has a hefty contingent of Mujahideen commanders and Taliban members, former communists who turned Pashtun chauvinists, and tribal leaders rooted in ethnic identity. These elements all grew up in Pakistani playpens some time or the other.

A last-minute closing of ranks between Mr. Qanooni and Tajik leader Burhanuddin Rabbani, on the one hand, and the consolidation of various progressive elements in Parliament who viewed a Sayyaf victory as a retrogressive development, on the other, would seem to have enabled Mr. Qanooni to scrape through.

What does Pakistan do now? The balance sheet of the war on terror reads dismal. Does the low intensity war make sense? The Taliban can surely create mayhem but cannot capture power. The U.S. is about to pass on the baton to NATO. Pakistan can end up annoying influential Western capitals.

Besides, there are discordant notes within the Afghan resistance. In his customary annual Id message on January 8, Gulbuddin Hekmatyar, who was in alliance with the Taliban, did some plain speaking about President Pervez Musharraf's Afghan policy. Mr. Hekmatyar said: "The Americans are well aware of everything happening inside Pakistan. The CIA gets to know about developments in the Pakistani President's office faster than news about happenings in the Afghan presidential palace. The CIA and FBI are active inside Pakistan as they are in Afghanistan. Their establishments in Pakistan are as active as in Afghanistan. There too, they can arrest people and lock them up in prisons at will. There too, they fire missiles into the houses of their opponents from their surveillance aircraft, but the Pakistani officials promptly announce that there was an explosion in a house used for making bombs in which a terrorist was killed.

"The Americans have asked the Pakistanis to give up Kashmir and promised that, in return, they will make the Durand Line permanent and will help them bring the tribal areas under Pakistani control, areas which the British failed to control. Officials in Islamabad have accepted this deal."

The Taliban's initial reaction to the political developments in Kabul has been rhetorical. "Amir-al-Momenin" Mullah Mohammad Omar said: "Now a fake parliament has been set up and U.S. Vice-President Dick Cheney inaugurated it, but everyone is aware that the Afghans have not given up their resistance to this fake process. The resistance is getting stronger and is spreading to all parts of the country day by day. We assure all Afghans and the Muslims of the world that the Americans, apart from such theatrical events, will never succeed . . . The Americans will be forced to withdraw their forces from Afghanistan just as they are forced to withdraw from Iraq. Our struggle will turn into a national movement because every zealous Afghan Muslim knows that our soil has been given to the Americans by a few puppets."

Much will now depend on what happens in Kabul. Mr. Karzai and Mr. Qanooni have been characterised as political "rivals." But a complex calculus of power is forming. Mr. Qanooni's political platform is far from irreconcilable with Mr. Karzai's.

True, Mr. Qanooni had reason to feel embittered that in the presidential election, he might have "secured the votes but Karzai got the victory." But today, he too is a stakeholder. True, Mr. Qanooni had not minced words in questioning Mr. Karzai's leadership qualities. But he never wanted Mr. Karzai's Government to collapse either, as that would be "tantamount to giving Afghanistan to Pakistan" (to quote him). Also, Mr. Qanooni

from his powerful post is finally getting the chance to realise his agenda of "national unity and stability and security."

Problem Areas

But there are problem areas. First, the power broker who counts most is 'Ustad' Rabbani. And, there is no certainty whatsoever that the 'Ustad' has forgiven those who unceremoniously forced him out of the presidential palace in Kabul in the winter of 2001 to make way for Mr. Karzai. Whether a coalition of conservative Mujahideen elements cutting across ethnicity would incrementally assemble around 'Ustad' Rabbani remains to be seen. He has extensive links with almost all Mujahideen leaders, including Mr. Hekmatyar or Mr. Sayyaf or Yunus Khalis—and also with Pakistani agencies. In the 1994–95 period, he even helped the Taliban. ('Ustad' Rabbani moved to Pakistan in 1973 as part of Zulfikar Ali Bhutto's strategy to exploit political Islam as an instrument of state policy *vis-à-vis* Afghanistan.) Prof. Rabbani is the seniormost Islamist leader in Afghanistan today. Yet he is out of power. There is something odd here. The 'Ustad' is a master tactician, who can be a dogged Afghan nationalist—if he chooses to.

Secondly, Mr. Qanooni must come up with something far better than Mr. Karzai's policies, which he himself has condemned as "driven by ethnicity and private gains." On the other hand, thanks to Mr. Karzai's ploys to create a pliable parliament, Mr. Qanooni is being handed down a factionalised legislature. He must now make it work. Thirdly, Mr. Qanooni has reservations about Mr. Karzai's Cabinet choices, which would come up for parliament's approval. He felt the Green Card holders from the Afghan *diaspora* who surrounded Mr. Karzai were out of touch with the realities of Afghan life.

Besides, Mr. Qanooni strongly feels that a parliamentary form of government suits Afghanistan's needs better. Mr. Karzai and his supporters, on the other hand, fought hard to enshrine in the constitution a very strong presidency. Equally so, the confusion in Iraq would have disillusioned the Americans too about the parliamentary form of government.

Not that Mr. Qanooni is prone to "anti-Americanism." He believes that an open-ended NATO presence suits Afghanistan's security needs. He has no problems if Afghanistan calls itself the U.S.' "strategic partner." But Mr. Qanooni regrets that Washington's policies take shape under "Pakistani influence," and "there are special groups in Pakistan who want to destroy Afghanistan's stability." He is on record that the Taliban's resurgence itself is not accidental but forms part of Islamabad's "strategic" plan of undermining Afghanistan's sovereignty. Of course, he has been critical of Mr. Karzai's ambivalent policy towards the Taliban.

Mr. Qanooni's election on the whole holds the potential for enhancing the "authority of the sovereign" in Afghanistan. But the sovereign is called upon to share power. Naturally, there is indignation that at this delicate juncture, Washington is inclined to announce "victory" in the Afghan war and march on.

Afghanistan's Drug Habit

Joel Hafvenstein

As if there hadn't been enough bad news from Afghanistan of late, now the country's drug dependency is back in the headlines. On Sept. 2, the head of the United Nations Office on Drugs and Crime reported that the shattered country is now producing 92 percent of the world's supply of illegal opium, up from 87 percent in 2004. This deplorable new record will not be reversed by more belligerent counternarcotics measures. Instead, America, NATO and the Afghan government must reform a vital but neglected institution: the local police.

In 2004, for the first time in history, farmers in every province of Afghanistan chose to cultivate opium poppies. The American and Afghan governments promised a major poppy eradication campaign. Aid agencies scrambled to create an economic alternative for the thousands of Afghans who depended on poppy farming to survive.

Thus in November 2004, I traveled to Lashkargah, the capital of Helmand Province, the opium heartland of Afghanistan, as the deputy leader of an "alternative livelihoods" project financed by the United States Agency for International Development. Our core team was made up of six Western aid workers, and we hired some 80 Afghan staff members.

In the long-term plan, alternative livelihoods meant helping Afghan farmers export high-value crops like saffron and cumin. It meant restoring the orchards and vineyards that had once made Afghanistan a power in the raisin and almond markets. It meant providing credit to farmers who had relied on traffickers for affordable loans.

In the short run, however, with the first eradication tractors already plowing up poppy fields, we had no time for those approaches. Instead, we created public-works jobs. Like a New Deal agency, we handed out shovels to thousands of local Afghans and paid them $4 per day to repair canals and roads. We found plenty of work on Helmand's grand but dilapidated irrigation system, a legacy of early cold-war American aid. By May 2005, we had paid out millions of dollars and had some 14,000 men on the payroll simultaneously. The program buoyed the provincial economy, and would have made a fine launching pad for long-term alternatives to poppy.

Security was our Achilles' heel. There was a new American military base by the graveyard on the edge of town, but the few score Iowa National Guard members there lacked the manpower and the local knowledge to protect us. We could not afford the professional security companies in Kabul, most run by brash veterans of Western militaries. Then, just before Christmas, some of our engineers were carjacked. We resorted to the only remaining source of protection: the provincial police.

We soon found that at their best, the Helmand police forces were half-organized militias with charismatic leadership and years of combat experience. At their worst, the policemen were bandits, pederasts and hashish addicts. Our local guard captain was one of the better ones, but he was still far from reliable.

Once I asked him what he earned as a district police commander. "The governor paid us no salary," he curtly replied. "The people gave us money. To thank us for solving their problems." I was never sure if we were paying him enough to solve our problems.

When the attacks came, our security was useless. On May 18, five of our Afghan staff members were murdered in the field. The next morning, one of the funeral convoys was ambushed, leaving six more of our workers and their relatives dead. The police responded with indiscriminate arrests and bluster, but they lacked the investigative skills to catch the killers.

We heard rumors that the attackers were Taliban troops—and indeed, the attacks were harbingers of the Taliban resurgence that Helmand has seen in the last year. We also heard that the Taliban had been paid by local drug barons to attack our project. All we knew was that we were targets, and that we could not protect ourselves. Within days, we had stopped all our projects and most of the staff went home.

To reduce Afghanistan's poppy cultivation, Western governments must keep their focus on improving security. Aid agencies and the Afghan government cannot foster alternatives to opium while under fire. In chaotic times, Afghan farmers are more likely to plant poppy, which offers the surest and highest returns on investment. Some remote areas of Afghanistan have grown poppy since the time of Alexander the Great, but in the irrigated plains of Helmand it caught on only during the breakdown of order in the 1980's. With security restored, the farmers of Helmand could rebuild their province and return to licit crops.

Local police forces are the weakest link in Afghanistan's security net. After the fall of the Taliban, the United States and NATO put most of their energy into building a professional Afghan Army. The police forces were essentially surrendered to local warlords—not through any malign plan, but by lack of money and attention.

Most Afghan policemen have now gone through a basic training course run by American and German police officers, but they return to units that are ill equipped, badly organized, founded on personal loyalty to a commander and accountable to no one.

The 4,500 British troops now fighting alongside Afghan soldiers in Helmand can defeat insurgents who muster in large numbers, but they cannot counter the Taliban's shrewder tactics—urban ambushes, suicide bombings and strikes on "soft" civilian targets like our project. For that, the police are necessary.

The Afghan Army and foreign powers must create space in which a professional, accountable police force can take root. This means continued military action against large Taliban incursions, diplomatic pressure on Pakistan to stop providing a haven for insurgents, and a focus on shielding the large cities of southern Afghanistan—Lashkargah, Kandahar and Ghazni—long enough for the Afghan government to establish the kernels of an improved police force there. It will also require an end to the impunity enjoyed by warlords and major traffickers, who can order an attack safe in the knowledge that the Taliban will be blamed.

The new Afghan police force needs clear lines of authority, formal disciplinary procedures and methods for internal oversight and public complaint. The officers need adequate pay and equipment, which can come only from Western sources, and better training in investigation and civilian protection. To ensure that all this makes a difference, the United States and its allies must commit experienced Western police officers to field-based mentoring programs with provincial police forces.

The poppy boom won't be solved by police reform alone, of course. The Afghan government must purge drug kingpins from the federal and provincial governments, and continue disarming militias (friendly as well as hostile).

Nothing has cost President Hamid Karzai more popularity in the south than the sense that unscrupulous gunmen are back in control. Security was the Taliban's main selling point when it took control of the country in the 1990's; it could be again.

Taliban Truce in District of Afghanistan Sets Off Debate

Carlotta Gall and Abdul Waheed Wafa

After a series of bruising battles between British troops and *Taliban* fighters, the Afghan government struck a peace deal with tribal elders in Helmand Province, arranging for a cease-fire and the withdrawal of both sides from one southern district. A month later, the ripples are still being felt in the capital and beyond.

The accord, reached with virtually no public consultation and mediated by the local governor, has brought some welcome peace for residents of the district, Musa Qala, and a reprieve for British troops, who had been under siege by the Taliban in a compound there for three months.

But it has sharply divided former government officials, legislators and ordinary Afghans.

Some say the agreement points the way forward in bringing peace to war-torn parts of the country. Others warn that it sets a dangerous precedent and represents a capitulation to the Taliban and a potential reversal of five years of American policy to build a strong central government. They say the accord gives up too much power to local leaders, who initiated it and are helping to enforce it.

"The Musa Qala project has sent two messages: one, recognition for the enemy, and two, military defeat," said Mustafa Qazemi, a member of Afghanistan's Parliament and a former resistance fighter with the *Northern Alliance*, which fought the Taliban for seven years.

"This is a model for the destruction of the country," he said, "and it is just a defeat for *NATO*, just a defeat."

As part of the deal, the district has been allowed to choose its own officials and police officers, something one member of Parliament warned would open a Pandora's box as more districts clamored for the right to do the same.

Some compare the deal to agreements that Pakistan has struck with leaders in its tribal areas along the Afghan border, which have given those territories more autonomy and, critics say, empowered the Taliban who have taken sanctuary there and allowed them to regroup.

"It is the calm before the storm," one senior Afghan military officer said of the accord.

Even President *Hamid Karzai*, who sanctioned the deal, has admitted to mixed feelings. "There are some suspicions in society about this," he said in a recent radio interview with Radio Free Europe.

"I trust everything these elders say," Mr. Karzai said, but he added that two recent episodes in the area—of killing and intimidation—gave pause and needed investigation.

For their part, foreign military officials and diplomats expressed cautious optimism, saying the accord had at least opened a debate over the virtues of such deals and time is needed to see if it will work. "If it works, and so far it appears to work, it could be a pointer to similar understandings elsewhere," said one diplomat, who would speak on the topic only if not identified.

The governor of Helmand, Mohammad Daud, brokered the deal and defended it strongly as a vital exercise to unite the Pashtun tribes in the area and strengthen their leaders so they could reject the Taliban militants.

Appointed at the beginning of the year, Mr. Daud has struggled to win over the people and control the lawlessness of his province, which is the largest opium-producing region as well as a Taliban stronghold.

Some 5,000 British soldiers deployed in the province this year as part of an expanding NATO presence have come under repeated attack. Civilians have suffered scores of casualties across the south as NATO troops have often resorted to airstrikes, even on residential areas, to defeat the insurgents.

It was the civilians of Musa Qala who made the first bid for peace, Mr. Daud explained.

"They made a council of elders and came to us saying, 'We want to make the Taliban leave Musa Qala,'" he said in a telephone interview from the provincial capital, Lashkar Gah. "At first we did not accept their request, and we waited to see how strong the elders were."

But the governor and the British forces soon demanded a cease-fire, and when it held for more than a month, they negotiated a withdrawal of British troops from the district, as well as the Afghan police who had been fighting alongside them. The Taliban then also withdrew.

Eventually the governor agreed on a 15-point accord with the elders, who pledged to support the government and the Afghan flag, keep schools open, allow development and reconstruction, and work to ensure the security and stability of the region. That included trying to limit the arming of people who do not belong to the government, namely the Taliban insurgents.

They drew up a list of local candidates for the posts of district chief and police chief, from which the governor appointed the new officials. They also chose 60 local people to serve as police officers in the district, sending the first 20 to the provincial capital for 20 days of basic training, according to provincial officials.

One energetic supporter of the deal is Abdul Ali Seraj, a nephew of King Amanullah, who ruled in the 1920s, and leader of the Coalition for National Dialogue With the Tribes of Afghanistan, which is working to bring peace through the tribal structures.

"Musa Qala is the way to do it," Mr. Seraj said. "Sixty days since the agreement, and there has not been a shot fired."

The agreement has been welcomed by residents of Musa Qala, who said in interviews by telephone or in neighboring Kandahar Province that people were rebuilding their houses and shops and planting winter crops, including the ubiquitous poppy, the source of opium.

The onset of the lucrative poppy planting season may have been one of the incentives behind their desire for peace, diplomats and government officials admitted.

Elders and residents of the area say the accord has brought calm, at least for now. "There is no Taliban authority there," said Haji Shah Agha, 55, who led 50 members of the Musa Qala elders' council to Kabul recently to counter criticism that the district was in the hands of the Taliban.

"The Taliban stopped fighting because we convinced them that fighting would not be to our benefit," he said. "We told the Taliban, 'Fighting will kill our women and children, and they are your women and children as well.'"

What the Taliban gained was the withdrawal of the British forces without having to risk further fighting. Meantime, the Taliban presence remains strong in the province, so much so that road travel to Musa Qala for a foreign journalist is not advised by *United Nations* security officials. While residents are happy with the peace, they do not deny that the militants who were fighting British forces all summer have neither disbanded nor been disarmed.

According to a local shopkeeper, Haji Bismillah, 40, who owns a pharmacy in the center of Musa Qala, the Taliban have pulled back to their villages and often come into town, but without their weapons.

"The Taliban are not allowed to enter the bazaar with their weapons," he said in a telephone interview. "If they resist with guns, the tribal elders will disarm them," he said.

He said the elders had temporarily given the Taliban "some kind of permission to arrest thieves and drug addicts and put them in their own prison," since the elders did not yet have a police force of their own.

The district's newly appointed police chief, Haji Malang, said the Taliban and the police had agreed not to encroach on each other's territory. "They have their place which we cannot enter, and we have our place and they must not come in," he said in a telephone interview this week.

Some residents said the deal would benefit the Taliban. "This is a very good chance for the Taliban," said Abdul Bari, 33, a farmer who accompanied a sick relative to a hospital in neighboring Kandahar province.

"The people now view the Taliban as a force, since without the Taliban, the government could not bring peace in the regions." he said. "It is not sure how this agreement will work, but maybe the Taliban will get more strength and then move against the elders."

Opponents of the agreement warned that the elders were merely doing the bidding of the Taliban and would never be strong enough to face down Taliban commanders.

"The Taliban reappeared by the power of the gun, and the only way to defeat them is fighting, not dealing," said Haji Aadil Khan, 47, a former police chief from Gereshk, another district of Helmand.

One event that has alarmed all sides was the killing and beheading of Haji Ahmad Shah, the former chief of a neighboring district, who returned to his home after the agreement was signed. Beheading is a tactic favored by some Taliban groups, and his friends say it is a clear sign that the Taliban are in control of the area. Elders of Musa Qala said that Mr. Shah had personal enemies and that they were behind the killing.

The governor, Mr. Daud, and the elders said a number of the opponents to the agreement were former militia leaders who did not want peace. "The people of Musa Qala took a step for peace with this agreement," said the chief elder, Haji Shah Agha. "The Taliban are sitting calmly in their houses."

Another elder, Amini, who uses only one name, said: "For four months we had fighting in Musa Qala and now we have peace. What is wrong with it, if we have peace?"

Tales of the Veil

Five Afghan women make a film on their fluid, intensely personal and often complex relationship to the chadori, revealing the stories hidden behind everyday lives.

TARAN N. KHAN

It started off rather ordinarily, when five women employees of a television station decided to work together on a short production. Initially they discussed making an anti-smoking feature, but started talking of other things. And then someone mentioned a *chadori* tale. Within seconds, the atmosphere in the room changed to electric excitement. Stories poured out, words tripping over words in their haste to be told. Their film, they eventually decided, would explore the relationship they themselves, as Afghan women, have with their *chadoris*. They called it "Remembering Chadori."

"You don't buy a *chadori* every day. It costs about five to six hundred Afghanis for a piece, and I'm talking about the ordinary ones, not one of your fancy coloured pieces. It lasts for at least four or five years, more if you're careful. Depends on how often you wear it too, of course. Some of us wear them just for certain *mehfils* (gatherings), or to weddings, or to visit some relatives who are like 'that'. If you're like Sameera-*jan* you wear it every day to work and to the market and (in a whisper) you hardly ever wash it! Still, with careful daily wear I'd say a sensible woman who takes care of these things should be able to maintain it for a few years at least."

Deceptive Appearance

"I like that their colour is blue, but I don't like the way they make me look broad, and that they are pleated. Abroad they have smarter styles, with more colours available and with better fitting. Those make you look good. During the Taliban years, some women would celebrate Eid or festivals by buying new *chadoris* rather than new clothes, since that was what you saw first and last of their appearance. So the style of the *chadori* became pretty important. Even now, the nice ones from Iran or the Gulf cost too much for me to afford, so I'm stuck with the home-grown variety that makes me look fat."

As the technology of representation reaches deeper into Kabul's society, interesting trends are emerging. Women who would resist being photographed earlier are ready to talk on camera provided they are in their *burqas*. The image is hilariously contradictory, since it defeats rather effectively the purpose of the visual medium. But it also indicates the nuanced nature of the relationship between the camera and its veiled subject. Watching their footage, the five women directors fall over themselves giggling. The visual on the monitor shows close shots of a woman glaring at the camera from under her *chadori*, abusing them violently. You cannot see her expressions, or even hear her clearly, but her anger is palpable in the furious quivering of her veil.

Fear and the *Chadori*

"Once I got on a crowded bus wearing my *chadori*. It was completely full, and I couldn't get a seat, so I had to travel standing while holding onto the hand strap for balance. Slowly the crowd swelled so much that I was caught in a crush of passengers. Or rather my *chadori* was caught from both the edges. Slowly I started to feel it being pulled off, ripping from the sides by the weight of the crowd. And all the while I was helplessly hanging onto the hand strap. This was before the Taliban had come to Kabul. After a while the crowd thinned out, and I was left standing with just the *topi*, the crown of cloth on top of my head. I have never felt so exposed; I realised that there was nothing covering me from the sides. Uff, how I cursed myself for being a *be-izzat*, *be-aabru* woman that day!"

"I never wore a *chadori* and I don't wear one now. My family is very *azaad* (liberal) and we didn't do these things, even before the Taliban. When they were in power I chose to stay home rather than go out wearing that thing. Once I fell very ill. My family tried to take me to the doctor's but I kept resisting.

I didn't want to go out looking like that. I suffered for a day or two but finally the pain became too much to bear and my determination cracked. So *majburan*, I wore a *chadori* much against my will and went to get myself some medicines."

One of the questions I often hear asked during discussions on *burqas* and Muslim women is—do they wear those things because they have to, or because they want to? I think of the women in my family who wore *burqas* each time they ventured out, as long as they lived. I think of their near-tactile dependence on the folds of their veils while passing through male domains. And of the joyous bursts of colour when they unveiled in a safely *zenana* area. I think of the women of Kabul who refused to take off their *chadoris* even after news of the Taliban's defeat reached them, because their clothes were too worn and dirty to be seen. And I remember marching in demonstrations protesting the bombings in Afghanistan, accompanied by hundreds of young Muslim women, many of whom adopted the headscarf during those days as a mark of solidarity with their Afghan sisters. Where does choice end and force begin? I think of my grandmother, sneaking off with her friends to forbidden cinema theatres in the blazing heat of summer afternoons, hiding from telltale neighbours and chance-met in-laws under the folds of their *burqas*. Sometimes prison, sometimes sanctuary, perhaps the answer lies in the shifting roles of the veil for women at different times.

Looking at Us Looking at Them

"We can tell each other apart under the *burqa*. If I see my friend walking towards me from a distance, and she is wearing a *burqa*, you think I can't recognise her? First it's the figure, then it's the way of walking, which doesn't change. Even if it does, you can recognise her from her shoes, her clothes that can be seen under the *burqa* and mostly her hands. It's important to learn how to do this and not ignore people you know and may meet outside just because they are covered."

"Men look more at women who are covered from head to foot. Say there is a wedding, and people are going in. We will focus on the reactions of the men standing outside. A woman will walk past, modestly dressed but not in a *chadori*. They will look at her, but not so much. Then will walk in someone with just her feet showing and they will peer at her feet as if they are the first pair they have seen in their lives. They will push and shove each other to catch a glimpse of her hands, her eyes, im-

agine the great beauty she must be, hiding behind her veil. Even if she is the most ordinary looking woman in the world, in their imaginations, she will be a queen! Imagine a room where there are only women. Men are not allowed. You can bet there will be a crowd of men outside, trying every trick they can to catch a glimpse of what's going on behind the curtains. It's the same with women behind veils. Mind you, women also look more freely from behind their *chadoris*. They can be more comfortable since they are in a way invisible and can boldly examine the world, and even the men looking at them."

Then and Now

"During the Taliban years my *chadori* used to hang near the door, it was always ready to go, at a moment's notice. Who could tell when you would need it next? Now it's lying at the back of my *almirah*, I rarely wear it except for special occasions. But I keep it in good condition because who knows when I may need it again?"

"Why are we calling it 'Remembering Chadori'? Because there is a difference between the way we see the *burqa* then and now. Then was during the Taliban days, when we had to wear them. Now is when we don't have to, but we do. It's the same thing, but it's very very different. It's the same *chadori*, maybe, but the memory of force makes it different. We remember ourselves wearing those forced *chadoris* in this film."

Reclaiming Images

Burqas are supposed to be particular to a particular religion and a region, but veils are universal. They extend over the stories of women worldwide, regardless of the prevailing dress code. Through this video project, this group of Afghan women revealed at least partially the stories hidden in their everyday lives. By reclaiming their own images, they foregrounded an often overlooked fact—that the relationship of women with their veils is usually fluid, intensely personal and always more complex than it appears. The telling of these *chadori* tales is an assertion of control over their own images. It is also an argument for a way of being that has the grace to listen to these stories without judgement. In effect, it is a call to remove the manifold veils of the mind and vision that intrude when audiences look at women in *chadoris*. That, when and if it happens, will be the true unveiling.

Nobel Comes Just in Time for Troubled Bangladesh

SOMINI SENGUPTA

The timing, Bangladeshis confess, could not have been better.

With a troubled election season around the corner, the Nobel Peace Prize comes to Bangladesh as it braces for battle with itself. Or as Muhammad Habibur Rahman, a retired chief justice, put it, "The country is in such doldrums, it's a shot in the arm."

This densely populated, grindingly poor country of 147 million people is frequently troubled by doldrums, natural and political. The latest is an impasse between the main political parties over who will take over at the end of next week, when the current Bangladesh National Party-led administration is to hand power to a caretaker government.

So bitter are the politics here that the law requires a caretaker to organize elections. The high-stakes haggling over who that should be this year has added to the usual level of distrust in a country where the widespread perception of corruption and the rivalry between the ruling party and the opposition have induced a long bout of political paralysis.

The opposition has threatened to boycott the elections, scheduled for early 2007. Its loyalists have clashed repeatedly with the police. Talks to resolve the standoff have proved futile.

But now there is the "Yunus effect," as some call it, named for Muhammad Yunus, the microcredit pioneer of Bangladesh and the winner of the 2006 Nobel Peace Prize.

Yunus has inspired jubilation amid the gloom. Shegufta Yasmeen, who waited to greet him one morning this week holding white gladioli, said he was "like the light of the moon in a dark room."

Yunus, for his part, has used his Nobel bully pulpit to gently goad his country's leaders to behave better. Engage in a marathon negotiating session, he has urged; work out a deal; exploit the euphoria his award has created. His name has even been floated as a substitute caretaker. He has expressed no enthusiasm for the job.

Since the announcement last Friday of the Nobel, which Yunus shares with his Grameen Bank, songs have been written in his honor. Banners and posters have gone up all over Dhaka, the capital. So many bouquets and wreaths have been dispatched to Grameen headquarters that it is a wonder there are any flowers left in Bangladesh.

Again and again, people here describe the Nobel as a prize second only to the country's freedom from Pakistan in 1971.

To recognize Grameen, of course, is to recognize how such nongovernmental organizations—Bangladesh seems to have more than its share—have stepped in to do a great many things that would normally be expected from government: building schools, offering health care and creating economic opportunities for the poorest in a country that is among the poorest in the world.

Instead, political deadlock has carried the day, pitting the country's two most powerful women against each other, and the legacies of their respective families.

Prime Minister Khaleda Zia rose to power after the assassination of her husband, Gen. Ziaur Rahman, the country's military ruler, in 1981. The opposition leader, Sheik Hasina Wazed, is the daughter of the founding prime minister, Sheik Mujibur Rahman.

Politics is a winner-take-all game in this country, and the stakes between them are high.

Yunus has called Bangladeshi politics "a bottleneck" to the country's aspirations. Transparency International's 2005 annual Perceived Corruption Index, based on surveys of businesspeople and analysts, listed Bangladesh at the bottom, with Chad.

"There's no ideological fight between them," Yunus said of the leaders in an interview here this week. "They go back to what your husband did, what your father did. They have to fight because they came into politics because of their legacy. There's no substance in the politics."

The two leaders are out of the country.

"Why don't you just sit down and settle the whole thing?" Yunus wondered aloud. "If they don't agree the situation is going to be very explosive. There will be political chaos."

He could hardly hide his distaste. "But they go their merry way."

A solution was possible, he insisted, indeed unavoidable. "After this euphoria, I don't think leaders have a chance to go to agitation," he said.

A former classmate and a retired police inspector, M. Aziz Ul Huq, said that Yunus was always an optimist. "A very rare quality, particularly in our country," he said.

Even more of a goad, Yunus has lately hinted at the prospect of starting a party. This year, he joined a citizens' group that toured the country calling for honest and competent candidates. It did not win him many friends from either of the main parties.

Even by the standards of Bangladesh, the elections are shaping up to be particularly troubling. In private, Bangladeshis say they worry not about whether blood will be spilled before the voting, but how much. Several hundred people were killed just before and after the last general elections, in 2001, and they were not laden with nearly as much controversy as these elections.

This time, the opposition Awami League has threatened to boycott, over the issue of the chosen caretaker and the composition of the election commission, both of whom it accuses of being partisan. The opposition leader, Sheik Hasina, has exhorted her followers to pour into the streets. The ruling party has blamed the Awami League for thwarting democracy.

The voter roll is also embroiled in controversy. It contains many more names than in the 2001 elections and represents roughly two-thirds of the total population—which a pre-election team dispatched by the National Democratic Institute for International Affairs, a nonprofit group, in September said "strains credibility."

A worry that Bangladeshis largely banished many years ago has recently resurfaced: Will the military step in if there is chaos?

Bangladeshis have been ground down by much more than election uncertainty. In September violent demonstrations over crippling power failures spilled into the streets of this capital. Garment workers went on strike demanding higher wages. Earlier, journalists and political party workers were attacked, some fatally.

In spring 2004, even the British high commissioner to Bangladesh, Anwar Choudhury, was injured in a grenade attack on the outskirts of Dhaka. Members of an outlawed Islamist group confessed to the attack last month. Bangladesh was struck by its first (and only) suicide bombing in December 2005. Earlier last year, militants set off more than 400 homemade bombs across the country.

The troubles eased, when the government arrested several members of a banned Islamist group, Jamaat-ul-Mujahedeen Bangladesh; five have been sentenced to death.

So while gushing comes easily to Bangladeshis, the rejoicing these days is all the more striking for the disquiet that they say they have lived with for many months—and may well have to live with for a while longer.

"We are a nation thirsty for recognition for something good," Mahfuz Anam, the editor of *The Daily Star*, an English-language newspaper, said, explaining the excitement of the last few days. "The euphoria is absolutely proportionate to the despondency that was there."

Poverty and Peace

The significance of the Nobel Peace Prize for 2006 is that it acknowledges a vital link. By awarding the prize in equal part to the Bangladeshi economist, Muhammad Yunus, and the Grameen Bank, which he founded in 1976, "for their efforts to create economic and social development from below," the Norwegian Nobel Committee has recognised that lasting peace is not possible without dealing with poverty. Professor Yunus's pioneering concept of microcredit, translated into action by the Grameen Bank, has given millions of poor people access to loans without collateral. The Bank has over six million members, 96 per cent of them women. It covers three quarters of Bangladesh's villages. It lends to nearly a million micro-enterprises. It recovers more than $5 billion every year. It has spawned innovative businesses, for example "telephone ladies"—the 100,000 village women who use their mobile phones to provide phone services in villages. Grameen has built houses and extended educational loans, particularly for girls. It will soon launch a business of providing nutritious food at affordable prices. Thirty years ago, microcredit was a concept unknown and unacceptable to the world's financial establishment. Today, it is operative in more than 100 countries. According to the 2005 State of the Microcredit Summit Campaign Report, 92 million families worldwide accessed microcredit by the end of 2004. Of these, 73 per cent were extremely poor at the time of their first loan.

These figures do not tell the full story. Critics of microcredit point out that commercial banks have exploited the concept by substituting these smaller and safer loans for rural credit, which is essential for farmers and rural enterprises but is also more risky. Another criticism is that the concept individualises the solution to poverty, thereby negating the possibility of social mobilisation and the need to change social structures. However, what the Bangladesh experience suggests is that programmes that empower women at the bottom combining with higher allocations for the social sector can make a real difference to the quality of life of the poor even under conditions of mass deprivation. This is reflected in the steady progress Bangladesh has made in the last two decades on the human development front where it has outpaced India. According to the United Nations Development Programme's Human Development Report 2005, Bangladesh ("moderate growth, rapid human development") is ahead of India in health, education, and gender equality. Professor Yunus and his Grameen Bank must be given some of the credit for this and therefore richly deserve the Peace Nobel.

Bhutan's Democratic Puzzle

The exotic, benign image of the Himalayan kingdom of Bhutan cannot conceal the battle between authoritarian politics and democratic dissent that is shaping its future, says Dharma Adhikari.

DHARMA ADHIKARI

These are truly extraordinary times for democracy in the Himalayas. A mass movement in Nepal effectively stripped King Gyanendra of his absolute powers in April 2006. In Bhutan, the eastern Himalayan kingdom, King Jigme Singhe Wangchuk declared in December 2005 that he would abdicate the throne and adopt a parliamentary system of government by 2008.

The 50-year-old king's announcement that he would step down in favour of his son Dasho Jigme Khesar Namgyel Wangchuk came as a shock to many. In combination with the trend of events in neighbouring Nepal, it seems evident that both kingdoms are democratising. But there is an important difference between Nepal's grassroots approach and the Bhutanese king's top-down devolution of power.

In Bhutan—a country more than double the size of Israel, and flanked by India and China—politics is not always what it is purported to be. Its tortuous history and its exclusionary politics defy the popular notions of democratic progress propagated in recent years by the palace and circulated by an international media always seeking "exotic" new locations and stories.

Indeed, reclusive, scenic Bhutan has frequently earned positive media spin for its efforts in preservation and modernisation: a culture untainted by modernity, the "land of the thunder dragon," a Buddhist Shangri-La that champions the royal philosophy of "gross national happiness" rather than gross national product, the only country to ban smoking, a country with almost two-thirds of its land under forest cover . . . not even open-Democracy is immune to the charming spin (see the article by Bhutan's foreign minister, Lyonpo Jigme Thinley, "Globalisation—the view from Bhutan" [25 October 2001]).

True, there are some genuinely "positive" stories coming out of Bhutan. The kingdom's economic indicators are relatively impressive in the developing world; the proposed adoption of a formal, written constitution and the holding of the first general elections are moves in the direction of parliamentary democracy; and King Wangchuk's relatively progressive image can appear a refreshing contrast to absolute monarchs from Brunei to Saudi Arabia to Swaziland, and perhaps even a reminder to the Burmese (Myanmar) junta that Buddhism is conducive to democracy.

Behind the smiles, however, is a more complex truth.

An Adolescent Monarchy

Bhutan, like Jordan, is a colonial monarchy. Established in 1907 by the British, it is one of the world's youngest monarchies. The exuberance that comes with an adolescent institution can be captivating, but unrestrained youthfulness can also lead to bravado, self-love and unnecessary squabbles.

Traditionally, political and social struggles in Bhutan were between Buddhist sub-sects and feudal warlords. The clash between the Mangol and Tibetan Buddhist sub-sects characterised the polity until 1616, when Shabdrung Ngawang Namgyal, a Tibetan Lama of Kagyupa school of Buddhism, founded modern Bhutan on the basis of a dual system of governance (spiritual and administrative order). The Buddhist theocracy, which partly inspired the utopian idea of Shangri-La, ended with Shabdrung's death in 1652; this unleashed a civil war between various sects that was to last two centuries. In 1907, Ugyen Wangchuk, a provincial governor of the Drukpa Kargyupa school of Tibetan Buddhism and the present king's great-grandfather, consolidated power over the country. As a reward for his loyalty, the British—then rulers of neighbouring India—designated Ugyen king.

But neither Ugyen Wangchuk (1907–1926) nor his son Jigme Wangchuk (1926–1952) nor his grandson Dorji Wangchuk (1952–1972) enjoyed absolute powers. In fact, to appease a decentralised and increasingly restless spiritual order, Dorji Wangchuk decreed in 1968 that the king would abdicate in favour of his oldest son if the *tshogdu* (national assembly) passed a vote of no confidence by a two-thirds majority against him. He also introduced the elections of national-assembly members via secret ballots.

Today, the power-struggle has reached an inevitable point—it is directly between the monarchy and the people.

The present king Singhe Wangchuk took the reigns of power in 1972. Soon after, he abolished the abdication system, hand-picked national-assembly members, and began the process of centralising power. For the first time in Bhutan's history, a ruler was able to create an elaborate royal family and a system of patronage and cronyism. The close-knit members of the extended royal family (Wangchuk has four wives, all of whom are sisters) dominate government and commerce.

The king also nurtured favouritism towards the ruling Ngalongs (westerners), at the expense of minorities such as Sarchops (easterners), Lhotshampas (Nepali-speaking southerners), and Doyas and Brokpas (scattered minorities). His racist motives became all the more apparent when in 1989 he issued a cultural decree called *driglam namzha* that promotes "one nation, one people." This anomalous edict makes it mandatory to everyone, irrespective of ethnicity and culture, to eat, sit, speak and dress the way the ruling Drukpas do. He introduced Dzongkha, a Tibetan dialect as a national language, and banned the teaching of other languages in schools, including the related Nepali language.

When the Lhotshampas refused to wear *gho* or *kira* (robe-like dresses) and protested against the discriminatory move, hundreds were tortured and jailed. They included Tek Nath Rizal a royal advisor, and now Bhutan's foremost pro-democracy leader. In 1990, more than 100,000 Nepali-speaking Bhutanese, comprising almost one-third of the country's (disputed) population of nearly half a million, were forcefully evicted from the country on the pretext that they were illegal immigrants, or *ngolops* (anti-nationals).

In fact, Nepalis have lived in Bhutan since 1624. Many more were lured by the Bhutanese government in large numbers as labourers and construction workers during the 19th and the first half of the 20th century.

King Wangchuk justified forceful depopulation on the grounds that a Nepali majority in Bhutan meant that the dragon kingdom would become another Sikkim, where the Nepali majority of the independent nation voted in 1975 to join the Indian republic.

The rebellion of the early 1990s also extended to the Sarchop, the second largest ethnic group and the original inhabitants of Bhutan. The Sarchop are of Indo-Burmese origin and speak non-Tibetan dialects, such as Tshangla. Many Sarchop fled the country to escape persecution, including Rongthong Kuenley Dorji, the exiled leader of the banned Druk National Congress (DNC) party. The persecution also extends to suppressing religious groups such as Christians and Hindus.

There have been fifteen rounds of bilateral talks between Bhutan and Nepal on the issue of the repatriation of the refugees living in the camps in Nepal. The last was in 2003, and little progress has been made.

Today, the refugees expelled by Bhutan—who include several of my Bhutanese extended family—languish in United Nations High Commission for Refugees (UNHCR)-managed camps in eastern Nepal. The "ethnic cleansing" of these now stateless people has been extensively documented by human-rights groups such as Amnesty International and Human Rights Watch, as well as independent scholars like Michael Hutt, Michael Aris, and Leo Rose.

An Exclusionary Politics

The exclusionary politics of King Wangchuk also became evident in his suppression of the popular Shabdrung legacy and his persecution of the Shabdrung reincarnations. DNC's Dorji, formerly close to the present king, recalls that Wangchuk once asked him not to explain the history of the Shabdrungs to the public. The last reincarnation Shabdrung Jigme Ngawang Namgyal Rinpoche—equivalent to the Dalai Lama lineage of Tibet and highly revered by Bhutanese—was an avid critic of the autocratic king. The Rimpoche lived in exile in India until his mysterious death on 5 April 2003.

Wangchuk's modernisation project, based on the post-colonial ethos of nation-building, did gain some momentum. Investment in quality tourism and modern infrastructure over the last few decades has brought the kingdom some world visibility and material progress. The United Nations human-development reports portray the country as a good performer among the least-developed countries (LDCs). However, the king's devotion to a narcissist view of culture and identity, and the king's feudal mindset, has caused much damage to regional peace, justice, human rights and democracy.

Today, the power-struggle has reached an inevitable point—it is directly between the monarchy and the people. It extends beyond the traditional elite. Already, there are many opposition parties in exile in Nepal and India, and the Bhutanese diaspora is abuzz with democratic discourse.

The king insists that democracy is an evolutionary process and that he will grant democracy to his subjects on a piecemeal basis, but he has also indicated that the impetus for his change of position is "contextual," not "consequential." Referring to developments in Nepal, where the Maoist insurgency has brought them close to power, he has asked: why wait for a revolution?

Bhutan's own history of long internal wars makes that a legitimate fear.

Indeed, the drafting of a constitution with provisions for democratic institutions and civil liberties is a monumental shift in a Bhutanese polity governed for so long by archaic decrees. However, there are doubts about the king's sincerity. Critics argue that just like during the guided *Panchayat* reign in Nepal (1960–90), the king hopes to use the constitution to circumvent a simmering upheaval and delay a truly representative democracy.

The constitution was drafted without representation from the dissident groups and remains vague about the monarch's prerogative powers. It also lacks a provision for an independent judiciary and fails to properly acknowledge religious, linguistic and cultural freedoms (among others). At best, it envisages a two-party oligarchy based on the *Drukpa* vision of a homogenous nationhood.

The first-ever democratic elections in Bhutan will be held only if the draft constitution is passed in a national referendum. This delaying tactic is already evident in the fact that on the recommendations of royal astrologers (who believe that the omens are not good for democracy at this time) the elections have been postponed until 2008.

The fundamentals of democracy—limited government and civil liberties—are essential in any form of democracy, even in the context of the cultural nuances of popular rule. Bhutan fails on both accounts. The launch of two private daily newspapers in the capital, Thimpu, does signal a first advance in press freedom. But Bhutan's government is in no mood to share power with the opposition (now mostly in exile), and it continues to deny basic rights to a large section of its population, particularly those living in refugee camps in Nepal and India. There cannot be a genuine democracy when more than a third of the entire population is displaced and disenfranchised.

The implication of this assessment is that unless the international community gets more involved and the refugee problem is resolved, genuine democracy in Bhutan is still a remote prospect.

An International Responsibility

Under the terms of a 1949 treaty, India manages the defence and foreign affairs of Bhutan, as well as being Bhutan's largest foreign donor. But India has dismissed the refugee problem as a "bilateral" issue, despite calls by the UNHCR and the European Union for its active involvement in mediating the issue.

India continues to appease the Thimpu regime in return for the latter's contribution to sustaining New Delhi's sphere of influence; it has been rewarded for its help in flushing out separatist Indian groups operating from their bases in southern Bhutan. Bhutan may have established diplomatic relations with twenty-two countries, and its educated elite may increasingly realise that the treaty of 1949 is discriminatory—but Bhutan has not been able to escape from India's shadow and act independently. The dragon kingdom has broken ranks with India only rarely in its votes at the United Nations, where it was admitted in 1971 thanks to New Delhi's influence. It does not have diplomatic relations with China, another regional power and India's rival.

In the early 2000s, Nepal's civil society and government have at least been able to draw international attention to the protracted problem of the refugees expelled from Bhutan. Amnesty International and Human Rights Watch have repeatedly called for an inclusive and transparent refugee-verification process, international monitoring and the involvement of third parties such as the UNHCR and refugees' representatives. The European Union passed a resolution on 18 July 2003 that called on both parties to actively support a just resolution of the problem. The resumption of EU aid to Nepal in June 2006 after its

democratic revolution is welcome; $2.5 million in food aid is designated for Bhutanese refugees.

Meanwhile, the United States does not have diplomatic relations with Bhutan, but it does have diplomatic obligations. America's stated polices towards south Asia—expanding freedom and promoting economic prosperity and peace—supply the rationale for a more progressive approach. The U.S. is aware of the problem but it could do more.

In 2000, towards the end of Bill Clinton's presidency, the US authorised part of a $22 million Balkan aid-package to Bhutanese refugees living in Nepal. At that time, the U.S. government hoped to "work with both countries for the just resolution of the humanitarian problem." That may not be much, but American concerns helped spur a series of bilateral talks between the two countries and the initiation of a verification process (aborted later as the political climate deteriorated). In May 2005, the U.S. ambassador to Nepal, James F. Moriarty, toured the refugee camps and assured people there that he would try to find a solution by holding talks with Nepal, India and Bhutan—"if possible."

The civil war in Nepal that has claimed 13,000 lives since 1996 pushed the once highly visible refugee issue on the back-burner. This stalemate has led to hopelessness and frustration among the refugees. Tek Nath Rizal, released under international pressure in 1999 after a ten-year imprisonment and now living in exile in Nepal, told me recently that the young refugees in the camps are fed up with their life in limbo. Sit-ins, peace marches to Bhutan (Indian police routinely arrest refugees who make the trek) and hunger-strikes have become routine forms of refugee protest.

The lack of economic freedom and of any semblance of progress in the bilateral talks makes it not unlikely that some refugees may make common cause with the Maoists in Nepal. Already, a Bhutanese Maoist outfit has become active. Rizal blames the international community for its inaction. "They have abandoned us," he said, and added: "How can Bhutan, that does not abide by international laws, continue to be a UN member?"

International inaction could lead to another Palestine, Kosovo, or Darfur, in an already volatile south Asia where the Nepali crisis may have eased but where Maoists in India (Naxalites) control a wide swathe of territory and the situation in Bangladesh remains highly volatile. All concerned parties—India, Nepal, Bhutan, the UNHCR, aid agencies and refugee representatives—must come together to deliberate how a workable, durable solution can be reached.

The refugee issue may be at the heart of Bhutan's problem at the moment, but it is only part of its democratisation puzzle. Bhutan's "gross national happiness" lies not in King Wangchuk's divisive politics, but ultimately requires a just and inclusive polity in which the royal regime respects diversity and listens to opposition leaders, parties and the international community. The king's abdication announcement may be alluring, but (as Tek Nath Rizal puts it) it does not mean he will begin to live the life of a hermit. In fact, the king himself has said that he will continue to be active in an advisory role after he surrenders formal power.

In the end, the key to Bhutan's future lies with New Delhi, but three other powers—the European Union, the United States and the United Nations—must also put pressure on India to initiate a genuine democratic process in Bhutan. The western democracies should be able to persuade India, the world's largest democracy, to side with freedom and dignity—not injustice and suppression—in the dragon kingdom.

DHARMA ADHIKARI teaches journalism and international media systems at Georgia Southern University in the United States. He is the founder and editor of www.Newslook.org. He grew up in India and Nepal, and became a Fulbright Scholar at the University of Missouri School of Journalism at Columbia, Missouri, where he also received his doctorate in journalism.

From *OpenDemocracy.net,* June 30, 2006. Copyright © 2006 by openDemocracy.net. Reprinted by permission.

Article 31

Protests in Paradise: Repression in the Maldives

The Maldives is a popular holiday destination, but is also a country with limited political freedom where people who are arrested are beaten up. They are held in detention for long periods without trial and are sentenced in unfair trials.

In recent weeks, the Government of the Maldives has been targeting journalists and members of the opposition Maldivian Democratic Party to try to stop a planned demonstration on Friday 10 November asking for constitutional reform.

The authorities have claimed that these actions represent a threat to the government. In the face of repressive measures against those planning the 10 November demonstrations, the opposition has called off the rallies. This is not the first time the government has targeted protesters.

In September 2003, people took to the streets after the killing of at least three prisoners by the National Security Service, which is under the President's command. Maldivian photo journalist Jennifer Latheef was one of the demonstrators.

The events of 20 September 2003 changed Maldivian photojournalist Jennifer Latheef's life forever—and made political history in the Maldives. This is her story:

It was around two o'clock in the afternoon when I heard the news. Evan Naseem, an inmate of Maafushi Prison, set on an atoll 18 miles south of our capital, Male, had died in prison the night before. He'd been the victim of a brutal beating by prison security guards. I decided to join the crowds already gathering in large numbers at the cemetery in Male for his funeral.

The place was packed when I arrived—people seemed to want to bear witness, to see for themselves the kind of things that can happen under a brutal regime. Torture is commonplace in Maldivian jails, and I have many friends and relatives who have lived in its shadow.

My paternal great-grandfather and my grandfather were both tortured to death in jail under the previous regime—that's why it's so hard to describe my feelings when I saw Evan Naseem's lifeless body. The simplest way to sum it up is to say that he became family from that moment on.

Then came more terrible news. Security officers at Maafushi jail, trying to quell an uprising in the wake of Evan's death, had opened fire on prisoners, killing three. Now the collective anger and horror slowly mounted until an entire community stood up to voice their protest against the brutality. People took to the streets; many vandalized and torched government property. Police stations and vehicles took the brunt of the anger.

My natural reaction to any kind of upset (in situations with family or friends, I mean) has always been to try to calm things down. Even before the rioting began, I had tried to talk to the police platoon of about 20 to 25 officers who had gathered near the hospital where victims of gun wounds were believed to have been taken.

The entire area was crowded with civilians. There had already been isolated incidences of attacks against the police—even those police in plain clothes. I felt that they were aggravating the situation by being there, and that they themselves were in danger.

When rocks started being thrown at the platoon, I headed for home—but not for long. It was very frustrating not knowing what was going on, and I couldn't reach anyone on the phone because the entire network was—conveniently—down. So I walked back to the hospital, past a police station in the process of being trashed, along with the police vehicles outside.

Eventually, I managed to get a ride to a friend's house—she agreed to come and meet me later back at the hospital, bringing other friends and a small, unobtrusive camera that I could use to document events. On my return, I passed another police station which had been also been systematically trashed. Everything inside had been dumped outside on the road and set on fire.

Later that evening, my friends and my sister in tow, we heard that another body was being taken to the cemetery in an ambulance. The main road, Majeedhee Magu, was already filling up with a long procession following behind.

I wormed my way in through the crowd to the foot of the slow-moving ambulance—and found my friend Zaid inside, hysterical and distraught because the dead body was his brother, Ameen, with a bullet through the back of his skull.

We got Zaid out of the ambulance and made our way back to our house. Inside, Zaid cried and we just hugged him. Then three of us took Zaid to the cemetery where we stayed for a while. Then curfew was announced and we had to be inside.

We decided to go to my friend Amani's house and stay up together. At her place, we watched BBC and constantly checked the internet. We also tried to tell as many people as we could outside the country about what had occurred. At six in the morning, when the curfew time was over, Marnie and I took Zaid back to the cemetery and we came home to sleep.

When I woke up, people were already saying that the police had arrested me. People had been calling my family and friends, saying that they had seen me being taken away. But I wasn't arrested until the next day, the 22nd of September, at 12:30 pm. And little did I know that this terrible day was only the beginning.

Jennifer Latheef is a 33 year old Maldivian photojournalist working for the daily Minivan News. She was sentenced to ten years' imprisonment on 18 October, 2005, convicted of 'terrorism' for taking part in the protest described above. Prior to sentencing she had been arrested and detained several times for her work as a human rights activist and member of the opposition, and placed under house arrest.

The main reason for her detention was her outspoken views critical of the Government of President Maumoon Abdul Gayoom.

In addition, her arrest was believed to be a measure by the government to limit the activities of her father, Mohamed Latheef, a Maldivian politician living in exile in Sri Lanka where he has been engaged in a campaign of peaceful political opposition to the Government of Maldives.

She was finally freed in August 2006, having again been placed under house arrest in December 2005. Amnesty took up her case in November 2003.

In Nepal, Time to Check the Dangerous Drift

The road map for the formation of an interim government with Maoist participation is more or less in place. But powerful forces are intervening to derail the process.

Siddharth Varadarajan

After moving forward quickly and purposefully towards the establishment of peace and democracy these past few months, Nepal's political parties have begun to stumble in the final crucial laps with a needless controversy over the disposition of Maoist arms.

At stake is the formation of an interim government consisting of the ruling Seven Party Alliance (SPA) and the Communist Party of Nepal (Maoist), which will have the mandate of conducting elections to a Constituent Assembly. The interim government will also have to administer the country till the formation of a new government elected on the basis of the Constitution which emerges from the Assembly's deliberations.

While it is the Constituent Assembly that will largely determine the political contours of the future Nepal, the credibility and structure of the interim government is equally important if the entire process is to be seen through to completion. As such, the full and unreserved participation of the Maoists and all other parties is essential. Indeed, the historic eight-point agreement, signed by Prime Minister Girija Prasad Koirala and CPN (M) leader Prachanda on June 16 explicitly commits the SPA and the Maoists to the establishment of an interim government on the basis of an interim constitution. Although that agreement explicitly provides for the United Nations to "help in the management of arms and armed personnel of both the sides and to monitor it in order to conduct elections for the Constituent Assembly in a free and fair manner," nowhere does it say that the surrender of arms by the Maoists is a precondition for the interim arrangement to go forward.

There is a good reason for this. By foregrounding the necessity of a political settlement between the SPA and the Maoists—through the instruments of an interim government and Constituent

Assembly—the June agreement makes it easier for the eventual settlement of the arms question. As a senior SPA leader told me during a visit to Delhi in July, insisting on the surrender of arms before a political settlement was like putting the cart before the horse. "Let us say they give up their weapons and then we fail to reach a political solution. It will not be difficult for them to pick up the gun again." As for ensuring a level playing field during the elections—a legitimate demand of the SPA, whose cadres might otherwise be intimidated by Maoist weapons—this would be taken care of by the U.N. monitoring of both Nepal Army soldiers and Maoist combatants.

As the prospects for durable political change strengthen, however, the old order and its backers have begun reasserting themselves. For example, hardly a day goes by without James F. Moriarty, the U.S. Ambassador to Nepal, warning the parties not to accept Maoist participation in government without disarmament first. So brazen has been his intervention in Nepal's internal affairs that a number of MPs have called for his expulsion from the country. Also involved in this anti-Maoist scare campaign are Army officers who have not yet reconciled themselves to the loss of the "Royal" prefix from the name of the Nepal Army.

After the eight-point agreement was signed, the first hitch arose when the Koirala Government—presumably under pressure from the U.S.—wrote to the U.N. in early July asking for help in the management and decommissioning of Maoist arms. This "misunderstanding" was eventually resolved with Mr. Koirala and Mr. Prachanda writing identical letters to Secretary-General Kofi Annan on August 9 inviting the U.N. to "deploy qualified civilian personnel to monitor and verify the confinement of CPN-M combatants and their weapons within designated cantonment areas" as well as "[m]onitor the Nepal Army to ensure that it remains in its barracks and its weapons are not used for or against any side."

The letters also requested the U.N. to continue its human rights monitoring through the Office of the High Commissioner for Human Rights in Nepal currently headed by Ian Martin, assist the monitoring of the 'Code of Conduct' during the Ceasefire, and "provide election observation for the election of the Constituent Assembly in consultation with the parties." Nowhere do the letters speak of decommissioning.

At a press conference in Kathmandu earlier this week, Mr. Martin acknowledged there was some confusion over the sequencing of what he called "arms management" issues and political issues. By this he meant the precise moment when the U.N. will step in to monitor the Nepal Army and Maoist combatants, in particular whether the monitoring would kick in before or after the formation of the interim government. While this sequencing is a matter for the SPA and Maoist leadership to sort out, the laying down of weapons by the Maoists is a diversionary question that will only undermine the prospects of the peaceful political transition both sides say they are committed to.

When Prime Minister Koirala and Mr. Prachanda get together later this month for their summit meeting, they must put an end to the dangerous drift that has set in on the formation of an interim government. The Interim Constitution Drafting Committee (ICDC) has done a commendable job in preparing a draft covenant to oversee the transitional period, including the formation of an interim government and the holding of elections to a Constituent Assembly. No doubt ambiguities abound, not least about how the issue of the mon-

archy is to be resolved, but none of these is intractable. With statesmanship and patience, which both the SPA and the Maoists have already displayed in abundance, the last remaining hurdles can be overcome.

India's Role

To the extent to which Washington has muddied the waters with its strident anti-Maoist campaign, however, India needs to counsel the SPA to stick to the path spelt out in the eight-point agreement of June 2006.

The inexplicable re-arrest in Chennai on Monday of Nepali Maoist leader C.P. Gajurel suggests the Manmohan Singh Government has still not realised the fragile nature of the transition Nepal is going through.

The Indian legal system can be chaotic and unpredictable but surely the Government of India knows how to negotiate its way through it.

In 2000, New Delhi pushed through the release of Masood Azhar. Unlike Azhar, who went on to found the Jaish-e-Mohammed, Mr. Gajurel is a political leader who has never been charged with a violent offence and who means India and its people no harm.

Ensuring his swift release—as well as his speedy, safe and honourable return to Kathmandu—would not only be the right thing to do but it would also send an important message: that India supports the formation of an interim government with the participation of all of Nepal's political parties, including the Maoists, and believes such a government offers Nepal its best chance for peaceful democratic change.

From Maoism to Fascism in the Himalayas?

Thomas A. Marks

It is an October replete with irony. The most definitive treatment to date on Mao Tse-tung's final crime against humanity, his "Great Proletarian Cultural Revolution," is out to solid reviews. Peru, in confirming the life sentence of Marxism's self-proclaimed "Fourth Sword," Comrade Guzman, has ensured that the country would not have on its streets a "democratic politician" whose only tangible achievement was to unleash the Maoist nightmare that left 60,000 of his countrymen dead. In Thailand, amidst the buffeting of democracy, the 14 October anniversary passed with hardly a thought. It was on that date, in 1973, that the authoritarian state crumbled, beginning the process through which democracy defeated Maoism. And in Nepal, the Maoists, sensing power just ahead, again issued a slew of statements denying that their Maoism and the catastrophe it has brought to the country has anything to do with the bloody 20th Century crimes of Marxism-Leninism.

What is striking in the Nepali scenario has been the crucial role played by the clueless united front allies of the Maoists, especially groups that bill themselves as 'civil society' or even as 'nonaligned'. They have lent critical strength to what otherwise would be a political movement n much the position as the Provisional Irish Republican Army (PIRA) prior to its participation in the peace process, when its front, the Sinn Fein, at peak garnered less than a fifth of the electorate.

What remains ill-understood is that the Maoists are not using even the same vocabulary, much less the same game plan, as the present political system. They continue to see themselves as a people's war on the offensive, and are simply proceeding along an avenue of approach complementary to armed action. Violence and non-violence are but two facets of a unified struggle, very much as, in boxing, feints and movement of the body are as necessary as punches thrown.

'People's war' is a strategy for armed politics. The mistake is to think it is merely 'war,' by which we normally mean action between armed forces. To the contrary, people's war is like any parliamentary campaign—except violence is used to make sure the vote comes out in your favour. Significantly, sub-state rebels such as the Maoists claim they are merely doing what the state itself has been doing all along. In Nepal, they claim, there never has been 'non-violent politics.' Rather, they assert, echoing Lenin, the democratic politics practiced by the 'old-order'—ancien regime—is but a façade for an oppression that is carried out using the violence of the state through its armed component, the security forces, as well as the 'structural violence' of poverty and injustice.

Thus the Maoists see themselves as engaged in a struggle for liberation, even of 'self-defense.' Such a struggle proceeds along different but orchestrated lines of operation. Use of violence, now 'in support,' is just one line of operation, which comprehends many forms of violence, from assassinations, such as that of Armed Police Force (APF) head, Krishna Mohan Shrestha, in 2003, to main force attacks, the large actions that seek to overrun District capitals. These forms of violence, in turn, were 'bundled' into campaigns, such as the campaign of terror that the Maoists used to eliminate all who opposed them in local areas, whether individuals or police. The family of Muktinath Adhikari, for instance, the teacher was hanged for the 'crimes' of teaching Sanskrit and failing to give 'donations' to the Party in early 2002, has recently surfaced to demand justice.

Yet such terror occurred for a reason: to clear the space for political action, to eliminate competitors. This is why Communist Party of Nepal—United Marxist-Leninist (CPN-UML, a parliamentary party,) activists were such particular targets. They advanced a competing programme which had won a majority of seats in Nepal's 3,913 Village Development Committees (VDCs). They had to be driven out so that the Maoist cadres would have uncontested access to the electorate. Only in this way could the Maoists mobilize a mass base using their own 'electoral platform,' if we may call it that—they call it their 'mass line.'

Of course, such methods are anathema to democracy as generally understood, even as certain portions of their (Maoist) party platform are attractive. It is for this reason that the Maoists have sponsored a multitude of front organizations, the wide variety, for instance, of ethnic and community rights organizations. On the surface, they are not Maoist, but in reality they are controlled by the Maoists. The student and labour organizations are especially prominent in this respect. The important thing about fronts is that they can present themselves as independent, even as they are being used to enhance Maoist strength. Lenin called those who unwittingly join such fronts, thinking they are acting on their own, "useful idiots."

Even as this goes on inside the country, the Maoists work outside. States tend to focus upon the tangible links, such as the Maoist presence in India. Much more important is their information campaign, designed to present their movement as almost benign. As states make mistakes, such as instances of indiscipline by military units, these are exploited to claim that the state itself is the problem, and terror is projected as a natural component of the solution. In the Nepal, the sheer level of terror inflicted by the Maoists has been quite forgotten in the rush to attack the Army, the APF, and the hapless police (who, recall, at one point in the conflict, had actually suffered a majority of all dead when considered as a proportion of the total victims).

For a Maoist movement, the goal is always power. This has been stated quite openly by all major Maoist figures. They must have power, because their 'end-state' is to refashion society. They are not seeking reintegration. That would be to accept the structure that exists and to play by the rules of that structure. Quite vocally, they reject the legitimacy of that structure and its rules. That is why they are adamant that there must be a constitutional convention. They see themselves in the driver's seat. They are like any political machine in a rough neighborhood—they can 'deliver' the vote. It is 'boss politics' played by 'big boy rules.'

In seeking 'peace' and proclaiming that they are 'not for violence,' what the Maoists mean is that they would much rather have the state deliver power to them (the Maoists), rather than make them (the Maoists) fight for it. They are not fools. They are not interested in dying. They are interested in 'building a new world.' Yet they hold that violence has been the indispensable tool for creating a new correlation of forces, a new electoral map, if you will. That is why they will not give up their weapons (alternatively, they say, all forces must lock up their weapons, but this does not include their local forces, their 'people's militia'). They have run the opposing parties out of the neighbourhood, and now they are demanding a vote. They do not see this as hypocrisy—they see it as doing precisely what the state has been doing in years past. But they hold that their motives are superior, because they aim to revolutionize society, to make Nepal a 'true' or 'authentic' democracy, because they are carrying out the will of history, "of the people."

Have they worked out the details of what this new democracy will look like? No, aside from vague notions of 'sectoral' representation. They have stated, as the Maoist chief, Pushpa Kamal Dahal @ 'Prachanda' recently did, that they oppose 'parliamentary republicanism,' by which they mean democracy as Nepal has, but with the Parliament sovereign. But they have not laid out what their 'real democracy' alternative will be. That is the beauty of being the political challenger. Today's realities are opposed with tomorrow's promises. This is what politicians always do, even those who run 'on my record.' The danger of left-wing ideologues, such as the Maoists, is that their worldview dramatically constrains their spectrum of possibilities.

They tend to think of fantasies, such as 'self-reliance' and 'independence,' as ends that can be achieved if only 'will' is harnessed. It was just such fantasies, implemented through violence, that gave us the astonishing crimes of the past century—crimes, it must be noted, the Maoists deny occurred. Yet there is no doubt what went on under Lenin, Stalin, and Mao (photos of all these individuals are used as veritable deities by the Maoists), any more than there is any question as to what occurred under Hitler or Pol Pot. What they shared was a startlingly similar worldview.

The Nepalese Maoists' way of dealing with this is, first, to deny reality (just as the leader of Iran seeks to deny the Holocaust); second, to claim that Nepal will be different (which is easily claimed, since there is a shocking lack of knowledge in Nepal of what has gone on globally in similar situations); and, finally, when all else fails, to claim that the critic has no right to speak. None of three ways, it bears reiterating, addresses the issue: the Maoists really have no answers to the challenges facing Nepal. They simply claim that they will do better than the bumbling (and bloody, they claim) incompetents who have preceded them.

The Maoists have used the monarchy as their foil. If the 'feudal monarchy' is swept away, they endlessly repeat, all will be well. In this, they certainly have been assisted by the tragic circumstances which placed the incumbent, King Gyanendra, on the throne. Similarly, they have been assisted by his errors in maneuvering through the maze of Nepali politics. However, having forced the monarch to a position most claim he should occupy, that of a ceremonial monarch in a parliamentary democracy, the Maoists are still left with the fundamental issue: what to do about Nepal? They see structural issues that can be addressed by 'will.' Most of us see a population that has exceeded the carrying capacity of the land.

Though marginal in an objective sense, Nepal and its troubles have implications for the region and beyond. The decimation of a democracy, the turning over of a people to the same tired solutions that have led to tragedy after tragedy, is of concern enough. Just as serious are the regional implications of allowing an armed, radical movement to force its way to power through terror.

India is the ultimate arbiter in Nepali affairs for reasons of geostrategic interest and Nepal's geo-fiscal realities. From Nepal's standpoint, this has not always worked out well. From India's standpoint, it has worked out reasonably enough. Nepal has steered clear of engaging in behaviour that threatens India's interests, and Nepalis have proved a valuable component of the Indian labour pool (including militarily, where Nepalis apparently comprise one-eighth of the manpower of India's infantry battalions). India's interest in the current situation is in having a stable neighbour, especially one that does not contribute to India's own growing Maoist problem. To achieve this goal, New Delhi desires in Nepal a functioning democracy committed to addressing the needs of its people. Balancing the elements of this general prescription has long been the challenge of Indian regional foreign policy and has led to some real flies-in-the-ointment at times.

Irony again surfaces, because it is India (not the Maoists) that has seen its policy of the past decade go awry. Hence it finds itself in bed with Maoist insurgents and in search of a 'soft landing.' New Delhi's strategy is to get one by facilitating in Nepal the creation of a 'West Bengal' or a 'Kerala'—States where the tamed Indian Left rules, where it continues with its nasty verbiage and bizarre worldview, but where it must respond to the realities of power and hence stays within the lanes on the national political highway. What New Delhi has overlooked is that such realities occur in India only because of the capacity of the national state to force compliance. Subtract the Indian military, paramilitary, and police forces from the equation, and India would be anarchy. Not surprisingly, that is the very term being used by many to describe the situation in Nepal.

As has been discussed previously by any number of sources, it is difficult to tell precisely where "our Indian friends," as Prachanda has taken to calling them, currently fit in. A number of elements figure into New Delhi's calculations. First, as the hegemonic power in an unstable subcontinent, India seeks restoration of order. Disorder produces refugees, unleashes intra-Indian passions, transfers elements of the conflict to Indian soil, and sucks New Delhi into foreign policy nastiness. Second, having opted for order, India has played a hand well known to its smaller neighbours: intervention. The only question has been how to intervene.

Here, there are several schools of thought. My past work in Sri Lanka has led to my being less than charitable as to Indian official motives. In the Sri Lankan case, New Delhi was into everything from supporting terrorism to running covert ops in a friendly, neighbouring democracy. Only when the Frankenstein it helped to create, the Liberation Tigers of Tamil Eelam (LTTE), turned on its former benefactor did logic and morality reassert themselves in New Delhi. In Nepal, it is perhaps too early to speak in such terms. What we know at the moment is that the weak position of the coalition government in New Delhi, combined with its normal 'Great Game' psychology and the eagerness of certain Indian personalities, especially on the Left, to expand their own role and spheres of involvement, led to a policy shift that supported the Seven Party Alliance and the Maoists (SPAM). It seems equally clear that India, as it did previously in Sri Lanka, went into the present endeavor quite misinformed by its alleged experts, not to mention its intelligence organs, and that it is quite ignorant as to the actual nature of the Maoists—no matter the efforts of those same personalities just mentioned to claim how wise, thoughtful, and caring Prachanda and other members of the Maoist leadership are.

In once again misreading the situation in a neighbouring state, India was initially and virtually pushed by the nationalism of the King. Whatever else he is, the monarch is a Nepali who does not think it is for India to dictate Nepali realities. Ironically, this is a position also held by the Maoists. They have simply realized, of late, that it is a position best relegated to the shadows. Better to rail against the old bugaboos of Indian politics, especially in unison with those who think the Cold War is still going on: 'America and world imperialism.'

As the US Ambassador to Nepal, James F. Moriarty, has made quite clear—and the cases of Hamas and Hezbollah illustrate well—there are consequences connected with actions that seek to talk peaceful politics but engage in behaviour labeled terrorist by virtually the entire world. It is noteworthy that, in their quest to carve out an identity as 'independent' actors, the Maoists claim to see exemplars in very unsavory types—Venezuela, Iran, Cuba, and North Korea. One can understand why these odious regimes are 'picked'—on the surface, they stand for a divorce from the present world-order, which Maoist dogma holds responsible, in league with the Nepali local representatives of 'world-capitalism' (that is, anyone who owns anything and makes a decent living), for the lack of development that is the country's present-day reality. In fact, Cuba and North Korea have long been economic basket-cases noted for their political repression, while Venezuela and Iran are political basket-cases determined to remain as such by exploiting a single resource, oil, something Nepal certainly does not have. Cases such as Brazil, Argentina, and Bolivia also offer a certain fascination for the Maoists, since these states claim to be 'socialist.' Each, though, has particulars not relevant to Nepal. Indeed, the most apt comparison for Nepal would seem to be to the Albania of the Cold War, when its lack of resources and close affinity with Maoist ideology reduced it to a complete backwater.

What now looms for India in Nepal is what Israel has faced with Hamas and Hezbollah, for example, thought they could be both in government and carry our terrorist actions. Their fellow citizens have paid a terrible price for such folly. Hamas is particularly tragic, because the Palestinians thought they could elect a group that both wanted to defy world norms and be supported by its money. The similarity to the Nepali case is compelling. Hamas and Hezbollah, one could argue, have behaved as the Nepali Maoists seem determined to behave: to participate in 'the system' only to use it for their own ends. Those 'ends,' obviously, have now made life even worse for the Palestinian and Lebanese populations.

In the Nepal case, it was disappointing and tragic that the SPA and the Palace could not have a meeting of minds. Parliamentary democracy should have been the ultimate bulwark against the Maoist challenge, but the very nature of Nepali parliamentary democracy, with its corruption and ineptitude, led to its marginalization. The increasingly bitter split between SPA and the King became all but inevitable in such circumstances, but personalities also played a central role, as they do in all that occurs in Nepal. It was the nastiness between Congress personalities, for instance, that incapacitated Government at the precise moment when focus and response were most needed against the insurgent challenge. India has sought to alter this reality long after the fact, by coming down squarely on the side of 'democracy.' Yet, as was the case in Sri Lanka, New Delhi's political class seems to have seriously miscalculated.

Though certain Indian commentators hold there are no connections between the Indian and Nepali Maoists, this has never been the case. Indeed, the two sides have openly discussed their linkages, and individuals from the two movements were apprehended or killed in operations "on the wrong side of the border." Only with a move to exploit the nonviolent line of operation did the Nepali Maoists stop claiming to be integrally linked not only with South Asian Maoism, through the Coordination Committee of Maoist Parties and Organisations of South Asia (CCOMPOSA), but also with global Maoist forces through the Revolutionary Internationalist Movement (RIM). Of course, these were never 'command' relationships, only liaison and, in the case of the Indian groups, some presence. It is naïve to claim the radical wing of a radical Maoist movement will simply salute and call it a day, even if the leadership decides reigning in the combatants is the best tactical course of action. Further, it is inevitable that any Maoist Government would encourage the usual flocking of Left Wing groupies that we see—and have seen—in every other case of a radical Government. Indeed, there already are here in Nepal the usual international activists supplying information to the Nepali left-wing press and even to the Maoists themselves.

There is, however, some hope for the Nepalese future. What is now happening politically should have been the earlier response to the Maoists, with the security forces providing the shield. Though a plan had, in fact, been drawn up, it was mechanical, devoid of substance, precisely because the mobilization that occurred in April 2006 was not used by Nepali democracy as its weapon. That is the irony of Nepali parliamentary democracy—it proved incapable of using mobilization of democratic capacity to defend itself. It did not do what the Thai, the Filipinos, the Peruvians, and the Sri Lankans (twice, against the Janatha Vimukthi Peramuna, JVP) did to defeat their Maoists. They brought reform to imperfect systems and made them better. They are still imperfect, as are all systems. But they are not man-eating systems as desired by the Left Wing, of which the Maoists are the premier representatives.

It should be obvious that the claim that there is 'no military solution' to insurgency is simply a canard. One hears it endlessly in Nepal, most often from 'the foreigners who would be gods,' as one acquaintance aptly put it. Armed capacity enables the campaign of reform, just as armed capacity is what enables the challenge to the old-order. In circumstances such as Nepal, no army can be committed simply to defend the status quo. It must be committed to defend transformation. That transformation, though, must look rather more like what can be seen in India and a lot less like that witnessed in Mao's China.

If Nepal wishes to move forward, it has all the pieces right before it on the table. This has been said before. What separates the sides is the Maoist notion that revolutionary transformation will now be delivered by surrender when force of arms could not take it. 'The people have spoken,' goes their claim. In reality, the people have spoken, but they have not at all supported what the Maoists have in mind, precisely because the Maoists have worked so hard not to let their vision and plans get out into the open. What Nepal needs now, more than ever, is equitable representation and good governance. What the Maoists keep demanding is retribution and marginalization of all who do not see a solution in their terms. There seems to be the idea that one can simply one day announce a decision has been reached, which will include a declaration that, in effect, a significant slice of the Nepalese old-order should present itself at the chopping block. To say that will not 'just happen' is not to be a pessimist or even a realist, but only to reiterate a point made previously in this publication: hope is not a method.

For reconciliation, all elements of society need to be engaged. At the moment, the Maoists and some misguided elements of SPA are proceeding in much the same fashion as did the Government of Sri Lanka, when it marginalized its Tamil population. Half of all Nepalis, in recent polls, said they would be content with a ceremonial monarchy; the security forces number more than 160,000 individuals in intact units. Yet there has been little effort to involve the forces represented by those statistics. For Nepal to move forward, to use a constitutional assembly as a basis for more equitable new arrangements, is a laudable goal. To think a socialist reshuffling of Nepal's demographic and physical pieces will produce a panacea is a pipe dream. On the contrary, in advancing their 'triumph of the will' solution, the Maoists seem quite unaware that they have fixed upon, as course of action, the very title of Hitler's most powerful fascist propaganda film.

Islam, Militarism, and the 2007–2008 Elections in Pakistan

Frédéric Grare

The year 2007 will be crucial for the future of democracy in Pakistan. If the election schedule announced by Parliamentary Affairs Minister Sher Afghan Niazi is followed, presidential elections will be held in the fall and the general and provincial elections will be held on January 30, 2008. All these elections will be carefully scrutinized by many in the United States and elsewhere, not least because they will include, among other political forces, a coalition of religious political parties, the Muttahida Majlis-e-Amal (MMA). Many commentators in the West believe that the Pakistani regime will portray the elections as a contest between Islamists represented by the MMA and the enlightened moderation of President Pervez Musharraf and the Pakistan Army. However, the reality is that the Islamic forces will not be a defining factor. They are a dependent variable whose power is largely determined by the army. The only real questions are whether the army's tactics for manipulating the 2007–2008 elections will differ from those used in 2002 and what role the Islamic parties will play in the process.

The MMA emerged from the Pak-Afghan Defense Council, a coalition of twenty-six Islamic organizations established in December 2000 to protest the decision by the United Nations to withdraw from Taliban-dominated Afghanistan. The council disbanded shortly after the fall of the Taliban in 2001. In January 2002, six of its major parties formed the MMA in order to participate in the general elections in October. The MMA comprises five Sunni organizations—the Jamiat Ulema-i-Islam Maulana Fazlur Rehman faction, the Jamiat Ulema-i-Islam Sami ul-Haq faction, the Jamiat Ulema-i-Pakistan, the Jamiat-i-Islami, and the Jamiat-al-Hadith—along with the Shiite group, Tehrik-i-Islami.

For many, the electoral success of the MMA in the 2002 general and provincial elections was both surprising and worrisome. It was, however, a blessing for the regime. A Supreme Court verdict of May 2, 2002 had required that elections be held to transition the country from military to civilian rule, but the elections for the National Assembly and the four provincial assemblies were held with the clear understanding that real power would not be transferred to civilians. The military's authority

and policies remained impervious to civilian challenge. Parliament had lost sovereignty under the Legal Framework Order (LFO) issued before the elections, which allowed the president to dissolve the National Assembly and created the National Security Council, a nonelected body intended to oversee the performance of the government.[1]

The apparent rise of Islamist power in these elections distracted international actors from the key fact that little real democratization was occurring. Much of the international community, especially the United States, was grateful to have Musharraf remain in power behind a facade of civilian rule. A year after the September 11, 2001, terrorist attacks on the United States, the outcome of the elections could be construed as validating the perception that Islamism was a force to reckon with in Pakistan and that the military was the ultimate institution able to prevent the country from going down the path of a Taliban-style Islamic "revolution."

This perception was carefully cultivated by the Pakistan regime itself. Even the diplomatic community could not totally ignore the fact that the elections had been rigged in favor of the Islamist parties, but the argument was soon refined. High-ranking officials started leaking the idea that yes, the Islamist victory in Balochistan and the North-West Frontier Province (NWFP) had been partly engineered but the result had surpassed expectations, suggesting that uncontrollable Islamic forces could possibly be unleashed throughout the country if international pressures on Pakistan went too far. As a result, the regime got some breathing space from its ally, the United States.

The 2007–2008 elections will take place in a different context, both international and domestic. Pakistan is no longer perceived as a pariah state but as a key ally of the United States in the war against terror. Pakistan's economic situation has improved. As a result, the usefulness of the Islamist organizations for the regime has decreased, and their role will have to be assessed differently.

Although Pakistan appears much less fragile than it did seven years ago, democracy has hardly improved. The next elections will not change this situation. For the military in general and President Musharraf in particular, the elections will be about consolidating their hold on power while maintaining a facade of democracy. For the mainstream political forces, particularly the opposition parties such as the Pakistan Peoples Party (PPP) and the Pakistan Muslim League Nawaz (PML-N), the elections will be about keeping (or not keeping) the promises of democratization and the return of their exiled leaders, Benazir Bhutto and Nawaz Sharif, respectively. For the general population, the elections will be, as usual, about living conditions and possibly another exercise in disillusionment. And for the international community—undoubtedly a stakeholder, though indirectly—the elections will most likely be another moment of imagined tension between democracy and stability.

One group will be uncertain of its fate and direction: the Islamic forces. The current legislature, whose term is ending, has been a difficult one for them. Although officially in the opposition, the MMA soon discovered that by criticizing the government and then bargaining for compromises, it became a key supporter of the regime. In particular, the MMA was instrumental in having the LFO passed in Parliament. Even though the MMA protested against democracy restrictions, it always provided the military with whatever support was needed. The MMA also channeled popular resentment when the government's actions did not match its rhetoric. The MMA was the pressure valve through which public frustration over contradictions in army policies could be released without risking true unrest because the MMA ultimately wanted to maintain the benefits of working with the government. Yet, as soon as the MMA established the formal legitimacy of the Musharraf government and the constitutional changes it sought, the military stopped favoring it.

For the MMA, the coming elections may well be a lose-lose situation; it might have to choose between marginalization and insignificance. Despite the supposed arbiter role that may eventually be attributed to the MMA by outside observers, it will be a dependent variable. It will no doubt retain some autonomy and try to enlarge its political space; however, it will most likely be able to do so only in the framework defined for it by the army. In no case will it be the master of its own destiny.

The situation of the MMA raises some serious issues regarding the nature of the relationship between the Islamists and the military. The mutual attempt of each to make the best possible use of the other is obvious here. Historically, however, the military has always gained much more politically from the relationship than the Islamists, who have had to pay the price of an increased dependence on the army for whatever support they received on the jihad's regional battlefields.

Delineating the process that led to this situation is the object of this paper. It seeks to identify not only the ideological evolution but also the tactical moves and eventual errors during the Musharraf period that led to the present domination of the MMA by the army. From there, it goes on to examine election and postelection scenarios.

The MMA and the 2002 Elections

The MMA was generally considered the great victor in the 2002 provincial and general elections. Many described its electoral performance as a surge of fundamental Islam. As table 1 shows, however, the MMA received only 11.10 percent of the vote in the general election, far behind the PPP of exiled former prime minister Benazir Bhutto (which received 25.01 percent), the pro-Musharraf Pakistan Muslim League Quaid-i-Azam (PML-Q, which received 24.81 percent), and the PML-N of exiled former prime minister Nawaz Sharif (11.23 percent). The seat distribution was, therefore, surprising: The PML-Q emerged as the single largest party, with 77 seats, but the MMA, despite winning only 11.10 percent of the vote, became the second-largest bloc,[2] with 53 seats out of 342 in the National Assembly.[3] The MMA's gains stemmed partly from post-election manipulations and the defections they generated from the PPP, which had initially gained 62 seats. More importantly, perhaps, the MMA was able to form the government in the two provinces bordering Afghanistan. In Balochistan, it did share power with the PML-Q, but in the NWFP it was able to form a government of its own.

Several arguments have been proposed to explain the rise of the MMA in the 2002 elections. Anti-Americanism was undoubtedly one factor—and candidates in the NWFP used this theme most effectively, probably because the local population was sensitive to the fate of the Pashtuns in Afghanistan. Official propaganda against the political class as well as the strategy of undermining the credibility of prominent personalities was

Table 1 Breakdown, by Party, of Voting and Seats in the Pakistan General Election, 2002

Party	Votes (Million)	Share of Total Vote (Percent)	Number of Seats Won*
PPP	7.39	25.01	62
PML-Q	7.33	24.81	77
PML-N	3.32	11.23	14
MMA	3.19	11.10	53

* The number of seats does not include the reserved seats for women and minorities, which are apportioned according to the percentage of votes obtained in the general vote.

Source: International Crisis Group, Pakistan: The Mullahs and the Military, ICG Asia Report 49 (Islamabad/Brussels: International Crisis Group, 2003), pp. 17–18.

another.[4] Still another factor was the absence from the campaign of issues relevant to the real concerns of the people, which led to the depoliticization of large segments of the population and to voter apathy.[5]

With the exception of the post-9/11 situation in Afghanistan, these explanations were not new; neither are they sufficient to explain the results of the 2002 elections. The gradual loss of faith in electoral politics can be observed from the beginning of the 1990s, with voter turnout constantly below 50 percent and dropping to a historic low of 35.4 percent in 1997. By contrast, in 2002, voters showed a slightly greater interest in the election in every single province of the country.[6]

Manipulations preceding the elections, which were reported by the European Union Election Observation Mission, offer a slightly different picture. According to the Election Observation Mission's final report, all parties raised concerns regarding the delimitation of the constituencies and accused the Election Commission of Pakistan of diluting strongholds of parties opposing the regime while favoring parties supporting the regime.[7]

Serious concerns were also raised regarding the quality of the voters registered.[8] The Election Observation Mission noted: "The electoral process was marked by the introduction of a new set of qualification criteria for the nomination of candidates, some of which [were] not in accordance with international standards or [were] clearly targeting specific prominent politicians."[9] For example, university bachelor's degrees were required, but madrassa diplomas were considered equivalent. This measure significantly advantaged the MMA, particularly in Balochistan, where some prominent nationalist leaders without university degrees were prevented from running in the election even though several had previously exercised the functions of governor or chief minister of the province. Rallies and the use of loudspeakers were forbidden during the entire campaign. The duration of the campaign itself was reduced to a minimum.

These restrictions were applied selectively. For example, the PML-N and the PPP were denied permission to organize rallies, but the MMA was allowed to. Moreover, because the MMA campaigned essentially in madrassas and mosques, in the context of its religious activities, it was relatively unaffected by the ban on rallies imposed by the military government.[10]

Religious Political Parties and the Military: Long-Term Trends and Tactical Mistakes

The MMA had participated in the elections on an anti-Musharraf platform, yet it was favored by the regime. The point here is not to suggest any hidden tension within the regime but to examine the nature of the alliance between the Islamists and the military. This relationship is at the crossroads of two radically opposite worldviews: The Islamists see power as a means to expand ideology, whereas the military sees ideology as a tool to strengthen its power and rationalize its expansionism. Thus, neither the existence of occasional meeting points nor the prevalence of a preexisting tension should come as a surprise.

Examined from the military's perspective, the situation is obvious. Mohammed Waseem observes: "The tussle over control of ideological power bases has been endemic to the politics of Pakistan."[11] He also notes:

> The ruling elite opted for Islam as an instrument of policy. It conceived religion as a counterweight to demands of leftist groups and ethnic parties to open up the state system to a wider section of the society. Under bureaucracy, and later the army, a democratic framework based on a mass mandate was considered dysfunctional. Therefore the state elite used Islamic ideology and shaped its idiom. It sought to control ever more aspects of Islamic theory and practice, by passing legislation in the name of Shariat, assuming control over madrasahs and shrines and influencing the growth patterns of Islamic groups and networks.[12]

But what one Pakistani author once qualified as "Islam from the cantonment"[13] is no more than a means of legitimating the regime. It has been demonstrated elsewhere that supporting the Islamist parties is a way of both weakening the mainstream parties and allowing the military to remain the ultimate arbiter of all Pakistani politics on the domestic front. A robust Islamist alternative is also a convenient foreign policy tool for convincing the international community that the army alone can contain the threat that the Islamists were supposed to represent.[14]

The motivations for this sometimes explicit but mostly implicit alliance are more enigmatic from the perspective of the religious political parties. It is sometimes argued that the Islamic establishment has reversed the relationship and has started to shape the political idiom according to its own preferences and politics. For some, "the emergence of the MMA as a serious power broker on the national scene in 2002 demonstrates the fact that now religion is seeking to define the state."[15] However, this does not mean that it can successfully do so. Pakistan's politics have turned the Islamic forces into a natural ally of the military, not necessarily into a peon of the army. On the contrary, it is the autonomy of the Islamic forces that makes their exploitation possible.

Ultimately, two main factors shape the relation of the Islamist parties with the military: their evolution toward what Olivier Roy qualifies as "Islamo-nationalism," that is, the combination of a pan-Islamist discourse with a practice that aims essentially at promoting the interest of the Pakistani state, perceived as the vector of the creation of the universal *ummah*;[16] and the relation of the Islamist parties to democracy. These two factors combine to define the Islamists' sphere of autonomy and their convergence of interests.

The Long Road Toward Islamo-Nationalism

It would not be useful here to rewrite the history of the ideological evolution of all the organizations that opposed the 1947 partition of the South Asian subcontinent because it broke the unity of the *ummah,* the community of the believers. Instead, it is sufficient simply to note how their involvement in Pakistan's politics led them to see the new state as a vector of the unity of the *ummah,* creating a convergence with the military that later led to a client-patron relationship.

This phenomenon is best understood through the evolution of the Jamiat-i-Islami (JI). As indicated above, the MMA is a coalition of six Islamist parties[17] formed to participate in the October 2002 elections. But, because of their importance for the coalition, two organizations stand out. The first, the Jamiat Ulema-i-Islam (JUI), a Deobandi organization,[18] is numerically the most important. The JUI is divided into the Jamiat Ulema-i-Islam Maulana Fazlur Rehman faction (JUI-F) and the Jamiat Ulema-i-Islam Sami ul-Haq faction (JUI-S), led by Fazlur Rehman and Sami ul-Haq, respectively. Holding forty-one seats in the National Assembly and twenty-nine of the MMA's seats in the legislature in the NWFP, the JUI-F is the larger of the two factions; it is also, numerically, the most important party of the coalition.[19]

The second organization, the JI, which some consider the main architect of official Islam in Pakistan, is more interesting for this study.[20] Having captured seventeen seats in the October 2002 general elections, the JI is only the second-largest component of the MMA, but its influence on the coalition is far greater than its numerical importance would suggest. Its evolution epitomizes in a sense the evolution of political Islam on the subcontinent, particularly in Pakistan.

The initial opposition by the founder of the JI, Sayyid Abul Ala Maududi, to the formation of the country of Pakistan was based on quasi-Marxist historical dialectic, whereby the struggle between Islam and non-Islam had replaced class struggle. Maududi believed that this "struggle between Islam and non-Islam would culminate in an Islamic revolution and the creation of an Islamic State which would in turn initiate large scale reforms in society thereby leading to a utopian Islamic order."[21] The success of the Islamic state would inevitably strengthen its legitimacy in the eyes of society. It was therefore logical to Islamize society before the creation of the state.

The leaders of the JI soon came to understand that without the support of the ulema, the army, and the bureaucracy their objective of establishing an Islamic state could not be realized, and they thus adjusted their political strategy. Although it had started as a revivalist movement, the JI became a political party. From then on, the objective of taking over the state machinery prevailed over ideological purity, and the JI started to compromise with those who, at least in theory, favored the ideal of an Islamic system.

Until the late 1970s, this led the JI to oppose both the army and the secular parties. But the military coup d'état of General Muhammad Zia ul-Haq changed the relations. The religious credentials of the dictator allowed for a mutually beneficial rapprochement. The JI thus entered the government. Moreover, through the conflict in Afghanistan, Zia ul-Haq was ready to give the JI a role in the management of Pakistan's foreign policy. The JI's political role did not last more than eight months, but Pakistan's continuous involvement in Afghanistan, Kashmir, and Central Asia resulted in a prolonged association with the army.

Other religious parties, with different ideological backgrounds, followed a similar evolution and were also later associated with both government and foreign policy management. For example, when the Pakistani Inter-Services Intelligence directorate preferred the Taliban over Gulbuddin Hekmatyar's Hizb-i-Islami movement in the mid-1990s, the two factions of the Jamiat Ulema-i-Islam became the military's proxy. As a result, the entire Islamist movement is now under military control in Pakistan.

Pakistan's Islamist Parties and Democracy

Even though the Pakistani Islamist movement is under military control, all the Islamist parties have uneasy relationships with the military. From their early confrontations with the army, they have retained the lesson that only through electoral politics can they one day expect to change the government. The main components of what is now the MMA had to camouflage their totalizing, and in many respects totalitarian, ideologies in favor of democratic discourse and practice because this became the condition for their political survival.

The Muhammad Ayub Khan years, which preceded the time of Zia ul-Haq, were the turning point for most of the Islamist parties. Like all political institutions, the Islamist parties were banned during the Ayub's martial law, but they continued to function under the cover of their social, educational, and religious activities. Because the dictator's economic policies proved successful, the only way the religious parties could attack the government was to demand that their civil rights—their democratic rights, in other words—be respected. Because sovereignty belongs to God only, democracy remained anathema from a theoretical point of view, but it constituted the primary condition for political survival. Defending democracy was the only strategy that these political groups could reasonably adopt.

Despite the religious sympathies of Zia ul-Haq, the Islamist parties had no other option but to adopt a similar strategy during Zia's martial law period. This period was particularly difficult for the JI because of the Islamization campaign launched by the military dictator. Having fought Bhutto with the slogan "Islam and Democracy," the JI also disapproved of Zia's coup, but suddenly it had to choose between the two. After promises that democracy would be restored, the JI agreed to participate in the government, but it left disillusioned only eight months later when it had become obvious that the dictator had no intention of holding the promised elections. Relations grew worse when the military ruler created a Sharia federal court in charge of ensuring that existing laws were in conformity with Islam but then exempted the decrees of martial law, the tax system, and the overall banking system from conformity with Sharia.

Since the death of Zia ul-Haq in 1988, all religious political parties have lived in this permanent tension between two series of contradictions. On one hand, they vitally need democracy to survive politically, but they have been unable to accommodate it during the rare periods of relative political freedom that the country has experienced. On the other hand, their Islamization agenda can partially materialize only with the support of the military, which provides the JI with an outlet by sending the Pakistan military to the hot spots of the subcontinent. In practice, strong antimilitary religious rhetoric barely hides the almost constant political and occasional "military" support for the army.

Pervez Musharraf and the MMA. Particularly significant for the JI's ambivalence about the military government was the attitude of the emir of the JI, Qazi Hussain Ahmed, after the 1999 military coup. Praising the army, and more specifically its chief, General Musharraf, "who had done an excellent job by dismissing the government of Nawaz Sharif," he demanded simultaneously "an evenhanded accountability and the constitution of an independent Election Commission to conduct free and fair polls in the country," the end of the state of emergency, and the return to democracy.[22] Qazi Hussain Ahmed also observed a few days later that in the past "martial law and military regimes had done nothing for the needful."[23] The JI's relations with the government soon turned sour, but the relationship continues even though the MMA has been largely marginalized.

Legal Framework Order. The postelection scenario is another indicator of the nature of the relationship between the Islamist coalition and the military. The debate over the LFO was one such occasion when the MMA was literally trapped by the army and lost what remained of its independence and political credibility.

Following the 2002 elections, the MMA refused to join a coalition with the pro-Musharraf parties. These parties were, nevertheless, able to form a government, thanks to a few PPP defectors who were rewarded with ministerial portfolios. The Pakistani president still needed a two-thirds majority to have the constitutional amendments contained in the LFO (which had been initiated before the election) approved by Parliament, and therefore he needed the support of the religious parties.

For fourteen months, the MMA sided with the secular opposition unified under the banner of the Alliance for the Restoration of Democracy (ARD).[24] They jointly refused the LFO and called for Musharraf's resignation. In December 2003, betraying its previous understanding with the ARD, the MMA announced that it accepted the LFO (slightly revised) because Musharraf promised that he would resign from his position of chief of army staff by December 31 of the following year.[25]

Whether the MMA leadership actually believed Musharraf's promise is a matter of debate. Although the content of the discussions between the military and religious leadership was not made public, there is little doubt that concessions were made regarding Islamization. The Hudood Laws, a code of honor that regulates male-female relations as well as marriages in Pakistan, had been discussed in the previous weeks, and a report from the chairperson of the Human Rights Commission was about to be released but was suddenly taken off the official agenda.

Politically the MMA was trapped. Having postured as being in opposition for fourteen months, it now appeared as the best support for the military regime. The MMA helped to institutionalize the presence of the army within Pakistan's political life through the creation of the National Security Council (NSC), a body in which the military predominated. It is true that the MMA could claim the creation of the NSC through a legislative process rather than a constitutional one as a major concession from the regime because it meant that the new body could be dissolved by a simple majority and not a two-thirds supermajority.[26] Given the army's degree of control over the political system, however, the concession was essentially cosmetic.

That the military no longer needed the MMA became obvious during the 2005 local elections. The Supreme Court suddenly disqualified candidates with madrassa degrees from running in elections unless they had studied and passed additional exams in English, Urdu, and Pakistan studies.[27] The International Crisis Group noted that this decision came against the backdrop of pressure by the regime on Akram Durrani, the NWFP MMA chief minister, and on Fazlur Rehman, the head of the JUI-F and leader of the opposition in the National Assembly, to end their boycott of the NSC.[28]

As a result of this and other manipulations, the MMA lost ground to the PML-Q in the NWFP, and the JI was ousted from Karachi by the Muttahida Quami Movement (MQM). Balochistan, where the JUI-F won six district *nazim* seats, was the only exception.[29] Given the nationalist insurrection in the province, the regime could not afford to favor the nationalist parties and other independent groups as it had done in the NWFP. The message was clear: With the threat of disqualification of MMA parliamentarians on educational grounds pending before the Supreme Court, the coalition could choose only between compliance with the military or political extinction.

Now that the military enjoyed a majority in the National Assembly sufficient to ensure the acceptance of whatever law it intended to pass as well as the institutionalism of its political role, it could do without the religious parties. Moreover, the now more vocal opposition from the MMA reinforced the international legitimacy of the regime. With the leaders of the mainstream opposition in exile and the MMA no longer able to form an alliance with the ARD, the regime had managed to marginalize its secular and religious oppositions alike.

Does the MMA Matter?

The question arises of the actual importance of the MMA (and consequently of the wisdom of policy dictated by fear of an increased importance of such a movement). Not only is the MMA unable to get substantial results without the firm hand of the military, but it also differs only marginally from the mainstream parties on a number of issues. Like mainstream groups, the MMA articulates the population's grievances vis-à-vis the regime. In January 2006, a resolution of the JI condemned Pakistan's "price hike, unemployment, inflation, social disparity and disappearing purchasing power."[30] Like its secular counterparts, whether in the government or in the opposition, the MMA often stops short of proposing any concrete alternatives.

Similarly, the MMA rightly condemns the democratic shortcomings of the regime. On January 3, 2006, for example, the *shura* of the JI passed a resolution in which most criticism could have been expressed by other opposition forces irrespective of their secular or religious character or by any independent observer. The same resolution condemned the military dictatorship for the paralysis of "all constitutional institutions" and the elimination of "the political system from the country besides causing irreparable damage to the independence, honor and reputation of the judiciary."[31]

Unlike the JI, the MMA's official motto is "Islam is the solution." The JI and its allies differ from the other opposition parties and the regime on two issues: Islamization and foreign policy. For most MMA members, Islamization and foreign policy are officially linked.

One should not be confused, here again, by the actors' discourse. Officially, Islamization is the main point of contention between the MMA and the regime. The coalition frequently blames the regime[32] for what it has termed a secularization program, accusing Musharraf of "forcing people to accept enlightened moderation" while the government cites militant Islamists as a danger that should make the United States hesitant to push democratization in Pakistan. But, once again, the social and, therefore, indirectly political roles of the MMA serve the regime. The Musharraf regime opposes Islamization only at the rhetorical level, and its secularization policies are, at best, limited. Musharraf has made significant concessions to the MMA by simply not changing the legislation regarding discrimination against gender or minorities.

More important is that, despite a number of claims and official texts, the regime has supported—at least passively—the madrassa network. What is at stake here is not the link between the madrassas and the jihadi organizations but, rather, the kind of education they disseminate and its social impact. Madrassa students are likely to graduate fully indoctrinated but not equipped with skills of value on the job market. By maintaining a substantial part of the population in such a state of semiliteracy, the regime guarantees its own stability; better-educated people might be in a position to ask for more accountability, a greater share of power, and a more equitable distribution of the country's economic resources.

The situation is similar in the foreign policy realm. During the past seven years, the MMA has often condemned the Musharraf regime for its alleged excessive compliance with its U.S. patrons, especially after September 11, 2001, and the U-turn in Pakistan's Afghan policy. By contrast, because they expect U.S. support in their electoral endeavors, the mainstream parties have not condemned the United States or have only criticized it slightly for supporting the regime. Yet the MMA has remained instrumental in implementing Pakistan's Kashmir and Afghan policies. JUI madrassas still provide Taliban manpower, and a number of militant groups, some of them close to the JI, remain active in Kashmir. At the political level, MMA propaganda generates the impression that both of these causes have popular support.

The 2007–2008 Elections: One Central Issue

The five years separating the last election from the upcoming one have, therefore, deeply changed Pakistan's political landscape. Several scenarios can be envisaged regarding the role of the Islamic forces in the upcoming elections as well as the outcome of these elections. All depend on one central issue: the president's decision whether to remain as chief of army staff. Elections for the presidency, the National Assembly, and the provincial assemblies are separate issues, although the president is elected by these bodies and the Senate. In other words, the coming elections are organizationally and politically linked.

Musharraf's mandate will end in April 2007, and he will eventually have to be reelected by the National Assembly, the Senate, and the four provincial assemblies.[33] It is therefore essential for Musharraf's political survival to ensure the victory of the PML-Q. His decision to run while retaining his post of chief of army staff will also influence his own prospects for reelection.

Remaining chief of army staff and rigging elections are the two conditions under which General Musharraf can retain power. Having no real political base, he has very little chance of being reelected as head of state if he does keep his post of chief of army staff. This applies whether or not he chooses to run for reelection before or after the general and provincial assembly elections. Only in his capacity as chief of army staff can he be reasonably certain of being obeyed and therefore followed, even by those whom he helped get elected.

The assumption that the elections will be rigged if Musharraf wants to retain power is not merely academic. Free and fair elections are almost unknown in Pakistan, but rigging elections has undoubtedly reached new levels under Musharraf, despite his recent protest that "Pakistan is a true democracy."[34] Manipulation of polls has included preelection division of existing districts as well as extension of chief-minister powers to remove *nazims,* with the effect that the latter became totally dependent on the provincial chief executive and, therefore, were rendered totally subservient. Although elections were supposed to be contested on a nonpartisan basis, both the president and the prime minister openly supported PML-Q candidates.[35] Polling was further rigged on election day. The International Crisis Group reported ballot stuffing and intimidation of opposition candidates by the police. In Balochistan, some opposition voters were detained, and some disappeared.[36] The monthly *Newsline* reported that in Gujrat (in Punjab), rival candidates of the PML-Q were arrested.[37]

Not only were the August and October 2005 local elections rigged to further weaken the mainstream opposition parties, but Musharraf also laid the groundwork for his supporters to dominate the forthcoming parliamentary elections.[38] Local elections were the first round of Musharraf's consolidation of power, as they ensured his control over the organization of the coming elections. Because the PML-Q won the elections, it will now be in charge of a majority of polling stations and therefore in a position to manipulate the results.

The regime has also taken care to choose a nonthreatening chief election commissioner, Qazi Mohammed Farooq, a former Supreme Court judge who, on May 12, 2000, validated the emergency proclaimed by Musharraf on the basis of the doctrine of "state necessity." Farooq is the author of a series of controversial decisions, all favoring the military. He is therefore no more likely than his predecessor, Justice Abdul Hameed Dogar, to challenge whatever fraud will take place. Against all evidence, Justice Abdul Hameed Dogar declared the 2005 local polls fair and transparent.

The MMA, like most other political parties in the country, is therefore most likely to ask for two things:

- That the series of elections scheduled for 2007 be held in the proper sequence (Musharraf's mandate will end on November 15, 2007, whereas the general and provincial elections are due 60 days after the termination of the assemblies mandates); and

- That Musharraf step down from his position as chief of army staff before his own bid for reelection.

Any other sequence will allow Musharraf to manipulate the election in his favor.

The JI has taken the lead in appealing for procedural reforms. The emir, Qazi Hussain Ahmed, who is also president of the MMA, continues to call for the resignation of Musharraf. In Lahore, on March 14, 2006, he warned that the MMA would boycott the next elections if they were held under the current Pakistani head of state, arguing that they would "not be genuine and fair" and would "consolidate the oppressive system."[39] In Peshawar, on March 26, he announced that all political and religious parties had agreed on a four-point agenda that envisages the resignation of Musharraf, the formation of a caretaker government, the restoration of the pre-1999 constitution, and the formation of an independent election commission.[40]

The U.S. Factor

The signal the United States sends to Pakistan's military rulers will be decisive for both the preelection situation and the election outcome. The central question here is not which particular political force may or may not win the election but, instead, the extent of the army's determination to consolidate its position within the country and orient Pakistan's foreign policy in a way that potentially collides with U.S. interests. Whether the army supports the Pakistani president or simply accepts the status quo will therefore be a true political choice between short- and longer-term interests.

There is little prospect that Musharraf will voluntarily resign his position as chief of army staff. The position of the U.S. administration will be decisive in determining the attitude of the Pakistani president. The intensity of the pressures and the nature of the demands on the Pakistani head of state will influence whether Musharraf retains his military position and will thus influence the position of the Islamist parties.

While he visited Pakistan on April 5, 2006, U.S. Assistant Secretary of State Richard Boucher stated that the Bush administration strongly favored civilian rule and civilian control of the military in Pakistan.[41] Acknowledging that General Musharraf's holding the dual offices of president and army chief negated "the spirit of democracy," Boucher declared that it remained to be seen how the issue would be addressed by the Pakistani president. Boucher remained evasive on the question of whether the United States would accept President Musharraf in uniform after the elections if he continued to hold both offices.[42]

This ambiguity illustrates the dilemma faced by the United States in its relations with Pakistan. Although the United States in principle favors a greater degree of democracy in the country (as stated in the new *National Security Strategy of the United States of America*[43]), the U.S. attitude will ultimately be decided by other considerations, such as the impact on the U.S. hierarchy of priorities of the most probable alternative. With the war on terror at the top of U.S. priorities for the South Asian region, tacit U.S. acquiescence to Musharraf retaining his uniform remains the most likely scenario.

Four Electoral Scenarios

Four different scenarios can be identified for the elections. Two depend not so much on whether the United States accepts Musharraf holding dual offices as on the intensity of the pressures his dual position will put on him and how those pressures are related to the extent of democratization in Pakistan.

Scenario 1: In Exchange for Implicit U.S. Acquiescence in Musharraf Continuing in Uniform, Musharraf Distances Himself Further From the Islamist Parties. This scenario reflects, to some extent, the existing reality. Soon after the LFO was passed in Parliament, General Musharraf started dissociating himself from religious parties that were increasingly becoming irrelevant, and they became more vocal against him. In the 2007 election scenario, increasing the distance would mean nothing worse for the religious parties than a few seats less in both the national and provincial assemblies.

Easy ways for the regime to weaken the religious parties would be to end the equivalence of madrassa certificates and university degrees or to suppress the law requiring a person to possess a university degree in order to be eligible to run for election. Such a measure would undoubtedly strengthen the regional parties countrywide but most notably in Balochistan and the NWFP. Given the present turbulence in Balochistan, such a decision is highly unlikely. The JUI will benefit from government support in the province.

Another possibility in the same context would be for the MMA to boycott the elections, as it is regularly tempted to do. Qazi Hussain Ahmed, the chairman of the MMA, has threatened to do so on several occasions, but a separate boycott by the MMA would almost inevitably provoke a split in the organization, which would then lose what is left of its political weight. Qazi Hussain has already made clear that the disintegration of the MMA is not an option.[44] As a matter of fact, despite many internal tensions, the MMA has proved to be much more cohesive than many initially believed it would be.[45] Moreover, having "demonstrated" its capacity to weaken the Islamic camp, the regime would feel internationally relegitimized.

The perspective would be different if the entire opposition decided to boycott the election, for it would demonstrate an absence of legitimacy of the regime that would be difficult for the United States and the European Union to ignore. This would not necessarily benefit the MMA because the opposition credentials of the ARD against the regime are much stronger, although the MMA has often been more vocal.

The dissociation between Musharraf and the MMA would benefit the MMA only in the case of an alliance between the regime and the liberal parties.[46] Such an alliance of all parties except the MMA (which, incidentally, U.S. diplomacy has been trying to promote for the past few years) would create a political vacuum that the MMA would be keen to fill, although it is highly improbable that it would be able to do so. With the exception of the regional parties, whose combined political weight is insufficient to challenge the central government, the MMA would be the sole real opposition. The population would become further depoliticized. The MMA would be unable to threaten the regime, but it would undoubtedly be legitimized in some segments of the population that otherwise have no ideological sympathy for the Islamists.

Scenario 2: Musharraf Continues in Uniform Despite U.S. Pressure and Decides to Favor the Islamist Parties to Ease the Pressure, Repeating the 2002 Scenario.

Such a scenario would undoubtedly benefit the MMA, which would feel strengthened and thus would be more assertive in its demands. Its actual political power would not necessarily be greater, but the regime would probably make additional compromises on Islamization, in particular on family laws and education.

This scenario is unlikely for at least two reasons:

- Technically, elections will have to be supervised by elected local bodies, whose majority, thanks to the rigged 2005 local elections, belongs to the PML-Q and will therefore be difficult to convince to favor candidates from other parties.

- The mechanism would be too transparent, even for international public opinion.

Yet the scenario cannot be totally dismissed as a real possibility if the regime feels threatened. Following Boucher's visit to Pakistan on April 5, 2006, the PML-Q central secretary and minister of state for information, Tariq Azim Khan, declared that the United States "cannot dictate [to] President Musharraf on the uniform issue,"[47] thus indicating that the regime would oppose such a move.

Moreover, the mainstream parties (PML-N and PPP) have threatened to boycott the elections if their leaders, former prime ministers Nawaz Sharif and Benazir Bhutto, are prevented from returning to Pakistan and a caretaker government is not formed.[48] For the MMA, such a boycott would result in a situation similar to the one generated by an alliance between the regime and these parties. The Islamist coalition would try to fill the political vacuum, although it would not have as much benefit as in a crisis of legitimacy generated by an alliance of the liberals and the military.

Scenario 3: Musharraf Disappears From the Political scene.

Although this scenario is not the most likely, it is not totally improbable and thus is worth examining. Notwithstanding death resulting from natural causes or accident, this scenario could result from two different politically meaningful situations: Musharraf could be assassinated, or the army could decide that he is no longer its best representative and force him to resign.

The assassination of Pakistan's head of state would most likely result in the cancellation or postponement of the elections. Whatever the army's decision, it would negatively affect the MMA, whose past and present links with jihadi movements would be examined with the blessing of the international community.

Much less clear would be the impact of a forced resignation of Musharraf, as happened to Ayub Khan. Such could be the case if, for example, the army decided that, given the current level of frustration in the country, it would be better off with a civilian assuming power but would be confronted with Musharraf unwilling to give up his position.

The situation in Waziristan and the current insurrection in Balochistan make this scenario improbable, as the army wants to avoid further disorder and uncertainty. Such a scenario would be more likely in the postelection period if, for example, Benazir Bhutto came back and was able to mobilize the population against the regime. Although not the most likely scenario, this possibility cannot totally be dismissed. The army might then be tempted to ask Musharraf to resign and let a civilian assume power while the army kept its control of the main levers of power.

Should Musharraf exit the political scene before the elections, it would probably lead to the closest possible approximation of a free and fair election. The military would be tempted to favor its preferred party but would be ready to accept the outcome of the election, providing that the winner would agree not to cross certain red lines concerning the role, budget, and prerogatives of the military and would not try to interfere with foreign policy.

In such a situation, the MMA would most probably emerge as a significant component of Pakistan's polity with its number of seats less than or equal to its current count, and it would remain an opposition party.

Scenario 4: Musharraf Resigns his Position of Chief of Army Staff, and the National and Provincial Elections are Held in a Free and Fair Manner.

This scenario is the least likely for it would almost automatically mean a normalization of Pakistan's political life. For the MMA, its impact would be similar to that of scenario 3.

Potential Impact of the Return to Pakistan of Nawaz Sharif and Benazir Bhutto on the Upcoming Elections

Unless he is forced to do so, General Musharraf is very unlikely to accept the return of either of the exiled former prime ministers, Nawaz Sharif and Benazir Bhutto. The unacceptability of Benazir Bhutto and her husband Asif Zardari to the military is well known, and additional charges against the couple were recently made public. Similarly, the negotiated exile of Nawaz Sharif is expected to cease only at the end of the decade. It is therefore improbable that he or his brother Shabaz, former chief minister of Punjab, will be allowed to return to Pakistan to run in the elections.

The government reaction (the announcement that the President would be re-elected by the current assemblies) to the signing by former prime ministers Nawaz Sharif and Benazir Bhutto on May 15, 2006, of the Charter of Democracy—a text calling for a number of constitutional amendments as well as legal and institutional changes to restore democracy, defining a code of conduct for the mainstream political parties, and excluding any recourse to the army against the parties[49]—is an indication of what could possibly happen in such an eventuality, even though the document is not a predictor that the two exiled leaders may be allowed to return to Pakistan for the elections, and there is no certainty that they will remain united.

Should they be allowed to return, the situation would become more complicated for the PML-Q and Musharraf. Although their return would not fundamentally alter any of the above scenarios, it would introduce an additional element of uncertainty.

In scenario 1 (in exchange for implicit U.S. acquiescence in Musharraf continuing in uniform, Musharraf distances himself further from the Islamist parties), the presence of either Sharif or Bhutto, or both, would facilitate Musharraf's plan by preventing the MMA from gaining ground in both Punjab and Sindh, which are their respective strongholds. It would, however, make life more difficult for him, for he would most likely have to face divisions within the PML-Q as some elements might be tempted once again to join the PML-N. Two cases could then be envisaged, depending on whether the PML-N and the PPP could sustainably unite against Musharraf. It would become extremely difficult for Musharraf to govern if they were able to muster such an alliance. If they cannot join forces, it would be difficult but not impossible for Musharraf to remain the arbiter.

Scenario 2 (Musharraf continues in uniform against U.S. pressure and decides to favor the Islamist parties to ease the pressure, repeating the 2002 scenario) would be much more difficult to implement should Sharif and Bhutto come back. The MMA obviously benefited from their absence in 2002. Although it is difficult to guess the margin by which the vote would be affected if the two leaders came back to contest the elections, the MMA would likely lose ground at least in Punjab and Sindh. Again, Musharraf's own position would depend on whether the PPP and the PML-N can unite.

In scenarios 3 (Musharraf disappears from the political scene) and 4 (Musharraf resigns his position of chief of army staff, and the national and provincial elections are held in a free and fair manner), the presence of Sharif and Bhutto only helps bring back the MMA to its natural modest electoral performance, which is nuanced only by circumstantial variations.

Finally, one should also consider the possibility of mass agitation if the elections are too blatantly rigged, in particular under scenario 1. In such a scenario the MMA could side with the opposition, being even the most vocal. Such a possibility would not necessarily benefit the MMA, however, because the logic of the situation would lead to either an army repression or new elections. In the case of repression, the MMA would most probably have to suffer from army subjugation like all political parties. In the case of fresh elections, the MMA would most likely lose badly in comparison with its 2002 performance.

Ultimately, for the MMA the most probable outcome of the 2007–2008 elections, which will be controlled by the PML, is a situation only marginally different from its present one. None of the scenarios proposed envisages a significant electoral gain for the Islamist coalition in the 2007 election, although the MMA could gain some seats in Punjab and Sindh if Nawaz Sharif and Benazir Bhutto are prevented from running. It is even more difficult to realistically envisage the situation that could potentially lead to an Islamist takeover unless it was engineered by the regime itself (that is, by the political wing of the Inter-Services Intelligence directorate), which would most probably prove internationally counterproductive.

Policy Implications

Whatever the prevailing scenario, the Islamic forces will be, ultimately, a dependent variable rather than a defining factor. In the months to come, the Musharraf regime is likely to try to convince the international community otherwise with a strategy opposite from the one it successfully used in 2002.

The MMA's success in the last general elections, following 9/11, was supposed to create the impression of a gradual yet inexorable trend toward extremism. The strategy this time could be to use extremism to discredit political Islam. The multiplication of sectarian incidents and the authorization to some previously banned sectarian organizations, such as the Sipah-e-Sahaba, to hold public rallies, although under a new name,[50] could be indicators of the government's willingness to use sectarian violence as an electoral tool. All over the country, sectarianism will contribute to creating an atmosphere of fear, a demand for law and order, and a rejection of religious violence. Fortunately for the regime, the situation in Waziristan, where the army seems unable to prevent the rise of the Taliban, will reinforce the threat perception.

Having increased the threat perception, the military will try to generate a secular front, playing on the frustrations generated by the 2002 general elections. If the 2005 local elections are any indication, we should witness a resurgence of the local nationalist parties. The Awami National Party will resurface in the NWFP, and the MQM will be allowed to continue terrorizing its political opponents in Karachi and elsewhere in Sindh. The same card will be more difficult to play in Balochistan because of the nationalist insurrection, but the regime may be tempted to exploit the divisions between tribal and non tribal leaders by asking the National Party, a non tribal organization, to join a vast anti-MMA coalition, at the same time making sure that the MMA gets enough seats in the provincial assembly to participate in the government. Overall, the PML-Q will get a majority and will be helped as much as necessary. The regional parties, however, will be there essentially to add credibility to the PML-Q victory.

Incidentally, it will be essential for the success of this strategy that the two leaders of the mainstream opposition, Nawaz Sharif and Benazir Bhutto, be prevented from running in the elections. The leader of the PPP in particular could constitute a real political threat for the regime because the PPP remains the number one party in the country. The regime will undoubtedly find allies in the regional parties and locally, with the MMA, because a too assertive PPP could engender a backlash.

The MMA will not disappear from the political scene. Depending on the evolution of alliances, it could even end up in a position similar to where it stood in 2002. But even a poor electoral performance would not spark a political confrontation with the military. The MMA's limited, yet real, popular support will make it essential for the army to assure itself that the MMA can be reactivated whenever necessary and can facilitate covert operations along the Afghan borders if need be. Politically, however, the MMA would likely return to its traditional position of opposition party with no other hope than being a catalyst for dissent and protest.

Whatever the MMA's ultimate electoral fate, it should not be the determinant of the international community's tolerance for the violation of democracy in Pakistan. Despite the blatant rigging of the 2002 elections, the international community remained mute, accepting a military dictator who promised to fight political Islam and promote "enlightened moderation" but then did neither. Just as the MMA's relative success in the 2002 election should not have determined policy toward Pakistan at that time, neither should the MMA's electoral defeat be the objective of any policy toward Pakistan in the coming months. Renouncing its own values will not serve the West but instead will reinforce the idea that the West applies a double standard when it comes to Islamic countries. The main illness of Pakistan is not Islamism, but militarism.

Notes

1. Mohammed Waseem, *The 2002 Elections in Pakistan* (Islamabad: Quaid-i-Azam University, International Relations Department, 2003), p. 30.
2. International Crisis Group, *Pakistan: The Mullahs and the Military,* ICG Asia Report 49 (Islamabad/Brussels: International Crisis Group, 2003), <http://www.crisisgroup.org/library/documents/report_archive/A400925_20032003.pdf>.
3. Ibid.
4. Waseem, *The 2002 Elections,* p. 33.
5. Ibid.
6. Ibid., p. 178, table 1.
7. EU Election Observation Mission to Pakistan, *Final Report of the European Union's Observation Mission to Pakistan: National and Provincial Assembly Election* (10 October 2002), p. 31, <http://ec.europa.eu/comm/europeaid/projects/eidhr/pdf/elections-reports-pakistan-02_en.pdf>.
8. Ibid., p. 32.
9. Ibid., p. 33.
10. International Crisis Group, *Pakistan: The Mullahs and the Military,* p. 16.
11. Waseem, *The 2002 Elections,* p. 55.
12. Ibid.
13. Jamal Malik, *Colonization of Islam: Dissolution of Traditional Institutions in Pakistan* (Lahore: Vanguard Books, 1996), p. 8.
14. Frédéric Grare, *Pakistan: The Myth of an Islamist Peril,* Policy Brief 45 (Washington, D.C.: Carnegie Endowment for International Peace, 2006), <http://www.carnegieendowment.org/files/45.grare.final.pdf>.
15. Waseem, op. cit., p. 56.
16. See Olivier Roy, "Le neo fondamentalisme islamique ou l'imaginaire de l'Oummah," *Esprit,* April 1996, p. 82.
17. For a brief review of each component of the MMA, see International Crisis Group, *Pakistan: The Mullahs and the Military,* pp. 5–6.
18. Deobandi organizations belong to the Hanafi legal school. They qualify themselves as deobandi as they feel connected one way or another with the theological seminary founded in 1867 in Deoband, near Delhi. According to Jamal Malik, "the core of affiliation comprised civil servants and merchants, while the students of the seminary basically originated from urban retail merchants, while the students of the seminary basically originated from urban retail merchant families, small landowners and also the poorer strata of society." Malik continues, "the role of the Prophet and the widespread cult of hereditary saints (pir) were demystified among the Deobandis. They do not project the solution of contemporary problems into the hereafter as other groups did. In this sense, they were vividly interested in the actual condition of life, *hic et nunc.*" They are politicized to a considerable degree. See Jamal Malik, *Colonization of Islam,* pp. 4–5.
19. International Crisis Group, *Authoritarianism and Political Party Reform in Pakistan,* ICG Asia Report 102 (Islamabad/Brussels: International Crisis Group, 2005), p. 13, <http://www.crisisgroup.org/library/documents/asia/south_asia/102_authoritarianism_and_political_party_reform_in_pakistan.pdf>.
20. Ibid.
21. Seyyed Vali Reza Nasr, *The Vanguard of Islamic Revolution: The Jamaat-i-Islami of Pakistan* (London: I. B. Tauris, 1994), p. 106.
22. *Pakistan Political Perspectives,* November 11, 1999, p. 44.
23. *Pakistan Political Perspectives,* December 12, 1999, p. 52.
24. See K. Alan Kronstadt, *Pakistan's Domestic Political Developments,* Report No. RL32615 (Washington, D.C.: Congressional Research Service, September 19, 2005), p. 16, <http://www.fas.org/sgp/crs/row/RL32615.pdf>.
25. Ibid.
26. Ibid.
27. Ibid., p. 22.
28. International Crisis Group, *Pakistan's Local Polls: Shoring Up Military Rule,* Asia Briefing 43 (Islamabad/Brussels: International Crisis Group, 2005), p. 6, <http://www.crisisgroup.org/library/documents/asia/south_asia/b043_pakistan_s_local_polls_shoring_up_military_rule.pdf>.
29. Ibid., p. 11.
30. Ibid.
31. *JI Media News,* "JI Shoora Resolution on Political Situation," January 2003, <http://www.jamaat.org/news/2006/jan/03/1001.html>.
32. Pakistan News Service, PakTribune.com, December 10, 2004.
33. On this occasion, each assembly accounts for the same number of seats as the smallest of the four provincial assemblies, to ensure equality between them.
34. "Pakistan Is a True Democracy," *Daily Times,* March 26, 2006, <http://www.dailytimes.com.pk/default.asp?page=2006/03/26/story_26-3-2006_pg7_1>.
35. International Crisis Group, *Pakistan's Local Polls,* p. 4.
36. Ibid., p. 10.
37. Zahid Hussain, "The Great Election Farce," *Newsline,* September 2005.
38. For a complete report on the rigging of the 2005 local elections, see International Crisis Group, *Pakistan's Local Polls.*
39. "MMA to Boycott Elections under Musharraf: Qazi," *JI Media News,* March 14, 2006, <http://www.jamaat.org/news/2006/mar/14/1002.html>.
40. "Qazi Demands Musharraf's Resignation, Caretaker Govt," *JI Media News,* March 26, 2006, <http://www.jamaat.org/news/2006/mar/26/1002.html>.
41. Qudssia Akhlaque, "U.S. Wants Civilian Rule: Boucher: Need for Free, Fair Polls Stressed," *Dawn,* April 6, 2006, <http://www.dawn.com/2006/04/06/top1.htm>.
42. Ibid.
43. *National Security Strategy of the United States of America* (Washington, D.C.: White House, March 2006), p. 39, <http://www.whitehouse.gov/nsc/nss/2006/>.
44. *Pak Tribune,* December 18, 2005.
45. M. M. Ali, "Democracy Is Back in Pakistan as Religious Parties Emerge as a Serious Political Force," *Washington Report on Middle East Affairs,* January–February 2003, pp. 34–35.
46. See *Daily Times,* April 7, 2006.
47. Pakistan News Service, PakTribune.com, April 7, 2006.
48. "Bhutto, Sharif Parties May Boycott Pakistan Polls," *Khaleej Times,* April 7, 2006.
49. "Text of the Charter for Democracy," *Dawn,* May 16, 2006, <http://www.dawn.com/2006/05/16/local23.htm>.
50. Azmat Abbas, "Warming up," *The Herald,* May 2006, pp. 30–31. According to the author, "the decision to allow the Millat-e-Islamia [the new name of the Sipah-e-Sahaba Pakistan] to start its activities without fear of harassment from law enforcement agencies was taken at a meeting held in March 2006."

FRÉDÉRIC GRARE is a visiting scholar with the Carnegie Endowment for International Peace, where he assesses U.S. and European policies toward Pakistan and focuses on the tension between stability and democratization in Pakistan, including challenges of sectarian conflict, Islamist political mobilization, and educational reform. Grare is a leading expert and writer on South Asia, having served most recently in the French Embassy in Pakistan and, from 1999 to 2003, in New Delhi as director of the Centre for Social Sciences and Humanities. Grare has written extensively on security issues, Islamist movements, and sectarian conflict in Pakistan and Afghanistan and has edited the volume *India, China, Russia: Intricacies of an Asian Triangle.*

Article 35

Textile Export Strategy

Prime Minister Shaukat Aziz asked the National Textile Strategy Committee (NTSC) on Thursday to submit its final recommendations by December 31 to make the textile industry sustainable and globally competitive. Going by the export trend, the core problem involves improving the industry's productivity in terms of quality and price. Despite the six-billion-dollar investment in modernisation, balancing and expansion or creation of new capacities over the last six years, growth in textile exports has been slowing down. According to latest reports, earnings from textile products dropped by 7.10 per cent during July–August to $1.625 billion compared to the corresponding period last year. The industry has not been able to face up to tough competition from the three major exporters in the region—China, India and Bangladesh—after the lifting of the textile quota on January 1, 2005. A recent UNDP report revealed that Pakistan is selling its textile products to the EU and the US at the cheapest rate in South Asia. An industry with the domestic advantage of a big cotton crop has a mere one per cent of the world market share in ready-made garments. The problems facing textile exports are industry-specific as well as related to the overall inefficiency of the economy. The All Pakistan Textile Mills Association wants incentives including duty-free import of machinery and spares to facilitate its members to make further investments. It is seeking concessions which it thinks are necessary to provide the industry an even playing field against its giant regional competitors, including Bangladesh which does not even produce cotton. On the agenda of the NTSC, which represents all stakeholders, are wide-ranging short- and long-term issues many of which have been neglected by both the industry and the government for a long time. While the government works on an ad-hoc basis, the industry has not been able to shake off cronyism completely. Chairing its first meeting, the prime minister asked the NTSC to critically study the Textile Vision 2015 guidelines and look at the industry's efficiency, including skill development and capacity building as well as its acquaintance with global market trends in higher-end products, especially women's garments. Fashion changes quickly, at least twice a year in developed markets, and the industry has not kept pace with it. Much of the value-addition is related to fabric and garment designing which is critical in boosting exports and needs to be pursued on a priority basis. Unfortunately, in this area the local industry is not part of the supply-chain management that enhances competitiveness. The agenda of the NTSC also includes topics like technological upgrading through value-chain product diversification and development of compatible infrastructure. With a paradigm shift taking place in the textile industry globally, the prime minister has emphasised that there is a need to take a fresh look at the national textile strategy. The government has just withdrawn its earlier condition of in-house facilities for extending a five per cent R&D support for home textiles. One hopes a part of the money thus gained will be channelled to the universities, as is the practice in developed countries. But perhaps the most important problem facing the textile industry is its archaic management system and paucity of upgraded trade skills. The family-managed textile companies have not been able to absorb modern corporate culture either in management or human resource development. To become globally competitive in price and quality, the industry has to move with the times.

For Pakistan, American Aid Is All Guns, No Butter

HELENE COOPER

Syed Jawad Ahsan's Valentine's Day this year was a heartbreaking window into the box in which this country is trapped.

Around 10:30 on Tuesday morning, Mr. Ahsan, chief executive of Irfan Textiles Pvt. Ltd., got into his car and headed for the factory just outside town where his workers, some 5,000 of them, stitch and weave underwear for Jockey. As he was leaving Lahore's outskirts, he saw some boys in the middle of the road, setting fire to car tires. A group of Sunni parties had called for yet another of the seemingly never-ending protests against the Danish cartoon caricatures of the Prophet Muhammad, and the boys had apparently decided that torching tires on their own turf would teach the West a thing or two.

Mr. Ahsan threw his car into reverse and started to back away. But behind him, another group had gathered, throwing rocks at a parked car, breaking its windows and slashing its tires. Frustrated, Mr. Ahsan turned left and made a quick exit, heading back to town. Using his cell phone, he called and left a message that I should meet him at his downtown office for our interview on Pakistan's textile industry. "I think it's safer for us in town today," he said.

An hour later, we were drinking Pepsi and eating crackers in his office in Lahore. Mr. Ahsan was visibly saddened. "Pakistan didn't used to be like this," he said. "All this extremism that you see here now is because of Afghanistan."

He meant the Afghanistan war that started in 1979, not the one that came after Sept. 11. The way Mr. Ahsan sees it, Pakistan before 1979 was a much more open society, with wine bars in the cities and a small measure of freedom. But when the Russians invaded Afghanistan, America responded by arming, and largely creating, the Islamist fighters who drummed up religious fire in their war to drive out the Russians. Next door, Pakistan became a front-line state, and American money flooded to the mujahedeen. Ever since, Pakistan has been home to a growing cadre of fundamentalist Islamists, many of them bent on jihad.

With the huge gap here between rich and poor, militants find young boys with nothing to do easy prey. Mr. Ahsan can't fathom why Americans aren't working on the economic conditions that breed discontent.

"We don't need more of your F-16's," he said. "What we need is trade in textiles. We need a free trade agreement, like the one you're going to give Egypt, like the one you gave Jordan, like the one you gave Morocco."

The United States agreed in 2005 to resume sales of F-16 fighter jets to Pakistan. The sales had been suspended for more than a decade because Pakistan began developing nuclear weapons. But Washington has refused to grant a bigger and far more important concession: duty-free access for Pakistani imports.

If there is a stronger case than Pakistan's for duty-free access, it is certainly hard to find. This place is a breeding ground for Muslim extremists, but it also has a population and government that has, by and large, maintained cordial relations with America. Pakistan's biggest industry is textiles, accounting for 45 percent of its manufacturing jobs, and its biggest market is the United States. Pakistani factories make everything from bras to shirts and sheets for companies like Wal-Mart, Polo Ralph Lauren and Martha Stewart Living Omnimedia.

Since Sept. 11, it's been an uphill battle for such Pakistani companies. American buyers have been skittish about trusting their orders to a place that looks like a war zone on TV. Meanwhile, other countries, including China, Bangladesh and India, have been quick to try to woo business away. The overwhelming belief here is that without duty-free access to the U.S. market, the textile and apparel industry here can't compete.

Mr. Ahsan says his knitwear exports are down 17 percent in the past year alone, and he believes that Pakistan's knitwear industry—the staple of its textile industry—is dying. This week, another knitting factory in Lahore became a casualty: 1,000 jobs will be eliminated, although the workers haven't yet been told.

It is the end of our interview, and Mr. Ahsan and I have spent as much time talking about religion and why Muslims are so upset about the cartoons as we have about trade and textiles. Reaching into his back pocket, he pulled out a Muslim prayer book—he said a friend had given it to him to help him get through the difficult times he is facing as he tries to keep his business together.

He said he was waiting to see whether President Bush's visit next month would produce any new American promises to help Pakistan on trade, but he admits that if past is prologue, Pakistan will come away empty-handed on what really counts. "Textile trade, not F-16's, is the only thing the U.S. should do if at all U.S. wanted to mellow extremism here," he said. "It must be employment."

I left him and headed to a Lahore suburb to meet some friends. About a half-hour later, the mob of boys, now thousands strong, reached Lahore's downtown area, which locals call the mall. They ransacked around 500 cars, burned 75 motorcycles and 10 other vehicles, and torched the Punjab Assembly. A bank security guard opened fire and killed two boys. Three others were shot and injured.

The mob then turned to the business district, setting fire to a Norwegian cell phone company's office and a KFC. Nestled between those two buildings was an office belonging to Mr. Ahsan and his brother. It, too, was burned down.

Letter from Sri Lanka: Tides of War

PHILIP GOUREVITCH

There was talk in Sri Lanka, not long after the tsunami, of an expensive coffin heading north. The story appeared in the press and was passed on in conversation, unencumbered by any trace of verifiable reality: *Did you hear . . . a coffin, very fancy . . . what to think?* Perhaps such a coffin existed, perhaps not. More than thirty thousand people had been killed on the island in the space of a few minutes when the Indian Ocean rose up and surged ashore under a bright, cloudless sky on the morning after Christmas; and Velupillai Prabhakaran, the leader of the secessionist Tamil Tigers, who control a sizable swath of northern Sri Lanka, had not been seen or heard from since. The coastal town of Mullaittivu, where Prabhakaran had his military headquarters in a network of underground bunkers, had been largely erased by the sea. An announcer on the state-owned radio, the Sri Lanka Broadcasting Corporation, speculated hopefully that, if so much of Mullaittivu was gone, perhaps its most notorious resident might be, too. For thirty years, since he took up arms against the government, which is dominated by the island's Sinhalese Buddhist majority, Prabhakaran, the self-styled Sun God of the Tamil Hindu minority, has been the defining figure of Sri Lankan history—a wearying chronicle of civil war, assassination, and terror. For a country dumbfounded by the senseless loss of life along its coasts, the rumor of the northbound coffin attached to the mystery of his absence to suggest the possibility of a single meaningful death.

Prabhakaran, who turned fifty last year, is one of the most bloody-minded and effective warlords in today's crowded field. Osama bin Laden is more infamous, on account of Al Qaeda's global reach and sensational operations, but Prabhakaran and his Tigers, in their determination to carve out an independent Tamil state in the north and east of Sri Lanka, have been every bit as bold. The Tigers, whose extremist ethnic nationalism is essentially secular, are often credited with inventing suicide bombing, and although that claim is surely exaggerated, they did develop the sort of explosive suicide vests favored by Palestinian terrorists, and they refined the technique of using speedboats as bombs to ram large ships, which was employed in 2000 by Al Qaeda agents in Yemen against the U.S.S. Cole. In 1991, long before female suicide bombers became a fixture of Middle Eastern terrorism, the Tigers deployed the woman who blew up

India's Prime Minister, Rajiv Gandhi. That was Prabhakaran's most notorious hit, but his suicide squad of Black Tigers has claimed more than two hundred and sixty bombings in the last two decades—an average rate of nearly one a month—injuring and killing thousands of people, the great majority of them civilians. "Of course we use suicide bombers," a Tiger official who was overseeing humanitarian relief for displaced tsunami survivors near Mullaittivu told me. "Because, as a revolutionary organization, we have limited resources."

Prabhakaran depicts his struggle as a quest to reclaim his people's historic homeland, but the idea of secession is actually a relatively recent phenomenon, a response to the government's discriminatory policies and its complicity in communal violence against Tamils during the decades following Sri Lanka's independence, in 1948, from British colonial rule. Until the early nineteen-eighties, most Tamils favored the establishment of a federal system that would grant them substantial local autonomy within a unified state; and, even as hope for a political solution gave way to Tamil militancy, armed struggle was widely seen as a means to force such an outcome. Prabhakaran, however, has always been hostile to the idea of power-sharing. He proclaims himself and his Tigers to be the only true representatives of Tamil political aspirations and has waged a systematic campaign—every bit as relentless as his war against the state—to eliminate Tamil rivals. Nevertheless, the Tigers have consistently had to resort to the forced recruitment of Tamil children, a practice barely distinguishable from outright abduction, to fill their fighting ranks and replenish their suicide brigades.

In Sinhalese, the name Sri Lanka means "blessed land," and in its physical aspects the country is a tropical paradise, hemmed by palm-shaded beaches and, in its interior, fragrant with the florid vegetation of astonishingly varied landscapes—salt marshes and mountain lakes, mist-shrouded tea plantations, glimmering paddies, and mahogany jungles. The contrast between the island's natural attractions and its repellently violent history was thrown into stark relief by the tsunami, which killed half as many people in one blow as three decades of war and terror had claimed. Yet this devastation was perfectly arbitrary, and it is a measure of the depth of Sri Lanka's troubles that for this reason the tsunami was widely regarded there not only as a disaster but also as an occasion for hope.

The President, Chandrika Bandaranaike Kumaratunga, articulated this unlikely optimism when she addressed the nation two days after the tsunami. Sri Lanka, she declared, had been "incredibly humbled" by the waves, which had dealt death and destruction to all ethnic groups indiscriminately. Never mind that Sinhalese, who count for nearly seventy-five per cent of the island's twenty million inhabitants, outnumber Tamils by roughly four to one, and that Tamils, in turn, outnumber the next largest minority group, Muslims, by three to one. "Nature does not differentiate in the treatment of peoples," the President said, and she urged Sri Lankans to follow nature's example. In fact, many had responded to the disaster by rushing to the aid of the afflicted without regard for their identity. There were stories of Sinhalese soldiers risking—and losing—their lives in efforts to rescue Tamil civilians; of Tamil businessmen carting meals to displaced Sinhalese survivors; and of Muslims buying up clothes and medicines to hand out to Hindus and Buddhists. It was only later that Sri Lankans had time to register their surprise at their own unthinking decency, and their relief at this discovery was compounded by a sense that the tsunami had saved the country from an imminent return to war.

Although a ceasefire between the government and the Tigers has held since early 2002, peace talks broke down the next year—with the Tigers demanding what amounts to self-rule, and the government refusing to grant it—and, in the unhappy deadlock that followed, both parties have been riven by internal disputes. On the government side, President Kumaratunga forged a new ruling coalition in April of last year with the People's Liberation Front (known by its Sinhalese initials as the J.V.P.), a small but aggressively divisive Communist party, which spikes its Marxism with an extremist strain of Sinhalese nationalism and Buddhist supremacism, and regards concessions to the Tigers as tantamount to treason. Kumaratunga, who first allied with the J.V.P. in 2001, has acknowledged that her affiliation with the party was a devil's bargain, made to retain power. This political realignment in Colombo, the capital, coincided with an armed revolt against Prabhakaran by one of his top commanders, a man known by the nom de guerre Colonel Karuna, who drew his support from his home area in eastern Sri Lanka, where Tamils had long felt exploited and ill served by the Tiger leadership. Karuna's aim was to secure autonomy for eastern Tamils from both the Tigers and the government, and although he could not prevail militarily against Prabhakaran, he remains at large—in hiding, and probably in exile—and the Tigers have been unable to re-establish dominion over large areas of the east. Karuna's rebellion dramatized the threat that peace poses to Prabhakaran's authority, and a month before the tsunami struck, when Prabhakaran delivered his annual Hero's Day speech, he declared himself fed up with the stalemate.

The Hero's Day oration, which is delivered at night, in a cemetery for martyred Tigers, lit by flaming torches, is often Prabhakaran's only significant public utterance in the course of a year, and his pronouncements have come to be seen as oracular. "We are living in a political void, without war, without a stable peace, without the conditions of normalcy, without an interim or permanent solution to the ethnic conflict," he began. He accused President Kumaratunga of rejecting the prospect of peace through her "unholy alliance" with the J.V.P. The Sinhalese and the Tamils, he said, were more polarized than ever—"two separate peoples with divergent and mutually incompatible ideologies, consciousness, and political goals"—and he concluded, ominously, "There are borderlines to patience and expectations. We have now reached the borderline." In the weeks before Christmas, assassinations and attacks involving Prabhakaran's forces and Karuna sympathizers escalated steadily in the east. Some Sri Lankans cancelled vacations in order to be at home if the war resumed; others made plans to leave the country.

"We were running at the rate of about a murder a day until the tsunami came along," Father Harry Miller, an American Jesuit missionary in the devastated east-coast city of Batticaloa, told me. Batticaloa, and the surrounding province, which shares its name, was the epicenter of Karuna's rebellion, a predominantly Tamil region where the ceasefire lines describe a confusing patchwork of government and Tiger territories. For dozens of miles before you reach Batticaloa city on the two-lane road that links it to Colombo—a slow, eight-hour drive away—the scrubby bush is punctuated by heavily fortified Army camps, and a pervasive military presence makes the government-controlled town feel like a place under occupation. Miller had heard the rumors that Prabhakaran might be dead, but he was not surprised when the Tiger leader reappeared in mid-January, without a word of consolation for his people's losses. Miller did not share President Kumaratunga's view of the tsunami as a cosmic corrective to what she called "a country where every aspect of life has been politicized," much less as a providential opportunity. The prevailing sentiment in Batticaloa, he said, was "We are victims again. We've had flood, we've had wars, we've had drought, we've had a cyclone. Victims again."

The defining catastrophe of post-colonial Sri Lankan history was an act of man, a law, promulgated in 1956, when the island was still called Ceylon. The law established Sinhalese as the sole official language (a status previously reserved for English). Sri Lanka's Sinhalese and Tamils both trace their origins to migrations from India, and, despite their different languages and religions, their coexistence had previously been untroubled by ethnic violence. The 1956 law, however, effectively transformed the parliamentary democracy into an instrument of Sinhalese nationalism and excluded Tamils and other minorities from careers in public service, access to many educational opportunities, and other rights and privileges to which citizenship supposedly entitled them.

The man behind the law was President Kumaratunga's father, Prime Minister S.W.R.D. Bandaranaike, the scion of a Sinhalese noble family, who was raised an Anglican and educated at Oxford. Although Bandaranaike had converted to Buddhism as a young man, he spoke English with greater ease than he did Sinhalese. In fact, he had to brush up on his native language before campaigning as a populist opposition leader, who mixed leftist rhetoric with nativism in order to tap the resentment of ordinary Sri Lankans toward the class from which he came, the British-educated élite. His Sinhalese-only policy coincided with celebrations in honor of the twenty-five-hundredth anniversary of the Buddha's enlightenment, and scholars tend to regard Bandaranaike's alienation of the Tamils as inadvertent. "He could just as well have included the Tamil poor in that anti-English campaign," the human-rights lawyer Radhika Coomaraswamy told me in Colombo. Coomaraswamy is a Tamil, and she said, "I don't see anti-Tamil sentiment at the core of the original Sinhalese nationalism. Tamils were just ignored, which may be an even greater insult."

Bandaranaike was unprepared when outraged Tamils took to the streets to protest the law and were met with violence from Sinhalese inflamed by the jingoism he had preached. Tamils were beaten (some of them to death), their homes were set ablaze, and their businesses were ransacked. Bandaranaike could not undo the damage. In 1957, he negotiated a pact with Tamil federalists that met many of their demands for regional autonomy. Sinhalese hard-liners protested, and in 1958 he repudiated the pact, and the country was again swept by violence, of which Tamils were overwhelmingly the victims. A year and a half later, Bandaranaike was shot dead by an apparently deranged Buddhist monk.

Bandaranaike was succeeded, the following year, by his widow, Sirimavo—the world's first female Prime Minister—who offered concessions to Tamil federalists and won their support during her campaign, then turned her back on them, triggering mass protests in the northern city of Jaffna. In 1962, the Army was sent in to quell the unrest, and although there was little violence between Sinhalese and Tamils during the next decade, the dispiriting effect of militarization in the north, coupled with official discrimination, was such that a generation of Tamils grew up with an acute sense of disenfranchisement. In the early nineteen-seventies, Sirimavo Bandaranaike hardened these feelings by elevating Buddhism to the equivalent of a state religion and by imposing harsh quotas on the number of Tamil students admitted to state universities. In the late sixties, half the students admitted to university programs in engineering and medicine were Tamils; by the end of the next decade, that number was closer to twenty per cent. In 1975, Velupillai Prabhakaran staged what he called his "first major military encounter," when he shot and killed the mayor of Jaffna, a close associate of the Prime Minister's, who had been on his way to pray at a Hindu temple.

Tamil militants had attempted to assassinate their politicians before, but none had succeeded, and Prabhakaran's example inspired others to take up arms in the name of Tamil self-determination. Some joined his tiny band of Tigers, who supported themselves by robbing banks and smuggling weapons from India. Others enlisted with competing Tamil guerrilla factions, which began claiming credit for assassinations and ambushes of politicians, policemen, and soldiers. Sinhalese agitators set off a new wave of anti-Tamil riots in 1977, and again in 1981, when the Jaffna library—the major repository of Tamil literature and history—was burned to a shell. Then, in July of 1983, the Tigers staged a carefully planned ambush of government forces near Jaffna, massacring thirteen officers. As news of the slaughter spread, the country was convulsed by the most hideous pogrom in its history, a wave of anti-Tamil violence so extreme that observers reached back to the horrors that accompanied India's partition, in 1947, for a fitting comparison.

As many as two thousand Tamils were hacked, bludgeoned, torched, or beaten and kicked to death by mobs. In Colombo, Sinhalese criminals in the high-security Welikade prison were allowed to slaughter dozens of Tamil political prisoners, and two days later another massacre of Tamils occurred in the same prison. Nearly eighty thousand Tamils fled their homes to hastily established refugee camps during those weeks, which became known as Black July; others piled into boats to seek asylum in India—the first great wave of an exodus that has, over the intervening decades of war, created a global diaspora of hundreds of thousands of Sri Lankan Tamils. Some Sinhalese were so disgusted by the horrors of 1983 that they, too, left the country. Johnny Attygale, a businessman whose father had served as Sri Lanka's police commissioner in the sixties, told me that he had been driving to the beach when a couple of frenzied Tamils appeared in front of his car, pursued by a lynch mob. He packed the men into his trunk and drove them to safety, then packed up his family and moved to Australia. "Bodies on the road, people being burned in the street—how do you explain that to your kids?" he asked.

To Prabhakaran, Black July was an affirmation of the Tiger cause—proof that the only hope for Sri Lankan Tamils was to establish an independent homeland by force. "The July holocaust has united all sections of the Tamil masses," he declared, and Tamil militants took to comparing their struggle to that of Palestinian nationalists and anti-apartheid South Africans. India's Prime Minister, Indira Gandhi, faced with a flood of Sri Lankan refugees and with discontent among sympathetic Indian Tamils, decided to train and arm Sri Lanka's Tamil militants (not only Tigers but a number of other factions as well). India's support for the rebels inspired more young Tamils to join the separatist fight, and Sri Lankans date the beginning of civil war to 1983, the year when the state's claim to be the representative government of all the island's people appeared most thoroughly discredited. Yet, as with so many armed liberation movements, the more the Tigers pressed their advantages and consolidated their power as a military and political force, the more they came to resemble—and then to exceed—the most repellent aspects of their enemies. Thirty years after Prabhakaran shot and killed the mayor of Jaffna, he is probably the world's most prolific political assassin. But the paradox of his monomaniacal pursuit of a Tamil homeland is that Tamils have borne the brunt of his violence.

Father Miller came to Sri Lanka from his home parish of New Orleans in 1948. "It was a brand-new nation with a beautiful administrative structure," he told me. "The British did a good job. They had trained people who knew how to keep accounts and write and type and file and everything else. There were people who'd studied in Oxford and Cambridge, and people trained at Sandhurst." Tea, rubber, and coconut plantations sustained a developing economy; a reliable rail system served the entire island; and most of the country was electrified. "We used to call Bangladesh bad off," Miller said. "We called them the basket case over the years. They never seemed to be able to get their act together. We've got to their stage now. They've gone forward, we've fallen back."

Miller was an undergraduate at Springhill College, a Jesuit school in Mobile, Alabama, when he volunteered as a missionary, and he packed his bags knowing that he was committing himself for life. Except for a stint in India in the early fifties, to complete his theological training, and a few years in other parishes in Sri Lanka, he has made his home in Batticaloa, teaching primary and secondary school—and for a decade serving as rector—at St. Michael's College, which is housed in a large Italianate building of ochre stucco and colonnaded terraces beneath red tile roofs, where he lives in a tower room, atop a steep and rickety wooden staircase. The office area of his L-shaped room is sparsely furnished, and the walls are barely adorned—a few pictures of Jesus hang on nails, along with a cross and a crude folk-art mask. His living quarters are even more ascetic: there is a narrow cot, a hot plate and washstand, and a clothesline, which, when I visited, was draped with a duplicate of the outfit he was wearing—a threadbare polo shirt and hiking shorts. Beneath his desk chair, a wooden prayer kneeler supported Miller's sandalled feet. He is a small, vigorous man, with thick workman's hands and a face that might fairly be called Roman on account of its sharp-featured, weathered intensity. Despite his Louisiana roots, he has a New England accent (a peculiarity he acknowledges yet cannot account for), but the most striking feature of his speech is the way he uses the first-person plural when describing the Batticaloa Tamil community, with which he has come to identify. "I've been here long enough," he said. "I say 'we' when I talk locally."

In the early days of the war, Miller told me, "one of the Sri Lankan colonels here gave me a nickname. I was a white Tiger, because I was always arguing the side of the Tamil people against the government." At that time, in the early eighties, the fighting was all in the north. But the government regarded Batticaloa as enemy territory nonetheless, Miller said, "and they came in and started arresting people right and left, in great numbers." Miller joined with other community leaders to document and contest instances of government abuse. In 1990, when the Tigers seized control of large areas of Batticaloa, Miller took to hounding them even more. "I object to both sides, and I'm talking on behalf of the people who are victims," he said. He was particularly incensed by the Tigers' forced conscription of Tamil children. "They had put in a rule," he explained. "Each family must give one child. And they were exacting that." He told me that when he went to the local Tiger commander to complain about a thirteen-year-old girl with a game leg and a fifteen-year-old boy with a terrible lung condition who had been taken from their families as recruits, the commander told him, "I don't have time for these minor matters."

Miller's sympathy for Tamil grievances was equalled by his disdain for the Tigers. "That leader, Prabhakaran, is a megalomaniac, and in anybody's books a mass murderer," he said. "Let me tell you one story. Mother and father have about five kids—three of them are girls, boys are younger fellows—and the Tigers go to the house, and say, 'You've got to give us one of the children.' The mother says, 'Never, never.' The father says, 'What are we going to do? We have to give them one of the children, that's all—we don't have a choice.' One day when the woman was away from home, they came and he was there, and he let one of the girls go. And the mother came back and she said, 'Where's the kid?' And he said, 'Well, they came and took her.' She said, 'You gave her?' He said, 'Yeah, what?' She

said, 'That's not even your child.' Now, they were not getting on well, and when she said, 'That's not even your child,' he went out and committed suicide. That's the level of pressure that they were able to put on people."

The Tiger commander in Batticaloa was Colonel Karuna, and when he turned against Prabhakaran, last year, the recruitment of children in his zone stopped. His declaration of independence inspired a number of Batticaloans to take to the streets and show their support by setting fire to the portraits of Prabhakaran that Karuna's men had, until the day before, required them to hang in their homes, and, before he went into hiding, Karuna disbanded the children's brigades. "He sent them home," Miller said. "The Tigers tried to get them back. They were going around in some of the villages with loudspeakers: 'We'd like to talk to you again, we need to bring things up to date, at least come and have a discussion with us.'" The tactic didn't work, but shortly after the tsunami UNICEF reported that Tiger recruiters were luring children from displaced-persons camps in the east.

Father Miller wasn't surprised. "Deep down inside, people realize that we haven't crossed that border yet to where we can say that there's going to be peace," he said. "We're going to go on killing each other, and there may come some time when it becomes so totally desperate that we get some good sense. I'm an optimist."

"Ceylon—the radiant, incomparable East," Mark Twain wrote when he paid a brief visit to the island in 1896, and his rhapsodic response to the place was typical of travellers' accounts through the years:

All the requisites were present. The costumes were right; the black and brown exposures, unconscious of immodesty, were right; the juggler was there, with his basket, his snakes, his mongoose, and his arrangements for growing a tree from seed to foliage and ripe fruitage before one's eyes; in sight were plants and flowers familiar to one in books but in no other way—celebrated, desirable, strange, but in production restricted to the hot belt of the equator; and out a little way in the country were the proper deadly snakes, and fierce beasts of prey, and the wild elephant and the monkey. And there was that swoon in the air which one associates with the tropics, and that smother of heat, heavy with odors of unknown flowers, and that sudden invasion of purple gloom fissured with lightnings—then the tumult of crashing thunder and the downpour—and presently all sunny and smiling again.

You could find much the same sort of gushing, albeit less memorably rendered, in most of the leading travel magazines last year: feature after feature touting Sri Lanka, post-ceasefire, as a hot (in every sense of the word) destination, where the suspended war provided a titillating whiff of adventure. Sri Lankans are prone to similar raptures about the Edenic luxuriance of their land. Their literature—heat-stunned and gin-soaked—is full of an aching auto-exoticism. Yet this fond self-regard contains a painful element of what another Southern writer, William Faulkner, called "a furious unreality," and nowhere is it more furious or unreal than in the Tiger-controlled territory.

To get there, you must cross what amounts to an international frontier in the middle of the kilometre-wide no man's land that bisects the island from coast to coast along the ceasefire line. Although the government of Sri Lanka refuses to recognize it, the Tigers have established their own state, with customs officials, a border control, a uniformed police force, and a full complement of ministries. The sheds on the Tiger side of the border crossing, where travel documents are examined, are plastered with posters celebrating the exploits of suicide bombers, and staffed by uniformed female cadres with braided pigtails looped and gathered on their heads, like helmets. The landscape on this side is indistinguishable from the rest of Sri Lanka, except that it is so sparsely populated as to seem abandoned, which in large stretches it is. The war damage is most striking in Kilinochchi, the political and economic capital of the Tiger zone. Three years ago, when the truce went into effect, there was hardly a roof left on any structure along Kilinochchi's main drag, and even now, after a fever of reconstruction, largely funded by overseas Tamil supporters of the war they have fled, ruins are everywhere. There are few private cars on the road, and a good many of them are archaic Morris Minors, jerry-rigged to run on kerosene, at perilously slow speeds. At the center of town, a side street leads to a complex of ultramodern hotel-like buildings, which make up the various departments of the Tigers' political commissariat. Here, the conspicuous absence of visible security measures—no guns or guards—signals the confidence of absolute authority.

Tiger apparatchiks are notoriously wary of the press. But after the tsunami they launched a charm offensive on foreign reporters, earning highly favorable reviews of the efficiency with which they orchestrated relief efforts. So, one evening, I was granted an audience with the head of the Tigers' political wing, S. P. Tamilchelvan, a slight, heavily mustached man, who is considered to be second only to Prabhakaran in the hierarchy. Tamilchelvan walks with a limp and the help of a cane, on account of an old combat injury. He does not speak English, or pretends not to (he clearly understands it). He received me in a bitterly air-conditioned conference room and was accompanied by his translator, George, an elderly rail of a man, who was extravagantly groomed, with gray hair slicked fiercely back, and profusions of equally gray hair sprouting from his ears in carefully combed tufts several inches long. George's English was as eccentric as his coiffure. When I posed a question—for instance, why had Prabhakaran failed to appear for weeks after the tsunami, giving rise to suspicions that he had been killed?—Tamilchelvan would answer at great length in Tamil, and then George would deliver his own baroque stem-winder:

> This is a story that has been in the spin for quite some time, not just since the tsunami but for two decades. Disappearance of the national leader takes place so many times, and people kill him several times, and there is a concerted effort on the part of the media in Colombo, and some racial elements in Colombo, political elements who have a wishful thinking of that to happen. So these are all planted by interested parties. Now we must understand the structure of the Liberation Tigers organization, the efficacy of the structure. How did it happen for a guerilla movement to transform itself into such a conventional army and while at the same time maintain structures that have been formulated to meet the day-to-day requirements of the people in a void that was made

by the government's absence to do such things during the past twenty-five years? So efficacy of the structures is now indicated by the leader's commands being taken into account immediately, and the response that came forward from all the units of the Liberation Tigers organization. And one walks into the street and sees how efficiently the mechanism is functioning . . . . Our leader never cares to pose for photographs in occasions, and show the world that he is living and he is distributing and he is participating in the effort. Those are all done within a framework that he himself has formulated . . . . A totally unprecedented contingency like this has been met squarely by the Tamil people and the Tamil Liberation Organization. So our leader never bothers much about this type of cynical reporting about the leader being conspicuously absent in places where he's needed. He is there.

Tamilchelvan sat expressionless during this outpouring, which went on for nearly five minutes. When I mentioned that most Americans think of the Tigers, if at all, as suicide bombers, George told me that Tamilchelvan said that this was "quite understandable," since Americans "are not in a position to discern the truth of any equation, since they are not familiar with the political situation." He urged me to consider that the government had deployed military personnel to attend to survivors of the tsunami in Tamil areas. "It is the very same military that was instrumental in hundreds of thousands of people being massacred overnight and end up in mass graves," he said, in a fit of impassioned exaggeration, and he warned, "If the administrators in Colombo do not think of removing that mind-set—the majoritarian, the supremacist, the military mind-set—then the paradigm is of course very gloomy." It was up to Colombo, he added, "to make a decision whether the Tamil people are again going to be asked to fight for their rights, or whether there is going to be accommodatingness in the center for devolving and sharing power."

On the way out of the conference room, Tamilchelvan's press officer wrote a letter for me in Tamil—a laissez passer—that gave me permission to visit Mullaittivu, Prabhakaran's seaside stronghold. I drove there the next day. Standing at the epicenter of the devastation, I could see from the surrounding grid of streets where block upon block of houses had stood, but what remained was just crumbled chunks of concrete, with here and there an isolated vestige of human design: a staircase lifting to nowhere, an iron gate opening to nothing, a bicycle twisted like a paper clip tossed aside by nervous hands, and a grand church signified by an ornate façade. The silence of the place was broken only by the relentless cawing of crows.

A minivan pulled up to the wreckage of the church, and a party of clergymen in flowing white vestments emerged to inspect the damage. One of them, distinguished by a crimson sash as a bishop, stopped to chat with me. At the same moment, a barefoot, severely bow-legged man appeared, heading toward me. He wore an indigo sarong and a light cotton shirt, and his eyes were bright with madness. He did not stop until he was almost standing on my toes. He offered his hand, which was eerily limp and weightless, and began to speak. The sharp, sweet smell of palm toddy filled the narrow space between us. His voice was high and a little hoarse, and he went on at length, staring into my face. "He is disturbed," the bishop explained. "He lost everything." The man continued his address, but he sounded different. The bishop chuckled. "He is talking no language," he said. "It's just made-up sounds." The madman smiled at me. I smiled back. Suddenly he reached up and felt my hair, then drew his hand back in a salute and, without another sound, wandered off into the ruins.

"People have a real psychosis now," the bishop said. But who knew what that man's story was? Perhaps his mind had been swamped by the tsunami, or perhaps he had always been mad, Mullaittivu's village idiot. Still, meeting him there made George's renditions of Tamilchelvan's soliloquies seem less strange. Recalling Black July, the Tiger spokesman had said, "Just because we were Tamils, we were assaulted, killed, and made to feel humiliated. To call ourselves Tamils was a matter that we were ashamed of—we were made to feel so small. That made the youths of that day, in the year 1983, to decide that the pursuit of learning, education, for purposes of prospering in our personal lives has no meaning as long as our brethren get killed in this manner, at the hands of a cruel military." He seemed to be saying that the Tigers had chosen to fight because they felt they had no alternative. They had agreed to the ceasefire for the same reason that the government had, because neither side could win the war. As I drove through the barricades and out of Tiger territory, it was almost impossible to imagine how Sri Lanka might be put back together again.

On my last day in Sri Lanka, I had lunch in Colombo with Dayan Jayatilleka, a Sinhalese political scientist and newspaper columnist. At one point, as he was telling me about himself, he smiled a little and said, "Oh, by the way, one thing I did over the last twenty years, I was indicted as a terrorist, under the Prevention of Terrorism Act, during the Emergency." This was in 1983, when Jayatilleka was twenty-five. The year before, he had been a doctoral student studying revolutionary political theory at SUNY-Binghamton, but Black July inspired him to turn his learning into action. "I not only had friends who died—close Tamil friends who were killed in the Welikade jail—I saw people killed on the street, and as a Sinhala I had a crisis of conscience," he said.

Jayatilleka and his comrades got armed and trained "in a very amateurish way" and set out to become urban guerrillas. "The idea was that the non-Tiger groups among the Tamils and the non-J.V.P. groups among the Sinhalese could link up and prevent this terrible polarization of fundamentalism on both sides," he said. "It was very utopian, and it didn't work. Some of us died, some of us went underground—like me, I was three years underground—some of us did time. We were caught between the state and these fanatical movements, and we got crushed." In 1986, when Jayatilleka was on the run from his terrorism indictment, he heard that Tigers were burning other Tamil militants in the streets of Jaffna, and that a Sinhalese student leader had been caught and murdered by J.V.P. thugs. "They cut his throat slowly. Apparently, they kept asking him where I was," Jayatilleka said. The shock of such killings sapped his appetite for armed struggle. "When we started out, none of us ever thought we'd ever be killed by other liberation fighters," he told me. "We thought we'd be killed by state forces, or tortured. We were all psyched up for that—that was the way the script was supposed to go. And then we were blind-sided by the J.V.P. and the Tigers."

In 1988, Jayatilleka negotiated an amnesty, and joined the government as a minister for Batticaloa province. He resigned after six months. "We were doing atrocious things at the time to anyone suspected of Tiger associations," he said. He described entering the provincial office one day and finding a teen-age boy, lying bound and beaten, face down on the floor. "I asked what he was doing there. They said, Oh, they were going to take him out to the swamp and shoot him in the back of the head. They didn't have a case against him of any kind. I managed to get him released—but how many more like him were there?"

That year, Jayatilleka's close friend and political comrade Vijaya Kumaratunga—a charismatic movie star, who had entered politics to promote a multi-ethnic, federalist policy for Sri Lanka—was shot in the face and killed in his driveway. Although no one was ever tried for the crime, the J.V.P. is widely assumed to have been responsible, which made it all the more shocking to many Sri Lankans when Vijaya's widow, now President Kumaratunga, allied with the party. Three days before Kumaratunga was elected, in December, 1999, she survived a Tiger suicide attack, which killed twenty-two others, wounded more than a hundred, and mutilated one of her eyes, but Jayatilleka, who despises the Tigers' barbarism, does not believe that personal animus to one extremist enemy can justify an alliance with another. "There is something that has been wrong for quite some time with the political system here," he said, and added, "It's a zero-sum game. Everybody here will ally with anyone else."

Sri Lanka's problem, as Jayatilleka sees it, is the absence of an overarching sense of national identity. Nobody in public life really talks about being Sri Lankan; there are only Sinhalese, Tamils, and Muslims. By way of contrast, he cited India, a state held together by a political understanding of itself as secularist and federalist. "Unlike Nehru, who had an idea of India, we went the other way," Jayatilleka said. "Our nationalism wasn't national in the sense of pan-Sri Lankan. Our nationalism took a cultural form—cultural, ethnic, religious." And, he said, "Anybody who looked like a true nationalist unifier got shot."

When I left Jayatilleka, I had an appointment to visit the Minister of Hindu Religious Affairs, Douglas Devananda, at his home office, a fortified compound on a quiet residential byway in central Colombo. The entry to the street was guarded by soldiers, who tugged aside a metal barricade to let me pass through an elaborate roadblock. Devananda, who spent many years as a Tamil guerrilla before he renounced violence and entered parliament, is the only former Tamil fighter in the government, and he has survived more assassination attempts than Rasputin endured. His home was hidden behind high walls posted with watchtowers and an iron gate piled high with sandbags and blockaded by oil drums filled with concrete. As I approached on foot, a narrow shutter slid open in the gate, and two eyes and a nose appeared in the window. "American?" a voice asked, and I was admitted.

Jayatilleka, who had received arms training from Devananda in the early eighties, had told me that I would find the minister surrounded by "heavy iron," and, sure enough, a half dozen fidgety young men wearing submachine guns were huddled in the entryway. One led me through a labyrinth of short hallways that switched this way and that at ninety-degree angles. There were more men with guns at every corner. Outside, rain was threatening, and the air in Devananda's den was heavy with dampness. As we progressed, the smell of mildew grew stronger, and mold stains claimed ever larger patches of wall. We passed a screened-off antechamber filled with parakeets, an atrium with a blue-tiled carp pond, and a dim room filled with tropical vegetation, where a chattering monkey sat on a rock clutching a gnawed orange. Finally, we reached a door studded with deadbolts, which clicked open by remote control from within, and there, at the back of a long, wide, windowless room, cluttered with furniture and stacked with papers, Devananda sat behind a desk: a big, bearded man, in a loose white V-necked undershirt and a green floor-length sarong, clutching two telephones to his head, one at each ear, while talking to a man standing next to him in a booming voice.

We sat on a rattan living-room set, where an aide brought us orange soda. Jayatilleka had said of Devananda, "When I needed a submachine, he gave me one," and, when I reminded Devananda of this, he let out a true belly laugh: "Ha-ha-ha-ha-ha—those days!" He had gone for his own training as a fighter—in 1978, and again in 1984—to Lebanon. "P.L.O., Al Fatah, George Habash," he said. Devananda had been a prisoner in the Tamil wards at the Welikade prison in 1983, when Sinhalese inmates began massacring his comrades with iron bars and blades and bludgeons. He survived by fighting off the attackers, hand to hand. Four years later, following his amnesty, when Devananda had become a government officer, he was asked by Tiger prisoners who were staging a hunger strike to come and talk to them. When he entered their cell, he was surrounded and attacked. A metal spike was driven into the back of his skull. A Sinhalese surgeon saved his life, but he describes himself as only eighty-five per cent recovered. At one point during my visit, an aide brought him a vial with a medicine dropper, which he used to lubricate his eyes. "This is unnatural tears," he explained. "If I want to cry, I put this, then I can cry. Ha-ha-ha-ha!"

He laughed again when he told me how last summer, on a day when he opened his office to his constituents, a young Tamil woman had refused to let his guards search her above the waist. Devananda told them not to seize her, in case she was wired as a bomb. Instead, he had his men lead her to a police station, where she blew herself up, killing four officers. It was the first suicide bombing in Sri Lanka since the ceasefire, but Devananda wasn't surprised. As a former guerrilla, he said, he knew Prabhakaran's mind. "It takes a snake to know a snake," he told me. He wriggled his hand through the air. "Prabhakaran doesn't want peace, he wants P-I-E-C-E—a piece of land to rule as a dictator," he said, and added, "I tell Tamils in my community that earlier, when we fought for liberation, we were in an iron handcuff. If tomorrow the Tigers lead, it's a golden handcuff. The difference is iron or gold, but the handcuff is the same."

Devananda claims that eighty per cent of Tamils want a federal solution but that most are too terrorized by the Tigers to say so. In last year's parliamentary elections, the Tigers bullied every Tamil candidate in the areas where they have influence

to swear allegiance to Prabhakaran's policies, and even then they resorted to fraud to insure victory for their candidates. Devananda read aloud from a report by European Union monitors, which said, "If the election results in the north and east had been a critical factor in determining who formed the government, it would have raised questions about the legitimacy of the final outcome. The events that took place in this part of Sri Lanka during the course of this election are totally unacceptable and are the antithesis of democracy."

Still, Devananda refused to call himself anti-Tiger. After all, he said, "If, tomorrow, Velupillai Prabhakaran genuinely comes for talks, I may give up politics." But, in the next breath, he added, "The reality is he won't come, and I also won't give up." Thinking as a snake who knows his kind, Devananda predicted that Sri Lanka would see a steady escalation of violence through the first half of this year, and so far he has not been wrong.

The killings began again in February, when a spate of tit-for-tat assassinations involving Tigers and Karuna's faction in the east broke the post-tsunami lull. The Tigers organized angry street protests, accusing the government of colluding with Karuna's cadres, and of failing to negotiate a mechanism for distributing aid to tsunami victims in Tiger areas. Throughout the spring, whenever President Kumaratunga declared herself ready to negotiate such an accord, the J.V.P. denounced her as a traitor; and when at last she succumbed to international pressure and agreed, in June, to an aid partnership with the Tigers, the J.V.P. quit the ruling coalition and persuaded the Supreme Court to suspend the pact, pending a review of its constitutionality. Meanwhile, in the north and the east, the killings have continued at a steadily intensifying rate—with a Tiger officer here, a couple of Karuna cadres there, and civilians inevitably picked off in the crossfire. Rather than bringing peace with unwanted force, the tsunami has become a new casus belli.

On the evening of April 28th, a prominent Tamil journalist named Dharmeratnam Sivaram—a founding editor of Tamil-Net, a widely read news Web site that is largely sympathetic to the Tigers—was accosted by four men outside a Colombo police station, bundled into a jeep, and driven away. The next day, policemen, responding to an anonymous tip, found his body in a high-security area behind the Sri Lankan parliament. Sivaram, who also wrote for the mainstream English-language newspaper, the *Daily Mirror,* had received death threats four years ago, after state media denounced him as a Tiger spy, and again last year, after he wrote about alleged ties between the government and Karuna. In May, 2004, his house had been ransacked by forty policemen, who claimed to be looking for arms. Sivaram's last column had been critical of Karuna's faction, and the stench of government collusion that clung to the circumstances of his murder further inflamed Tamils in Tiger areas. There has barely been a day since without violence.

"The fascist enemy cannot be fought by imitating him. He can be fought only by maintaining a moral and ethical superiority, as exemplified in an open, pluralistic society," Dayan Jayatilleka wrote in his column, when he heard of Sivaram's death. He counted the journalist as a friend, and his column concluded with an homage: "Sivaram challenged us with his writing. He was an uppity Tamil: confident, aware of Sinhala society and political trends, knowledgeable of international affairs. He held up a mirror before us. He was the Other in our midst. Now that he is dead, this is a lonelier place."

In his next column, Jayatilleka lashed out at the "cowardice" of Sinhalese commentators, who derided Sivaram's ideas after he was dead, but never "took him on in print when he was alive"—or did so only "in the safety of a language he couldn't respond in because he did not know it." Rather than blaming the dead journalist for failing to denounce the crimes of his side, Jayatilleka said, the Sinhalese should ask themselves what offenses they have chosen to ignore. He posed as "the final question" of his friend's life a conundrum that belongs equally to every side in every ethnic-nationalist conflict on earth: "Had we been Tamil, are we sure we would not have been Sivarams?"

A Crisis and an Opportunity in Sri Lanka

The SLMM report, detailing the violations of the ceasefire agreement by the LTTE and the Government, underlines the need for a speedy return to the dialogue table.

B. MURALIDHAR REDDY

The latest ruling by the Sri Lanka Monitoring Mission (SLMM), on the major violations of the Cease Fire Agreement (CFA) by the Government and the Liberation Tigers of Tamil Eelam from July 22 to September 26, throws light on the growing humanitarian crisis in the island nation.

It squarely blames the LTTE for creating a situation, by closing the Mavil Aru sluice gates on July 22, that led to a major military offensive by the Government. However, the SLMM seems to suggest that having completed a successful operation, the Government is in no mood for talks now.

The SLMM ruling particularly makes sad reading coming as it does nearly three weeks after the September 12 declaration in Brussels of the Co-Chairs of Sri Lanka announcing the willingness of both parties to return to the dialogue table "unconditionally." Implied in the readiness conveyed by the two parties to resume talks was the commitment to cease hostilities. Yet, as if not taking chances, the Co-Chairs, reflecting the sentiments of the 58-odd donor countries, had appealed to all the parties concerned to put a stop to the violence and pave the way for meaningful negotiations.

This appeal does not seem to have made the desired impact. At least not yet, despite Colombo's confirmation that it had received "positive signals" from the LTTE leadership on resumption of the stalled talks, albeit on the Government's terms.

Terrible Impact

The impact of the hostilities on ordinary citizens is difficult to imagine. Says the newly appointed SLMM chief, Maj. Gen. Lars Solvberg: "As a result of these actions over 200 civilians have been killed and several thousands are internally displaced creating a serious humanitarian crisis in the eastern and northern parts of Sri Lanka." Conservative United Nations estimates suggest that in the phase of unrest from April alone more than 2.25 lakh people have been rendered homeless.

Reports from Jaffna town and the Jaffna peninsula, virtually cut off from the rest of the country because of the closure of the A9 highway for nearly two months now, speak of severe food and medicine shortages. Educational institutions have been shut down and students face the threat of losing a precious academic year. A litre of petrol in Jaffna town reportedly cost Sri Lankan Rs. 500 in the second and third weeks of September.

The SLMM report noted:

The humanitarian crisis in many areas in the North and in the East is steadily worsening with limited supplies being brought up to Jaffna and into various LTTE areas leaving thousands of people without basic necessities and paralysed economic activity. Aid agencies are in general prevented from going into LTTE areas. With the monsoon season on its way it is likely that the conditions of people in general will get worse.

The situation in the Jaffna peninsula continues to be tense with intensified fighting between the LTTE and the security forces along the FDL [forward defence line] and a high number of assassinations and abductions. There are no indications that this will change in the upcoming week. The humanitarian situation is affected and there are indications of food, fuel and basic needs shortages, despite provisions coming in by boat. Curfew is lifted twelve hours a day in the whole area, apart from areas being closed for cordon-and-search when incidents have happened. It is expected that curfew hours will remain the same in the upcoming week.

According to the Government Agent there are approximately 10,000 civilians who have registered to be transported by ship to Colombo via Trincomalee. The population on the peninsula seems to be pessimistic when it comes to ending the confrontations.

The growing crisis makes it imperative for the Government and the LTTE to heed the counsel from the international community and head towards the dialogue table. There is no dearth of voices within and outside the Mahinda Rajapaksa Government urging it not to let go of the military edge gained over the Tigers easily and rush into talks. But while the Tigers' military challenge should be met squarely, the misery of the thousands caught in the crossfire cannot be ignored.

As things stand, President Rajapaksa has everything going for him. For the first time in the country's history, the ruling Sri Lanka Freedom Party (SLFP) headed by him, and the Opposition United National Party, have joined hands in the quest for a common approach to the country's problems. It is a tribute to the large-heartedness of Ranil Wickremesinghe, the UNP chief and former Prime Minister, that he has responded to the President's appeal for a common minimum programme despite provocations by the managers of the ruling party. Since the November 2005 Presidential election, the SLFP has liberally poached from the rank and file of the UNP.

Though many continue to be sceptical of the ultimate outcome, the coming together of the archrivals has had an electrifying impact on politics in the island nation. The ultra-nationalist Janatha Vimukthi Peramuna, an electoral alliance partner of the SLFP, is furious.

The SLFP-UNP unity could go a long way in containing the war-mongers and in halting the campaign for a de-merger of the north and the east. There is a consensus within and outside Sri Lanka that the de-merger now could only heighten tensions and that the need of the hour for the Government is to expedite the process of resolving the ethnic conflict.

The Rajapaksa regime has the backing of the international community too in its war against the LTTE and can bank on it for any help. This is evident from a series of developments, particularly in the current year, such as the decision of the European Union to ban the LTTE and Prime Minister Manmohan Singh's refusal to meet a delegation of the pro-LTTE Tamil National Alliance last week.

The Sri Lankan Government should make the most of the situation and respond at the earliest to the Brussels declaration on a range of issues. The LTTE should understand the futility of the politics of blood and agree to a dialogue with sincerity.

The SLMM report summarises the expectations of the world from both the parties. It says: "The SLMM would like to underline that the gravity of the violations committed have led to a dangerous escalation in hostilities . . . It is important that the parties realise the seriousness of the current situation and do whatever in their power to move forward instead of engaging in military confrontation."

Glossary of Terms and Abbreviations

Al-Qaeda "the Base;" a loose collection of Islamic terrorist cells held together by their fundamentalist zeal to resist the encroachment of Western secularist power and values on the Muslim community (Ummah), and by financial support from contributions to Salafiyyah mosques throughout the world and from patrons like Osama bin Laden.

Asoka A Mauryan emperor in northern India from 268 to 232 B.C. Overcome with remorse about deaths caused by his military conquests, he abandoned warfare as an instrument of imperial power and adopted the Buddhist Dharma as the standard for his rule. He enforced this expectation in a series of edicts carved into stones and pillars throughout his kingdom. His example is recognized today in the adoption of the lion capital on one of his pillars as the insignia of the Republic of India.

Ayodhya, Uttar Pradesh A small city in the eastern part of India's largest state which became a national pilgrimage center as the birthplace of Lord Ram with the rise of Hindu religious nationalism in the 1980s. The destruction of the Babri Mosque there by Hindu pilgrims in 1992 led to communal riots throughout India and abroad. *See* Babur.

Babur The first of the Moghul emperors, who engaged in a military conquest of northern India from 1526 to 1529. It was during his brief reign that the Babri Mosque was built in Ayodhya, purportedly on the site of an earlier Hindu temple, the destruction of which, in December 1992, led to communal riots across India. Akbar, the greatest of the Moghul monarchs, who ruled from 1556 to 1605 and completed the Moghul conquest of northern India, was Babur's grandson.

Bharatiya Janata Party (BJP) "Indian Peoples Party" grew as a Hindu nationalist party out of the heartland of the Gangetic plain to become the only party to challenge Congress Party hegemony on a national level. Led by Atal Behari Vajpayee, it attained leadership in Parliament with the support of a 19-party coalition in 1998, and with a 24-party coalition in 1999. Riding high on a platform of Hindu nationalism and economic reform, it lost to the Congress Party in the elections in 2004.

Brahmin The priestly community, ranked highest on the varna caste scale.

Buddhism A religious faith that started in India in the sixth century B.C. by Siddhartha Gautama, who renounced his royal heritage to seek enlightenment for the salvation of all humankind. The attainment of Nirvana (his death) is placed at 483 B.C. This faith extended throughout Asia in two major traditions: Theravada ("Teaching of the Elders") to Sri Lanka and Southeast Asia; and Mahayana ("Great Vehicle") to China and Japan. Tibetan Buddhism is a subset of the Mahayana tradition. Theravada has been called Hinayana ("Lesser Vehicle") by Mahayana Buddhists to distinguish that tradition from their own.

Chola A Tamil dynasty centered in the Tanjavur District of the current state of Tamil Nadu, which dominated that part of south India from A.D. 880 to 1279. The temples built and the bronzes cast under the patronage of the Chola kings remain some of the most beautiful and cherished works of Indian art.

Congress Party As the successor of the Indian National Congress in 1935, under the leadership of Jawaharlal Nehru, it led to the independence of India in 1947, and to the Republic of India in 1950. The party remained in power in Parliament for 45 years, led by Nehru's daughter, Indira Gandhi, after his death in 1964, and by his grandson Ranjiv Gandhi, after her death in 1984. Narasimha Rao became prime minister after the death of Ranjiv Gandhi in 1991, until 1996. Nehru's granddaughter-in-law, Sonia Gandhi, elected president of the party in 1998, led it to victory in the parliamentary elections in 2004.

Dalits The "broken" or "oppressed"; this is the name preferred by those traditionally known as scheduled castes, outcastes, or untouchables, members of the lowest-rank communities in the classical caste system, below the four ranks of priests, rulers, citizens, and laborers on the varna social scale. Mahatma Gandhi, deeply concerned about removing their oppression, called them *Harijans,* "children of God."

Dharma Translated as "law, justice, duty, cosmic order," the moral standard by which society and an individual's life are ordered and given meaning.

Godhra, Gujarat A small city in a growing industrial state in which Mahatma Gandhi was born, where a gang of slum dwelling Muslims set fire to a railway car full of pilgrims returning from Ayodhya on February 27, 2002. The death of 59, including women and children, led to violent reprisals against Muslims in the city, which killed more than 1,000 Muslims, and left many more homeless.

Green Revolution An upsurge in agricultural production that followed the introduction of high-yielding hybrids of rice and grains, developed by the Rockefeller Foundation in Mexico and the Philippines, into South Asia during the 1950s and 1960s.

Harappa and Mohenjo Daro The two largest cities excavated during the 1930s in the Indus River Valley to reveal an ancient urban culture that began around 3000 B.C. It flourished for 1,000 years and then inexplicably disappeared.

Herat A 5000-year-old city along the silk route to China, in a fertile valley in the northwestern corner of Afghanistan. Long a center of Afghan Sufi religious life, art and poetry, it was decimated by Genghis Khan in 1222, damaged by the British in 1885, and heavily bombed and mined by the Soviets in 1979. Ismael Khan led the city's insurrection against the Soviets in 1979, and served as governor of Herat Province from 1993–1998 and 2001–2004.

Hindi The prevalent language and literature of northern India.

Hindu One who follows the faith of Hinduism.

Hinduism The dominant religion of India, emphasizing Dharma, with its ritual and social observances and often mystical contemplation and ascetic practices.

Hindutva "Hindu-ness;" a political platform of the Hindu nationalist Bharatiya Janata Party, which aspires to rule India according to the classical norms of Great Tradition, i.e., pre-Islamic, India.

Hurriyat Conference The consolidation of some 23 Kashmiri Muslim insurgent groups in 1993 to seek an end to Indian military occupation and an independent Islamic Kashmiri homeland. Many in these groups are committed to finding a peaceful resolution and are in dialogue with the government of India.

Glossary of Terms and Abbreviations

Others have received monetary support, arms, and training from Pakistan as well as the support of *jihadis* from all over the Islamic world.

Indian National Congress An association of educated Indians and sympathetic Europeans who gathered in Bengal in 1885 to seek admission for qualified Indians into the British Indian Civil Service. In the early twentieth century, this association became the bearer of the independence movement of the subcontinent from British colonial rule. Following the establishment of a provisional government in 1935, it evolved into the Congress Party.

Islam A religious faith started in Arabia during the seventh century A.D. by the prophet Mohammad.

Islamization A policy adopted by General Mohammad Zia-al-Haq of Pakistan in the late 1970s to win political support for his martial rule from a growing Islamic fundamentalist movement in his country, spurred by the Soviet military incursion into neighboring Afghanistan.

Jain A religious faith started in India by Mahavira in the sixth century B.C. Its primary teachings include the eternal transmigration of souls and the practice of nonviolence toward all living creatures.

Jajmani A barter system of economic activity in the village, in which villagers provide their services on a regular basis to particular land owners—their patrons—in exchange for fixed portions of the annual harvest.

Jati An extended kinship group, usually identified with a traditional occupation, that defines the parameters of accepted marriage relationships. It is the unit that is ranked in the hierarchical social (caste) structure of a village and that moves within that structure.

Jihad "Struggle;" the quest to become part of a pure Muslim community (*Ummah*) by practicing an exemplary religious life in submission to Allah and by protecting it from all that would deny or destroy it. In the twentieth century, it took on the obligation among fundamentalist Muslims to become religious warriors, *jihadis*, on behalf of the faith.

Khalistan An independent state in the South Asian subcontinent for Sikhs.

Koran The sacred scripture of the Islamic faith, the teachings of Allah (God) as revealed to His prophet Mohammad in the seventh century A.D.

Ladakh The easternmost and highest region of the state of Kashmir-Jammu, inhabited mostly by Buddhists.

Lama A leader of a Tibetan Buddhist monastic community (sangha).

Lashkar-e-Taiba (Army of the Righteous) is a militant wing of a large Pakistan Sunni religiously fundamentalist organization, Markaz-ud-Dawa-wal-Irshad. Committed to restoring Islamic rule over all of India, it has been actively supporting the insurgency in Kashmir to free Muslims from Indian military occupation since 1993. It was declared a terrorist organization by the United States in 2001, and banned by the Pakistan Government in 2002. Identified with many terrorist acts in India, including the bombing of commuter trains in Mumbai on July 11, 2006, it played a major role in fund raising and relief work following the massive earthquake in Pakistan in October 2005. It is also known as Jamaat ud-Dawa (Party of the Calling).

Liberation Tigers of the Tamil Nation (LTTE) The militant separatist organization of Tamil-speaking Hindus in northern Sri Lanka. This insurgency sprang up in the 1980s under the leadership of V. Pirapaharan to seek by force a homeland independent of Sinhalese domination. Its violent ravaging, including suicide bombings, continued until it declared a cease-fire in December 2001 and entered into peace negotiations under Norwegian auspices with the Sri Lankan government in September 2002.

Lok Sabha and Rajya Sabha The two houses of Parliament in the Republic of India: "The House of the People" has 545 members elected directly by voters on the district level; "The Council of States" has 250 members, 12 appointed by the president and 238 elected by state legislatures.

Loya Jirga A council of Afghan chieftains and clan leaders called by claimants to regional power to recognize their authority to rule. Such a council was convened in June 2002 under United Nations auspices in Kabul to create a provisional government to restore civil order to the war-ravaged country of Afghanistan.

Mahabharata The Great Epic of India, with more than 90,000 stanzas, composed around the third century B.C. The longest poem in the world, it is the story of five brothers' struggle to wrest their father's kingdom from their cousins. This epic contains the *Bhagavad Gita,* a discourse between one of the brothers, Arjuna, and his charioteer, Krishna, on the eve of the culminating battle with their cousins, when Arjuna is overcome by concerns about appropriate behavior and quality of life.

Mahar A depressed (untouchable) community in the state of Maharashtra, which converted to Buddhism in October 1956 as an initiative to free themselves as a community from the social burden of untouchability, under the leadership of Dr. B. R. Ambedkar.

Mahatma Literally "great souled one"; a title given to Mohandas Gandhi by Rabindranath Tagore in 1921 and adopted by the people of India to express their belief in Gandhi's saintliness.

Mandala An intricate visual symbol developed in the Tibetan Buddhist tradition, revealing elaborate patterns of many shapes and colors, intended to lead its creator and observer into supranormal levels of consciousness.

Moghuls Islamic invaders of Turkish descent who established the longest dynastic imperial rule in the Great Central Plain of South Asia, from A.D. 1526 to 1857.

Mohajirs "Immigrants"; those Muslims who moved from their homelands in India at the time of partition in 1947 to settle in Pakistan. Because they have retained many of the customs as well as the language (Urdu) of their former homes, even today they remain a distinctive community and political force, as the Mohajir Quami Movement (MQM) in Pakistan.

Monsoon An annual torrential rainfall, which normally begins during the month of June, when the prevailing winds shift to the west, gather clouds with water from the Arabian Sea, and deluge the subcontinent with rain as the clouds rise over the Himalayan Mountains. The dramatic shift from the torrid dry heat of late spring to this stormy wet season and the lush growth that it provides has an immense impact on the economies, the literature, and the consciousness of South Asian peoples. Raja Rao gives a brief, gripping description of the coming of the monsoon on page 50 of his novel *Kanthapura* and in his notes, pages 215–216.

Mujahideen Militant tribal leaders in Afghanistan who joined in alliance to protect their authority from national and foreign (Soviet) incursion.

Muslim One who submits to the supreme will of Allah (God), as revealed to the prophet Mohammad; one who practices Islam. Sometimes spelled Moslem.

Naxalites A loose collection of militant groups in central India inspired by the Maoist revolution in China, who attack any element of the Indian establishment in the name of the landless and the tribal people of that region. Their name comes from an uprising of a tribal community in the village of Naxalbari in western Bengal in 1967. Though mostly active in the 1960's and 70's, now largely fragmented, small bands of the People's War Group or the Maoist Communist Centre still attack landlords and politicians sporadically in Andhra Pradesh, Jharkhand, Orissa and Bihar.

Nirvana Literally, "blowing out, extinguishing"; the ultimate enlightenment of Buddhism: departure from the relentless transmigratory cycle of births and deaths into nothingness.

Pali One of many regional Indo-European languages (called Prakrits) spoken in the northern plains region of South Asia following the Aryan Invasion (ca. 1700 B.C.) and before the evolution of the subcontinent's modern languages, following the twelfth century A.D. It was the language in which the earliest documents of the Buddhist faith were composed in northern India.

Panchayat Literally, "council of five." This traditional leadership of elders in the jati kinship group was adopted in the Panchayat Acts in state legislatures during the 1950s as the appropriate form of democratically elected village government in the Republic of India.

Parsi A member of the Zoroastrian faith, the ancient religion of Persia. Most of the Parsis in South Asia live in Bombay (Mumbai) and Karachi.

Pathans Tribal peoples in the northwest corner of the subcontinent who speak the Pushtu language.

Punjab Translated as *panch* ("five") and *ap* ("water"), designates the land in the western portion of the Great Central Plain through which the five rivers forming the Indus River System flow. The province that had this name during the British Indian Empire was divided between India and Pakistan in 1947.

Purana "Tradition," a genre of Sanskrit religious texts of different sects of Hinduism from the Classical Period (A.D. 300 to 1200), setting forth their primary myths and teachings; also the accounts in local languages of the sacred significance of religious sites, temples, places of pilgrimage, etc.

Rabindranath Tagore An outstanding Bengali poet and educator (1861–1941), whose collection of poems, *Gitanjali,* published in English translation in 1912, won the Nobel Prize for Literature.

Raj Translated as "rule" or "king," a term that designates political sovereignty. (The word *reign* comes from the same Indo-European root.) "Raj" is used with "British" to identify the British colonial government in India; it is used with *maha* ("great") to identify rulers of the Indian princely states; and it is used with *swa* ("self") to mean self-rule or independence. Swaraj also has the connotation of self-discipline, which is an important aspect of Mahatma Gandhi's concept of independence.

Ramayana An epic Sanskrit poem, composed around the second century A.D. and attributed to Valmiki, describing the ordeals of the ideal prince Rama. Most of the text describes his ultimately successful quest for his faithful wife Sita, who was abducted by the demonic King Ravana.

Rashtriya Swayamsevak Sangh (RSS) An organization founded in 1925 to train Hindus to seek independence from the British Raj by whatever means necessary and to further Hindu nationalistic objectives. Recognized as a militant alternative to Mahatma Gandhi's nonviolent movement, it is today a significant political force within the Bharatiya Janata Party (BJP).

Rg Veda The first of the four Vedas, which are the earliest and most sacred of the writings of the Hindus. Around 1000 B.C., it was compiled into an anthology of 10 books containing 1,028 hymns.

Salt March An act of nonviolent civil disobedience (*satyagraha*) led by Mahatma Gandhi in 1930. He and his followers marched from his *ashram* at Sabarmati 241 miles to Dandi on the coast to evaporate salt from the sea, in order to protest the British tax on salt.

Sangha A Buddhist community of holy men and women who follow the Buddha's path called Dharma. The Buddha, Dharma, and Sangha are called the "three jewels of the Buddhist faith."

Sanskrit Translated as "made together, formed, perfected," as descriptive of the classical language of India as structurally perfected.

Satyagraha Literally, "holding the truth," the name that Mahatma Gandhi adopted while in South Africa to describe his nonviolent civil protest against the South African government's oppression of the people from India. Gandhi's translation of this term as "soul force" affirms that, even early in his public career, he understood such action to be primarily religious and only secondarily political.

Shariah "The Path to the Water Hole"; Islamic sacred laws, based upon the Koran as revealed to Mohammad and the *Sunnah*, the record of his exemplary life. These laws are affirmed by the Sunni followers of Islam to be divinely inspired and immutable guides for Muslims' everyday life.

Shia Followers of Islam (approximately 15 percent of Muslims) who differ from the Sunnis in their belief that the traditions of Islam are sustained by a divinely inspired succession of Imams (religious leaders) who are descended from Ali ibn Abi Talib, the cousin and son-in-law of the Prophet Mohammad. He was elected the fourth Caliph in the Sunni succession and was assassinated in A.D. 661. Especially sacred to this tradition is the 10th day of the Arab month of Muhurram (Ramadan), on which Ali's son, Husain, the third Shia Imam, was killed on the plain of Kerbala. This community developed with the rise of the Safavid Empire in Persia in the sixteenth century. Today Shia live mostly in Iran and southern Iraq.

Shiva Literally, "auspicious"; the name of God in one of the two main sects of Hinduism: Shaivism (from Shiva) and Vaishnavism ("followers of Vishnu").

Sufi A person of the Islamic faith who affirms through religious discipline and mystical experience the spiritual union of self with God.

Sunnah "Custom"; practices of the Prophet Mohammad remembered by his early followers as the guide for an ideal Islamic life.

Sunni The tradition of the majority of Muslims, based on strict adherence to the Sunnah of the Prophet Mohammad.

Taliban "Seekers of religious knowledge"; members of a militant and exceptionally conservative freedom force named after the Pathan students of Islam from Kandahar who started a fundamentalist crusade to free Afghanistan from foreign and modern corruptions of their faith and traditional way of life.

Tsunami An enormous ocean wave created by an earthquake on an ocean floor. Occurring with some frequency in the Pacific

Ocean, the Indian Ocean tsunami on December 26, 2004, was the result of a totally unexpected earthquake that measured 9.0 on the richter scale along the Sunda trench west of Sumatra in Indonesia. The worst tsunami in history, it extended across the entire Indian Ocean to the coast of Africa, causing death and damage in 13 countries. Indonesia reported a death toll of over 110,000. On the eastern shore of Sri Lanka it killed 38,000; along the coast of Tamil Nadu, in India, 7,968 and the Indian Andaman and Nicobar Islands, 1,837, with 5,625 missing; and in Thailand, an estimated 11,000 deaths.

Upanishads A collection of profound religious teachings that form the last stage in the development of Vedic literature, beginning with the *Rg Veda* and continuing with the *Brahamanas*, which are manuals for the performance of Vedic sacrifices.

Varna Originally translated as "class," later as "color"; the fourfold division of classical Indian society, ranked on a purity–pollution scale: priests, rulers, citizens, and laborers. The untouchables and tribals are a fifth group, known as outcastes, ranked below the laborers.

Vellalas Among Tamil-speaking peoples, the dominant landholding and cultivating communities, similar to the Jat communities in the Hindi-speaking regions of the subcontinent.

Vishnu Receiving somewhat minor attention as a solar deity in the *Rg Veda,* Vishnu became recognized as Supreme Lord of the universe, its creator and preserver during the classical period (A.D. 300–1200). He is worshipped widely throughout Hinduism through His incarnations (*avatars*), of whom Rama and Krishna are the most prevalent.

Yoga A highly disciplined set of exercises to identify, nurture, and develop different parts of one's natural body, breathing, nervous system, and consciousness. Practice of this discipline leads to the integration of one's total self—physical, mental, and spiritual, the unconscious as well as the conscious.

Bibliography

GENERAL WORKS

Basham, A.L., *The Wonder That Was India*, (Columbia, MO: South Asia Books, 1995). A comprehensive introduction to classical India.

Baxter, Craig, et al, *Government and Politics in South Asia*, (Boulder, CO: Westview Press, 5th ed., 2001).

Bose, Ashish and Mahendra K. Premi (eds), *Population Transition in South Asia*, (Columbia, MO: South Asia Books, 1992).

Cohen, Myron L., *Asia, Case Studies in Social Sciences*, (Armonk, New York: M. E. Sharpe, 1992). A Guide for Teaching, Columbia Project on Asia in the Core Curriculum.

deBary, W.T. (ed), *Sources of Indian Tradition*, (New York: Columbia University Press, 1988) Translations of primary texts from the Vedic Period to Independence.

Dittmer, Lowell, *South Asia's Nuclear Security Doctrine: India, Pakistan and China*, (Amonk, New York, M.E. Sharpe, 2005).

Embree, Ainslie T. & Carol Gluck (eds), *Asia in Western and World History*, (Amonk, New York, M. E. Sharpe, 1993). A Guide for Teaching, Columbia Project on Asia in the Core Curriculum.

Ganguly, Sumit, *Conflict Unending, India-Pakistan Tensions since 1947*, New York,:(Columbia University Press, 2002).

Ganguly, Sumit and Devin T. Hagerty, *Fearful Symmetry: Indai-Pakistan Crises in the Shadow of Nuclear Weapons*, (New Delhi: Oxford University Press, 2006).

Leonard, Ann, *Seeds: Supporting Women's Work in the Third World*, (New York: Feminist Press, 1989). Chapters on Credit Organization in Madras, India; Non-craft Employment in Bangladesh; and Forest Conservation in Nepal.

Kenoyer, Jonathan M., *Ancient cities of the Indus valley civilization*, (Karachi: Oxford University Press. Islamabad: American Institute of Pakistan Studies, 1998).

Lewis, Todd and Theodore Riccardi, *The Himalayas: A Syllabus of the Region's History, Anthropology, and Religion*, (Ann Arbor, MI: Association of Asian Studies, 1995).

McIntosh, Jane, *A Peaceful Realm: The Rise and Fall of the Indus Civilization*, (Boulder, CO: Westview Press, 2001).

Miller, Barbara Stoler (ed), *Masterworks of Asian Literature in Comparative Perspective*, (Amonk, New York: M.E. Sharpe, 1993). A Guide for Teaching, Columbia Project on Asia in the Core Curriculum.

Mines, Diane P. and Lamb, Sarah, (eds) *Everyday Life in South Asia*, (Bloomington: Indiana University Press, 2002).

Robinson, Francis, (ed), *The Cambridge Encyclopedia of India, Pakistan, Bangladesh, Sri Lanka, Nepal, Bhutan, and the Maldives*, (Cambridge: Cambridge University Press, 1989).

Robinson, Francis, *Islam and Modern History in South Asia*, (New Delhi: Oxford University Press, 2001).

Schwartzberg, Joseph, *A Historical Atlas of South Asia*, (New York: Oxford University Press, 1993).

Sen, Amartya, *Development as Freedom*, (Anchor Books, 2000).

Tambiah, S.J. *Leveling Crowds, Ethno-Nationalist Conflicts and Collective Violence in South Asia*, (Berkeley, CA: University of California Press, 1997).

Weiner, Myron, *The Global Migration Crisis: Challenge to States and to Human Rights*, (New York: Addison-Wesley, 1995).

Weiner, Myron and Ali Aanuazizi (eds), *The Politics of Social Transfromation in Afghanistan, India and Pakistan*, (Syracuse: Syracuse University Press, 1993).

NATIONAL HISTORIES AND ANALYSES

AFGHANISTAN

Ewans, Martin, Sir, *Afghanistan: A Short History of its People and Politics*, (New York: Harper Collins, 2002).

Girardet, Edward R. et al., *Afghanistan: Crosslines Essential Field Guides to Humanitarian and Conflict Zones*, (Geneva: Crosslines Publishing, 2004).

Hosseini, Khalied, *The Kite Runner*, (New York: Riverhead Books, 2003). A novel of an emigrant's childhood in Kabul and his return during Taliban rule.

Kaplan, Robert D., *Soldiers of God, With Islamic Warriors in Afghanistan and Pakistan*, (New York: Vintage, 2001).

Magnus, Ralph H. & Eden Naby, *Afghanistan: Marx, Mullah, and Mujahid*, (Boulder, Colorado: Westview, 2002).

Maley, William, *The Afghan Wars*, (New York: Palgrave, 2002).

Rashid, Ahmed, *Taliban: Militant Islam, Oil & Fundamentalism in Central Asia*, New Haven, CT: Yale University Press, 2001).

Rubin, Barnett R., *The Fragmentation of Afghanistan: State Formation and Collapse in the International System*, (New Haven, CT: Yale University Press, 2002).

Skaine, Rosemarie, *The Women of Afghanistan Under the Taliban*, (New York: McFarland, 2001).

BANGLADESH

Bornstein, David, *The Price of a Dream, The Story of the Grameen Bank*, (Chicago: University of Chicago Press, 1997).

Faraizi, Amiul H., *Bangladesh: Peasant Migration and the World Capitalist Economy*, (New York: Apt Books, 1993).

Gardner, Katy, *Global Migrants, Local Lives; Travel and Transformation in Rural Bangladesh*, (Oxford: Clarendon Press, 1997).

Ghosh, Amitav, *The Hungry Tide*, (New York: Harper Collins, 2004). A novel of life on the Sundarban islands on the south coast of Bangladesh.

Hossain, Rokeya Sakhawat, *Sultana's Dream*, (New York: The Feminist Press, 1988). Bengali Muslim writer on purdah and dream of its reversal.

Kramsjo, Bosse, *Breaking the Chains: Collective Action for Social Justice Among the Poor in Bangladesh*, (New York: Intermed Technology Development Group of North America, 1992).

McCahill, Bob, *Dialogues of Life, A Christian Among Allah's Poor*, (Orbis Books, 1995).

Nasrin, Taslima, *Meyebela, My Bengali Childhood* (Steerforth Press, 2002).

Yunus, Muhammad, *Banker to the poor: micro-lending and the battle against world poverty*, (New York: PublicAffairs, 1999).

BHUTAN

Armington, Stan, *Lonely Planet: Bhutan*, (Oakland: Lonely Planet, 2002).

Hutt, Michael, *Unbecoming Citizens–Culture, Nationhood, and the Flight of Refugees from Bhutan*, (New Delhi, Oxford University Press, 2003).

Sinha, A.C., *Bhutan: Ethnic Identity and National Dilemma*, (New York: Apt Books, 1991).

Zeppa, Jamie, *Beyond the Sky and the Earth: a Journey into Bhutan*. (New York: Riverhead Books, 1999).

INDIA

Agarwal, Bina, *A Field of One's Own: Gender and the Land Rights in South Asia*, (Cambridge: Cambridge U Press, 1994).

Bondurant, Joan, *Conquest of Violence* (Princeton: Princeton University Press, 1988).

Brass, Paul, *The Politics of India Since Independence*, (Cambridge: Cambridge U Press, 1990).

Chandra, Sharat, *Population Pattern and Social Change in India*, (Columbia, MO: South Asia Books, 1992).

Cohen, Stephen P., *India: Emerging Power*, (Washington, D.C.: Brookings Institution Press, 2001).

Crosette, Barbara, *India: Facing the Twenty-first Century*, (Bloomington: Indiana U Press, 1993).

Dalton, Dennis, *Mahatma Gandhi, Nonviolent Power in Action*, (New York, Columbia U Press, 1995).

Das, Gurcharan, *India Unbound: The Social and Economic Revolution from Independence to the Global Information Age*, (New Delhi: Viking, Penguin Books India, 2000. New York: Alfred A. Knopf, 2001).

Dash, Narendra K., *Encyclopaedic Dictionary of Indian Culture*, (Columbia, MO: South Asia Books, 1992).

Dirks, Nicholas, *Castes of Mind: Colonialism and the Making of Modern India*, (Princeton: Princeton University Press, 2001).

Eck, Diana, *Darshan— Seeing the Divine Image in India*, (New York, Columbia U Press, 1985).

Embree, Ainslie, *Utopias in Conflict, Religion and Nationalism in Modern India*, (Berkeley: U of Cal Press, 1990).

Ericson, Eric, *Gandhi's Truth*, (New York: Norton, 1970).

Gandhi, Mohandas K., *An Autobiography: The Story of My Experiments With Truth*, (Boston: Beacon, 1957).

Ganguli, Sumit (ed), *India as an Emerging Power*, (Portland: Frank Caso, 2003).

Hopkins, Thomas, *The Hindu Religious Tradition*, (Belmont, CA: Dickenson, 1971).

Ikram, S.M., *Muslim Civilization in India*, (New York: Columbia University Press, 1964).

Jacobson, Doranne, *India: Land of Dreams and Fantasy*, (Columbia, MO: South Asia Books, 1992).

Khilnani, Sunil, *The Idea of India*, (London: Hamish Hamilton, 1997; New York: Farrar, Straus & Giroux, 1998).

Knipe, David, *Hinduism, Experiments in the Sacred*, (New York: Harper, 1990).

Mehta, Suketu, *Maximum City: Bombay Lost and Found*, (New York: Alfred A Knopf, 2004).

Naipal, V.S., *India: A Million Mutinies Now*, (New York: Viking, 1992).

Nehru, Jawaharlal, *The Discovery of India*, (New York: John Day, 1946).

Raja Rao, *Kanthapura*, (New York: New Directions, 1963). A novel describing the impact of Mahatma Gandhi on a South Indian village.

Rudolph, Lloyd and Suzanne, *The Modernity of Tradition*, (Chicago: U of Chicago Press, 1984).

Sarkar, Jadunath, *India Through the Ages*, (New York: Apt Books, 1993).

Sen, Amartya, *The Argumentative Indian: Writings on Indian History, Culture, and Identity*, (London: Allen Lane, 2005; New York: Farrar, Straus & Giroux, 2005).

Seth, Vikram, *A Suitable Boy*, (Perennial, 1994). A monumental novel about pursuing the choice of a husband in 1950s north India.

Sharma, S.N., *Personal Liberty Under Indian Constitution*, (Columbia, MO: South Asia Books, 1991).

Spear & Thapar, *A History of India*, 2 vols., (Baltimore: Penguin, 1965).

Srinivas, M.N., *Social Change in Modern India*, (Berkeley: U of Cal Press, 1969).

Tully, Mark, *The Defeat of a Congressman : and Other Parables of Modern India*, (New York: Knopf: Distributed by Random House, 1992).

Varshney, Asutosh, *Ethnic Conflict and Civic Life: Hindus and Muslims in India*, (New Haven: Yale University Press, 2002).

Webster, John C.B., *A History of the Dalit Christians in India*, (San Francisco: Mellen Research University Press, 1992).

Weiner, Myron, *The Indian Paradox: Essays on Indian Politics*, (Newbury Park, CA: Sage, 1983).

Wiser, William and Charlotte, *Behind Mud Walls*, (Berkeley: U of Cal Press, 1972). A classic description of an Indian village in 1930 and 1960, with a new chapter on 1984.

Wolpert, Stanley, *India*, (Berkeley: U of Cal Press, 1991).

Wolpert, Stanley, *Nehru, A Tryst with Destiny*, (New York: Oxford University Press, 1996).

Zaehner, R.C., *Hinduism*, (New York: Oxford University Press, 1970).

Zimmer, Heinrich, *Myths and Symbols in Indian Art and Civilization*, (New York: Harper, 1946).

MALDIVES

Balla, Mark, *Maldives and Islands of the East Indian Ocean: A Travel Survival Kit*, (Oakland: Lonely Planet Publishing, 1993).

Camerapix, *Maldives*, (Edison, NY: Hunter Poblishing, 1993).

Gayoon, Maumoon Abdul, *The Maldives: A Nation in Peril* (Ministry of Planning Human Resources and Environment, Republic of Maldives, 1998).

Phandnis, Urmilov, *Maldives: Winds of Change in an Atol State*, (New Delhi: South Asian Publishers, 1985).

NEPAL

Connell, Monica, *Against a Peacock Sky*, (New York: Viking, 1992). An anthropologist's account of her year in a western Nepali village.

Gregson, Jonathan, *Massacre at the Palace: the Doomed Royal Dynasty of Nepal*, (New York: Talk Miramax Books, 2002).

Guneratne, Arjun, *Many Tongues, One People: The Making of Tharu Identity in Nepal*, (Ithica: Cornell University Press, 2002).

Gyawali, Dipak, *Water in Nepal*, (Lalitpur: Himal Books, 2001).

Hutt, Michael, *Himalayan People's War: Nepal's Maoist Rebellion*, (Bloomington: Indiana University Press, 2004).

Rose, Leo E. & John T. Schulz, *Nepal: Profile of a Himalayan Kingdom*, (Boulder, Colorado: Westview, 1980).

PAKISTAN

Bhutto, Benazir, *Daughter of Destiny, An Autobiography*, (New York: S & S Trade, 1990).

Burki, Shahid Javed, *Pakistan: Fifty Years of Nationhood*, (Boulder, Colorado: Westview, 1998).

Jaffrelot, Christophe, (ed), *Pakistan, Nationalism without a Nation*, (New Delhi: Manohar, 2002).

Jones, Owen Bennett, *Pakistan, Eye of the Storm*, (New Haven: Yale University Press, 2002).

Kux, Dennis, *The United States and Pakistan: 1947–2000: Disenchanted Allies*, (Princeton: Woodrow Wilson Center Press, 2001).

Weaver, Mary Anne, *Pakistan, In the Shadow of Jihad and Afghanistan*, (New York: Farrar, Straus & Giroux, 2002).

SRI LANKA

De Silva, Kingsley, *Reaping the Whirlwind: Ethnic Conflict, Ethnic Politice in Sri Lanka*, (Columbia, MO: South Asia Books, 1998).

Ludowyk, E.F., *The Footprint of the Buddha*, (London: George Allen & Unwin, 1958).

Jayaweera, Swarna, (ed), *Women in Post-Independence Sri Lanka*, (Thousand Oaks, CA: Sage Publications, 2002).

Ondaatje, Michael, *Anil's ghost*, (New York : Alfred A. Knopf : Distributed by Random House, 2000). A novel of a Sinhalese forensic anthropologist who returns home to document human rights abuses in the Civil War.

Rahula, Walpola, *History of Buddhism in Ceylon*, (Colombo: M.D. Gunasena, 1956).

Tambiah, S.J., *Sri Lanka, Ethnic Fratricide and the Dismantling of Democracy*, (Chicago: U of Chicago Press, 1991).

Wickremeratne, Ananda, Paul J. Griffiths, *The Roots of Nationalism in Sri Lanka*, (Columbia, MO: South Asia Books, 1996).

Index